3D User Interfaces

3D User Interfaces

Theory and Practice

Doug A. Bowman
Ernst Kruijff
Joseph J. LaViola, Jr.
Ivan Poupyrev

✦Addison-Wesley

Boston • San Francisco • New York • Toronto • Montreal
London • Munich • Paris • Madrid • Capetown
Sydney • Tokyo • Singapore • Mexico City

For Dawn, Drew, and Caroline, my true joys on this earth.

—*Doug*

To my family, for their faith, affection, and support.

—*Ernst*

To my family, with love—they are my life.

—*Joe*

To my parents, for bringing me up.

—*Ivan*

Contents

Contents

Foreword

Three-dimensional user interfaces are finally receiving their due! Research in 3D interaction and 3D display began in the 1960s, pioneered by researchers like Ivan Sutherland, Bob Sproull, Fred Brooks, Andrew Ortony, and Richard Feldman. Although many commercially successful 3D applications exist—computer-aided design and simulation, radiation therapy, drug discovery, surgical simulation, scientific and information visualization, entertainment—no author or group of authors has written a comprehensive and authoritative text on the subject, despite a continuing and rich set of research findings, prototype systems, and products.

Why is that? Why is it that this book by Doug Bowman, Ernst Kruijff, Joe LaViola, and Ivan Poupyrev is the first thorough treatment of 3D UIs?

Perhaps it was our digression during the last 20 years to the WIMP GUI. After all, the Windows, Icons, Menus, and Pointers GUI is used very widely by millions of users. Mac OS and Microsoft Windows users know it well, as do many UNIX users. Indeed, every user of the Web works with a GUI, and this year there are many hundreds of millions of them. Two-dimensional GUIs will be with us for a long time. After all, a lot of the workaday world with which we deal is flat—not just our Web pages but our documents, presentations, and spreadsheets too. Yes, some of these can be extended to 3D, but most of the time, 2D is just fine, thank you very much. Furthermore, pointing and selecting and typing *are* relatively fast and relatively error-free—they work, and they work well.

Perhaps it is that not as many people use 3D GUIs as use the 2D WIMP GUI, and so they are not thought to be as important. But the above list of 3D applications involves multibillion-dollar manufacturing industries, such as aerospace and automotive, and equally large and even more important activities in the life-saving and life-giving pharmaceutical and health care industries.

Perhaps it was that we needed the particular set of backgrounds that Doug, Joe, Ivan, and Ernst bring to the table. Doug comes out of the GVU Center at Georgia Tech, where he worked on 3D UIs with Larry Hodges and others and learned the value of careful user studies and experimentation, and he is now a member of an influential HCI group at Virginia Tech; Joe works at Brown with Andy van Dam, a long-time proponent of rich 3D interaction; Ivan comes from the HIT Lab at the University of Washington, where he worked with Tom Furness and Suzanne Weghorst, and now works with Jun Rekimoto at Sony CSL; and Ernst works with Martin Goebel in the VE Group at Fraunhofer IMK in Germany.

Whatever the case, I am excited and pleased that this team has given us the benefit of their research and experience. As I reviewed the draft manuscript for this book, I jotted down some of the thoughts that came to my mind: comprehensive, encyclopedic, authoritative, taxonomic; grounded in the psychological, HCI, human factors, and computer graphics literature; grounded in the personal research experiences of the authors, their teachers, and their students.

I myself have long preached the importance of integrating the study of the computer with the study of the human. Indeed, this is the key premise on which I built the GVU Center at Georgia Tech. This book certainly follows that admonition. There are numerous discussions of human issues as they relate to 3D navigation and interaction, drawing on references in psychology and human factors.

This is indeed a book for both practitioners and researchers. The extensive literature reviews, examples, and guidelines help us understand what to do now. Combined with the research agenda in Chapter 13, The Future of 3D User Interfaces, the material also helps us have a sense of what it is that we do not yet know.

I particularly commend to readers the Chapter 11 discussion of evaluating 3D UIs. We in the computer graphics community have tended to design devices and techniques and then "throw them over the wall" to the user community. This is not the route to success. Careful study of user needs coupled with evaluation as part of the ongoing design cycle is much more likely to lead to effective techniques. The authors, all of whom have grappled with the difficult task of designing 3D interfaces, know from first-hand experience how crucial this is. Their section 11.4, on the distinctive characteristics of the 3D interface evaluation process, is a wonderful codification of that first-hand knowledge.

Thanks to Doug and Ernst and Joe and Ivan!

Jim Foley
GVU Center
College of Computing
Georgia Tech
March 2004

Preface

An architect sits in her home office, putting the final touches on the design of the new entrance to the city park. A three-dimensional virtual model of the park appears in front of her on the desk's surface. She nudges a pathway slightly to the right to avoid a low-lying area, and then makes the model life-size so she can walk along the path to view the effect. "Those dark colors on the sign at the entrance are too foreboding," she thinks, so she quickly changes the color palette to brighter primary colors. She looks up and notices that the clients are arriving for the final design review meeting. They are located in other offices around the city, but they can all view the 3D model and make suggested changes, as well as communicate with one another. "What's the construction plan?" asks one of the clients. The architect starts an animation showing the progress of the project from start to finish. "That first step may not work," says the client. "The excavation is much too close to the existing playground. Let me show you." He looks out his window, which has a view of the park, and overlays the virtual construction plan on it. "You're right," says the architect, "let's plan to move the playground slightly—that will be much cheaper than changing the construction site." After viewing the effects of the change, all agree that this plan will work, and the meeting adjourns.

This scenario and others like it illustrate the enormous potential of 3D environments and applications. The technology to realize such a vision is available now, although it will certainly be improved. But the scenario also leaves out a great deal of information—information that is crucial to making this dream a reality. How did the architect load the park model, and how does she manipulate her view of it? What technique is used to change the pathway? How can multiple clients all manipulate the model at the same time? How do the participants appear to each other in the virtual space? How is the speed and playback of the animation controlled? How did the client instruct the system to merge the real and virtual scenes?

These questions all relate to the design of the *user interface* (UI) and *interaction techniques* for this 3D application, an area that is usually given only a cursory treatment in futuristic films and books. The scenarios usually either assume that all interaction between the user and the system will be "natural"—based on techniques like intuitive gestures and speech— or "automatic"—the system will be so intelligent that it will deduce the user's intentions. But is this type of interaction realistic, or even desirable?

This book addresses the critical area of *3D UI design*—a field that seeks to answer detailed questions, like those above, that make the difference between a 3D system that is usable and efficient and one that causes user frustration, errors, and even physical discomfort. We present practical information for developers, the latest research results, easy-to-follow guidelines for the UI designer, and relevant application examples. Although there are quite a few books devoted to UIs in general and to 2D UI design in particular, 3D UIs have received significantly less attention. The results of work in the field are scattered throughout numerous conference proceedings, journal articles, single book chapters, and Web sites. This field deserves a reference and educational text that integrates the best practices and state-of-the-art research, and that's why this book was created.

How This Book Came to Be

The story of this book begins in April 1998, when Ivan Poupyrev and Doug Bowman were doctoral students at Hiroshima University and Georgia Tech respectively, working on 3D interaction techniques for object manipulation in virtual environments (VEs). We started a lively email discussion about the design and usability of these techniques and about 3D UIs in general. Ivan, who was at the time a visiting research student at the University of Washington, suggested that the discussion would be even more profitable if other researchers in this new area could join in as well, and so the 3DUI mailing list was born. Since that time, over 100 researchers from around the globe have joined the list and participated in the discussion (to see an archive of all the list traffic or to join the list, check out http://www.3dui.org). Joe LaViola and Ernst Kruijff were two of the first people to join the list.

In August of that same year, Doug forwarded to the list a call for tutorials for the upcoming IEEE Virtual Reality Conference. After some discussion, Joe, Ivan, and Ernst agreed to join Doug to organize a tutorial on "The Art and Science of 3D Interaction." The tutorial was a big hit at the conference in Houston, and the four of us continued to present courses on the topic at ACM Virtual Reality Software and Technology 1999, IEEE VR 2000, and ACM SIGGRAPH 2000 and 2001.

After developing a huge amount of content for the notes supplements of these courses, we decided it would be silly not to compile and expand all of this information in book form. Furthermore, there was no way to include all the information available on 3D UIs in a one-day course. And that's why you're holding this book in your hands today—a book containing information on 3D UIs that can't be found in any other single source.

What's in the Book

The title of this book emphasizes that we have written it for both academics/researchers and practitioners/developers—both those interested in basic research and those interested in applications. Most chapters of the book integrate both theory and practical information. We intend the book to be used both as a textbook (see suggestions below) and as a reference work.

Theory-related content includes the following:

- Sections on the psychology and human factors of various 3D interaction tasks
- Information on different approaches for the evaluation of 3D UIs (Chapter 11)
- Results from empirical studies of 3D interaction techniques
- A research agenda for 3D interaction (Chapter 13)
- Lists of recommended further reading at the end of most chapters
- A comprehensive bibliography of important research articles

Practice-related content includes the following:

- Principles for choosing appropriate input and output devices for 3D systems (Chapters 3 and 4)
- Details and helpful tips for the implementation of common 3D interaction techniques
- Guidelines for the selection of interaction techniques for common 3D tasks
- Case studies of 3D UIs in real-world applications

The book is organized into five parts. Part I introduces the topic of 3D UIs. Part II discusses the input and output device technology used in the development of 3D UIs, with an emphasis on the impact of these devices on usability and performance. Part III presents a wide range of 3D interaction techniques for the common tasks of navigation, selection and manipulation, system control, and symbolic input. In Part IV, we discuss the design, development, and evaluation of complete 3D UI metaphors and applications. Finally, Part V considers the future, with chapters on 3D interaction in augmented reality applications and a research agenda for 3D UIs. The appendix includes information on required mathematical background and is followed by a bibliography of 3D UI references.

Throughout the book, we offer several special features. First, most chapters contain numerous *guidelines*—practical and proven advice for the designer and developer. Guidelines are indicated in the text like this:

> Follow the guidelines in this book to help you design usable 3D UIs.

We also include implementation details for many of the most common and useful interaction techniques. We describe these algorithms using a combination of textual and mathematical descriptions (to avoid a bias toward any particular development tool or programming style).

How to Use the Book and Related Material

If you are a 3D UI developer: Professional developers can use the book for inspiration and guidance in the design, implementation, and evaluation of applications with 3D UIs. In the design process, developers can consider overall UI metaphors from Part IV, choose specific interaction techniques from Part III, and match these with appropriate input and display devices from Part II. The design guidelines from all of these sections should help developers make rational, informed decisions. The implementation of the 3D UI can benefit from the textual and mathematical descriptions of interaction techniques we provide in Part III. Finally, developers can choose evaluation methods and assess the usability of their applications based on the information in Chapter 11.

If you are a teacher: The book can also be used as a textbook in several different types of university-level courses. A graduate course on 3D UI design could use it as a primary textbook. A more generic virtual environments course could use Parts I, II, and III of this book as an introduction to the basic technology and techniques used in VE interaction. An undergraduate HCI course could pull information from Parts I and IV in a module on 3D interfaces and their differences from traditional UIs. Implementation of common techniques from Part III could enhance a course on interactive 3D graphics.

If you are a researcher: This book can serve as a comprehensive reference guide for researchers engaged in 3D UI design or evaluation, the investigation of 3D applications, or the use of VEs or augmented reality. The research agenda in Chapter 13 also provides researchers and research students with a list of important questions to be addressed in the field. It could even be used as the starting point for a PhD student looking for a topic related to 3D UIs.

3D UI design is a fast-moving and evolving field. Therefore, we are committed to updating the material in this book. One way we will do this is through the book's official Web site at http://www.3dui.org. This site will contain information and links related to the latest 3D UI research and applications, organized in the same manner as the book so you can easily find new information about the topics in a particular part or chapter. The site will also allow you to join the 3DUI mailing list. We also ask for your help in keeping the book up to date. Send us your comments, clarification questions, or links to additional information by visiting the Web site above and using the online feedback form. Or email us directly at 3dui@3dui.org. Your comments will help us update the Web site, as well as future editions of this book.

Acknowledgments

This book would not have been possible without the hard work, support, and intelligence of a large group of people.

First, we offer our gratitude to the reviewers who gave their time and energy in improving the quality of the book. Their comments and suggestions have made the book more complete, more readable, and more useful. Thanks to Ben Shneiderman, Harry Hersh, D. Jay Newman, Jeff Pierce, Dieter Schmalstieg, and Bob Zeleznik for providing this invaluable service. Special thanks go to Jim Foley for his encouragement and support.

Next, we would like to thank our editor at Addison-Wesley, Peter Gordon, for his invaluable advice and encouragement. The rest of the staff, including Bernie Gaffney, Amy Fleischer, Julie Nahil, Heather Mullane, and Curt Johnson have also been extremely helpful. Thanks also to Simone Payment and Carol Lallier for their competent and professional work during the production phase.

All of us would like to personally thank our colleagues in the 3D UI community for their fruitful discussions and collaborations. They include Mark Mine, Robert Lindeman, Matthew Conway, Ken Hinckley, Shumin Zhai, Kiyoshi Kiyokawa, Chris Shaw, Mark Billinghurst, Rudy Darken, Pablo Figueroa, and Bernd Fröhlich.

Portions of this material are based upon work supported by the National Science Foundation under Grants No. DUE-0127326 and IIS-0237412. Any opinions, findings and conclusions, or recommendations expressed in this material are those of the author(s) and do not necessarily reflect the views of the National Science Foundation (NSF).

Doug Bowman: I would like to thank my wife, Dawn, for her unfailing love and support, as well as my extended family and friends, especially those at Grace Covenant Presbyterian Church. Much gratitude is due to Joe, Ivan, and Ernst for seeing this project through and for all their years of friendship and collaboration. Thanks also go to my colleagues and students at Virginia Tech, including Chris North, Ron Kriz, Mehdi Setareh, Walid Thabet, Thomas Ollendick, David Cox, Debby Hix, John Kelso, Joe Gabbard, Chad Wingrave, Jian Chen, Nicholas Polys, Wendy Schafer, and Marcio Pinho. Past colleagues at Georgia Tech also deserve thanks. They include Larry Hodges, Drew Kessler, David Koller, Donald Johnson, Donald Allison, Brian Wills, Jean Wineman, Jay Bolter, Elizabeth Davis, Albert Badre, and Ben Watson.

Ernst Kruijff: First of all, my thanks go to Doug, Ivan, and Joe for their great cooperation, help, and extensive discussions. Thanks also go to my parents, my brother, and my sister-in-law for their support, each in their own way. Furthermore, my thanks go to all of my colleagues at the VE group of IMK, especially Martin Goebel for being a great chief, Gerold Wesche, Andreas Simon, Gernot Goebbels, Stefan Conrad, Aeldrik Pander, and Steffi Beckhaus for their past and current cooperation and help during the making of this book and its instigators, the courses we (the authors) gave together. My thanks also go to my past colleagues at Bauhaus University, especially the members of igroup, in particular Holger Regenbrecht. Furthermore, thanks to all the students who helped in many projects, especially Stefan Hansen, Arnold Mueller, Jakob Beetz, and Hartmut Seichter. Finally, my thanks go to Dieter Schmalstieg for being patient with my PhD efforts.

Joe LaViola: I would like to thank my PhD thesis advisor, Andries van Dam, for his forgiveness and patience and for putting up with someone as hardheaded as me. Thanks also to my mom and dad, Jamie, Nick, Heidi, and my friends Don Carney and Dave Gondek for their love and support throughout the writing of this book. My colleagues Robert Zeleznik, Daniel Keefe, Daniel Acevedo Feliz, Andrew Forsberg, Loring Holden, Tim Miller, Steve Dollins, Lee Markosian, David Karelitz, Tim Rowley, Christine Waggoner, and all the members of the Brown University Computer Graphics Group past and present also deserve thanks. Finally, thanks to my coauthors for their hard work and dedication.

Ivan Poupyrev: I would never have been able to work on this book without the help and support I received from many people I was fortunate to meet. I am deeply indebted to Professor Tadao Ichikawa, who supervised my PhD thesis at Hiroshima University. I am also thankful to Professor Masahito Hirakawa for his help and support, as well as to my fellow students and researchers Bryn Holmes, Olivier Liechti, and Numada Tomokazu. I am grateful to the Japanese government for providing me with the Monbusho Scholarship for conducting graduate studies in Japan.

While working on my PhD thesis, I had the exceptional opportunity to spend almost three years at the Human Interface Technology Laboratory (HITL) at the University of Washington. The HITL experience made an enormous impact on me and formed me as a researcher. For this, I will always be grateful to Suzanne Weghorst, the Director of Research at the HITL, who invited me in summer 1995 to join HITL first as a summer intern and then as a visiting researcher; and Professor Tom Furness III, Director of HITL, who believed in me and provided invaluable moral and financial support. I was very fortunate to meet and work with Mark Billinghurst; our collaboration and friendship extended well beyond my stay at the HITL. I am also deeply thankful to Edward Miller for his help in developing a number of HITL 3D UI projects, in particular the V3D interface toolkit, as well as to Jerry Prothero and Hunter Hoffman for late-night discussions of chess, psychology, and the meaning of life; Tony Emerson for finding everything that I ever needed; Ann Elias for all her generous help while I at was the HITL; Mark Phillips, Jennifer Feyma, and Chris Airola for being friends and giving me life outside the lab.

The augmented reality chapter of this book includes a significant amount of work that I did while at the ATR Media Integration and Communication Research Labs in Kyoto. I am very thankful to all the amazing people I met and worked with there: Ryohei Nakatsu, Jun Ohya, Nobuji Tetsutani, Jun Kurumisawa, Tatsumi Sakaguchi, Keiko Nakao, Lew Baldwin, Desney Tan, Sidney Fels, Michael Lyons, Tal Shalif, Parham Zolfaghari, Christa Sommerer, and many others.

Finally, I am thankful to my family and friends in Russia, particularly my parents and brother, Pavel Poupyrev; my first research advisers, Vladimir Lischouk, Dinara Gazizova, and Vladimir Lukin; as well as to Sergei Tsimbalist, Vadim Malishev, Vitaly Lazorin, Constantin Guzovski, and Elena Krupskaya.

It is impossible to mention everyone in Japan, the United States, and Russia who helped, supported, and inspired me. Without this help, support, and inspiration I would not be able to take even my current modest steps toward designing and exploring future interaction technologies. My deepest gratitude and appreciation goes to all of you.

PART I

Foundations of 3D User Interfaces

Part I introduces you to the topic of 3D user interfaces (UIs). Chapter 1 explains what 3D UIs are and why they are important. It also introduces some key terminology used throughout the book and describes some applications that use 3D UIs. Chapter 2 provides a brief history of 3D UIs and a "roadmap" of related areas, positioning the topics covered in this book within a larger context.

CHAPTER 1

Introduction to 3D User Interfaces

On desktop computers, good user interface (UI) design is now almost universally recognized as a crucial part of the software and hardware development process. Almost every computing-related product touts itself as "easy to use," "intuitive," or "designed with your needs in mind." For the most part, however, desktop user interfaces have used the same basic principles and designs for the past decade or more. With the advent of virtual environments (VEs), augmented reality, ubiquitous computing, and other "off-the-desktop" technologies, three-dimensional (3D) UI design is now becoming a critical area for developers, students, and researchers to understand. In this chapter, we answer the question, What are 3D user interfaces? and provide an introduction to terminology that is used throughout the book. We describe the goals of 3D UI design and briefly look at some application areas for 3D user interfaces. Keeping these applications in mind as you progress through the book will help provide a concrete reference point for some of the more abstract concepts we discuss.

1.1. What Are 3D User Interfaces?

Modern computer users have become intimately familiar with a specific set of UI components, including input devices such as the mouse and keyboard, output devices such as the monitor, interaction techniques

3

such as drag-and-drop, interface widgets such as pull-down menus, and interface metaphors such as the desktop metaphor.

These interface components, however, are often inappropriate for the nontraditional computing environments and applications under development today. For example, a wearable-computer user may be walking down the street, making the use of a keyboard impractical. A head-mounted display in an augmented reality application may have limited resolution, forcing the redesign of text-intensive interface components such as dialog boxes. A virtual reality application may allow a user to place an object anywhere in 3D space, with any orientation—a task for which a 2D mouse is inadequate.

Thus, these nontraditional systems need a new set of interface components: new devices, new techniques, new metaphors. Some of these new components may be simple refinements of existing components; others must be designed from scratch. Most of these nontraditional environments work in real or virtual 3D space, so we term these new interfaces *3D user interfaces* (a more precise definition is given in section 1.3).

In this book, we describe and analyze the components (devices, techniques, metaphors) that can be used to design 3D user interfaces. We also provide guidance in choosing the components for your particular system based on empirical evidence from published research, anecdotal evidence from colleagues, and personal experience.

1.2. Why 3D User Interfaces?

Why is the information in this book important? We have five main motivations for producing this book:

3D interaction is relevant to real-world tasks Interacting in three dimensions makes intuitive sense for a wide range of applications (see section 1.4) because of the characteristics of the tasks in these domains and their match with the characteristics of 3D environments. For example, VEs can provide users with a sense of *presence* (the feeling of "being there"—replacing the physical environment with the virtual one), which makes sense for applications such as gaming, training, and simulation. If a user is immersed and can interact using natural skills, then the application can take advantage of the fact that the user already has a great deal of knowledge about the world. Also, 3D UIs may be more direct or immediate; that is, there is a short "cognitive distance" between a user's action and the system's feedback that shows the result of that action. This can allow users to build up complex mental models of how a simulation works, for example.

The technology behind 3D UIs is becoming mature User interfaces for computer applications are becoming more diverse. Mice, keyboards, windows, menus, and icons—the standard parts of traditional WIMP (Windows, Icons, Menus, and Pointers) interfaces—are still prevalent, but nontraditional devices and interface components are proliferating rapidly. These include spatial input devices such as trackers, 3D pointing devices, and whole-hand devices that allow gesture-based input. Multisensory 3D output technologies, such as stereoscopic projection displays, head-mounted displays (HMDs), spatial audio systems, and haptic devices are also becoming more common.

3D interaction is difficult With this new technology, new problems have also been revealed. People often find it inherently difficult to understand 3D spaces and to perform actions in free space (Herndon et al. 1994). Although we live and act in a 3D world, the physical world contains many more cues for understanding and constraints and affordances for action that cannot currently be represented accurately in a computer simulation. Therefore, great care must go into the design of user interfaces and interaction techniques for 3D applications. It is clear that simply adapting traditional WIMP interaction styles to 3D does not provide a complete solution to this problem. Rather, novel 3D UIs based on real-world interaction or some other metaphor must be developed.

Current 3D UIs either are simple or lack usability There are already some applications of 3D user interfaces used by real people in the real world (e.g., walkthroughs, psychiatric treatment, entertainment, and training). Most of these applications, however, contain 3D interaction that is not very complex. More complex 3D interfaces (e.g., modeling and design, education, complex scientific visualizations) are difficult to design and evaluate, leading to a lack of usability. Better technology is not the only answer—for example, 30 years of VE technology research have not ensured that today's VEs are usable. Thus, a more thorough treatment of this subject is needed.

3D UI design is an area ripe for further work Finally, development of 3D user interfaces is one of the most exciting areas of research in human–computer interaction (HCI) today, providing the next frontier of innovation in the field. A wealth of basic and applied research opportunities are available for those with a solid background in 3D interaction.

It is crucial, then, for anyone involved in the design, implementation, or evaluation of nontraditional interactive systems to understand the issues discussed in this book.

1.3. Terminology

The technology sector loves acronyms and jargon, and precise terminology can make life easier as long as everyone is in agreement about the meaning of a particular term. This book is meant to be accessible to a broad audience, but we still find it useful to employ precise language. Here we present a glossary of some terms that we use throughout the book.

We begin with a set of general terms from the field of HCI that are used in later definitions:

human–computer interaction (HCI) The process of communication between human users and computers (or technologies in general). Users communicate actions, intents, goals, queries, and other such needs to computers. Computers, in turn, communicate to the user information about the world, about their internal state, about the responses to user queries, and so on. This communication may involve explicit dialog, or turn-taking, in which a user issues a command or query, the system responds, and so on, but in most modern computer systems, the communication is more implicit, freeform, or even imperceptible (Hix and Hartson 1993).

user interface (UI) The medium through which the communication between users and computers takes place. The UI translates a user's actions and state (inputs) into a representation the computer can understand and act upon, and it translates the computer's actions and state (outputs) into a representation the human user can understand and act upon (Hix and Hartson 1993).

input device A physical (hardware) device allowing communication from the user to the computer.

degrees of freedom (DOF) The number of independent dimensions of the motion of a body. DOF can be used to describe the movements of input devices, the motion of a complex articulated object such as a human arm and hand, or the possible movements of a virtual object.

output device A physical device allowing communication from the computer to the user.

interaction technique A method allowing a user to accomplish a task via the UI. An interaction technique includes both hardware (input/output devices) and software components. The interaction technique's software component is responsible for mapping the information from the input device (or devices) into some action within the system, and for mapping the output of the system to a form that can be displayed by the output device (or devices).

usability The characteristics of an artifact (usually a device, interaction technique, or complete UI) that affect the user's use of the artifact. There are many aspects of usability, including ease of use, user task performance, user comfort, and system performance (Hix and Hartson 1993).

usability evaluation The process of assessing or measuring some aspects of the usability of a particular artifact.

Using this HCI terminology, we define *3D interaction* and *3D user interface:*

3D interaction Human–computer interaction in which the user's tasks are performed directly in a 3D spatial context. Interactive systems that display 3D graphics do not necessarily involve 3D interaction; for example, if a user tours a model of a building on her desktop computer by choosing viewpoints from a traditional menu, no 3D interaction has taken place. On the other hand, 3D interaction does not necessarily mean that 3D input devices are used; for example, in the same application, if the user clicks on a target object to navigate to that object, then the 2D mouse input has been directly translated into a 3D location, and thus 3D interaction has occurred.

3D user interface (3D UI) A UI that involves 3D interaction.

Finally, we define some technological areas in which 3D UIs are used:

virtual environment (VE) A synthetic, spatial (usually 3D) world seen from a first-person point of view. The view in a VE is under the real-time control of the user.

virtual reality (VR) Synonymous with *VE*. We use the term *VE* in this book because the term *VR* is associated with unrealistic hype generated by the media.

augmented reality (AR) A real-world environment that is enhanced (augmented) with synthetic objects or information.

mixed reality (MR) A continuum including both VEs and AR. An environment's position on the continuum indicates the level of "virtuality" in the environment (with the extremes being "purely virtual" and "purely physical"). Mixed reality systems may move along this continuum as the user interacts with them (Milgram and Kishino 1994).

ubiquitous computing (UbiComp) The notion that computing devices and infrastructure (and access to them) may be mobile or scattered throughout the real environment so that users have "anytime, anyplace" access to computational power (Weiser 1991).

1.4. Application Areas

Before we discuss the components of 3D UIs, it will be helpful for you to have an idea of the types of applications that employ 3D interaction. Keep these application examples in mind as you read through the various sections of the book (a more complete list of application areas can be found in Chapter 2). Although many of the examples we discuss in the book come from VEs, the principles we discuss can be applied in a wide variety of applications. Here are some examples:

- *Design and prototyping:* A 3D UI can be used to allow designers of real-world artifacts to work directly in a realistic 3D context. For example, an architect can navigate through a proposed new building and make changes to its design directly rather than working in the traditional 2D medium of drawings and plans (Bowman, Wineman et al. 1998). The scenario in the preface illustrates the types of design problems and tasks a 3D UI might help to address.

- *Psychiatric treatment:* People with strong fears of certain objects or situations are often treated with "exposure therapy" in which they are gradually presented with increasing levels of the fear-inducing stimulus. VEs can be used for "virtual exposure therapy" (Hodges et al. 1995), where the stimulus is synthetic rather than real. This can be less expensive, less embarrassing, and less dangerous. A 3D UI can be used to allow the patient to interact with the environment. For example, someone with a fear of snakes might be able to pick up and handle a virtual snake with a combination of 3D input devices and a realistic toy snake.

- *Scientific visualization:* Scientists and engineers run experiments and simulations that produce huge amounts of data. This data can be visualized using 3D graphics, providing understanding and insight that could not be obtained from looking at numeric results. With 3D UI components, the user can interactively navigate through the data, query various points in the visualization, or even steer the simulation computation (Bryson 1996).

- *Heritage/tourism:* Visiting historical sites can often be disappointing. Buildings have crumbled, cities have grown up around the site, and information is difficult to obtain. Augmented reality technology can address some of these issues by allowing a visitor to see directly what the site might have looked like in earlier times. The combination of real-world images and synthetic images seen from a first-person point of view can be quite compelling. For example, 3D UIs can be used to set the time period the user wants to view or to navigate through text, audio, or image information related to the site (Gleue and Dahne 2001).

- *Collaborative work:* More and more of our work is done in groups or teams, and often these groups are geographically scattered rather than located in a single office. This situation has led to the rise of a whole new software industry focused on collaborative applications, including videoconferencing, online presentations and classes, and collaborative document editing. There are a number of ways 3D UIs can be used for collaborative work (Prince et al. 2002). For example, a virtual meeting can be held in a 3D environment, providing more of the spatial and visual richness of a face-to-face meeting, or collaborators can enter a 3D environment to work together on the design of a new car.

1.5. Conclusion

In this chapter, we discussed briefly the area of 3D UI design—its importance, terminology, and applications. In Chapter 2, we step back to look at the bigger picture—the history of and context for 3D UIs.

CHAPTER 2

3D User Interfaces: History and Roadmap

Three-dimensional UI design is not a traditional field of research with well-defined boundaries. Like human–computer interaction (HCI), it draws from many disciplines and has links to a wide variety of topics. In this chapter, we briefly describe some of the history of 3D UIs to set the stage for the rest of the book. We also present a 3D UI "roadmap" that positions the topics covered in this book relative to associated areas. After reading this chapter, you should have an understanding of the origins of 3D UIs and the relation of 3D UI design to other fields, and you should know what types of information to expect from the remainder of this book.

2.1. History of 3D UIs

The graphical user interfaces (GUIs) used in today's personal computers have an interesting history. Prior to 1980, almost all interaction with computers was based on typing complicated commands using a keyboard. The display was used almost exclusively for text, and when graphics were used, they were typically noninteractive. But around 1980, several technologies, such as the mouse, inexpensive raster graphics displays, and reasonably priced personal computer parts, were all mature enough to enable the first GUIs (such as the Xerox Star). With the advent of GUIs, UI design and HCI in general became a much more important research area because the research affected everyone using computers. HCI is an interdisciplinary field that draws from existing knowledge in perception, cognition, linguistics, human factors, ethnography, graphic design, and other areas.

In a similar way, the development of the 3D UI area has to a large degree been driven by technologies, including 3D graphics technology, augmented reality and virtual environment (VE) technology, and flight simulator technology, to name a few. As each of these technologies matured, they enabled new types of applications, leading in turn to previously unexplored user tasks, new challenges in UI design, and unforeseen usability issues. Thus, 3D UI research became necessary. In the rest of this section, we chronicle the development of one of these areas—virtual environments, to be precise—and show how advances in VEs produced a need for 3D UI research.

In the late 1960s, Ivan Sutherland developed the first head-tracked, head-mounted display (Sutherland 1968) and a vision for the use of this new technology to enable a whole new type of computing (Sutherland 1965). Sutherland was ahead of his time, but finally in the late 1980s and early 1990s, it became more practical to build VE systems. The technologies that enabled this vision included 3D stereoscopic computer graphics, miniature CRT displays, position-tracking systems, and interaction devices such as the VPL DataGlove. Interestingly, when VEs first entered the public consciousness through Jim Foley's article in *Scientific American* (Foley 1987), the cover image showed not a display system or a complex graphical environment, but rather the DataGlove—a "whole-hand" input device allowing users to interact with and manipulate the virtual world.

At first, VEs were strictly the domain of computer scientists and engineers (mostly in the graphics community) and was used for relatively simple applications. Visualization of 3D scientific datasets, real-time walkthroughs of architectural structures, and VE games were interesting and useful applications, and they provided plenty of research challenges (faster, more realistic graphics; more accurate head-tracking; lower latency; better VE software toolkits; etc.). These applications, however, were relatively impoverished when it came to user interaction. The typical application only allowed the user to interactively navigate the environment, with a few providing more complex interaction, such as displaying the name of an object when it was touched. As VE technology continued to improve, however, researchers wanted to develop more complex applications with a much richer set of interactions. For example, besides allowing an architect to experience his building design in a virtual world, we could allow him to record and play audio annotations

about the design, to change the type of stone used on the façade, to move a window, or to hide the interior walls so that the pipes and ducts could be seen. At this point, some VE researchers realized that they didn't know enough about interface design to make these complex applications usable. Technology had improved to a point where such applications were possible, but more than technology was needed to make them plausible.

Fortunately, because of the earlier focus on interfaces for personal computers, the field of HCI was already relatively mature when VEs experienced their "interface crisis." HCI experts had developed general principles for good interface design (e.g., Nielsen and Molich 1992), product design and development processes aimed at ensuring usability (e.g., Hix and Hartson 1993), and models that explained how humans process information when interacting with systems (e.g., Card et al. 1986).

The application of existing HCI knowledge to VE systems helped to improve their usability. But there were some questions about VE interfaces on which traditional HCI was silent. Consider the architectural design example again. Suppose the architect wants to move a doorway and change the door's paint color. An HCI expert would tell us that the movement task would best be accomplished by direct manipulation (like dragging an icon on your computer desktop), since that would provide direct and continuous feedback to the user. But how should a direct manipulation interface be implemented in a VE? How does the architect select the door? Once the door is selected, how does he move it? How do the architect's hand and body motions map to the movement of the door? Again, the HCI expert might suggest that for the painting task, we need a simple menu selection mechanism, perhaps based on a real-world metaphor such as paint sample cards. But what does a menu look like in a VE? How does the user activate the menu and select an item within it? Where does the menu appear in the 3D world?

Questions such as these indicated that a new subfield of HCI was needed to address the issues specific to the design of interfaces for 3D VEs. In parallel, other technologies, such as interactive 3D graphics for desktop computers, augmented reality, and wearable computers, were also being developed, and researchers found that developing UIs on these platforms was also problematic. The common theme of all of these interactive technologies is interaction in a 3D context. Thus, the new subarea of HCI is termed *3D interaction, 3D user interface design,* or *3D HCI.*

In the next section, we look at the types of research problems addressed and approaches used in 3D UI work and position them with respect to related work in other fields.

2.2. Roadmap to 3D UIs

To help you understand the material in this book in its proper context, it's important to discuss what types of work are part of the 3D UI area, what disciplines and areas make up the background for 3D UI work, and what impact 3D UIs have on other areas. In this section, therefore, we present brief snapshots of a wide variety of areas with some connection to 3D UIs. Figure 2.1 illustrates our basic organizational structure. In the following lists of topics, we provide at least one important reference for most topics or, if applicable, a pointer to a particular chapter or section of the book where that topic is covered.

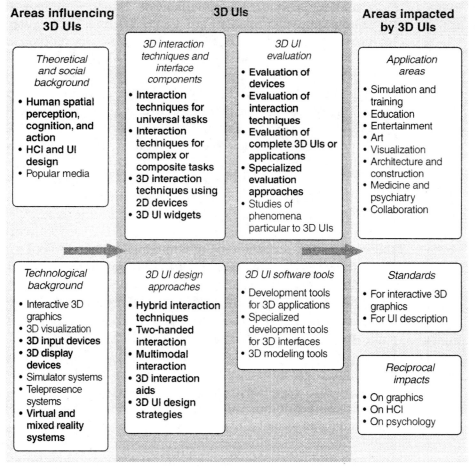

Figure 2.1   *Roadmap to 3D UIs. Topics shown in darker text are covered in this book.*

2.2.1. Areas Informing the Design of 3D UIs

We can draw upon many areas of research when considering the design of 3D UIs. The following sections discuss the theoretical and social background as well as the technological background for the topics covered in this book.

Theoretical and Social Background

Human spatial perception, cognition, and action The defining feature of 3D UIs is that users are viewing and acting in a real or virtual 3D space. Thus, psychology and human factors knowledge about spatial perception; spatial cognition; and human navigation, movement, and manipulation in 3D space contain critical background information for 3D UI design. Examples of such knowledge and theories include

- Visual perception and 3D depth cues (e.g., Bruce and Green 1990; Kosslyn 1993; see Chapter 3, section 3.2.2)
- Human spatial abilities and individual differences in abilities (e.g., Shephard and Metzler 1971)
- Building spatial knowledge about 3D environments (e.g., Thorndyke and Hayes-Roth 1982; see Chapter 7, section 7.2)
- Spatial sound perception (e.g., Durlach 1991; see Chapter 3, section 3.3.1)
- Properties of manual reaching and grabbing (e.g., MacKenzie and Iberall 1994; Marras 1997; see Chapter 5)
- Cognitive planning of actions (e.g., Card et al. 1983)
- Presence (e.g., Slater et al. 1994)

Basic principles of HCI and UI design A great deal of knowledge, theory, and practical advice has been generated by researchers in HCI. Although some is particularly focused on traditional desktop UIs, much can be generalized to apply to 3D UIs as well. Examples include

- Generic heuristics or guidelines for UI design, such as visibility, affordances, and constraints (e.g., Nielsen and Molich 1992; Norman 1990)
- Models and theories of HCI, such as activity theory, GOMS (Goals, Operators, Methods, and Selection Rules), and scenario-based design (e.g., Bødker 1991; Card et al. 1980; Rosson and Carroll 2001)

- UI design and evaluation techniques such as hierarchical task analysis, ethnographic analysis, heuristic evaluation, cognitive walkthrough, and usability studies (as found in HCI textbooks such as Shneiderman [1998]; see Chapter 11)

Popular media A very different source of inspiration and vision for 3D UI work has been popular books (especially science fiction), films, and other media. Much of this vision has involved fully "natural" interaction with intelligent interfaces in perfectly realistic environments. Some specific examples are

- Books such as *Snow Crash* (Stephenson 1992), which describes the "Metaverse," a futuristic, realistic version of the Internet; *Neuromancer* (Gibson 1984), which coined the term *cyberspace;* and *Disclosure* (Crichton 1994), which features a VE with natural physical movement and natural language interaction.
- Television shows such as *Star Trek: The Next Generation,* which features the "Holodeck."
- Films such as *The Matrix,* which envisions an entire race of people living unsuspectingly in a thoroughly realistic virtual world.

Technological Background

Interactive 3D graphics Producing realistic but synthetic 3D images on a computer screen has been a focus of computer science research for almost 50 years. One particular line of research has focused on interactive 3D graphics—images that are rendered in real time so that users can interact with them directly. This technology provides the environment in which 3D UI designers do their work. Some representative advances in interactive 3D graphics are

- Fast line and polygon rendering algorithms (e.g., Bresenham 1965)
- Texture-mapping procedures (e.g., Watt and Watt 1992)
- Real-time lighting methods (e.g., Bishop and Weimer 1986)
- Dedicated graphics processors for fast hardware-based rendering (e.g., Olano and Lastra 1998)
- Algorithms for drawing stereoscopic images (e.g., Davis and Hodges 1995)

3D visualization An important application area for 3D computer graphics has been visualization—changing abstract data into a perceptual form so that humans can use their well-developed visual sense to find patterns, detect anomalies, and understand complex situations. Research in visualization includes

- Principles of visual data representation (e.g., Tufte 1990)
- General information or data visualization techniques (e.g., Ware 2000)
- Scientific visualization techniques (e.g., McCormick et al. 1987)

3D input devices Computer systems have traditionally used text-based input (keyboards), and 1- (dials, sliders) or 2-DOF (mouse, joystick, trackball) input devices. Three-dimensional input devices provide more DOF for the user to control simultaneously. They are important for 3D UIs because users want to specify points, directions, gestures, and other actions in 3D space in order to accomplish complex 3D tasks. Examples of 3D input device types include

- Tracking devices (Welch and Foxlin 2002; Meyer and Applewhite 1992)
- Multiple-DOF joysticks (e.g., Zhai et al. 1999)
- Isotonic 3D input devices (e.g., Simon and Fröhlich 2003)

We discuss 3D input devices in Chapter 4.

3D display devices All visual displays used with computers today are capable of displaying 3D graphics. Often, however, 3D UIs make use of more advanced displays that provide stereo viewing (slightly different images for the left and right eyes, producing an enhanced depth effect) or immersion (being surrounded by a graphical environment). In addition, many 3D UIs make use of nonvisual displays—displays that present information to other senses. Here is a short list of such advanced 3D displays:

- Stereoscopic displays for desktop computers (e.g., Schmandt 1983)
- Walkaround 3D displays (e.g., Bimber et al. 2001)
- Head-mounted displays (e.g., Melzer and Moffitt 1996)
- Projection-based immersive displays (e.g., Cruz-Neira et al. 1993; Krüger et al. 1995)

- 3D spatial sound systems (e.g., Kapralos et al. 2003)
- Force-feedback, tactile, and other haptic displays (e.g., Burdea 1996)

Chapter 3 presents details on a wide range of 3D display devices.

Simulator systems Before VR, simulator systems pioneered the use of large, interactive displays of 3D computer graphics. Simulators have been used for many applications, including flight simulation, tank and military vehicle simulation, space vehicle simulation, and simulators for entertainment (e.g., Pausch et al. 1993).

Telepresence systems Telepresence systems allow a user in one real-world location to feel as if he were in a different real-world location. They combine sensors (cameras, microphones, etc.) on the remote side with displays (visual, auditory, haptic) and interactive controls (e.g., for rotating the camera) on the local side. Telepresence technology is similar to VR (see below) in many ways (e.g., Stassen and Smets 1995).

Virtual reality systems Immersive VR systems combine interactive 3D graphics, 3D visual display devices, and 3D input devices (especially position trackers) to create the illusion that the user is inside a virtual world. In particular, head tracking produces the effect that the world completely surrounds the user—when the user turns her head to the right, new images are rendered showing the part of the world to the user's right. Because the images are always located at the correct position around the user, they appear to form a seamless 3D environment. Some important VR systems have included

- Sutherland's original head-mounted display system (Sutherland 1968)
- VPL's HMD and DataGlove (Zimmerman et al. 1987)
- The Cave Automatic Virtual Environment (CAVE), originally developed at the University of Illinois-Chicago's Electronic Visualization Laboratory (Cruz-Neira et al. 1993)

2.2.2. 3D UI Subareas

In this section, we describe the various subparts of the field of 3D UIs. These subareas, described only briefly here, make up the bulk of the content of this book. We provide references in this section only when a topic is not covered later in the book.

3D Interaction Techniques and Interface Components

Just as 2D UIs are built from components like windows, scrollbars, menus, and drag-and-drop, 3D UIs are built from a large number of techniques and components.

Interaction techniques for universal tasks (Chapters 5–9) Selection, manipulation, travel, wayfinding, system control, and symbolic input are common, low-level user tasks in 3D interfaces. For each of these tasks, there is a large number of possible interaction techniques (combinations of input device and UI software).

Interaction techniques for complex or composite tasks More complex tasks in 3D UIs are composed of the universal tasks described above. For example, the task of changing an object's color might involve choosing a "color picker" item from a menu (system control), pointing out an object (selection), and positioning a marker in a 3D color space (manipulation). The low-level interaction techniques for these subtasks can be composed to form a high-level interaction technique for the composite task.

3D interaction techniques using 2D devices (Chapter 5, section 5.4.7) A special category of 3D interaction techniques are those that operate in a 2D input context (i.e., on the desktop). For example, in 3D modeling programs running on desktop computers, we need a way to map 2D mouse input to the 6 DOF of a 3D object.

3D UI widgets (Chapter 8, section 8.3) Not all 3D interaction is "natural," operating directly on the objects in the world. For many complex tasks, we need specialized objects that are not part of the environment but that help the user to interact with the environment. For example, a virtual knife might help a designer to slice through an automobile model to see a particular cross-section, or a small icon representing a piece of paper could be attached to a building to indicate the presence of textual information about it.

3D UI Design Approaches

Low-level interaction techniques and interface components are the building blocks of complete 3D UIs, but it is not trivial to put these elements together in a usable and understandable way. Thus, we need higher-level approaches or strategies for building 3D interfaces.

Hybrid interaction techniques One way to improve on the usability of individual interaction techniques is to combine the best parts of existing techniques. For example, the HOMER manipulation technique (see Chapter 5, section 5.4.5) is a hybrid of two other types of techniques: raycasting and arm-extension.

Two-handed interaction (Chapter 10, section 10.2.3) 3D UIs can take advantage of a much richer set of inputs than can 2D interfaces. One powerful approach is to develop interactions that allow the user to use both hands in a complementary way. Taking this approach even farther, 3D UIs can be designed around "whole-body" interaction.

Multimodal interaction (Chapter 8, section 8.7) Another design strategy that makes sense for 3D UIs is to use many different input and output "modalities"—so-called *multimodal interaction*. For example, combining hand-based gestures with speech input provides a powerful and concise way to specify complex actions.

3D interaction aids (Chapter 8, section 8.6, and Chapter 10, section 10.2.1) Purely virtual 3D interaction can be very powerful and flexible, but it can also be frustrating and imprecise. Including physical objects ("props") in a 3D UI helps ground the user and constrains the interaction. For example, placing a 2D menu on a physical 2D surface helps the user find the menu and make a precise selection. Including physics (forces, collisions, etc.) or constraints (snapping, grouping, etc.) in a 3D world can also make interaction easier.

3D UI design strategies (Chapter 10) Overall strategies for designing 3D UIs include

- Using real-world metaphors that help guide the user to the correct actions
- Applying principles of aesthetics and visual design
- Basing UI design on formal taxonomies of devices or interaction techniques
- Basing UI design on guidelines developed by researchers
- Using "magic" to allow the user to go beyond the perceptual, cognitive, or physical limitations of the real world
- Intentionally violating assumptions about the real world in the virtual world

3D UI Software Tools

Tools are needed to turn conceptual UI designs into concrete prototypes and implementations. This subarea has not received as much attention as design, but there are a few important categories of tools.

Development tools for 3D applications A wide variety of software libraries, toolkits, application programming interfaces (APIs), and integrated development environments (IDEs) exist that allow programmers to develop 3D applications. Typically, these applications are written in a standard programming language such as C++ and make use of special APIs for 3D graphics (e.g., OpenGL), 3D device drivers, and so on.

Specialized development tools for 3D interfaces Very few tools are designed specifically to aid the implementation of 3D UIs. Some 3D toolkits include a few default interaction techniques or interface widgets. Also, some work has been done on 3D UI description languages. Standards such as Virtual Reality Modeling Language (VRML) and Extensible 3D (X3D) include some interaction functionality, although the implementation of this functionality is left up to the browser or viewer developers.

3D modeling tools All 3D UIs include 3D geometric objects and/or scenes. We are not aware of any 3D modeling tools aimed specifically at 3D UI visual design, but modeling tools used in other domains, such as animation, architecture, and engineering, can also be used to develop the objects and elements in a 3D UI. Common tools today include AutoCAD, 3D Studio Max, and Maya.

3D UI Evaluation

Just as in traditional HCI, usability evaluation is a critical part of 3D UI design. Evaluation helps designers pursue good ideas and reject poor ones, compare two or more alternatives for a particular UI component, validate the usability of a complete application, and more. We cover 3D UI evaluation in detail in Chapter 11.

Evaluation of devices In 3D UIs, evaluation must start at the lowest level because all the UI components are novel and unfamiliar. Thus, comparisons of the usability of various input and output devices are necessary. For example, one might compare the performance of different device types for a simple 3D rotation task (Hinckley, Tullio et al. 1997).

Evaluation of interaction techniques As new 3D interaction techniques are developed for universal or composite tasks, formative usability studies can help to guide the design of these techniques. When there are many possible techniques for a particular task, a comparative evaluation can reveal the tradeoffs in usability and performance between the techniques.

Evaluation of complete 3D UIs or applications At a higher level, usability evaluation can be used within the design process (formative evaluation) or at its end (summative evaluation) to examine the quality of a fully integrated UI or complete 3D application.

Specialized evaluation approaches Some researchers have investigated generic methodologies for evaluating the usability of 3D interfaces. For example, in testbed evaluation (Chapter 11, section 11.6.1), researchers compare interaction techniques by having subjects use them in a wide variety of different tasks and situations so that a complete picture of the technique's quality is obtained.

Studies of phenomena particular to 3D UIs Most usability evaluations measure things like time to complete a task, perceived ease of use, or error rates. There are some metrics, however, that are unique to 3D UIs. One of these is *presence*—the feeling of "being there" that you get when immersed in a virtual 3D world (Slater et al. 1994). Because presence is not a concept that applies to most UIs, researchers have only recently begun to define it precisely and devise methods for measuring it. Another unique phenomenon is *cybersickness*—feelings of physical discomfort brought on by the use of immersive systems (Kennedy et al. 2000). Again, precise definitions and metrics for cybersickness are just beginning to emerge.

2.2.3. Areas Impacted by 3D UIs

This section addresses the impact of 3D UIs on other domains. This impact is felt mainly in the applications that are enabled by 3D UIs.

Application Areas

Simulation and training Three-dimensional environments based on virtual or augmented reality can be used for simulations of military operations, robotic agent actions, or the spread of a disease within the body, just to name a few. Training in a 3D environment for tasks such as surgery, spacewalks, or aircraft piloting is also a very popular application area.

Education Students can learn topics from Newton's laws to environmental design in 3D worlds. If the worlds are highly interactive, students can experiment with a range of situations to help them construct their own mental models of how something works.

Entertainment Three-dimensional environments already provide the context for the most popular video games on desktop computers. When 3D interaction is added, allowing more direct involvement in the world, and when many players can all be immersed in the same environment, the possibilities are endless. A famous example of the potential of this application area is the DisneyQuest attraction at Disneyworld in Florida.

Art Three-dimensional worlds provide artists a new canvas for new types of expression. Although some of today's 3D art is passive, most of it is interactive, responding to viewers' positions, gestures, touch, speech, and so on.

Visualization Scientists, engineers, business analysts, and others all work with large, complex, 3D (or higher-dimensional) datasets. Exploring these datasets visually, querying them to extract information, and navigating to find patterns in them is another powerful application of 3D interaction.

Architecture and construction Architectural design and construction projects are organized around large 3D environments, but most tools currently used in these domains are 2D (drawings or text). With 3D interfaces, architects can visualize and modify their designs directly, contractors can address the coordination of construction equipment on a worksite, or interior designers can try hundreds of combinations of wall colors, furniture, and lighting and see the results immediately.

Medicine and psychiatry Three-dimensional applications are being used in the medical domain for telemedicine (remote diagnosis and treatment), 3D visualization of medical images such as MRIs, and psychotherapy for anxiety disorders such as phobias, just to name a few examples. All of these applications require a usable 3D interface.

Collaboration Today's workgroups are often scattered around the globe. Technologies such as augmented reality, with an appropriate 3D UI, can allow such groups to work together as if they were located in the same place. For example, a group of stakeholders could discuss the design of a proposed new feature at a park, as we suggested in the preface.

Standards

There are no "standard" 3D UIs today in the sense of de facto standards (such as the desktop metaphor) or in the sense of documented standards (such as ISO standards). However, 3D UI work has had a small impact (that will continue to grow) on certain areas of standardization.

For interactive 3D graphics The World Wide Web Consortium (W3C) defines international standards for many aspects of the Internet, including interactive 3D graphics. This work has led to the VRML specification, and its successor, X3D. These standards provide a well-defined method for describing interactive 3D environments and indicate the features and functionality that 3D Web browsers need to implement. Although they focus on geometry, appearance, and organization, these standards do include some interactive components, and more are being added all the time.

For UI description The HCI community has worked to develop methods for the abstract, platform-independent description of UIs, and several have been produced for 2D GUIs (e.g., Hartson and Gray 1992). Although these could not yet be called standards, that is their intent. The 3D UI community has also seen the need for such description languages (e.g., Figueroa et al. 2001), and we expect that this will be a focus area in the future.

Reciprocal Impacts

Finally, we note that 3D UI research has influenced some of the areas from which it sprang. These "reciprocal impacts" indicate that 3D UI work has had an effect beyond itself, revealing gaps in our knowledge of other areas.

On graphics To be usable, 3D UIs often require complex visuals. For example, the principle of feedback indicates that the visual display should show the user information about his actions both during and after the user's input. This means that during 3D object manipulation, we should provide the user with sufficient depth and position cues to understand where the object is in relation to the target location. These cues might include subtle lighting effects, realistic shadows, or various levels of transparency, all of which require complex real-time graphics algorithms. In this and many other ways, the requirements of 3D UIs can drive graphics research.

On HCI The study of 3D UIs has revealed many areas not addressed by traditional HCI. For example, what metrics should be used to indicate the usability of a system? In 2D UIs, metrics like speed, accuracy, satisfaction, and perceived ease of use are sufficient; in 3D UIs, we also need to assess things like physical comfort and presence. The development of heuristics or guidelines for good UI design is another area that has been studied thoroughly in traditional HCI but that requires further thought and expansion for 3D UIs.

On psychology As we noted above, the design of 3D UIs is heavily dependent on information from perceptual and cognitive psychology. In an interesting way, even these areas have benefited from 3D UI research. One issue in perceptual psychology, for example, is the design of valid and generalizable experiments studying visual perception, because it's very hard to tightly control what a person sees in a real-world setting and because some visual stimuli are hard to produce in the real world. In a synthetic 3D VE, however, we can remove all the real-world visual stimuli and replace it with anything we like, producing an extremely powerful environment for studying visual perception.

2.3. Scope of This Book

This book is about the design of 3D interfaces, and therefore we focus on the content that is specific to 3D UIs. This roughly corresponds to the topics in section 2.2.2 (3D UI Subareas). We also discuss briefly some of the background and application topics from sections 2.2.1 and 2.2.3 when appropriate.

Of course, this book can't cover everything in the roadmap. Some specific items that are not covered include

- An in-depth discussion of presence and cybersickness
- Technical information on the design or workings of various devices
- Graphics algorithms and techniques for rendering 3D environments
- Information on the usage of particular 3D toolkits, APIs, or modeling programs

For information on these topics, refer to the references above and to the recommended reading lists in each chapter.

For a visual representation of the book's coverage, see Figure 2.1. The items shown in black text in the figure are discussed in some detail, while the gray items are not covered or are mentioned only briefly.

We already noted that there are several different platforms for 3D UIs, including VEs, mixed or augmented reality, and traditional desktop computers. In this book, we strive to be as general as possible in our descriptions of interaction techniques and UI components, and the principles and guidelines we provide are usually applicable to any 3D UI. However, we recognize that there are some interaction techniques that are specifically designed for one platform or another. Since we come from a background of research in immersive VEs, many of the examples we use and specific technique descriptions are slanted in that direction. We do cover some desktop-specific techniques in Chapters 5 and 6, and augmented reality techniques in Chapter 12, but not at the same depth as our coverage of VE techniques.

For a more thorough treatment of desktop techniques for 3D interaction, we recommend *3D User Interfaces with Java3D* (Barrilleaux 2000), which specifically addresses techniques for desktop 3D UIs and provides more implementation details.

2.4. Conclusion

In this chapter, you've taken a tour through some of the history of 3D interaction and seen glimpses of the many facets of this rich and interesting area. In Part II, we dive into the details of the technological background for 3D UI design.

PART II

Hardware Technologies for 3D User Interfaces

One way to describe human–computer interfaces is as a means of communication between a user (or users) and a system. The user must communicate commands, requests, questions, intent, and goals to the system. The system in turn must provide feedback, requests for input, information about the system state, and so on. We can think of this communication process as a series of *translations*. The user and the system do not speak the same language, so the interface must serve as a translator or intermediary between them. In fact, there are multiple translation steps involved (Figure P.1): the user first translates her goals into actions; next, the input device translates those physical actions into an electronic form for the system; finally, the system deciphers those signals based on the current system state. Typically, the system responds in some way to the input of the user, and so there must be some transformation of the input to produce the output—this is called a *transfer function*. To communicate this output to the user, the system translates the information into a digital display representation that is again translated by output devices into a form the user can perceive (e.g., light or sound), and finally, the user translates those perceptions into a meaningful semantic representation. The translations that occur between input devices and output devices are also known as *control-display mappings.*

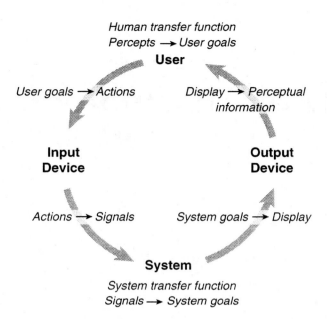

Figure P.1   *Human–computer communication through devices and translations.*

In the end, though, all of this communication must use physical devices—hardware that serves as the medium of communication between the parties. This part of the book provides an overview of the hardware devices used to realize 3D UIs. Chapter 3 covers *output devices,* which present, or display, information to the user's perceptual system. Although visual displays are the most prominent type of output device for 3D UIs, we also cover auditory and haptic displays. In Chapter 4, we discuss *input devices*—the means by which the user gives information to the system. The goal of these chapters is to give you an idea of the types of technologies commonly used in 3D UIs and to help you choose devices for your applications, not to provide an exhaustive survey of current devices or to discuss the design of 3D input/output devices.

CHAPTER 3

3D User Interface Output Hardware

This chapter begins our discussion of the hardware commonly used in 3D user interfaces. We examine visual, auditory, and haptic display devices and see how they affect 3D UI design and development. Additionally, we describe the characteristics of different output devices and develop some general strategies for choosing appropriate hardware.

3.1. Introduction

A necessary component of any 3D UI is the hardware that presents information to the user. These hardware devices, called *display devices* (or *output devices*), present information to one or more of the user's senses through the human perceptual system; the majority of them are focused on stimulating the visual, auditory, or haptic (i.e., force and touch) senses. In some rare cases, they even display information to the user's olfactory system, or sense of smell (Davide et al. 2001). Of course, these output devices require a computer to generate the information through techniques such as rendering, modeling, and sampling. The devices then translate this information into perceptible human form. Therefore, displays actually consist of the physical devices *and* the computer systems used in generating the content the physical devices present. Although the focus of this chapter is on display devices, we do provide references to relevant material on topics such as graphical and haptic rendering, as well as material on 3D sound generation.

Display devices need to be considered when designing, developing, and using various interaction techniques in 3D UIs, because some interaction techniques are more appropriate than others for certain displays. Therefore, an understanding of display device characteristics will help the 3D UI developer make informed decisions about which interaction techniques are best suited for particular display configurations and applications.

In this chapter, we explore different display device types (specifically visual, auditory, and haptic devices) and styles that are commonly found in 3D UIs. This is the first of two chapters that deal specifically with hardware technology (see Chapter 4, 3D User Interface Input Hardware). Note that this chapter is not meant to be a detailed exposition of the connections between display devices and human sensory systems. However, we do discuss fundamental concepts of the human visual, auditory, and haptic systems as needed to help illustrate the differences among various display types. See Stanney (2002), Sherman and Craig (2003), and Durlach and Mavor (1995) for more details on the human sensory system and its relationship to display technology.

3.1.1. Chapter Roadmap

In section 3.2, we begin by looking at visual display devices. We first examine visual display device characteristics, then discuss visual depth cues. Next, we present the many different types of visual display devices commonly found in 3D UIs and discuss how they affect 3D UI design. In section 3.3, we examine auditory displays by describing a variety of important spatial audio cues, then discuss how 3D sound is typically generated. Next we present the pros and cons of different sound system configurations and discuss the benefits of sound in 3D UIs. In section 3.4, we discuss haptic display devices, beginning with an examination of haptic cues. Next, we discuss different haptic display device characteristics, the different types of haptic display devices, and their use in 3D UIs. Finally, in section 3.5, we present some guidelines and strategies for choosing display devices for particular systems or applications.

3.2. Visual Displays

Visual displays present information to the user through the human visual system. Visual displays are by far the most common display devices used in 3D UIs. As stated in the introduction to this chapter, display devices require the computer system to generate digital content that the display device transforms into perceptible form. For visual display devices in 3D UIs, real-time computer graphics rendering techniques are used to produce the images that the display device presents to the user. Many different real-time rendering techniques have been developed over the years. The details of these techniques are beyond the scope of this book; however, Akenine-Möller and Haines (2002), Watt and Watt (1992), and Slater, Steed, and Chrysanthou (2002) all provide comprehensive treatments for interested readers.

3.2.1. Visual Display Characteristics

A number of important characteristics must be considered when describing visual display devices. From a 3D interface perspective, we discuss a visual display's

- field of regard and field of view
- spatial resolution
- screen geometry
- light transfer mechanism
- refresh rate
- ergonomics

Other characteristics include brightness, color contrast, and gamma correction.

Field of Regard and Field of View

A visual display device's field of regard (FOR) refers to the amount of the physical space surrounding the user in which visual images are displayed. FOR is measured in degrees of visual angle. For example, if we built a cylindrical display in which a user could stand, the display would have a 360-degree horizontal FOR.

A related term, field of view (FOV), refers to the maximum number of degrees of visual angle that can be seen instantaneously on a display. For example, with a large, flat projection screen, the horizontal FOV might be 80 or 120 degrees depending on the user's position in relation to the screens because the FOV varies with the user's distance from the screen. A display device's FOV must be less than or equal to the maximum FOV of the human visual system (approximately 200 degrees) and will be lower than that if additional optics such as stereo glasses are used.

A visual display device can have a small FOV but still have a large FOR, as in the case of a tracked head-mounted display (see section 3.2.3). For a head-mounted display, the FOV might be 40 degrees, but because the device is attached to the user's head, with the display always in front of the user's eyes, the synthetic imagery is always perceived by the user regardless of her position or orientation (i.e., the user could make a 360-degree turn and always see the visual images). Thus, the FOV α is always less than or equal to the FOR β. In general, the user at each instant can view α degrees out of the full β degrees available to her.

Spatial Resolution

The spatial resolution of a visual display is related to pixel size and is considered a measure of visual quality. This measure is often given in dots per inch (dpi). The more pixels displayed on the screen, the higher the resolution, but resolution is *not* equivalent to the number of pixels (a common misuse of the term). Instead, resolution depends on both the number of pixels and the size of the screen. Two visual display devices with the same number of pixels but different screen sizes will not have the same resolution, because on the large screen, each individual pixel takes up a larger portion of the screen than on the small screen. Therefore, the smaller screen will actually have higher resolution than the larger screen when both have an identical number of pixels.

The user's distance to the visual display device also affects the spatial resolution on a perceptual level. The further the user is from the display, the higher the *perceived* resolution because individual pixels are not distinguishable. This is similar to the effect of viewing paintings from the pointillist movement (Kieseyer 2001). As the viewer gets close to the painting, she can see the individual dots on the canvas, but as she moves away from it, the dots disappear and the individual dots fuse together to form a cohesive image. This phenomenon is often a problem with head-mounted displays because the user's eyes must be very close to the display screens, causing degradation in the perceived spatial resolution.

Screen Geometry

Another visual display characteristic that plays a role in visual quality is screen shape. Visual displays come in a variety of different shapes (see section 3.2.3), including rectangular, L-shaped, hemispherical, and hybrids. Nonrectangular screen shapes require nonstandard projection algorithms, which can affect visual quality. For example, hemispherical displays can suffer from visual artifacts such as distortion at the edges of the display surface, resulting in lower overall visual quality.

Light Transfer

Perhaps the most important visual display characteristic when considering 3D UI design is the how the light actually gets transferred onto the display surface. There are a number of different ways to transfer the light, including front projection, rear projection, laser light directly onto the retina, and the use of special optics. The light transfer method often dictates what types of 3D UI techniques are applicable. For example, when using a front-projected display device, 3D direct manipulation techniques do not work well, because the user's hands can get in the way of the projector, causing shadows to appear on the display surface.

Refresh Rate

Refresh rate refers to the speed with which a visual display device refreshes the displayed image from the frame buffer and is usually reported in hertz (Hz, refreshes per second). Note that refresh rate is not to be confused with frame rate, the speed with which images are generated by the graphics system and placed in the frame buffer. Although a graphics system could generate images at a rate higher than the refresh rate, the visual display can show them only at its refresh rate limit. The refresh rate of a visual display is an important characteristic because it can have a significant effect on visual quality. Low refresh rates (e.g., below 50–60 Hz) can cause flickering images depending on the sensitivity of a particular user's visual system.

Ergonomics

Finally, visual display ergonomics is also an important display characteristic. We want the user to be as comfortable as possible when interacting with 3D applications, and we want the visual display device to be as unobtrusive as possible. Comfort is especially important when a user has to wear the display on his head.

3.2.2. Depth Cues

Because 3D UIs are used primarily in 3D applications, the user must have an understanding of the 3D structure of the scene; in particular, understanding visual depth is crucial. Depth information will help the user to interact with the application, especially when performing 3D selection, manipulation, and navigation tasks (see Part III of this book). Therefore, understanding what depth cues the visual system uses to extract 3D information and how visual displays provide such cues is another important tool for characterizing these devices. Visual depth cues can be broken up into four categories:

- monocular, static cues
- oculomotor cues
- motion parallax
- binocular disparity and stereopsis

We briefly describe these cues and discuss their relevance to visual displays. Note that more detail on visual depth cues can be found in May and Badcock (2002); Wickens, Todd, and Seidler (1989); Sedgwick (1988); and Sekuler and Blake (1994).

Monocular, Static Cues

Monocular, static depth cues refer to depth information that can be inferred from a static image viewed by a single eye. Because they can be seen in a still picture, static cues are also called pictorial cues. These cues include relative size, height relative to the horizon, occlusion, linear and aerial perspective, shadows and lighting, and texture gradients.

With no information about the absolute size of an object, its *relative size* can be used as a depth cue. For example, if a scene contains a group of increasingly smaller circles placed against a blank background, the smaller circles appear to be farther away (see Figure 3.1). An object's *height relative to the horizon* can influence a viewer's depth perception. Objects viewed below the horizon in the lower part of the visual field appear closer to the viewer than objects higher in the visual field. This effect is reversed for objects above the horizon.

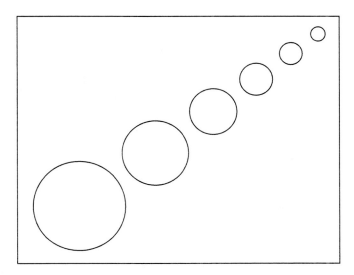

Figure 3.1   *Relative size as a visual depth cue.*

Occlusion (also called contour interruption or interposition) is the phenomenon in which an object closer to the user partially obstructs the view of an object farther away. When one opaque object occludes another, the user knows the first object is nearer (see Figure 3.2).

Linear perspective is the phenomenon that makes parallel lines appear to converge as they move away from the viewer. The closer the lines get to one another, the farther they appear to be from the viewer. In addition to showing occlusion, Figure 3.2 shows an example of linear perspective.

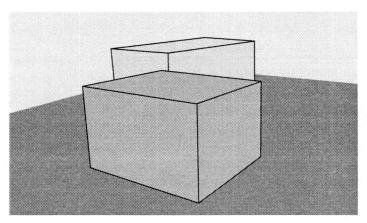

Figure 3.2   *Occlusion and linear perspective.*

Figure 3.3 *How shadows give the illusion of depth: the rectangle on the right appears to be much higher off the page than the rectangle on the left.*

Note that linear perspective does not require an object's contours to be straight; they can be of any shape as long as they are equally spaced (e.g., a winding roadway). *Aerial perspective* (also called atmospheric attenuation) is a cue that gauges relative distance by measuring the scattering and absorption of light through the atmosphere. For example, a nearer object will have more color saturation and brightness, while a more distant object will be duller and dimmer.

Shadows and lighting also play a role in helping the viewer to determine depth. *Shadows* convey depth as they fall on other objects or are cast from an object to adjacent surfaces. The viewer estimates the location of the light sources in the scene to determine how far an object is from an adjacent surface (see Figure 3.3). *Lighting* conveys depth because objects that have more illumination are generally perceived to be closer to the viewer.

Many surfaces and objects have patterns associated with them. When these patterns are projected onto a 2D surface, the density of the surface or object texture increases with distance between the surface and the viewer. This phenomenon is called an object's *texture gradient* and provides relative depth cues (see Figure 3.4).

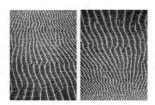

Figure 3.4 *Effects of texture gradient: the image on the right is simply the left image inverted. In both cases, depth is conveyed.*

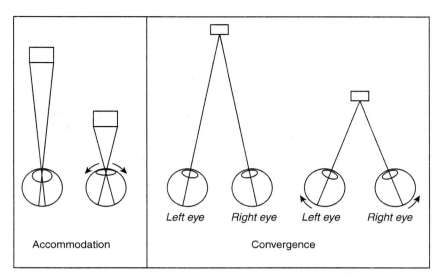

Figure 3.5 *Accommodation (left image) and convergence (right image): the arrows indicate the stretching of the eye lens for accommodation and the rotating of the eyes for convergence.*

Oculomotor Cues

Oculomotor cues (illustrated in Figure 3.5) are depth cues derived from muscular tension in the viewer's visual system, called accommodation and convergence. *Accommodation* is the physical stretching and relaxing of the eye lens caused by the eye muscles when focusing on an image. The state of these eye muscles in stretching and relaxing provides the viewer a cue as to the distance of the focused object. When an object is far away, these muscles relax, resulting in the lens being more spherical. When an object is close to the viewer, the eye muscles pull on the lens, flattening it out. *Convergence* is the rotation of the viewer's eyes so images can be fused together at varying distances. The muscular feedback from this rotation is also a cue as to the depth of the object. A viewer's two eyes converge when viewing near objects and diverge when viewing far objects.

Motion Parallax

Depth information is conveyed when objects are moving relative to the viewer (i.e., stationary-viewer motion parallax), when the viewer is moving relative to stationary objects (i.e., moving-viewer motion parallax), or through a combination of the two. *Motion parallax* causes objects closer to the viewer to move more quickly across the visual field and objects farther

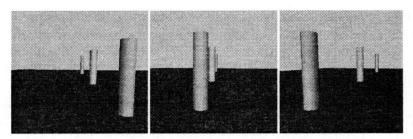

Figure 3.6   *A sequence of images illustrating motion parallax. As the viewer moves from left to right, the cylinder closest to the viewer appears to move the most, while the cylinder farthest away from the viewer appears to move the least. (Image courtesy of Joseph LaViola Jr.)*

away from the viewer to move more slowly (see Figure 3.6). As an example, consider someone in a moving car. As the car moves, objects such as streetlights and telephone poles that are on the side of the road appear to be moving very quickly past the viewer, while objects farther away from the car, such as a tall building or mountain, appear to move much more slowly. Motion parallax is called a *dynamic* depth cue, because it requires a moving image. In an otherwise sparse 3D environment, motion parallax can provide excellent depth information to the viewer.

Binocular Disparity and Stereopsis

Most people view the world with two eyes, and each eye sees a slightly different image. *Binocular disparity* refers to the difference between these two images. A great way to understand binocular disparity is to focus on a near object (such as your finger) and alternate opening and closing each eye. The differences between the two images will be readily apparent.

Binocular disparity tends to be much more pronounced the closer the object is to the viewer. The fusion of these two images (through accommodation and convergence) provides a powerful depth cue by presenting a single *stereoscopic* image. This effect is referred to as *stereopsis.* Note that if the two images cannot be properly fused (e.g., when an object is very close to the viewer) *binocular rivalry* can occur, which causes the viewer to see one image but not the other or a part of one image and a part of the other.

Depth Cue Relevance and Relationship to Visual Displays

A visual depth cue's strength varies depending on visual circumstances. Stereopsis is a very strong visual depth cue with objects in close proximity to the viewer (no more than 30 feet away), because there is very little binocular disparity with objects that are farther away. Because the oculomotor cues are linked to binocular disparity, they are also effective only for objects that are short distances from the viewer. In contrast, motion parallax can be a very strong visual cue, perhaps stronger than stereopsis, when objects are viewed at a wide range of depths. Of the monocular static cues, occlusion is the strongest.

In terms of visual displays, the monocular depth cues can be synthetically generated with almost any visual display device, assuming appropriate rendering hardware or software. In addition, motion parallax cues can be generated when the viewer and/or objects move through the world. Stereopsis usually requires special-purpose visual display devices, and the display system must produce a left- and a right-eye image with correct geometric properties (i.e., varying binocular disparity depending on object depth).

As for oculomotor cues, visual display devices that allow for stereo viewing also provide a proper convergence cue. However, accommodation cues are generally not present in stereoscopic displays, because graphically rendered objects are always in focus at the same focal depth—the depth of the screen (Cruz-Neira et al. 1993). In fact, the lack of accommodation cues with the majority of stereo visual display devices causes the accommodation–convergence mismatch illustrated in Figure 3.7. Because the graphics are displayed on a fixed screen, the user must focus at that depth to see the graphics sharply. However, the left- and

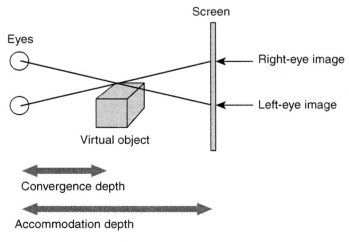

Figure 3.7 *Accommodation–convergence mismatch.*

right-eye images are drawn so that the user's eyes will converge to see the object at its virtual depth. When the virtual object depth and the screen depth are different, the user's oculomotor system sends conflicting signals to the brain about the distance to the object. In general, autostereoscopic devices (see the next section), do not have this cue conflict.

3.2.3. Visual Display Device Types

We now examine many different types of visual displays used in 3D UIs, which include the following:

- monitors
- surround-screen displays
- workbenches
- hemispherical displays
- head-mounted displays
- arm-mounted displays
- virtual retinal displays
- autostereoscopic displays

We look at specific examples and identify the advantages and disadvantages of each visual display type with respect to 3D interaction.

Monitors

Conventional monitors are commonly used in many different kinds of 3D applications, including modeling, scientific visualization, and computer games. They are relatively inexpensive and can provide monocular and motion parallax depth cues. Stereopsis can also be achieved using a standard monitor and some additional hardware (stereo glasses and a stereo-capable graphics card). Note that some monitors do not need any special hardware for stereopsis. These monitors are autostereoscopic in nature (discussed later in this section). In order to achieve high stereo quality, a monitor must have a high refresh rate because the display of the two images (one for each eye) effectively halves the refresh rate. As a rule of thumb, a monitor with a refresh rate of 100 Hz or better is usually acceptable for obtaining well-perceived stereo images. As a result of this requirement, liquid crystal display (LCD) monitors are rarely used with

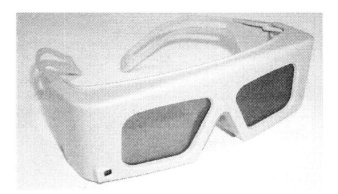

Figure 3.8 *Active stereo glasses for viewing stereoscopic images. (Photograph courtesy of Joseph J. LaViola Jr.)*

stereoscopic applications because their refresh rates are currently limited (approximately 85 Hz maximum).

Besides an appropriate monitor, a pair of stereo glasses is also needed to achieve stereoscopic viewing. These glasses can be either active or passive. Active stereo glasses, often called shutter glasses, are synchronized to open and close their shutters at a rate equal to the refresh rate of the visual display (temporal multiplexing). An example of active stereo glasses is shown in Figure 3.8. The images for the left and right eye are rapidly alternated on the screen, and the shutter glasses block one eye's view in a coordinated sequence to prevent it from seeing the other eye's view. Infrared signals are sent to the glasses to maintain this synchronization. If the signal is blocked, the shutter glasses stop working and the stereo effect is disrupted. As a general guideline, 3D UIs should discourage the user from moving his hands or other physical objects into the line of sight of the glasses and emitters.

Passive stereo glasses use either polarization or spectral multiplexing. *Polarization multiplexing* filters the two separate, overlaid images with oppositely polarized filters. For example, one filter could be horizontally polarized and the other vertically polarized so that each eye sees only one image. *Spectral multiplexing* (i.e., anaglyphic stereo) displays the two separate, overlaid images in different colors. The glasses use colored filters so light from any color other than the filter's color is effectively washed out. For example, blue and red anaglyph stereo glasses would allow only blue light to pass through the blue filter and only red light to pass through the red filter, so that each eye sees only its own image.

Anaglyph stereo is relatively inexpensive to produce, but it obviously has color limitations.

In general, active stereo is considered to achieve the highest stereo quality, but passive stereo has its place because the passive stereo glasses are inexpensive compared to shutter glasses and because there are no synchronization issues between the glasses and the generated images (i.e., no infrared emitter is needed).

A monitor coupled with a pair of stereo glasses (see Figure 3.9) makes for a simple yet effective visual display for 3D and VE applications. When a user is head-tracked (see Chapter 4 for information on user tracking), moving-viewer motion parallax becomes even easier to achieve. Such a setup is commonly referred to as fishtank virtual reality (Ware et al. 1993). These configurations are relatively inexpensive compared to other visual display devices, such as workbenches and surround-screen devices (see descriptions later in this section), and they provide excellent spatial resolution. They also allow the use of virtually any input device and can take full advantage of the keyboard and mouse. This flexibility provides the 3D UI developer with more input-device-to-interaction-technique mappings than do other visual display systems, because the user can see the physical world and is usually sitting at a desk. On the other hand, monitors are not very immersive, and the user has a very limited range of movement due to their small FOR. This limitation prohibits the use of many physically based travel techniques (see Chapter 6) and restricts the user's ability to use her peripheral vision. Additionally, because of the visual display's size, physical objects used for interaction often occlude the visual display, which can break any stereo illusion.

Figure 3.9   *A monitor equipped with stereo glasses. (Photograph courtesy of Daniel Acevedo Feliz, Brown University Computer Graphics Group)*

Surround-Screen Displays

A surround-screen display is a visual output device that has three or more large projection-based display screens (often between 8 and 12 feet in width and height) that surround the human participant (Figure 3.10 shows an example). Typically, the screens are rear-projected so users do not cast shadows on the display surface. However, in some cases, the floor of a surround-screen device can use front-projection as long as the projector is mounted such that the user's shadow is behind the user (e.g., as in Figure 3.10). Because there are multiple screens, either a large graphics workstation or a PC cluster is used to generate the images.

The first surround-screen VR system was developed at the Electronic Visualization Laboratory at the University of Illinois at Chicago. This system was called the CAVE (Cruz-Neira et al. 1993) and consisted of four screens (three walls and a floor). Since that time, a number of other surround-screen devices have been developed, including the C2, the C6, and the GROTTO, all with similar configurations.

There have been a number of interesting variations on the basic structure of a surround-screen display. For example, the Computer-driven Upper Body Environment (CUBE) is a 360-degree display environment composed of four 32- by 28-inch rear-projected Plexiglas screens. Users stand inside the CUBE, which is suspended from the ceiling, and physically turn around to view the screen surfaces. The screens are approximately one foot from the user's face and extend down to his or her midsection. It was developed at the Entertainment Technology Center at

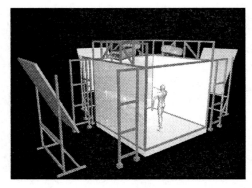

Figure 3.10 *A surround-screen VR system. The image shows a four-sided device (three walls and a floor). A projector mounted above the device projects images onto the floor (not pictured). (3D model courtesy of Mark Oribello, Brown University Graphics Group)*

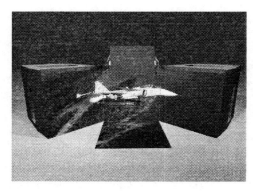

Figure 3.11   *The RAVE can be used as a large single-wall display, surround-screen device, or an L-shaped cove. (Photograph courtesy of Fakespace Systems)*

Carnegie Mellon University and represents a small, personalized version of a surround-screen display.

Figure 3.11 shows the RAVE, a reconfigurable advanced visualization environment. It is designed to be a flexible display device that can be used as a 30-foot flat wall, a 30-foot variable-angle immersive theater, a CAVE-like four-screen immersive environment, an L-shaped cove with separate 10-foot wall, or three separate 10-foot review walls.

There are a number of advantages to using a surround-screen display system. They typically provide high spatial resolution and a large FOR. In addition, such devices also have a large FOV, allowing the user to utilize his peripheral vision. Like a monitor, surround-screen devices provide monocular depth cues and motion parallax, and when the user is tracked and wears stereo glasses, the device also provides additional motion parallax cues and stereopsis respectively. In contrast with fishtank VR, a tracked user in a surround-screen display has much better moving-viewer motion parallax because the user can actually walk around in the device. As an example, a user could walk around a virtual chair projected in the center of the display and see the sides and back of the chair. The user does not have this capability with a fishtank VR setup. Stereopsis issues with surround-screen devices are also similar to those found with a stereo monitor configuration. Surround-screen stereo can be done actively with shutter glasses or passively with polarized glasses and special polarized lenses for the projectors. Most current systems use the former approach. Additionally, real and virtual objects can be mixed in the environment. For example, a tractor's cockpit could be brought into the display so an operator could test out its controls while driving through virtual farmland.

One of the biggest disadvantages of surround-screen display devices is that they are expensive and often require a large amount of physical space. For example, a 10- by 10- by 10-foot four-walled CAVE requires a room at least 30 feet long, 22 feet wide, and 12 feet high to handle the display screens and the mounted projectors. Another problem with these systems, as well as any projection-based display system, is that users can have difficulty seeing objects in stereo under certain conditions. When the user gets close to the display or when objects appear to be right in front of the user, it becomes increasingly difficult to use the visual system's accommodation and convergence capabilities to fuse the two images together. Eye strain is a common problem in these situations.

When more than one person inhabits a surround-screen device, they all view the same screens. However, images are rendered from the tracked user's perspective. If an untracked viewer moves in the device, there will be no response from the virtual environment (i.e., the images will be distorted). As the tracked user moves, all nontracked users effectively see the environment through the tracked user's perspective, which can cause cue conflicts and lead to cybersickness (LaViola 2000a). This problem is a fundamental limitation of surround-screen displays, as well as any visual display device that claims to accommodate multiple users, and is a disadvantage compared to the unlimited number of active viewpoints when using multiple head-mounted displays. If nontracked users stay close to and look in the same direction as the tracked user, they can get a rough approximation of the correct viewpoint, but this is not a completely satisfactory solution.

Techniques have been developed to increase the number of active viewpoints. Currently, a maximum of two active stereoscopic viewpoints (Agrawala et al. 1997) or four monoscopic viewpoints (Blom et al. 2002) are possible at any one time. The basic approach to adding more than one active viewpoint is to render images from two or more tracked users and then synchronize the images with the shutter glasses. For example, to allow two active stereoscopic viewpoints, the graphics must be rendered and displayed four times (once for each eye of the two viewers) per frame. The shutter glasses then must be modified so that for one viewer, the left and right eyes switch between the ON/OFF and OFF/ON states while the second viewer's glasses are turned completely off. Then, the second viewer's glasses are in the ON/OFF and OFF/ON states while the first viewer's glasses are turned completely off. Of course, when using this approach, the refresh rate for each eye is cut in half because each eye will see only one of four images displayed—this may cause flicker problems. The frame rate will also be affected, because the rendering engine must perform twice as many computations.

Although physical objects do not have to be represented as graphical objects in surround-screen display systems, an important issue with using physical objects in this type of display device is the physical/virtual object occlusion problem. The problem arises when the user tries to move a physical object behind a virtual object. Visually, the physical object will appear in front of the graphical object because the graphical object is actually being projected on the screen. This is a common problem with any projection-based display device, and it can lessen the immersive experience and break the stereo illusion.

Workbenches

Another type of projection-based display is the Responsive Workbench, originally developed by Krüger and Fröhlich (1994). This display device was designed to model and augment interaction that takes place on desks, tables, and workbenches. Today, such devices go by many different names, such as Immersadesk, VersaBench, Baron, and VisionMaker. Figure 3.12 shows two workbench displays with differing characteristics. The picture on the left shows a standard single workbench with the display oriented almost vertically. The image on the right shows a small

Figure 3.12   *Workbench style displays. (Photographs courtesy of Fakespace Systems)*

workbench that has a pressure-sensitive display surface for 2D input, which lets users write on the screen surface and makes it easier to utilize both 2D and 3D interaction techniques. An L-shaped workbench with two screens is also a common configuration.

In general, workbenches provide relatively high spatial resolution and make for an intuitive display for certain types of applications. Relative to surround-screen displays, workbench screen sizes are smaller, which improves visual quality. Workbenches also can provide the same visual depth cues that surround-screen displays and monitors do (assuming appropriate stereo and user-tracking hardware). In many device designs, the display can be rotated so the screen's orientation relative to the user is anywhere from completely horizontal to fully vertical, making the device quite flexible. For example, a horizontal configuration is ideally suited to a surgical training application, while a 35-degree orientation would be useful in a drafting or 3D modeling application.

As with a surround-screen display, the device accommodates multiple users but with the same viewpoint constraints described in the previous section. In general, users have limited mobility when interacting with a workbench because the display is not head-coupled like a head-mounted display (discussed later in this section) and does not enclose them like a surround-screen display. Therefore, as with monitors, the range of viewpoints from which a user can see 3D imagery is restricted because for some viewpoints, all or part of the screen is not visible. For example, it would not be possible for a user to see the bottom of a stationary graphical object with a completely horizontal workbench, because the display surface would no longer be in the user's FOV. From a 3D interaction perspective, then, physically based travel techniques are not appropriate when using a workbench, because the user has little maneuverability compared to other display devices. However, most direct selection and manipulation techniques (see Chapter 5) work well because most of the workbench screen real estate is within arm's reach.

Hemispherical Displays

Hemispherical displays are projection-based devices that use special software and optics to display images in a 180- by 180-degree field of view with projection diameters of varying sizes. For these types of devices, a wide-angle lens is attached to the projector, which distorts the output image. Spherical mapping software is used to predistort the image so that it appears correctly on the curved screen. An example of a smaller

Figure 3.13   *A hemispherical display. (Photograph courtesy of Elumens Corporation)*

hemispherical device (a projection diameter of 4 feet) that acts as a personalized display is shown in Figure 3.13. The user sits in front of a small table and can interact with 3D applications using a keyboard and mouse or 3D input devices. Hemispherical displays with much larger projection diameters have been developed to accommodate multiple users, but they have the same active viewpoint restrictions that all monitors and projection displays do.

These display devices can provide the same visual depth cues that appropriately equipped surround-screen displays, workbenches, and monitors afford. In addition, they are often front-projected, which makes the display brighter than most rear-projected devices. However, direct 3D selection, manipulation, and navigation techniques may not work well, because moving too close to the display surface casts shadows on the screen, breaking the stereo illusion and possibly occluding virtual objects. For these types of devices, indirect techniques such as virtual laser pointers or keyboard- and mouse-based video game–style controls work best. Another problem with hemispherical displays is that spatial resolution and image quality are usually not uniform across the display. In general, the center of the hemisphere has higher resolution and quality, while these values decrease toward the screen's edges.

Head-Mounted Displays

Our discussion of visual display devices has so far focused on stationary displays (i.e., displays that do not move with the user). In this section and the next two, we examine visual displays in which the user's head is attached (coupled) to the visual display device. One of the most common head-coupled display devices used for VE applications is the head-mounted display (HMD). An HMD is a sophisticated piece of equipment because it requires the complex integration of electronic, optical, mechanical, and even audio components (some HMDs support 3D stereo sound). As such, many different HMDs have been designed and developed over the years. Regardless of internal design, an HMD's main goal is to place images directly in front of the user's eyes using one (for monoscopic viewing) or two (for stereoscopic viewing) small screens. A combination of refractive lenses and/or mirrors (depending on the optical technique used) are used to present and sometimes magnify the images shown on the screens (see Stuart [1996] for more details on the physical design of HMDs). An example of an HMD is shown in Figure 3.14.

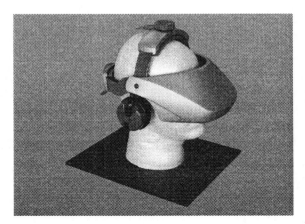

Figure 3.14 *A head-mounted display. (Image courtesy of Fifth Dimension Technologies: www.5dt.com)*

Most HMDs use either LCD or cathode ray tube (CRT) screens. An alternative, however, is the head-mounted projective display (HMPD). In HMPDs, small LCD projectors are attached to the HMD, and these project the graphical images into the real environment. Retroreflective material (a special bendable material that reflects light back in the direction it came from regardless of its incident angle with the screen surface) is placed strategically in the environment so that the user sees the graphics reflecting off the material. HMPDs thus are a hybrid between conventional HMDs and projection displays (Hua et al. 2001). HMPDs are ideally suited to collaborative applications in mixed reality (see Chapter 12) because using retroreflective screens provides correct occlusion cues for both virtual and real objects and because each participant has his own individually correct viewpoint (Hua et al. 2002).

In terms of visual depth cues, as with other display systems, tracked HMDs allow for all the monoscopic and motion parallax depth cues. Stereoscopy is produced differently with HMDs than with projection-based displays and monitors. With non-head-coupled devices, stereo is produced using temporal multiplexing (i.e., drawing images for the left and right eye on the same screen sequentially). With an HMD, stereopsis is achieved by drawing two separate images on two separate screens—one for each eye. As a result, the graphics engine driving the HMD must be able to support two separate simultaneous display channels. Because not all commodity graphics hardware supports two channels, most HMDs allow the same image to be displayed on both screens, resulting in monoscopic viewing.

One of the biggest advantages of HMDs is that the user can have complete physical visual immersion (i.e., a 360-degree FOR) because the user always sees the virtual world regardless of head position and orientation. Although, in general, HMDs block out the real world, a camera is sometimes mounted on the HMD, allowing it to display both real-world video and graphical objects. In addition, some HMDs offer see-through options. This type of technology is used in augmented and mixed reality systems (see Chapter 12).

Even though tracked HMDs have a 360-degree FOR, many of them have small FOVs (between 30 and 60 degrees horizontal), which can cause perception and performance problems. Even high-end HMDs have limited FOVs when compared to surround-screen displays. According to Neale (1998), restricted FOVs can impede a user's ability to acquire spatial information and develop spatial cognitive maps of unfamiliar spaces. Small FOVs may also produce distortions in perception of size and distance. These types of problems can hinder the user's experience with the application and make wayfinding (see Chapter 7) difficult.

HMDs have other benefits when compared to projection-based displays and monitors. HMDs do not suffer from the active viewpoint problem that plagues projection-based displays and monitors, because each user can have his own HMD with his own tracked view of the virtual world. Of course, multiple HMDs require multiple graphics engines to drive them, and this can get costly as the number of participants increases. Multiple viewers also cannot see each other when wearing HMDs.

HMDs have both pros and cons when it comes to stereoscopic viewing. Because they use one screen per eye, HMDs eliminate the need to do temporal multiplexing. A potential problem with stereoscopic HMDs is that each person has a different interocular distance (the distance between the two eyes), meaning that stereo images have to be separated by that distance for correct binocular stereopsis. Many HMDs do not provide a way to adjust for interocular distance, making stereo viewing problematic for some users. Additionally, because the images the user sees are always in focus and have the same focal depth, accommodation and convergence cue conflicts can occur when users look at objects with different virtual depths, causing eye strain and discomfort. This phenomenon also occurs with projection-based displays and monitors but may be more pronounced with HMDs because the screens are close to the user's eyes. Omura, Shiwa, and Kishino (1996) developed a system to alleviate this problem by incorporating movable relay lenses into an HMD. The lenses are continuously adjusted based on gaze direction. The screen surface appears at the same distance as the user's convergence point, creating a display with matched accommodation and convergence cues. However, these types of display systems are still in the early stages of development.

HMDs have the advantage of being more portable, brighter, and less expensive as compared to projection-based displays. However, projection-based displays and monitors generally have higher spatial resolutions than HMDs because the display screens have to be small and lightweight to keep the overall weight of the HMD low. Weight restrictions are one of the main reasons that most HMDs use lighter, but lower-quality, LCD screens over higher-quality but heavier CRT screens. Ergonomically, the weight and shape of an HMD must be considered because a heavier HMD can cause strain in neck muscles from extended use. HMDs may not fit every user, because everyone has different head sizes and shapes.

Because the real world may be completely blocked from the user's view, interaction while wearing an HMD often requires some type of graphical representation of either one or both hands, or the input device used. These graphical representations can be as simple as a cube or as sophisticated as a hand model containing thousands of polygons. HMDs also limit the types of input devices that can be used because the user cannot physically see the device in order to use it. More details on head-mounted displays can be found in Melzer and Moffitt (1996).

Arm-Mounted Displays

An arm-mounted display is simply a visual display device attached to an armature. Typically, these devices have a counterweight on the opposite side of the display to make it easier to manipulate. For example, the arm-mounted display shown in Figure 3.15 is called a Binocular Omni-Orientation Monitor (BOOM), developed by Bolas (1994). Using the counterweight makes it possible for this device to use better optics and heavier, higher-quality display screens (i.e., CRTs), providing greater resolution. The BOOM supports up to 1280×1024 pixels per eye, which is

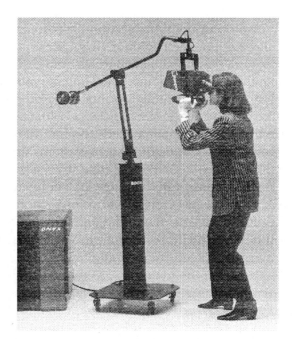

Figure 3.15   *An arm-mounted display called the Binocular Omni-Orientation Monitor. (Photograph of the Boom 3C courtesy of Fakespace Labs, Mountain View, California)*

Figure 3.16   *An arm-mounted display called the BOOM-Chameleon. (Photograph courtesy of Alias)*

better than most average-quality HMDs, which typically provide 800 × 600 pixels per eye. This device also uses mechanical tracking technology (see Chapter 4) to track the user's head position and orientation. The BOOM is not the only type of arm-mounted display. Tsang and colleagues (2002) developed an arm-mounted device that attaches a flat panel display to an armature (Figure 3.16). This display enables the metaphor of a "window" into the 3D virtual world.

The BOOM provides the same visual cues that HMDs do and suffers from many of the same problems. However, because the user does not have to wear the device, it is easy to operate, allows for different users to trade places quickly, and avoids the ergonomic issues of differing user head size and shape. Arm-mounted displays are typically attached to a large stand, so the user's movement is limited. Users can move in a relatively small area (e.g., a 6-foot diameter with the BOOM) around the center of the stand, which limits the use many of the physically based navigation techniques described in Chapter 6. Another disadvantage with arm-mounted displays is that the user must have at least one hand on the device to move it around the environment, which can limit various types of two-handed interaction.

Virtual Retinal Displays

The virtual retinal display (VRD), also called the light-scanning display, was invented at the Human Interface Technology Lab in 1991 (Tidwell et al. 1995). It is based on the idea that images can be directly displayed onto the retina. With a VRD, photon sources are used to generate coherent beams of light (e.g., lasers), which allow the system to draw a rasterized image onto the retina. In order to generate full-color images, three light sources are needed (red, green, and blue), while monochrome versions of the VRD require only one. These light beams are intensity-modulated to match the intensity of the image being rendered, meaning that is possible to produce fully immersive and see-through display modes. The light beams then scan across the retina to place each image point, or pixel, at the proper position. With one current version of the display, the viewer sees an image equivalent to a 14-inch monitor viewed from 2 feet away.

VRDs have the potential to be very powerful visual displays for 3D applications because they can provide a high FOV (almost approaching human vision) with bright, high-resolution, stereo images. A head-tracking device could also be added to a VRD to provide a fully immersive FOR and motion parallax based on head motion. The picture at the top of Figure 3.17 shows an example of what a lightweight, dual-eye VRD might look like. The two bottom pictures show examples of existing VRDs. Both of these displays are see-through. The one on the bottom left projects retinal images to only one eye, and the one on the bottom right projects images to both eyes.

One of the major issues with existing VRDs is a lack of eye tracking. If users move their eyes while using a VRD, they can lose all or part of the image, because the retinal beams are projected to a single location. However, work by Chinthammit, Seibel, and Furness (2002) has alleviated this problem through the development of an eye-tracking system that allows VRD images to be coupled to a user's eye movements.

Another issue with VRDs that present stereo images to the user is the accommodation–convergence problem that plagues stereoscopic displays. As stated in previous sections, accommodation and convergence cue conflicts can occur because the images the user sees are always in focus and have the same focal depth. Research by McQuaide and colleagues (2002) uses a VRD and deformable membrane mirror (a

Figure 3.17 *The top picture shows a lightweight dual-eye prototype of a VRD; the two bottom pictures show some existing light-scanning devices. (Photographs courtesy of Microvision)*

microelectromechanical system) to dynamically change the focal plane, which would enable the viewer to see 3D objects using the natural accommodative response of the visual system. Although this work is in its early stages, it shows great promise in helping to overcome one of the fundamental limitations with today's stereoscopic display systems, enabling the use of all the visual depth cues.

Unfortunately, there has been little work done with VRDs in the context of 3D UIs. However, VRDs like the one shown on the bottom left of Figure 3.17 are used in augmented reality applications in the medical, aerospace, and defense industries. For example, an airplane maintenance technician could use a VRD to access repair information while examining an airplane wing. As such, the technician is performing 3D interaction with the real world and using the visual display as an assistant in the repair process (see Chapter 12 for more information on augmented reality interfaces). For VEs, one could speculate that the advantages and disadvantages that accompany 3D UIs when using HMDs would also be applicable to virtual retinal displays.

Autostereoscopic Displays

In this last section on visual displays, we discuss *autostereoscopic* display devices, which generate 3D imagery without the need for special shutter or polarized glasses. These displays mainly use lenticular, volumetric, or holographic display technology, and we describe these below. However, other techniques for creating autostereoscopic displays exist as well, including the diffractive-optical element approach, integral imaging, parallax illumination, and barrier grids. A discussion of these techniques goes beyond the scope of this book, but Pastoor and Wöpking (1997) provide a nice survey of these autostereoscopic display technologies.

Lenticular displays (see Figure 3.18) use either a vertical grating or a cylindrical lens array in front of the display screen. With the vertical grating approach, one eye sees odd pixels through the grating, while the other eye sees even pixels. The cylindrical lens array approach directs different 2D images into different subzones, and these zones are projected out at different angles. When the viewer's head is positioned correctly in front of the display, each eye sees a different image, allowing for binocular disparity. These techniques have the drawback that the user must be in a stationary position. Extensions to the basic approach do allow for user movement and the maintaining of motion parallax (see Perlin et al. [2000] and Schwerdtner and Heidrich [1998] for more detail).

Figure 3.18   *A lenticular display. (Photograph courtesy of SeeReal Technologies GmbH)*

According to Blundell and Schwarz (2000), a volumetric display device permits the generation, absorption, or scattering of visible radiation from a set of localized and specified regions within a physical volume (holographic displays can also fit into this definition). In other words, volumetric displays create "true" 3D images by actually illuminating points in 3D space. This is in contrast to other stereoscopic displays, which provide the illusion of 3D images but are actually projected onto a 2D surface. Volumetric displays generate 3D imagery using a number of different methods. Two of the most common use either a swept- or a static-volume technique (Balakrishnan et al. 2001).

Swept-volume techniques sweep a periodically time-varying 2D image through a 3D spatial volume at high frequencies. Displays using swept-volume techniques (see Figure 3.19) have a mechanical component because they essentially spin a 2D screen within the viewing volume to create the 3D image. Static-volume techniques create 3D images without the need of mechanical motion within the viewing volume. One static-volume approach uses two intersecting invisible laser beams to create a single point of visible light. This allows the drawing of voxels (3D pixels) inside the volume by controlling when and where the lasers intersect. Rapidly scanning these intersection points in a predefined way enables the drawing of a true 3D image (Ebert et al. 1999). Other static-volume approaches use a high-speed projector with a stack of air-spaced liquid crystal scattering shutters (multiplanar optical elements), which act as an electronically variable projection volume. The high-speed projector projects a sequence of slices of the 3D image into the stack of scattering

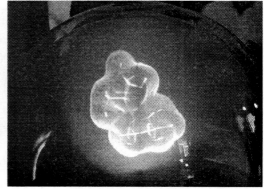

Figure 3.19 *A volumetric display system that uses the swept-volume technique. On the left is the display device, and on the right, a volumetric image. (Photographs courtesy of Actuality Systems)*

Figure 3.20   *A volumetric display that uses a multiplanar, static-volume approach to generate 3D images. (Photograph courtesy of LightSpace Technologies)*

shutters, and each slice is halted at the proper depth (Sullivan 2003). Figure 3.20 shows a display using this static-volume approach.

Holographic displays are similar to volumetric displays in that they both produce true 3D images. However, these displays use different techniques to generate them. Holographic displays produce 3D imagery by recording and reproducing the properties of light waves (amplitude, wavelength, and phase differences) from a 3D scene. The process involves a computational step in which a 3D description of a scene is converted into a holographic fringe pattern (a diffraction pattern that captures light from different directions), and an optical step that modulates the fringe pattern and turns it into a 3D image. Lucente (1997) provides a detailed introduction to the steps involved in generating 3D images using holographic displays.

An important concept to understand about volumetric and holographic displays is that because they produce true 3D imagery, they do not suffer from the active viewpoint problem that plagues projection-based displays and monitors. Therefore, the number of viewers with the correct perspective is basically unlimited. In addition, with these devices, no trackers are needed to maintain moving-viewer motion parallax. They also do not suffer from the accommodation–convergence cue conflicts that accompany more traditional stereoscopic displays. However, current volumetric displays have the problem that they cannot provide many monocular depth cues, such as occlusion and shading. Additionally, both volumetric and holographic displays generally can display images only within a small working volume, making them inappropriate for immersive VEs or augmented reality.

As with VRDs, there has been little 3D interface work with lenticular and holographic displays. However, the same interfaces that work for rear-projected displays should also work for lenticular displays. Volumetric displays have an interesting characteristic in that many of them have an enclosure around the actual 3D imagery, making for interesting interface possibilities. Balakrishnan, Fitzmaurice, and Kurtenbach (2001) built volumetric display prototypes to explore these issues. They have developed a set of UI design options specific to these displays for performing tasks such as object selection, manipulation, and navigation (see Balakrishnan et al. [2001] for more details).

3.3. Auditory Displays

Auditory displays are another approach to presenting information (sound) to the user, but they are overlooked in many 3D UIs (Cohen and Wenzel 1995). One of the major goals of auditory displays in VEs is the generation and display of spatialized 3D sound, enabling the human participant to take advantage of his auditory localization capabilities. *Localization* is the psychoacoustic process of determining the location and direction from which a sound emanates (Sherman and Craig 2003). Having this feature in a 3D application can provide many important benefits to the 3D UI designer.

Note that the topic of auditory displays and 3D sound generation is a very large and active field, and going into intense detail on the subject is beyond the scope of this book. For more details on 3D sound and audio displays, Blauert (1997), Begault (1994), Shilling and Shinn-Cunningham (2002), and Kapralos, Jenkin, and Milios (2003) all provide comprehensive introductions.

3.3.1. 3D Sound Localization Cues

As with the visual system, the auditory system provides listeners with a number of different localization cues that allow them to determine the direction and distance of a sound source. Although there are many different localization cues, the main ones that apply to 3D UIs (Shilling and Shinn-Cunningham 2002) are

- binaural cues
- spectral and dynamic cues

- head-related transfer functions (HRTFs)
- reverberation
- sound intensity
- vision and environment familiarity

We briefly describe these cues and discuss their relative strengths, which often depend on sound-source distance. More details on localization cues and spatial hearing can be found in Gelfand (1998) and Yost (1994).

Binaural Cues

Binaural cues arise from a comparison of the sound waves received by each ear. Depending on the location of the sound source, one ear may receive a sound earlier than another. The difference in time between the arrival of the sound to each ear is known as the interaural time difference (ITD) and is an important cue for determining the sound source's lateral location (i.e., whether the sound source is to the left or the right of the listener). Similarly, because the ears are separated by the listener's head, higher-frequency sound waves (above 2 kHz) are reflected and diffracted by the head so that less acoustic energy reaches the far side of the head, causing an *acoustic shadow.* Therefore, the relative intensities of the sound vary for each ear depending on the lateral location of the sound source. The difference in sound intensities arriving at each ear is called the interaural intensity difference (IID) and is another important cue for determining a sound source's lateral location.

The fundamental problem with binaural cues is that there are locations relative to the listener's head where ambiguous situations occur (in the absence of any other cues). These situations occur whenever two different sound-source locations provide similar values for the ITD and IID. This phenomenon occurs primarily in two cases. First, when the sound source is directly in front, behind, above, or below the listener, the sound waves will reach each ear at approximately the same time, and the sound's intensity will be approximately the same for both ears, resulting in IIDs and ITDs that are close to zero. Second, for sound sources that are more than about 3 feet from the listener, there are a set of points that approximate a hyperbolic surface symmetric with the interaural axis (i.e., the axis that runs through the user's two ears), which provide roughly the same ITD and IID values (Kendall 1995). In these situations, other cues are needed to localize sound sources.

Spectral and Dynamic Cues

One of the ways a listener can deal with ambiguous binaural cues is with dynamic movement of the listener's head or the sound source itself. For example, if the sound source was directly in front of the listener, a leftward rotation of the head would result in the ITD and IID favoring the right ear, thus helping to break the ambiguity. However, investigations into moving sound sources have shown that dynamic movement is still a fairly weak cue (Shilling and Shinn-Cunningham 2002).

The primary cue for resolving sound-source locations in regions of binaural ambiguity is the spectral content of the signals reaching the ears. These cues arise because of the interaction of the sound wave and the outer ear (called the pinna) and depend on the relative position of the sound source to the listener's head. In other words, the frequency spectrum of a sound source varies with respect to source distance because of absorption effects (Kapralos et al. 2003). Spectral cues do have their drawbacks in that they occur only at relatively high frequencies (above 6 kHz).

Head-Related Transfer Functions

Head-related transfer functions (HRTFs) are the spatial filters that describe how sound waves interact with the listener's torso, shoulders, head, and particularly the outer ears. The outer ears are relatively complex anatomical structures with many notches and grooves that heighten or suppress sound waves at mid and high frequencies depending on the location and frequency content of the sound source. Therefore, HRTFs modify the sound waves from a sound source in a location-dependent manner. These modified sound waves provide a localization cue to the listener.

One of the interesting properties of HRTFs is that they contain most of the spatial information contained in real-world listening conditions. ITD and IID cues are encoded within the relative phase and magnitude of filters for the left and right ears. In addition, spectral information and sound intensity is present in the absolute frequency-dependent magnitudes of the two filters (Shilling and Shinn-Cunningham 2002). HRTFs also provide cues that help listeners deal with the ambiguous cases for binaural cues. However, HRTFs have their complications in that they are listener-specific, making them difficult to generalize, and they generally do not contain any reverberation information, which is another important cue for localizing sound sources.

Reverberation

In natural environments, many different factors may affect the sound waves emanating from a sound source, including atmospheric properties (temperature, humidity, etc.) and various objects, which can absorb these waves and reflect them in different directions. Therefore, sound waves emanating from a sound source can reach the listener both directly and indirectly (e.g., off the walls, furniture, ceiling, etc.). *Reverberation* is the collection of these reflected waves from various surfaces within a space and acts as an important acoustical cue for localizing sound sources.

Reverberation as a cue does little if anything to aid the listener in the perception of a sound source's direction, but it does aid in the perception of source distance (Shilling and Shinn-Cunningham 2002). In addition, it also provides information about the size and configuration of a listening environment.

Sound Intensity

A sound's intensity (which is perceived as loudness) is a primary cue for determining a sound source's distance because it will decrease as the distance to the source increases. Because of the simplicity of simulating this cue, it has often been used in 3D auditory displays (Begault 1994).

Vision and Environmental Familiarity

In many cases, the visual system can be used in conjunction with the auditory system to form spatial percepts (Welch and Warren 1986), which can be used to determine a sound's location. Of course, these percepts are useful only if the sound source is within the user's FOV. In addition, a listener's prior experience with a particular sound and environment can affect the listener's ability to determine the sound source's location. This can be very important in 3D and VE applications where wayfinding (see Chapter 7) is needed.

3.3.2. 3D Sound Generation

Before 3D sound can be used in a 3D UI, it must be generated in some way. This generation process is important because it can have an effect on the quality of the interface and the user's overall experience with the application. There are many different techniques for generating 3D sound, and we briefly describe two of the most common. The first is 3D sound sampling and synthesis, and the second is auralization.

3D Sound Sampling and Synthesis

The basic idea behind 3D sound sampling and synthesis is to record sound that the listener would hear in the 3D application by taking samples from a real environment. For example, with *binaural audio recording,* two small microphones are placed inside the user's ears (or in the ears of an anthropomorphic dummy head) to separately record the sounds heard by left and right ears in the natural environment. All of the 3D sound cues discussed in section 3.3.1 are present in these recordings, which are capable of producing very realistic results. However, the main problem with this type of sound generation is that it is specific to the environmental settings in which the recordings were made. Therefore, any change in the sound source's location, introduction of new objects into the environment, or significant movement of the user would require new recordings. Unfortunately, these changes will occur in most 3D applications, making this basic technique impractical for the majority of situations.

An alternative approach, which is one of the most common 3D sound generation techniques used in 3D applications today, is to imitate the binaural recording process by processing a monaural sound source with a pair of left- and right-ear HRTFs corresponding to a desired position within the 3D environment (Kapralos et al. 2003). With these empirically defined HRTFs, real-time interactivity becomes much more feasible because particular sound sources can be placed anywhere in the environment and the HRTFs will filter them accordingly to produce 3D spatial audio for the listener.

As with binaural recording, there are some important issues that need to be considered with the HRTF approach. In general, HRTF measurements are taken in echo-free environments, meaning that they will not produce reverberation cues. Additionally, as with binaural recording, one pair of HRTFs applies to only one position in the environment, which means that many HRTF pairs are needed in order to have spatial audio in the whole space. Ideally, HRTF measurement should be done for all possible points in the space, but this is highly impractical because of time and resource constraints. One approach to dealing with this problem is to use interpolation schemes to fill in the HRTF measurement gaps (Kulkarni and Colburn 1993). The other major issue with using HRTF measurements for generating spatialized sound is that there is a large variation between the HRTFs of different subjects. These differences are due to variations in each listener's outer ears, differences in measurement procedures, and perturbations in the sound field by the measuring instruments (Carlile 1996). One method for dealing with these variations is to use generic HRTFs. These HRTFs are constructed in a number of ways, including using an anthropomorphic dummy head or averaging the responses of several listeners (Kapralos et al. 2003).

Auralization

Auralization is the process of rendering the sound field of a source in space in such a way as to simulate the binaural listening experience through the use of physical and mathematical models (Kleiner et al. 1993). The goal of auralization is to recreate a listening environment by determining the reflection patterns of sound waves coming from a sound source as they move through the environment. Therefore, this process is very useful for creating reverberation effects.

The two main computer-based approaches to creating these sound fields are wave-based modeling and ray-based modeling. With wave-based modeling techniques, the goal is to solve the wave equation so as to completely re-create a particular sound field. In many cases, there is no analytical solution to this equation, which means that numerical solutions are required. In the ray-based approach, the paths taken by the sound waves as they travel from source to listener are found by following rays emitted from the source. The problem with the ray-based approach is that these rays ignore the wavelengths of the sound waves and any phenomena associated with them, such as diffraction. This means this technique is appropriate only when sound wavelengths are smaller than the objects in the environment but larger than the roughness of them (Huopaniemi 1999). Other material on auralization and its use in VEs can be found in Dobashi, Yamamoto, and Nishita (2003); Naer, Staadt, and Gross (2002); Tsingos and colleagues (2001); and Funkhouser, Min, and Carlbom (1999).

3.3.3. Sound System Configurations

The 3D sound generated using any of the many techniques available can then be presented to the user. The two basic approaches for displaying these signals are to use headphones or external speakers, and there are advantages and disadvantages to each.

Headphones

A common approach to the display of 3D sound is to use stereophonic headphones that present different information to each ear. Note that if

3D sound is not required in the 3D UI, monophonic (presenting the same information to each ear) headphones will work just as well, but for the purposes of this discussion, when we refer to headphones, we are referring to the stereophonic variety. Headphones have many distinct advantages in a 3D UI. They provide a high level of channel separation, which helps to avoid *crosstalk*, a phenomenon that occurs when the left ear hears sound intended for the right ear, and vice versa. They also isolate the user from external sounds in the physical environment, which helps to ensure that these sounds do not affect the listener's perception. They are often combined with visual displays that block out the real world, such as HMDs, helping to create fully immersive experiences. Additionally, headphones allow multiple users to receive 3D sound (assuming that they are all head-tracked) simultaneously, and they are somewhat easier to deal with because there are only two sound channels to control.

The main disadvantage of headphones is a phenomenon called inside-the-head localization (IHL). IHL is the lack of externalization of a sound source, which results in the false impression that a sound is emanating from inside the user's head (Kendall 1993). IHL occurs mainly because of the lack of correct environmental information, that is, lack of reverberation and HRTF information (Kapralos et al. 2003). The best way to minimize IHL is to ensure that the sounds delivered to the listener are as natural as possible. Of course, this naturalness is difficult to achieve based on our previous discussions on the complexity of 3D sound generation. At a minimum, having accurate HRTF information will go a long way toward reducing IHL. Including reverberation can basically eliminate IHL at a cost of reduced user localization accuracy (Begault 1992). Another minor disadvantage of headphones is that they can be cumbersome and uncomfortable to wear for extended periods of time. According to Begault (1994), other than the IHL problem and possible comfort issues, headphone displays are superior devices for conveying 3D spatialized sound.

External Speakers

The second approach to display 3D sound is to use external speakers placed at strategic locations in the environment. This approach is often used with projection-based visual displays. The main limitation with this approach is that it makes it difficult to present 3D sound to more than one head-tracked user (external speakers work very well for nonspatialized sound with multiple users). On the other hand, with external speakers, the user does not have to wear any additional devices.

The major challenge with using external speakers for displaying 3D sound is how to avoid crosstalk and make sure the listener's left and right ears receive the appropriate signals. The two main approaches for presenting 3D sound over external speakers are with transaural audio and amplitude panning. *Transaural audio* allows for the presentation of the left and right binaural audio signals to the corresponding left and right ears using external speakers (Kapralos et al. 2003). Although transaural audio overcomes IHL, it requires some type of crosstalk cancellation technique, which can be computationally expensive, to ensure that the ear does not receive unwanted signals. See Gardner (1998); Mouchtaris, Reveliotis, and Kyrakakis (2000); and Garas (2000) for details on different crosstalk cancellation algorithms. *Amplitude panning* adjusts the intensity of the sound in some way to simulate the directional properties of the ITD and IID. In other words, by systematically varying each external speaker's intensity, a phantom source is produced in a given location. Although amplitude panning produces a robust perception of a sound source at different locations, it is very difficult to precisely control the exact position of the phantom source (Shilling and Shinn-Cunningham 2002). See Pulkki (2001) for details on many different amplitude panning techniques.

A final issue when using external speakers is speaker placement because sounds emanating from external speakers can bounce or be filtered though real-world objects, hampering sound quality. For example, in a surround-screen system, placing the speakers in front of the visual display could obstruct the graphics, while placing them behind the display could muffle the sound.

3.3.4. Audio in 3D Interfaces

There are several different ways 3D interfaces can use audio displays, including

- localization
- sonification
- ambient effects
- sensory substitution
- annotation and help

Localization

As stated at the beginning of section 3.3, the generation of 3D spatial sound creates an important audio depth cue, providing the user with the ability to use her localization skills and giving her an aural sense of the virtual environment. Three-dimensional sound can be used in a variety of ways in 3D interfaces, including audio wayfinding aids (see Chapter 7), acoustical cues for locating enemies in games and training applications, to help in target acquisition, and others.

Sonification

Sonification is the process of turning information into sounds (the audio equivalent of visualization). It can be useful when trying to get a better understanding of different types of data. For example, in a 3D scientific visualization application for examining fluid flow, a user could move her hand through a portion of the dataset, and sounds of varying frequency could be generated to correspond to varying flow speeds.

Ambient Effects

Ambient sound effects can provide a sense of realism in a VE. For example, hearing birds chirping and the wind whistling through the trees helps to augment an outdoor wilderness environment, and hearing cars traveling down city streets could make a city environment more compelling.

Sensory Substitution

In the case of audio displays, *sensory substitution* is the process of substituting sound for another sensory modality, such as touch. This substitution can be a powerful tool in 3D interfaces when haptic feedback (see section 3.4) is not present. For example, a sound could substitute for the feel of a button press or physical interaction with a virtual object, or it could let the user know an operation has been completed.

Annotation and Help

Recorded or synthesized speech can play a role as an annotation tool in collaborative applications, such as distributed model viewers, and in providing help to users when interacting in the 3D environment is unclear.

3.4. Haptic Displays

The last type of display device that we examine in this chapter is the haptic display. Haptic displays try to provide the user with the sense of touch by simulating the physical interaction between virtual objects and the user. The word *haptic* comes from the Greek word *haptesthai,* meaning "to touch," but is used to refer to both force (joint/muscle) and tactile (skin-based) feedback (Burdea 1996). Therefore, depending on the haptic display, these devices provide the user with a sense of force, a sense of touch, or a combination of the two. Haptic displays also can be considered, in many cases, to be both input and output devices because of their physical connection to the user. Because of this connection, many haptic display devices are also tracking devices (see Chapter 4), so they can provide the necessary information, such as user position and orientation, to the display system to generate the appropriate force and tactile feedback.

An important component of a haptic display system (besides the actual physical device) is the software used to synthesize forces and tactile sensations that the display device presents to the user. The software used in these interfaces is called *haptic rendering* software and includes many different algorithmic techniques taken from physics-based modeling, simulation, and others. Haptic rendering is an active field, and there has been a lot of work done in the area. However, for the purposes of this chapter, we focus on the physical output devices instead of the haptic display system as a whole. See Burdea (1996), Basdogan and Srinivasan (2002), and Sherman and Craig (2003) for more details on haptic rendering algorithms, haptic devices, and the human haptic system.

3.4.1. Haptic Cues

The human haptic system is a complex integration of perceptual receptors in the joints, tendons, muscles, and skin that receive various forms of stimulation, providing a sense of force and touch. The two fundamental cues a human participant uses in haptic perception are tactile and kinesthetic cues (Sherman and Craig 2003).

Tactile Cues

Tactile cues (taction) are perceived by a variety of cutaneous receptors located under the surface of the skin that produce information about surface texture and temperature as well as pressure and pain. Mechanoreceptors determine mechanical action (i.e., force, vibration, slip), thermoreceptors detect changes in skin temperature, and nocireceptors sense pain (Burdea 1996). If the stimulus is greater than a particular receptor's threshold, then a response is triggered as an electrical discharge and subsequently sent to the brain. Tactile receptors are found in varying concentrations in different areas in the body. See Loomis and Lederman (1986) for more details on tactile cues.

Kinesthetic Cues

Kinesthetic cues are perceived by receptors in the muscles, joints, and tendons of the body to produce information about joint angles and muscular length and tension. Kinesthetic cues help to determine the movement, position, and torque of different parts of the body, such as the limbs, as well as the relationship between the body and physical objects, through muscular tension. Kinesthetic cues can be both active and passive. Active kinesthetic cues are perceived when movement is self-induced, and passive kinesthetic cues occur when the limbs are being moved by an external force (Stuart 1996). In addition, tactile mechanoreceptors also produce kinesthetic cues due to stretching skin receptors associated with object movement (Burdea 1996). See Clark and Horch (1986) for more details on kinesthetic cues.

Effects of Tactile and Kinesthetic Cues on Haptic Perception

Both tactile and kinesthetic cues are important in haptic perception. In many simple tasks, one cue is more important than another. For example, feeling the surface texture or determining the relative temperature of an object uses taction as the dominant cue. On the other hand, determining the length of a rigid object using a pinching grasp would predominantly use kinesthetic cues (Biggs and Srinivasan 2002). However, in more complex tasks, both haptic cues are fundamental. As an example, consider a handshake between two people. In this case, both kinesthetic and tactile cues play an important role. The tactile cues provide information about the temperature of the other person's hand as well as pressure from the handshake. The kinesthetic cues provide information about the position and movement of each person's hand, arm, elbow, and shoulder plus information about any forces that the other person is applying.

Human Motor Subsystem

In addition to tactile and kinesthetic cues, the human haptic system also includes a motor subsystem, which enables control of active exploration of the environment, that is, control of body postures and motions together with the forces of contact with objects (Srinivasan and Chen 1993). Understanding this subsystem can be useful for designing haptic devices, because such an understanding provides information about human motor capabilities used in the real world, such as maximal force exertion, force tracking, force control bandwidth, and others. See Burdea (1996) for more information on the human motor subsystem and how it relates to haptic device design.

3.4.2. Haptic Display Characteristics

Haptic displays have many different characteristics we can use to describe them. These characteristics help to determine a haptic device's quality and provide information on how it can be utilized in 3D interfaces. In this section, we discuss three of the most common characteristics, including

- haptic presentation capability
- resolution
- ergonomics

See Sherman and Craig (2003) for more information on haptic display characteristics.

Haptic Presentation Capability

One of the most important haptic display characteristics is its presentation capability. In other words, what types of information does the haptic display output to the user? For example, a display might provide tactile or kinesthetic cues, or both. If the device provides tactile cues, what receptors does it target? If the device is designed to output kinesthetic cues, how many points of force does it provide? In either case, what parts of the body (hands, feet, arms) is the display designed for? If the display provides kinesthetic cues, is it active (actively generating forces) or passive (a simple physical prop)? Additionally, how big is the display, and what is the range of motion the display affords? Answering these questions helps to determine the type of haptic display and the display's application compatibility.

Resolution

The resolution of a haptic display device is an important consideration both spatially and temporally. The *spatial resolution* of a haptic display refers to the minimum proximity of the stimuli presented to the user. For example, the forearm is less sensitive to closely placed stimuli than are the fingertips (Sherman and Craig 2003). Therefore, a tactile device designed for the fingers should have much higher spatial resolution than one designed for the forearm. The *temporal resolution* of a haptic display refers to the refresh rate of the display. In force displays, a low temporal resolution can adversely affect quality, causing unintended vibrations and making virtual objects feel softer than intended. In many cases, force displays need refresh rates of up to 1000 Hz to provide quality output (Massie 1993).

Ergonomics

Because haptic displays generate forces and tactile information and have a close coupling to the user, ergonomics plays a vital role in characterizing these displays. As a result, safety is an important concern for any user working with a haptic device. For example, many tactile displays use electrical stimulation to stimulate tactile receptors. Care must be taken not to use too much current, or injury can result. In addition, many high-fidelity force displays can exert forces that are unsafe for the participant, and if there are errors in the haptic rendering software, injury could also result.

In addition to safety issues, user comfort is another concern with haptic displays. Many haptic devices (especially more complex devices with multiple force contacts) require a significant time period to attach the device to the user. Once the device is attached to the user, its weight can be burdensome, and it can be difficult to perform anything but the intended haptic tasks. Regardless of the haptic display used, the user's comfort and safety must be a primary concern.

3.4.3. Haptic Display Types

Many different haptic displays have been developed through the years in both research and industrial settings. Many of them have evolved from work done in telerobotics (Biggs and Srinivasan 2002). There have also been a number of attempts to classify haptic displays. For example, they are often categorized based on the types of actuators (i.e., the components of the haptic display that generate the force or tactile sensations) they use. See Burdea (1996) for a comprehensive introduction to actuator technology.

For the purposes of our discussion, haptic display devices can be placed into one of five categories:

- ground-referenced
- body-referenced
- tactile
- combination
- passive

In this section, we briefly describe some of the devices that fall into these categories.

Ground-Referenced Haptic Devices

Ground-referenced feedback devices (also called world-grounded) create a physical link between the user and a ground point. These devices can be grounded to a desktop, wall, ceiling, or floor, and this helps to support their weight. Note that because these devices are fixed to the physical environment, their range is often limited. Different types of ground-referenced displays include force-reflecting joysticks, pen-based force-feedback devices, stringed devices, motion platforms, and large articulated robotic arms. Ground-referenced displays typically use electric, pneumatic, or hydraulic actuator technology.

Force-reflecting joysticks as well as force-feedback steering wheels are often used in computer games and in-flight simulators. These devices are relatively inexpensive. Pen-based haptic displays allow for interaction with a familiar device such as a stylus. An example of such a display is shown in Figure 3.21. String-based feedback devices use thin steel cables (or strings) to apply forces to the user's hand. As a result, these devices are lightweight and can also support a large workspace (Ishii and Sato 1994). Ground-referenced feedback also includes devices such as treadmills, motion platforms, and other locomotion devices for traveling through 3D environments (see Chapter 6 for more details). Finally, there are large, articulated arms that are grounded to the floor or ceiling. They generate much higher levels of force, which means safety is a much more critical issue. Additionally, they can provide a fairly large range of motion

Figure 3.21 *A ground-referenced force-feedback device. (Photograph courtesy of SensAble Technologies)*

for the user. Examples of this type of device are the Argonne Remote Manipulator (Brooks et al. 1990) and the SARCOS Dextrous Arm Master (Burdea 1996)—arm exoskeleton force displays that can apply forces to the hand, elbow, and shoulder.

Body-Referenced Haptic Devices

In contrast to ground-referenced haptic displays, body-referenced feedback places the haptic device on some part of the user's body. In other words, the haptic display is grounded to the user in some way. The main benefit of body-referenced displays is that they provide the user with much more freedom of motion than do ground-referenced displays. However, the user has to bear the weight of the device. Therefore, these displays have weight and size limitations, making them more difficult to design. This type of display typically uses electrical or pneumatic actuator technology.

Body-referenced displays come in two varieties. The first type is the arm exoskeleton (i.e., external force-feedback systems). These devices are similar to ground-referenced arm exoskeleton force displays except they are grounded to the user's back rather than the floor, ceiling, or wall. The second type of body-referenced display is the hand-force-feedback

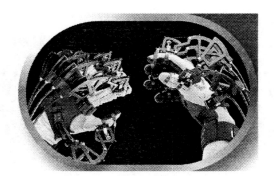

Figure 3.22   *A body-referenced force-feedback device. (Photograph reproduced by permission of Immersion Corporation, © 2004 Immersion Corporation. All rights reserved)*

device. Such devices are grounded to the user's forearm, palm, or back of the hand, depending on the design. These displays typically use cables, tendons, and pulleys to transmit forces to the hand and fingers, with the actuators placed remotely. An example of such a device is shown in Figure 3.22; this device can produce forces that prohibit the user from bending the fingers (e.g., if the user is grasping a virtual ball). Another approach to hand-force-feedback devices involves putting the actuators in the user's palm, reducing the overall complexity of the devices (Burdea et al. 1992). Regardless of the type of body-referenced haptic display, because they are worn by the user, they typically take some time to put on and calibrate.

Tactile Devices

Tactile displays utilize different kinds of actuators to stimulate the user's tactile sense. These displays are generally much smaller and more lightweight than force displays. The different types of tactile actuators include inflatable bladders, vibrators, pin arrangements, electrical currents, and temperature-regulating devices (Burdea 1996). For example, many console video game systems such as the Microsoft Xbox and the Sony Playstation utilize vibrotactile actuators in their game pads in order to simulate collisions. Other types of tactile displays (see Figure 3.23) place vibrotactile actuators on the fingertips and use them to present tactile information to the user. Yet another type uses electrotactile stimulation to stimulate the eighth cranial nerve located behind the wearer's ear. These electrical signals provide the user not with a tactile sensation, but with vestibular stimulation, which can create a sensation of motion.

Figure 3.23   *A tactile device that puts vibrating actuators on the fingertips and the palm of the hand. (Photograph reproduced by permission of Immersion Corporation, © 2004 Immersion Corporation. All rights reserved)*

Combination Devices

Because of the complexities of simulating force and touch sensations, most haptic and tactile devices focus on producing feedback within one of the three haptic display categories above. However, combining different types of feedback can create stronger haptic sensations. Figure 3.24 is an example of such a device that combines ground-referenced and body-referenced feedback styles. Another example of a combination display uses a body-referenced hand-force device coupled with tactile feedback for the user's fingertips (Kramer 1993).

Passive Haptic Devices

The haptic devices we have seen thus far have all been active devices that generate forces or tactile sensations using some type of actuator technology plus haptic rendering. Another class of haptic devices are those that have a passive quality. Their unique characteristic is that they convey a constant force or tactile sensation based on the geometry and texture of

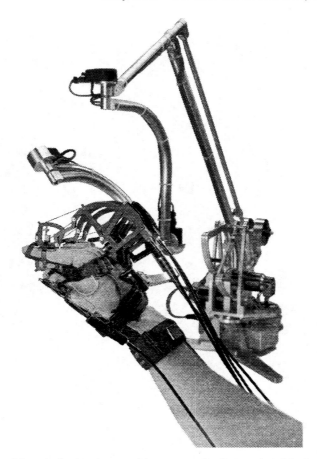

Figure 3.24   *A haptic device that combines ground-referenced and body-referenced force feedback. (Photograph reproduced by permission of Immersion Corporation, © 2004 Immersion Corporation. All rights reserved)*

the particular object. For example, a real cup or hammer can be used to provide a fully realistic haptic sensation when the virtual world contains a virtual cup or hammer. Passive haptic devices are not necessarily restricted to handheld objects. They can be larger, such as tabletops or desks as well.

Passive haptic devices (or "props") are very specific in that they often are the physical objects that they are used to represent. As a result, they have been shown to be effective in improving the perceived fidelity of VEs (Insko 2001). Of course, their underlying limitation is their specificity. Refer to Chapter 10 for a thorough discussion on passive haptic devices used in 3D interfaces.

3.4.4. Haptic Displays in 3D Interfaces

The ability to present haptic feedback to the user in a 3D application is a powerful tool. From an immersive standpoint, haptic displays can help to improve the realism of a VE (Biggs and Srinivasan 2002). Of course, realistically simulating the haptic cues of real-world objects using these displays is difficult to do—"getting it right" is quite challenging. A poor-quality display can actually hinder the immersive experience. Additionally, these devices can be quite cumbersome and difficult to wear and operate.

From a 3D UI perspective, a natural use of haptic feedback from devices like the ones shown in Figures 3.22 and 3.24 is simply for grabbing and manipulating virtual objects using direct manipulation. Ground-referenced devices like the one shown in Figure 3.21 have been used in surgical training (Körner and Männer 2003), molecular docking (Brooks et al. 1990), and 3D modeling and painting applications (Foskey et al. 2002). Tactile feedback can be used to simulate the feeling of different surfaces. For example, a user might want to feel the surface textures of different countertops in a kitchen design application. In another example, a tactile display could be used to help a firefighter determine a doorknob's temperature in the context of a training simulation. This type of feedback can also be used as a way to signal the user that an interaction task has been invoked or completed. Finally, passive haptic devices can also be used in 3D interfaces as props that provide weight and texture, and represent an inexpensive way to display haptic cues to the user.

3.5. Design Guidelines: Choosing Output Devices for 3D User Interfaces

Choosing the appropriate output devices for a 3D application is a difficult task, and unfortunately, there is no single rule of thumb telling developers which output devices to use.

Tables 3.1, 3.2, and 3.3 present summaries of the advantages and disadvantages of the output devices we have discussed in this chapter and can be used as a quick guide for starting the process of choosing an appropriate output device for a 3D UI.

Table 3.1   *Visual display devices: pros and cons, visual depth cues supported.*

Visual Display Types	Pros and Cons	Visual Depth Cues Supported
Monitors	+ Relatively inexpensive + Very high spatial resolution + Can use virtually any input device − Small FOR/FOV − No peripheral vision − Not very immersive − Physical/virtual object occlusion problem	• Monocular • Stereopsis if using stereo-capable monitor • Limited motion parallax when tracked because of limited mobility • Convergence if using stereo • No accommodation
Surround-screen displays	+ Large FOV/FOR + Makes use of peripheral vision + Real and virtual objects easily mixed in 3D application − Requires large amount of physical space − Expensive device − Limited to 4 tracked viewers in mono, 2 in stereo per device − Physical/virtual object occlusion problem	• Monocular • Stereopsis • Full motion parallax when tracked • Convergence if using stereo • No accommodation
Workbenches	+ Generally higher spatial resolution than surround-screen devices + Devices can be tilted to mimic desks and easels + Some devices permit 2D input on display surface − No peripheral vision − Limited to 4 tracked viewers in mono, 2 in stereo per device − Physical/virtual object occlusion problem	• Monocular • Stereopsis • Limited motion parallax when tracked because of limited mobility • Convergence if using stereo • No accommodation

Visual Display Types	Pros and Cons	Visual Depth Cues Supported
Hemispherical displays	+ Brighter images due to front projection + Large FOV − Spatial resolution not always uniform across display surface − Front projection makes direct manipulation difficult − Limited to 4 tracked viewers in mono, 2 in stereo per device − Physical/virtual object occlusion problem	• Monocular • Stereopsis • Limited motion parallax when tracked because of limited mobility • Convergence if using stereo • No accommodation
Head-mounted displays	+ 360-degree FOR + Portable device + No physical/virtual object occlusion problems − Small FOV − Lower spatial resolution than projection-based devices − Ergonomic issues due to weight and fit of device − Limited peripheral vision	• Monocular • Stereopsis if using stereo-capable HMD • Full motion parallax when tracked • Convergence if using stereo • Accommodation possible in research prototype
Arm-mounted displays	+ Easy to manipulate because of counterweight + 360-degree FOR with BOOM + High spatial resolution because heavier optics can be used − User must have one hand on device in order to operate it − Limited user mobility − Limited peripheral vision	• Monocular • Stereopsis if the device is stereo-capable • Limited motion parallax when tracked to limited mobility • Convergence if using stereo • Accommodation possible
Virtual retinal displays	+ Bright, high-resolution images + Potential to have FOV matching human visual system + 360-degree FOR − Current systems designed primarily for mobile computing only − Needs eye tracking − Little work done with 3D UIs	• Monocular • Stereopsis if using stereo-capable VRD • Full motion parallax when tracked • Convergence if using stereo • Accommodation possible in research prototype

continued

Table 3.1   *continued*

Visual Display Types	Pros and Cons	Visual Depth Cues Supported
Autostereoscopic displays (lenticular)	+ No glasses required to see stereo + High spatial resolution – Limited sweet spot – Limited FOV and FOR – Limited to 4 tracked viewers in mono, 2 in stereo per device – Physical/virtual object occlusion problem	• Monocular • Stereopsis • Limited motion parallax when tracked • Convergence • No accommodation
Autostereoscopic displays (volumetric and holographic)	+ Produce true 3D imagery + Unlimited active viewers (all will see correct perspective) + No accommodation–convergence cue conflicts + No trackers needed – Limited FOV, FOR, and display area – Little work done with 3D UIs	• Monocular only with some devices • Stereopsis • Motion parallax • Convergence • Accommodation

Table 3.2   *Pros and cons of using headphones or external speakers in a 3D sound display.*

Auditory Display Types	Pros and Cons
Headphones	+ High level of channel separation + Isolate users from external sounds + Multiple users can hear 3D sound (provided they are tracked – Inside-the-head localization – Uncomfortable to wear for extended periods of time
External speakers	+ User does not need to wear any additional devices – 3D sound generation more difficult – Need to worry about crosstalk

Table 3.3   *Pros and cons of different haptic display device types.*

Haptic Display Types	Pros and Cons
Ground-referenced	+ Often produce high levels of force if needed + Don't have to wear them + Accurate trackers − Limited movement when using them
Body-referenced	+ More freedom of motion + Provide more control with direct manipulation of virtual objects − User has to bear weight of device − Can be burdensome to put on
Tactile	+ Smaller and more lightweight when compared to force displays + Useful for simulating touch + Can stimulate vestibular nerve − Difficult to get sensations correct − Often stimulate only small area of skin
Hybrid	+ Useful for combining tactile and force feedback − More complex devices − Can be burdensome to wear
Passive	+ Useful when haptics is required for a specific object or physical proxy + Easy to design and use − Constant force and tactile sensations − Limited by specificity

Although there are many factors to consider when choosing output devices, such as finances, restrictions from available input devices, and ergonomics, the most important consideration is the application itself.

> Analyze the application's goals and its underlying operations and tasks to obtain direction in choosing an appropriate output device.

As an example, consider a medical visualization tool that allows doctors to teach medical students about various surgical procedures.

Because of the collaborative nature of this application, an HMD or simple monitor would probably not be appropriate, since a group of people needs to see the display simultaneously. In this case, a large-screen display is probably the best choice. In contrast, an application used in phobia treatment, such as Georgia Tech's Virtual Vietnam (Hodges et al. 1999), requires an individual user to be completely immersed in the environment with the real world blocked out. Clearly, an HMD or six-sided surround-screen display is the best choice for this application. As a final example, a holographic or volumetric display might be the best choice for an exhibit in a museum, because users do not need to wear any special glasses for the 3D stereo effect and because an unlimited number of viewers can get correct views simultaneously.

Choosing an audio display is a somewhat easier task because it often enhances an application's effectiveness. Of course, choosing the appropriate audio configuration, whether it is headphone-based or a multiple speaker system, still depends on the type of application and on the other devices used.

With haptics, the display choice often depends on the type and accuracy of the feedback required. In some applications, a tactile sensation is enough to give the user a sense that there is something tangible about the objects they see and interact with. However, if the application requires a real force, such as a molecular docking application (Brooks et al. 1990) in which users try to fit different molecules together, a ground-referenced force-feedback device is more appropriate.

The examples presented thus far are more about common sense than any scientific discovery. However, another approach to determining the most appropriate display device for a given application is through empirical study. Bowman, Datey, and colleagues (2002) have begun to develop guidelines for choosing appropriate display devices by examining interaction techniques across different display platforms. In an initial experiment, they compared users' preferences for real and virtual turns in an HMD and a four-sided surround-screen display. The results showed that users had a preference for real turns in the HMD and for virtual turns in the surround-screen display.

> Visual display devices with a 360-degree FOR should be used in applications in which users perform frequent turns and require spatial orientation.

In another set of empirical studies, Swan and colleagues compared a monitor, surround-screen display, workbench, and a large wall display for the task of navigating in a battlefield visualization application. For this particular application, the results showed that users were faster at performing the navigation tasks on the desktop than with the other display devices, indicating that a conventional 3D desktop display is more appropriate for map-based visualization applications. For more details on the study, see Swan et al. (2003).

Kasik and colleagues (2002) also performed empirical evaluations on different visual display devices. They compared a high-resolution 20-inch monitor, a hemispherical display, and a large 50-inch flat screen panel by testing how quickly and accurately users found objects of interest in sophisticated 3D models. Users performed better with the monitor than with the flat panel or the hemispherical display, indicating that higher spatial resolution was an important factor in their search tasks. Other anecdotal evidence from subjective studies (Demiralp et al. 2003) indicates that higher spatial resolution and crispness is important to users in scientific visualization.

> For visual search and pattern identification tasks in 3D environments, choose a display with high levels of spatial resolution, such as a monitor.

Although these empirical studies are quite powerful, their results should be used with caution because these studies are often designed for specific tasks and applications, making them difficult to generalize. Nevertheless, the development of guidelines based on empirical results should continue to be an important area of 3D UI research and will help to make it easier to determine the best display devices for given applications.

3.6. Conclusion

Output devices are not the only important hardware component used in 3D UIs. Input devices, the devices used to perform actions and tasks within the applications, are equally important. The choice of input device can affect the choice of output device, and vice versa. In the next chapter, we continue our examination of hardware used in 3D UIs by exploring the many different input device varieties and how they affect 3D UI design.

Recommended Reading

For thorough expositions on computer graphics rendering, we recommend the following:

Akenine-Möller, T., and E. Haines (2002). *Real-Time Rendering*, 2nd ed., AK Peters.

Slater, M., A. Steed, and Y. Chrysanthou (2002). *Computer Graphics and Virtual Environments: From Realism to Real-Time*, Addison Wesley.

Watt, A., and M. Watt (1992). *Advanced Animation and Rendering Techniques: Theory and Practice*, ACM Press.

A general discussion on human perception (including vision, audition, touch, smell, and taste) can be found in the following:

Sekuler, R., and R. Blake (1994). *Perception*, McGraw Hill.

Information on visual depth cues can be found in the following:

May, J., and D. Badcock (2002). Vision and Virtual Environments. *Handbook of Virtual Environments: Design, Implementation, and Applications.* K. Stanney (Ed.), Lawrence Erlbaum Associates, 29–64.

Sedwick, H. (1988). Space Perception. *Handbook of Perception and Human Performance.* K. Boff, L. Kaufman, and J. Thomas (Eds.), John Wiley & Sons, Volume 1, 1–21.

Wickens, C., S. Todd, and K. Seidler (1989). Three-Dimensional Displays: Perception, Implementation, Applications. Ohio, CSERIAC SOAR-89-01 Wright Patterson AFB.

A thorough discussion of the design of head-mounted displays can be found in the following:

Melzer, J., and K. Moffitt (1996). *Head-Mounted Displays: Designing for the User,* McGraw-Hill.

Details on autostereoscopic techniques and true 3D displays can be found in the following:

Blundell, B., and A. Schwarz (2000). *Volumetric Three-Dimensional Display Systems,* John Wiley & Sons.

Pastoor, S., and M. Wöpking (1997). 3-D Displays: A Review of Current Technologies. *Displays* 17: 100–110.

Comprehensive introductions to 3D spatialized audio displays can be found in the following:

Begault, D. R. (1994). *3D Sound for Virtual Reality and Multimedia,* Academic Press.

Blauert, J. (1997). *Spatial Hearing: The Psychoacoustics of Human Sound Localization,* MIT Press.

Kapralos, B., M. Jenkin, and E. Milios (2003). Auditory Perception and Virtual Environments, Dept. of Computer Science, York University, CS-2003-07.

Shilling, R., and B. Shinn-Cunningham (2002). Virtual Auditory Displays. *Handbook of Virtual Environments: Design, Implementation, and Applications.* K. Stanney (Ed.), Lawrence Erlbaum Associates, 65–92.

Information on 3D spatialized sound rendering can be found in the following:

Dobashi, Y., T. Yamamoto, and T. Nishita (2003). Real-Time Rendering of Aerodynamic Sound Using Sound Textures Based on Computational Fluid Dynamics. *ACM Transactions on Graphics* 23(3): 732–740.

Funkhouser, T., P. Min, and I. Carlbom (1999). Real-Time Acoustic Modeling for Distributed Virtual Environments. *Proceedings of SIGGRAPH '99,* ACM Press, 365–374.

Naer, M., O. Staadt, and M. Gross (2002). Spatialized Audio Rendering for Immersive Virtual Environments. *Proceedings of the ACM Symposium on Virtual Reality Software and Technology (VRST 2002),* ACM Press, 65–72.

Tsingos, N., T. Funkhouser, A. Hgan, and I. Carlbom (2001). Modeling Acoustics in a Virtual Environment Using the Uniform Theory of Diffraction. *Proceedings of SIGGRAPH 2001,* ACM Press, 545–552.

Details of haptic display device technology and haptic cues can be found in the following:

Biggs, S. J., and M. A. Srinivasan (2002). Haptic Interfaces. *Handbook of Virtual Environments.* K. Stanney (Ed.), Lawrence Erlbaum Associates, 93–115.

Burdea, G. (1994). *Force and Touch Feedback for Virtual Reality,* Wiley Interscience.

Information on haptic and tactile rendering algorithms can be found in the following:

Basdogan, C., and M. A. Srinivasan (2002). Haptic Rendering in Virtual Environments. *Handbook of Virtual Environments: Design, Implementation, and Applications.* K. Stanney (Ed.), Lawrence Erlbaum Associates, 117–134.

Burdea, G. (1994). *Force and Touch Feedback for Virtual Reality,* Wiley Interscience.

Sherman, B., and A. Craig (2003). *Understanding Virtual Reality,* Morgan Kauffman Publishers.

Finally, two interesting papers that exemplify the nuances of empirical studies for display device evaluation are these:

Pausch, R., D. Proffitt, and G. Williams (1997). Quantifying Immersion in Virtual Reality. *Proceedings of SIGGRAPH '97,* ACM Press, 13–18.

Robertson, G., M. Czerwinski, and M. van Dantzich (1997). Immersion in Desktop Virtual Reality. *Proceedings of the 1997 ACM Symposium on User Interface Software and Technology (UIST '97),* ACM Press, 11–19.

CHAPTER 4

3D User Interface Input Hardware

This chapter continues our discussion of the hardware commonly used in 3D UIs. We examine a variety of input devices that are used in both immersive and desktop applications and their effect on 3D UIs. We also examine how to choose input devices for different 3D applications by looking at some important device attributes, taxonomies, and evidence from empirical studies.

4.1. Introduction

As we saw in Chapter 3, choosing appropriate output devices is an important component of designing, developing, and using a 3D application because they are the primary means of presenting information to the user. An equally important part of 3D UI design is choosing the appropriate set of input devices that allow the user to communicate with the application. For example, we might need to track the user's head or let him interact with the application using his voice. Perhaps our 3D UI has specific needs, such as letting users throw 3D virtual paint around using a paint bucket, or providing a way to record handwritten notes. As with output devices, there are many different types of input devices to choose from when developing a 3D UI, and some devices may be more appropriate for certain tasks than others.

This chapter is meant as a guide to the types of input devices available and how they are used in 3D UIs. As with the previous chapter, this chapter is not meant to be a fully exhaustive discussion on all the input devices ever developed or the technical details of input device design; rather, it presents a representative sample of devices commonly found in 3D applications. See Sherman and Craig (2003) and Burdea and Coiffet (2003) for other expositions on 3D input hardware.

We encourage you to think about the content in this chapter while exploring the rest of the book and especially when thinking about interaction techniques. This interaction technique/input device connection is important because of the distinction between the two. Input devices are just the physical tools that are used to implement various interaction techniques (Foley and Wallace 1974). In general, many different interaction techniques can be mapped onto any given input device. The question is how natural, efficient, and appropriate the mapping between a given input device and a given technique will be.

4.1.1. Input Device Characteristics

Many different characteristics can be used to describe input devices. One of the most important is the degrees of freedom (DOF) that an input device affords. A degree of freedom is simply a particular, independent way that a body moves in space. A device such as a tracker generally captures three position values and three orientation values for a total of six DOF. For the most part, a device's DOF gives an indication of how complex the device is and the power it has in accommodating various interaction techniques.

Another way to characterize input devices is by the input type and frequency of the data (i.e., reports) they generate. Data reports are composed of either discrete components, continuous components, or a combination of the two. Discrete input device components typically generate a single data value (e.g., a Boolean value or an element from a set) based on the user's action. They are often used to change modes in an application, such as changing the drawing mode in a desktop 3D modeling program, or to indicate the user wants to start performing an action, such as instantiating a navigation technique. Continuous input device components generate multiple data values (e.g., real-valued numbers, pixel coordinates, etc.) in response to a user's action and, in many cases, regardless of what the user is doing (tracking systems and bend-sensing gloves are examples). In many cases, input devices combine discrete and continuous components, providing a larger range of device-to-interaction technique mappings.

Input devices can also be described based on how much physical interaction is required to use the device. For example, *purely active* input devices are devices that require the user to actually perform some physical action before data is generated. In other words, the input device will not provide any information to the computer unless it is manipulated in some way. Otherwise, the device just sits there and does nothing. Purely active input devices can have both discrete components (e.g., buttons) and manually driven continuous components, which means that the user must manipulate the component in order to generate the device's continuous behavior. Trackballs, sliders, and dials are examples of manually driven continuous components, and they allow the user to generate sequences of values from a given range.

Purely passive input devices do not require any physical action for the device to function. In other words, these devices continue to generate data even if they are untouched. Of course, users can manipulate these devices like active input devices, but this is not a necessity. They are sometimes called *monitoring* input devices (Sherman and Craig 2003), and they are very important in many 3D UIs. For example, a tracker is a device that will continually output position and/or orientation records even if the device is not moving. These devices are important when we want to know where something is in the virtual space and we do not want to have to keep asking for it. A perfect example of this is head tracking, which is a requirement for 3D audio displays and active viewer motion parallax in visual displays.

Finally, input devices can be categorized by their intended use. For example, some devices are designed to specifically determine position and/or orientation information (locators), while others are designed to produce a real number value (valuators) or to indicate a particular element of a set (choice). Other input device characteristics include whether the device measures relative (i.e., the difference between the current and past measurement) or absolute (i.e., measurements based on a constant point of reference) values, is a direct or indirect controller, or allows for position or rate control (Jacob 1996).

4.1.2. Chapter Roadmap

Most of this chapter contains a discussion of a variety of different input devices used in 3D interfaces and how they affect interaction techniques. These devices are broken up into the following categories:

- desktop input devices
- tracking devices
- 3D mice
- special-purpose input devices
- direct human input

In section 4.2, we discuss devices that have been traditionally used in 2D desktop applications but work well in 3D UIs and 6-DOF devices that were designed specifically for 3D desktop interaction. In section 4.3, we examine user tracking devices, which are very important when we want to know a user's or physical object's location in 3D space. Section 4.4 presents a variety of 3D mice, which are defined to be devices that combine trackers with a series of buttons and other discrete components in a given configuration. In section 4.5, we present a hodgepodge of specialized input devices that do not fit well into our other categories. Finally, section 4.6 describes direct human input, which includes speech, bioelectric, and brain input. After we explore this collection of input devices, section 4.7 provides valuable information on strategies for building custom input devices. In section 4.8, we present some ideas and guidelines for choosing input devices for a particular task or application.

4.2. Desktop Input Devices

There are many input devices that are used in desktop 3D UIs. Many of these devices have been used and designed for traditional 2D desktop applications such as word processing, spreadsheets, and drawing. However, with appropriate mappings, these devices also work well in 3D UIs and in 3D applications such as modeling and computer games. Some desktop input devices have also been developed with 3D interaction in mind. These devices can provide up to 6 DOF, allowing users to manipulate objects in 3D space, and are specifically designed for interaction on the desktop. Of course, most of these devices could also be used in more immersive 3D UIs that use surround-screen displays or HMDs, although some would be more appropriate than others.

In this section, we discuss

- keyboards
- 2D mice and trackballs

- pen-based tablets
- joysticks
- 6-DOF devices for the desktop

In general, these devices are purely active because the user must physically manipulate them to provide information to the 3D application.

4.2.1. Keyboards

The keyboard is a classic example of a traditional desktop input device that contains a set of discrete components (a set of buttons). They are commonly used in many desktop 3D applications from modeling to computer games. For example, the arrow keys are often used as input for simple travel techniques in first-person shooter computer games. Unfortunately, bringing the standard keyboard into more immersive 3D environments is not practical when users are wearing HMDs or in surround-screen environments, because users are typically standing. However, some less immersive workbench and personalized hemispherical displays (see Figure 3.13 in Chapter 3) can make use of traditional keyboards.

Because entering alphanumeric characters is important in many immersive 3D applications that use HMDs and surround-screen displays, other less conventional devices are needed in these environments. An example of such a device is the chord keyboard, which was first introduced by Engelbart and English (1968). This device is held in one hand, and the user presses combinations of keys as a single chord for alphanumeric input. See Chapter 9 on symbolic input for a more detailed discussion of these devices.

4.2.2. 2D Mice and Trackballs

Two-dimensional mice and trackballs are another classic example of desktop input devices made popular by the Windows, Icons, Menus, and Pointers (WIMP) interface metaphor (van Dam 1997). The mouse is one of the most widely used devices in traditional 2D input tasks and comes in many different varieties. The trackball is basically an upside-down mouse. Instead of moving the whole device to move the pointer, the user manipulates a rotatable ball embedded in the device. One of the advantages of the trackball is that it does not need a flat 2D surface to operate, which means that it can be held in the user's hand and will still operate correctly. Regardless of the physical design of the mouse or trackball, these devices have two essential components. The first is a manually continuous 2D locator for positioning a cursor and generating 2D pixel coordinate values. The second is a set of discrete components (usually one to three buttons). Mice and trackballs are relative devices that report how far they move rather than where they are. As with keyboards, they are commonly used in many different 3D applications and provide many different choices for mapping interaction technique to task. For example, they are often combined with keyboards in computer games to enable more complex travel techniques. The keyboard may be used for translation while the mouse or trackball is used to rotate the camera so the user can see the 3D environment (e.g., look up, look down, turn around). More details on how mice and trackballs (and 2D locators in general) are used in 3D interaction techniques can be found in Chapters 5 and 6.

Mice and trackballs have the same problem as the keyboard in that they are not designed to be brought into more immersive 3D environments. Because a mouse needs to be placed on a 2D surface in order for the locator to function properly, it is difficult to use with these displays. Since the trackball can be held in one hand and manipulated with the other, it can be used in immersive 3D environments, and it has also been successfully incorporated into a 3D interface using a workbench display (Forsberg et al. 1997). However, in most cases, 3D mice are used in immersive 3D interfaces because of their additional DOF. Section 4.4 discusses 3D mice.

4.2.3. Pen-Based Tablets

Pen-based tablets (see Figure 4.1) and handheld personal digital assistants (PDAs) generate the same types of input that mice do, but they have a different form factor. These devices have a manually continuous component (i.e., a 2D locator) for controlling a cursor and generating 2D pixel coordinate values when the stylus is moving on or hovering over the tablet surface. Additionally, the stylus or the tablet itself can have various buttons for generating discrete events. In contrast to mice, pen-based tablets are absolute devices, meaning that the device reports where the stylus is in relation to the tablet surface. Large pen-based tablets are not appropriate for most fully immersive visual displays because of their weight, but smaller tablets and PDAs have been integrated successfully into 3D UIs in these environments (Poupyrev, Tomokazu et al. 1998; Watsen et al. 1999). Larger pen-based tablets can be used in 3D applications

Figure 4.1 *A large pen-based LCD tablet allowing the user to draw directly on the screen. (Photograph courtesy of Wacom Technology and @Last Software)*

where the user is sitting, such as with desktop 3D displays, some workbench and single-wall displays, and small hemispherical displays. These types of devices are becoming more popular in both desktop 3D and immersive VE applications, because they give the user the ability to interact with a "pen and paper" interface, and they allow the user to bring 2D interaction techniques such as handwriting and menu-based techniques into 3D environments (Forsberg et al. 1998; Poupyrev, Tomokazu et al. 1998; Watsen et al. 1999).

4.2.4. Joysticks

Joysticks are another example of input devices traditionally used on the desktop and with a long history as a computer input peripheral. These devices are similar to mice and pen-based tablets in that they have a combination of a manually continuous 2D locator and a set of discrete components such as buttons and other switches. However, there is an important distinction between the mouse and the joystick. With a mouse, the cursor stops moving as soon as the mouse stops moving. With a joystick, the cursor typically continues moving in the direction the joystick is pointing. To stop the cursor, the joystick's handle must be returned to the

Figure 4.2   *Simple joysticks have evolved into sophisticated game controllers. (Photograph courtesy of Joseph J. LaViola Jr.)*

neutral position. This type of joystick is commonly called an *isotonic joystick*, and the technique is called rate control (as opposed to position control). Many console video game systems make use of different joystick designs in their game controllers (see Figure 4.2). Joysticks can also be augmented with haptic actuators, making them haptic displays as well (Burdea 1996).

Isometric joysticks have also been designed. Isometric devices have a large spring constant so they cannot be perceptibly moved. Their output varies with the force the user applies to the device. A translation isometric device is pushed, while a rotation isometric device is twisted. A problem with these devices is that users may tire quickly from the pressure they must apply in order to use them. Figure 4.3 shows an example of such a device.

Joysticks have been used as input devices in computer games for many years. They are frequently used in driving and flight simulation games, and when integrated into game controllers, they are the input device of choice with console video game systems. Additionally, they are sometimes used in CAD/CAM applications. Because joysticks are designed primarily for desktop applications and console video game systems, they are rarely used in 3D UIs that employ HMDs or surround-screen visual displays. However, because many joysticks are handheld, they could easily be brought into these types of environments.

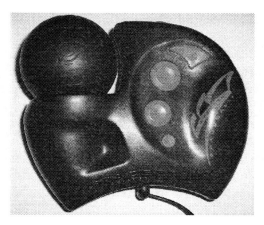

Figure 4.3 *An isometric 3D input device. (Photograph courtesy of Andrew Forsberg, Brown University Graphics Group)*

4.2.5. Six-DOF Input Devices for the Desktop

The devices we have discussed so far can all be used in 3D interfaces, and they can allow the user to interact with 3D objects, but they were not specifically designed for this purpose. Figure 4.4 shows two examples of 6-DOF input devices that were developed specifically for 3D interaction on the desktop. Slight push and pull pressure of the fingers on the cap of the device generates small deflections in x, y, and z, which moves objects dynamically in the corresponding three axes. With slight twisting and tilting of the cap, rotational motions are generated along the three axes. The particular devices shown in Figure 4.4 also have a series of buttons,

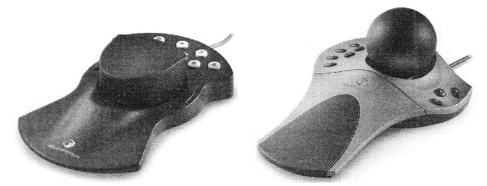

Figure 4.4 *Two 6-DOF desktop input devices: the SpaceMouse Plus and the Space-Ball 5000. (Developed by 3Dconnexion)*

which can be programmed with any frequently used function or user-defined keyboard macro.

This type of device is commonly used in desktop 3D applications for manipulating virtual objects. They were originally developed for tele-robotic manipulation and are used today by 3D designers and artists with CAD/CAM and animation applications. They do not replace the mouse; rather, they are used in conjunction with it. One hand on the motion controller positions the objects in 3D space, while the other hand with the mouse can simultaneously select menu items and edit the object. These devices are rarely used in more immersive environments because the device works best when grounded and not carried in the user's hands. Additionally, they can be difficult to use when trying to make fine manipulations, and it takes practice to become proficient with them.

4.3. Tracking Devices

In many 3D applications, it is important for the UI to provide information about the user or physical object's location in 3D space. For example, an application might need the user's head position and orientation so that full motion parallax and stereoscopic depth cues can be included in the application. In another case, the UI might require information about the bending of the user's fingers so that a virtual hand corresponding to the user's physical hand can be rendered. In most cases, we want this information sent to the 3D application automatically without the user having to signal the computer system to collect it. Therefore, most of these devices are purely passive and generate information continuously. In this section, we examine three of the most common tracking devices:

- motion trackers
- eye trackers
- data gloves

We also explore their relationship to 3D UIs.

4.3.1. Motion Tracking

One of the most important aspects of 3D interaction in virtual worlds is providing a correspondence between the physical and virtual environments. As a result, having accurate tracking is a crucial part of making interaction techniques usable within VE applications. In fact, motion tracking is fundamental to many interaction techniques described in Part III of this book. The critical characteristics of motion trackers include their range, latency (delay between the time a motion occurs and when it is reported), jitter (noise or instability), and accuracy. Currently, there are a number of different motion-tracking technologies in use, which include

- magnetic tracking
- mechanical tracking
- acoustic tracking
- inertial tracking
- optical tracking
- hybrid tracking

See Foxlin (2002); Welch and Foxlin (2002); and Allen, Bishop, and Welch (2001) for more details on motion-tracking technology.

Magnetic Tracking

Magnetic trackers use a transmitting device that emits a low-frequency magnetic field. A small sensor, the receiver, determines its position and orientation relative to this magnetic source. The range of such trackers varies, but they typically work within a radius of 4 to 30 feet. Figure 4.5 shows an example of a magnetic tracking system. It uses a small transmitter and receivers and has better accuracy than larger-range systems. However, its range is limited to a 4-foot radius, which means the device is not appropriate for large display environments such as surround-screen visual displays or even HMDs where the user needs a lot of space to roam. It is used primarily with conventional monitors (for fishtank VR) and small workbench displays where range of the device is not a critical factor.

In general, magnetic tracking systems are accurate to within 0.1 inch in position and 0.1 degree in orientation. Their main disadvantage is that any ferromagnetic or conductive (metal) objects present in the room with the transmitter will distort the magnetic field, reducing the accuracy. These accuracy reductions can sometimes be quite severe, making many interaction techniques, especially gesture-based techniques, difficult to use. Distortions can be handled with calibration routines and filtering algorithms (Kindratenko 2000), but doing so can increase start-up time and online computational overhead.

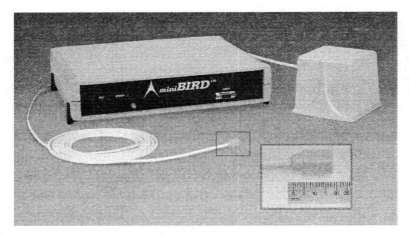

Figure 4.5   *A magnetic tracker consisting of an electronics unit, a magnetic field generator (on the right), and receivers (the small sensors connected to the front of the electronics unit, also shown in the inset) that track the user or object. (Photograph courtesy of Ascension Technology Corporation)*

Mechanical Tracking

Mechanical trackers have a rigid structure with a number of interconnected mechanical linkages combined with electromechanical transducers such as potentiometers or shaft encoders. One end is fixed in place, while the other is attached to the object to be tracked (usually the user's head or hand). As the tracked object moves, the linkages move as well, and measurements are taken from the transducers to obtain position and orientation information. Arm-mounted visual displays use this type of tracking technology (see Figures 3.15 and 3.16 in Chapter 3). Additionally, many ground-referenced force-feedback devices (see section 3.4.3 in Chapter 3) are mechanically based, making them trackers as well as force displays. Mechanical trackers are very accurate and transmit information with very low latencies. However, they are often bulky, limiting the user's mobility and making it difficult to use physically based navigation techniques (see Chapter 6).

Acoustic Tracking

Acoustic tracking devices (see Figure 4.6) use high-frequency sound emitted from source components and received by microphones. The source may be on the tracked object, with the microphones placed in the

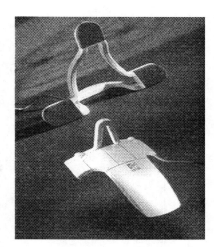

Figure 4.6 *An acoustic tracking device (the Fly Mouse). The mouselike device generates the acoustic signals from which the receiver determines position and orientation information. (Photograph courtesy of Logitech International)*

environment (an *outside-in* approach), or the source may be in the environment, with the microphones on the tracked object (an *inside-out* approach). The dominant approach to determining position and orientation information with acoustic tracking is to use time-of-flight duration of ultrasonic pulses. In other words, the distance between emitter and receiver can be determined by the time it takes for an ultrasonic pulse to travel from source to destination multiplied by the speed of sound. From this distance, position can be estimated, and with more receivers, a set of three points can be used to determine orientation using triangulation.

The advantages of acoustic tracking systems are that they are relatively inexpensive and lightweight. However, these devices often have a short range and low sampling rates (compared with optical and inertial trackers, which can have sampling rates above 1 KHz). In addition, their accuracy suffers if acoustically reflective surfaces are present in the room. Another disadvantage of acoustic tracking is that external noises such as jingling keys or a ringing phone can cause interference in the tracking signal and thus significantly reduce accuracy. As with any tracking system that has accuracy problems, many interaction techniques are difficult to use if an ultrasonic tracker loses signal, has significant jitter, or suffers from distortions anywhere within the tracking range (distortions usually increase significantly as the user moves toward a tracking boundary).

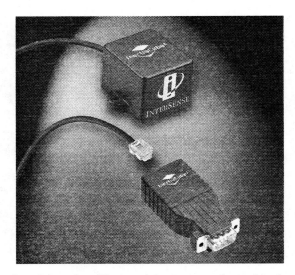

Figure 4.7   *An inertial tracker. The inertial sensors are located in the cube shown in the picture. (Photograph courtesy of InterSense, Inc.)*

Inertial Tracking

Inertial tracking systems (see Figure 4.7) use a variety of inertial measurement devices, such as angular-rate gyroscopes and linear accelerometers. These devices provide derivative measurements (i.e., gyroscopes provide angular velocity, and linear accelerometers provide linear acceleration), so they must be integrated to obtain position and orientation information. Because the tracking system is in the sensor, range is limited to the length of the cord that attaches the sensor to the electronics unit (wireless tracking is also possible with these systems). In addition, these devices can produce measurements at high sampling rates. Inertial tracking systems were originally used in ships, submarines, and airplanes in the 1950s (Welch and Foxlin 2002). However, the weight of these devices prohibited their use in motion tracking until they became small enough to fit in microelectronic mechanical systems (MEMS).

The major limitation of inertial trackers is that they suffer error accumulation from sensor biases, noise, and drift (see Foxlin [2002] for a detailed discussion on error accumulation). Error accumulation can be severe with linear accelerometers, which is why most purely inertial tracking systems track only orientation. Although there are inertial navigation systems that can track position and orientation, they are used on ships and submarines, where tracking error within a mile is often acceptable, in contrast to the subcentimeter accuracy required in 3D UIs. Gyroscopes also suffer from error accumulation, but this is less severe, and there are methods for compensating for this problem. For example, inertial trackers often handle error accumulation by using a gravitometer and compass measurements to prevent accumulation of gyroscopic drift.

Not tracking position severely limits what the interface designer can do in terms of using common interaction techniques. However, orientation-only tracking systems can be used in VEs for head tracking where the user will basically stand in one place and look around. A virtual travel technique (Chapter 6) can be used in this case to allow translation through the environment.

Optical Tracking

Another approach to position and orientation tracking of users and physical objects is from measurements of reflected or emitted light. These types of trackers use computer vision techniques and optical sensors such as cameras, infrared emitters, or lateral effect diodes, which generate signals proportional to the position of incoming light along one axis (i.e., 2D displacement measurement). A variety of different cameras can be used, from simple desktop webcams to sophisticated high-resolution cameras with high sampling rates and pixel densities.

Like acoustic trackers, optical tracking systems use either outside-in or inside-out configurations. Outside-in systems have their sensors mounted at fixed locations in the environment, and tracked objects are marked with active or passive landmarks such as retroreflective markers or colored gloves. The number and size of these landmarks vary depending on the type of optical tracking system and how many DOF are required. In some cases, no landmarks are used at all (Starner et al. 1998). Inside-out systems place optical sensors on the user or tracked object while the landmarks are placed in the environment. There are many different landmarks that can be used, such as active LED beacons (Welch et al. 2001) or passive fiducials such as cards with recognizable patterns (Foxlin and Naimark 2003).

Setting up vision-based tracking systems can be difficult because many parameters must be set in order to track the user or physical objects properly. These parameters include the number of cameras, the placement of the camera, what visual background is put up, and the design and placement of landmarks—whether they are in the environment or on the tracked user or object.

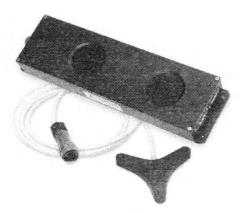

Figure 4.8   *An optical tracking device. The user wears the triangular sensor for tracking, and the scanner generates laser beams throughout the environment. (Courtesy of Ascension Technology Corporation)*

Figure 4.8 shows an example of an optical tracking device. It delivers accurate position and orientation tracking without environmental interference or distortion. Its miniaturized scanner reflects laser beams throughout the workspace. Each sensor, attached to a tracked object, instantly picks up the laser beams. Signals are then directed back to the scanner's DSP electronics for processing and transmission to the computer. Another vision-based approach is the HiBall system (see Figure 4.9), composed of a set of small, high-speed cameras, which are aligned in a self-contained housing and affixed to the user's head (Welch et al. 2001). A set of LEDs are placed in the environment, and their positions are surveyed. The LEDs are flashed at high speed in a specific known sequence, and providing the camera can see enough LEDs, the position and orientation of the tracker can be calculated directly through triangulation.

Theoretically, vision-based tracking systems have a clear advantage in that the user can be completely untethered from the computer. However, in practice this is often not the case. The tracking systems in Figures 4.8 and 4.9 both have wires that attach to the device even though they are vision-based solutions. Even if the tracking system allows the user to be completely untethered, other input or output devices (an HMD or force-feedback display, for example) will require tethering between user and machine. With wireless technology becoming more powerful, these limitations are receding, making fully untethered systems more practical (Liebe et al. 2000; Hogue et al. 2003), especially in conjunction with projection-based displays (see Chapter 3, section 3.2.3).

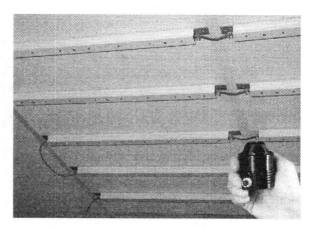

Figure 4.9 *The HiBall Tracking System. The LED beacons are mounted on the ceiling, and the camera device is located in the handheld object. (Photograph of the HiBall-3000 Tracker courtesy of 3rd Tech, Inc.)*

The major disadvantage of vision-based trackers is occlusion. In many cases, the camera cannot pick up information about parts of the user's body that are occluded by other parts. For example, it is difficult to extract information from all of the fingers when the hand is oriented in certain ways. Adding more cameras and landmarks can help to reduce the occlusion problem, but this increases the complexity of the tracking algorithm.

Hybrid Tracking

Hybrid trackers put more than one tracking technology together to help increase accuracy, reduce latency, and provide a better overall 3D interaction experience. In general, the individual tracking technologies are used to compensate for each other's weaknesses. An example of such a device is shown in Figure 4.10. This example combines inertial and ultrasonic tracking technologies. The inertial component measures orientation, and the ultrasonic component measures position, enabling the device to attain 6 DOF. Moreover, information from each component is used to improve the accuracy of the other. As a side note, this tracking system has the added advantage of being wireless, with the user wearing a small battery-powered electronics box on her belt (Wormell and Foxlin 2003). The major difficulty with hybrid trackers is that more components produce more complexity. The extra complexity is warranted, however, if tracking accuracy is significantly improved.

Figure 4.10   *A wireless inertial/ultrasonic tracker. (Photograph courtesy of Inter-Sense, Inc.)*

Another type of hybrid tracking combines video cameras and structured digital light projectors. Combining these two technologies allows for the capture of depth, color, and surface reflectance information for objects and participants in the environment. This approach was used at the University of North Carolina at Chapel Hill in its Office of the Future project (Raskar et al. 1998). An idealized drawing is shown in Figure 4.11.

Figure 4.11   *A stylized drawing of the Office of the Future. The room uses both cameras and structured light to track the user and perform scene acquisition. (Artwork by Andrei State, © University of North Carolina at Chapel Hill)*

Finally, hybrid trackers may incorporate other technologies into their devices, such as global positioning systems (GPS). GPS is often used in conjunction with accelerometers or gyroscopes for tracking in large-scale, outdoor, augmented reality environments, where it is impossible to fix sources or receivers to the environment (see Chapter 12 for more information on augmented reality).

4.3.2. Eye Tracking

Eye trackers are purely passive input devices used to determine where the user is looking. Eye-tracking technology is based primarily on computer vision techniques: the device tracks the user's pupils using corneal reflections detected by a camera. Devices can be worn (Figure 4.12) or embedded into a computer screen, making for a much less obtrusive interface. Other eye-tracking techniques include electro-oculography, which measures the skin's electric potential differences using electrodes placed around the eye, and embedding mechanical or optical reference objects in contact lenses that are worn directly on the eye (Duchowski 2003).

From a generic interaction perspective, eye-tracking systems have been used both as an evaluation tool and to interact with an application. For example, these devices are used to collect information about a user's eye movements in the context of psychophysical experiments, to get

Figure 4.12 *This user-worn eye-tracking device uses corneal reflections and pupil tracking to determine eye position. (Photograph courtesy of SR Research, Ltd.)*

application usage patterns to help improve the interface, or for training in visual inspection tasks (Duchowski et al. 2001). Eye-tracking systems are also used as input devices. An example would be a user controlling a mouse pointer strictly with his eyes. In the context of 3D interface design, active eye-tracking systems have the potential to improve upon many existing 3D interaction techniques. For example, there are numerous techniques that are based on gaze direction (e.g., gaze-directed steering, gaze-directed manipulation), which use a head-tracker as an approximation to where the user is looking. Because the gaze vector is accurate only if the user is looking straight ahead, usability problems can occur if the user looks in other directions while keeping the head stationary. Eye-tracking devices might help improve these gaze-directed techniques, because the actual gaze from the user can be obtained. See Duchowski (2003), Wilder et al. (2002), and Jacob (1995) for more information on eye-tracking systems and their use in 3D applications.

4.3.3. Data Gloves

In some cases, it is useful to have detailed tracking information about the user's hands, such as how the fingers are bending or if two fingers have made contact with each other. Data gloves are input devices that provide this information. Data gloves come in two basic varieties: bend-sensing gloves and Pinch Gloves. In this section, we examine both of these glove types and also a research prototype that was developed to combine bend-sensing and pinch functionality.

Bend-Sensing Gloves

Bend-sensing data gloves are purely passive input devices used to detect hand postures (static configurations) and certain gestures (a series of postures). For example, the device can distinguish between a fist, a pointing posture, and an open hand. The raw data from the gloves is usually given in the form of joint angle measurements, and software is used to detect postures and gestures based on these measurements.

Many data gloves have been developed over the years using various kinds of sensors. For example, light-based sensors use flexible tubes with a light source at one end and a photocell at the other (Defanti and Sandin 1977). As the fingers are bent, the amount of light that hits the photocells varies, producing a measurement. Another light-based approach uses optical goniometer sensors consisting of flexible tubes with a reflective interior wall, a light source at one end, and a photosensitive detector on

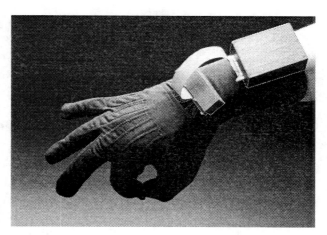

Figure 4.13 *A bend-sensing data glove. (Photograph courtesy of Fifth Dimension Technologies, www.5dt.com)*

the other, which detects both direct and reflected light rays (Zimmerman, Lanier et al. 1987). Depending on the bending of the tubes, the detector changes its electrical resistance as a function of light intensity. These types of light-based sensors were used in older, first-generation data gloves. Today, more sophisticated sensor technology is used, such as fiber-optic sensors, resistive ink sensors, and strain-gauge bend sensors (Kramer 1991). Regardless of the type of sensor used, they are usually embedded in the glove or placed on the outer surface of the glove.

Data gloves typically have anywhere between 5 and 22 sensors. For example, a glove that has 5 sensors will usually measure one joint in each finger, while a glove with 18 sensors could measure at least two joints in each finger, abduction between fingers, wrist roll and yaw, and others. An example of a 16-sensor glove that uses fiber-optic sensors is shown in Figure 4.13.

From a 3D UI perspective, data gloves are commonly used for hand gesture and posture recognition, which can be applied to a variety of different interaction techniques. For example, a flick of the wrist could indicate the user wants to delete an object. A pointing posture could indicate a travel technique such as steering (Chapter 6). Often, hand postures and gestures are used as system commands in the context of system control techniques (see Chapter 8 for more details). Note that to recognize some gestures (such as a waving hand), a motion tracker must be attached to the data glove.

In some 3D UIs, a virtual representation of a user's hand or hands is required. Data gloves with an associated tracking system can provide such a representation. In general, these types of representations are useful when the real world is completely blocked from the user's view (e.g., when using an HMD), and the user needs to see her hands in the scene with other virtual objects. For instance, a user might wish to get an understanding of where her hands are in relation to various dials and controls in a virtual car's interior.

One of the major advantages of bend-sensing gloves is that they provide a large number of DOF, making it possible to recognize a variety of hand gestures and postures as well as providing a representation of the user's hand in the 3D application. However, the user does have to wear the device, and there will always be a significant portion of the population for which the glove does not fit well. In addition, bend-sensing gloves sometimes need calibration on a user-by-user basis.

Pinch Gloves

The Pinch Glove (see Figure 4.14) system is an input device that determines if a user is touching two or more fingertips together. These gloves have a conductive material at each of the fingertips so that when the user pinches two fingers together, an electrical contact is made. These devices are often used for performing grabbing and pinching gestures in the context of object selection, mode switching, and other techniques (see Bowman, Wingrave et al. [2002] for details).

Figure 4.14   *A Pinch Glove is a user-worn discrete input device. (Photograph courtesy of Joseph J. LaViola Jr.)*

An interesting characteristic of this device is that the conductive cloth is also found on the back of the glove along the user's fingers and thumb, as shown in Figure 4.14. If a tracker is attached to the user's fingertip, for example, the user can make gestures that can be interpreted as simple sliders by simply making a cloth contact with the tracked fingertip and one of the cloth strips on the back of the other glove. When contact is made, the system can determine the location of the tracked fingertip as the user slides up and down the cloth strip. If another tracker is attached to the other glove, it is trivial to determine if the user's finger is moving toward the wrist or away from the wrist when making the gesture. This simple technique has been used to adjust object size or increase and decrease parameter values (LaViola 2000b).

Pinch Gloves are extremely light, reducing user fatigue in comparison to handheld input devices. They also provide for two-handed interaction (see Chapter 10). There are literally thousands of different pinching combinations that can be made using this device, which allows for a large design space of input-device-to-task mappings. However, only a handful of them are useful and ergonomic. Additionally, with extended use, the cloth contacts often deteriorate, making the gloves unusable.

Combining Bend-Sensing Data and Pinch Input

Both the Pinch Gloves and bend-sensing gloves have limitations. Although it is possible to determine if there is finger contact (e.g., index finger to thumb) with a bend-sensing glove, some form of hand gesture recognition is required, which will not be as accurate as the Pinch Glove (which has essentially 100% accuracy, assuming the device is functioning properly). Conversely, one can get an idea of how the fingers are bent when using Pinch Gloves, but they provide only very rough estimates. Ideally, a data glove should have the functionality of both bend-sensing gloves and Pinch Gloves.

The Flex and Pinch input system is an example of an input device that combines the functionality of the Pinch Glove system with the bend-sensing technology of a data glove (see Figure 4.15). The pinch buttons, which are connected to a microcontroller, are made from conductive cloth and can be placed anywhere on the bend-sensing glove. This combination of hand-generated discrete and continuous events can make certain interaction techniques easier to perform, such as locking during a scaling operation or starting and stopping an object selection operation (LaViola 1999b).

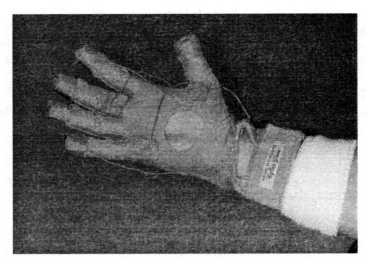

Figure 4.15   *The Flex and Pinch input system combines bend-sensing input with discrete buttons. (Photograph courtesy of Joseph J. LaViola Jr.)*

4.4. 3D Mice

In the last section, we described tracking devices that are used to monitor the user or physical objects in 3D space. In many cases, specifically with motion trackers (see section 4.3.1), these tracking devices are combined with other physical device components, such as buttons, sliders, knobs, and dials, to create more functionally powerful input devices. We call these devices *3D mice* and define them broadly as handheld or worn input devices that combine motion tracking with a set of physical device components.

The distinguishing characteristic of 3D mice, as opposed to regular 2D mice, is that the user physically moves them in 3D space to obtain position and/or orientation information instead of just moving the device along a flat surface. Therefore, users can hold the device or, in some cases, wear it. Additionally, with orientation information present, it is trivial to determine where the device is pointing (the device's direction vector), a function used in many fundamental 3D interaction techniques (see Chapters 5 and 6). Because of their generality, they can be mapped to many different interaction techniques, and in one form or another, they are often the primary means of communicating user intention in 3D UIs for VE applications.

4.4.1. Handheld 3D Mice

A common design approach for 3D mice is to place a motion tracker inside a structure that is fitted with different physical interface widgets. Actually, one of the first 3D mice to be developed used no housing at all. The "bat" (Ware and Jessome 1988), so named because it is a mouse that flies, was developed by Colin Ware in the late 1980s. It was simply a 6-DOF tracking device with three buttons attached to it. Such a device is rather easy to build with a few electrical components (provided you have the tracking device). A more sophisticated and elegant version of the bat is shown in Figure 4.16. This device houses a motion tracker in a structure that looks like a simple remote control. It is commonly used in conjunction with surround-screen displays for both navigation and selection of 3D objects.

The physical structure that houses the motion tracker is often a replication of an input device used in the real world. For example, the 3D mouse shown in Figure 4.17 is modeled after an air force pilot's flight stick. Some 3D mice have also been developed to look like their 2D counterparts. For example, the Fly Mouse (see Figure 4.6) looks similar to a conventional 2D mouse, but it uses acoustic tracking, has five buttons instead of two, and can also be used as a microphone for speech input.

The Cubic Mouse (shown in Figure 4.18), originally developed at Fraunhofer IMK, is a 3D mouse designed primarily as an interactive prop for handling 3D objects. It is ideally suited for examining volumetric data because of its ability to intuitively map to the volume's coordinates and

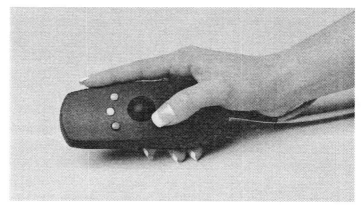

Figure 4.16 *The Wanda input device. (Photograph courtesy of Ascension Technology Corporation)*

Figure 4.17   *A 3D joystick modeled after a flight stick. (Built by VP Integrated Solutions as a large-scale visualization device)*

act as a physical proxy for manipulating it (Fröhlich and Plate 2000). The device consists of a box with three perpendicular rods passing through the center, an embedded tracker, and buttons for additional input. The Cubic Mouse does have a disadvantage in that the three orthogonal rods can get in the way when the user is holding the device in certain configurations.

Figure 4.18   *The Cubic Mouse. (Photograph courtesy of Fakespace Systems)*

Aside from the Fly Mouse (shown in Figure 4.6), the 3D mice we have shown thus far have all been tethered. Many current 3D mice, however, are completely wireless, often making use of 6-DOF optical tracking. For example, the Bug (Stefani et al. 2003) is an ergonomically designed wireless device with two buttons and a slider. It looks similar to a desktop mouse but features three spherical markers (used by the optical tracking system to measure position and orientation) protruding from the device.

4.4.2. User-Worn 3D Mice

Another approach to the design of 3D mice is to have the user wear them instead of hold them. Assuming the device is light enough, having the device worn on the user's finger, for example, makes the device an extension of the hand. Figure 4.19 shows the Ring Mouse, an example of such a device. It is a small, two-button, ringlike device that uses ultrasonic tracking that generates only position information. One of the issues with this device is that it has a limited number of buttons because of its small form factor.

The FingerSleeve, shown in Figure 4.20, is a finger-worn 3D mouse that is similar to the Ring Mouse in that it is small and lightweight, but it adds more button functionality in the same physical space by using pop-through buttons (Zeleznik et al. 2002). Pop-through buttons have two clearly distinguished activation states corresponding to light and firm finger pressure.

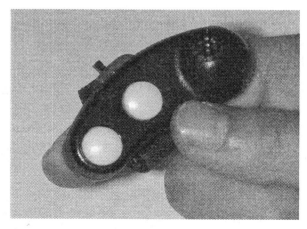

Figure 4.19 *The Ring Mouse input device uses acoustic tracking and is worn on a user's index finger. (Photograph courtesy of Joseph J. LaViola Jr.)*

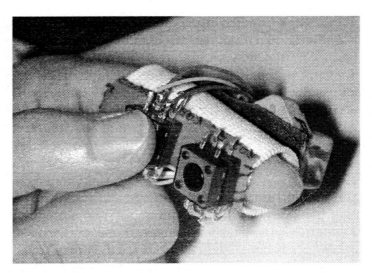

Figure 4.20   *A user pressing one of the multilevel buttons on the FingerSleeve. (Photograph reprinted from Zeleznik et al. [2002], © 2002 IEEE Press)*

The device can be worn on the index finger of either the left or right hand and is made of an elastic fabric and a small piece of flexible plastic that can be found at any arts and crafts store. The fabric is sewn into a sleeve with a varying diameter that fits snugly for most users. The plastic is sewn onto the front of the sleeve to provide a solid mount for pop-through buttons, and the buttons are glued into place a few millimeters apart on top of the plastic. A 6-DOF tracker is secured to the back of the sleeve using Velcro. See Zeleznik and colleagues (2002) for more details.

4.5. Special-Purpose Input Devices

Many other types of devices are used in 3D interfaces. These devices are often designed for specific applications or used in specific interfaces. In this section, we present some examples of these special-purpose devices.

ShapeTape (shown in Figure 4.21) is a flexible, ribbonlike tape of fiber-optic curvature sensors that comes in various lengths and sensor spacing. Because the sensors provide bend and twist information along the tape's length, it can be easily flexed and twisted in the hand, making it an ideal input device for creating, editing, and manipulating 3D curves (Grossman et al. 2003). In addition, the device can be used in system control (see Chapter 8) by recognizing different gestures made by the tape

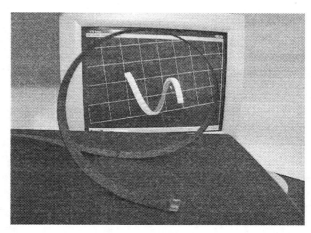

Figure 4.21 *ShapeTape used in manipulating 3D curves. (Photograph courtesy of Measurand, Inc., www.measurand.com)*

(e.g., quickly moving the endpoints of the tape together or apart). Note that in some cases, other input devices (the bat, for example) can be attached to the tape to increase functionality (Balakrishnan, Fitzmaurice et al. 1999).

In many surround-screen display configurations where the floor is actually a display surface, users must wear slippers when they enter the device to avoid making scuff marks and tracking in dirt. An input device called the Interaction Slippers (Figure 4.22) takes advantage of the need for slippers in these environments.

Figure 4.22 *A user wearing Interaction Slippers. (Photograph reprinted from LaViola et al. [2001], © 2001 ACM Press)*

The Interaction Slippers (LaViola et al. 2001) embed a wireless track-ball device (the Logitech Trackman) into a pair of common house slippers. The slippers use wireless radio technology to communicate to the host computer. The Trackman is inserted into a handmade pouch on the right slipper and rewired. Two of the Trackman's three buttons are connected to a pair of conductive cloth patches on the instep of the right slipper. On the instep of the left slipper, two more conductive cloth patches are attached (as shown in Figure 4.22). Touching a cloth patch on the left slipper to a cloth patch on the right slipper completes the button press circuit. This design enables two gestures corresponding to heel and toe contacts respectively. The slippers were designed for interacting with the Step WIM navigation technique, in which a miniature version of the world is placed on the ground under the user's feet, allowing him to quickly travel to any place in the VE. LaViola and colleagues (2001) describe the slippers in more detail.

An example of an input device that was specifically developed for a particular 3D application is the CavePainting Table (see Figure 4.23) used in CavePainting (Keefe et al. 2001), a system for painting 3D scenes in a VE. The CavePainting Table uses a prop-based design that relies upon multiple cups of paint and a single tracked paintbrush. These paint cup props stay on a physical table that slides into the surround-screen device and also houses knobs and buttons used for various interaction tasks. In conjunction with the table, a real paintbrush is augmented with a single

Figure 4.23   *The CavePainting Table used in the CavePainting application. (Photograph reprinted from Keefe et al. [2000], © 2001 ACM; reprinted with permission)*

button that turns the "paint" on and off. The bristles of the brush are covered with conductive cloth, and users can dip the brush into the paint cups (which are lined with conductive cloth as well) to change brush strokes. A tracked bucket is used to throw paint around the virtual canvas.

In some cases, making a simple addition to an existing input device can create a powerful tool for interacting in 3D applications. For example, when interacting with 3D applications that utilize workbench-style displays, attaching a motion tracker to a piece of Plexiglas can create a useful tool for interacting in 2D and 3D. In addition, these devices can also have touch-sensitive screens (see Figure 4.24). Such a device allows the user to perform 2D interaction techniques, such as writing and selection of objects and commands from 2D palettes, as well as 3D interaction techniques, such as volumetric selection by sweeping the device through the virtual world (see Schmalstieg, Encarnação et al. [1999], Coquillart and Wesche [1999], and Williams et al. [1999] for more details). This "pen-and-tablet" metaphor has been used extensively in 3D UIs and is discussed in detail in Chapter 10.

The last input device we discuss in this section is the Control Action Table (CAT), which was designed for use in surround-screen display environments (Hachet et al. 2003). This freestanding device (shown in Figure 4.25) looks like a circular tabletop. The CAT uses angular sensors to detect orientation information using three nested orientation axes. The device also has an isometric component; the tabletop is equipped with a potentiometer that detects forces in any 3D direction. Thus, the user can push or pull on the device for translational movement. Additionally, the CAT has a tablet for 2D interaction mounted on the tabletop, which

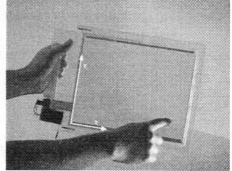

Figure 4.24 *Transparent palettes used for both 2D and 3D interaction. (Williams et al. 1999; photographs courtesy of Fakespace Labs, Mountain View, California)*

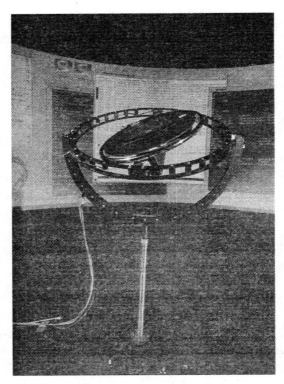

Figure 4.25 *The CAT is designed for surround-screen display environments. It combines 6-DOF input with 2D tablet interaction. (Photograph courtesy of the Iparla Team [LaBRI–INRIA])*

makes it unique because it supports both 6-DOF and 2D input in the same device. Other advantages of the CAT include the ability to control each DOF individually and its *location persistence* (meaning that its physical state does not change when released). The CAT does have some inherent limitations because the nature of the nested orientation axes can make some orientations hard to specify, and in certain configurations (e.g., when the tabletop is vertical), translational movement can be difficult to perform as well.

4.6. Direct Human Input

A powerful approach to interacting with 3D applications is to obtain data directly from signals generated by the human body. With this approach, the user actually becomes the input device. For example, a user could stand in front of a camera and perform different movements, which the computer would interpret as commands (Lucente et al. 1998). Other types of direct human input for 3D UIs include speech, bioelectric, and brain computer input and we focus on these types in this section.

4.6.1. Speech Input

Speech input provides a nice complement to other input devices. It is a natural way to combine different modes of input (i.e., multimodal interaction) to form a more cohesive and natural interface. In general, when functioning properly, speech input can be a valuable tool in 3D UIs, especially when both of the user's hands are occupied. Beyond choosing a good speech recognition engine, there are many other important issues to consider when using speech for a 3D interface (LaViola 1999a).

There are tradeoffs that must be made when dealing with speech input. One important issue is where the microphone is to be placed. Ideally, a wide-area microphone is used so that the user need not wear a headset. Placing such a microphone in the physical environment could be problematic because it might pick up noise from other people or machines in the room. One of the big problems with using speech input is having the computer know when to and when not to listen to the user's voice. Often, a user is conversing with a collaborator with no intention of issuing voice commands, but the application "thinks" the user is speaking to it. This misinterpretation can be very troublesome.

One of the best ways to avoid this problem is to use an implicit or invisible push-to-talk scheme. A traditional push-to-talk scheme lets the user tell the application when he or she is speaking to it, usually by pushing a button. In order to maintain the naturalness of the speech interface, we do not want to add to the user's cognitive load. The goal of implicit push-to-talk is to embed the "push" into existing interaction techniques so the user does not have the burden of remembering to signal the application that a voice command is about to be issued. As an example, consider a furniture layout application in which a user wants to place different pieces of furniture into a room or other architectural structure. The user wishes to put a table into a kitchen. To accomplish this task, the user must create the object and then place it in the room. The user shows where the table should be placed using a laser pointer and then says, "Give me a table, please." The act of picking up the laser pointer signals the application that the user is about to ask for an object. This action "piggybacks" the voice command onto the placement task, making the push-to-talk part of the technique implicit. More information on speech input can be found in Chapters 8 and 9.

4.6.2. Bioelectric Input

NASA Ames Research Center has developed a bioelectric input device that reads muscle nerve signals emanating from the forearm (see Figure 4.26). These nerve signals are captured by a dry electrode array on the arm. The nerve signals are analyzed using pattern recognition software and then routed through a computer to issue relevant interface commands. Figure 4.26 shows a user controlling a virtual 757 aircraft (Jorgensen et al. 2000). This type of device could also be used to mimic a real keyboard in a VE.

4.6.3. Brain Input

The goal of brain–computer interfaces is to have a user directly input commands to the computer using signals generated by the brain (Millán 2003). A brain–computer interface can use a simple, noninvasive approach

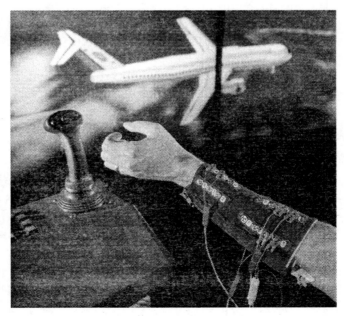

Figure 4.26   *A bioelectric control device attached to a user's wrist. (Photograph courtesy of NASA Ames Research Center)*

by monitoring brainwave activity through electroencephalogram (EEG) signals. The user simply wears a headband or a cap with integrated electrodes. A more invasive approach would be to surgically implant microelectrodes in the motor cortex. Of course, this approach is still not practical for common use but might be appropriate for severely disabled people who cannot interact with a computer in any other way. Research has shown that a monkey with microelectrodes implanted in its motor cortex can move a mouse cursor to desired targets (Serruya et al. 2002). These types of interfaces are still in their infancy, but the underlying potential of such an interface is immense, not only for 3D interfaces but for all other types of computer interaction as well.

An example of a brain–computer interface device is shown in Figure 4.27. This device uses a brain–body actuated control technology that combines eye movement, facial muscle, and brainwave biopotentials to generate input signals. It has three sensors in a headband, and its interface unit amplifies and translates the brainwave, facial muscle, and eye-movement data into separate frequencies and transmits them to a PC serial port. Software processes and displays these frequencies and 10 continuous command signals, which can then be sent to applications for navigating through a VE, interacting with a computer game, or a variety of other tasks. Although this device represents only the beginning of brain–computer input devices, it shows the potential of this technology for taking computer interaction to a whole new level. More information on brain–computer interfaces can be found in Millán (2003).

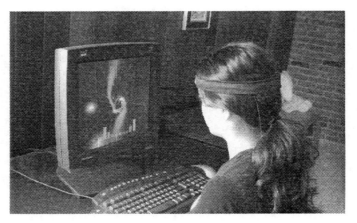

Figure 4.27 *The user wears a headband that reads brainwave biopotentials to generate input. (Photograph courtesy of Brain Actuated Technologies, Inc.)*

4.7. Home-Brewed Input Devices

In some situations, commercial, off-the-shelf input devices may not be adequate for a given 3D application or task. For example, the 3D UI designer may want to better exploit a user's feet in navigating through a VE or have discrete button functionality on a bend-sensing data glove. Such situations provide an opportunity for exploring the in-house development of novel devices that are specifically suited to given interaction techniques. Creating home-brewed input devices often aids the 3D UI designer in developing new interaction techniques and improving upon existing ones. They can also provide the user with more expressive power in specific 3D applications and with new methods of expression that existing input devices do not afford (LaViola et al. 2004).

The 3D UI researcher and practitioner can go a long way toward developing these augmented and novel devices using simple electronic components and household items. In fact, this home-brewed style of input device design and prototyping has produced many of the commercial input devices sold today. We have already seen devices such as the bat, the Cubic Mouse, the FingerSleeve, and the CAT, all of which were designed and built by researchers in small academic research labs. In this section, we briefly discuss some strategies for making custom input devices by first presenting some ideas on building the physical devices and then discussing methods for creating the interface between devices and the computer.

4.7.1. Strategies for Building Input Devices

There are a variety of strategies for constructing home-brewed input devices. One of the first things to consider is the device's intended functionality, because doing so helps to determine what types of physical device components will be required. For example, the device might need to sense forces, motion, or simply button presses. Based on the intended device functionality, the device developer can choose appropriate sensors, whether they are digital (output of 0 or 1) or analog (output of a range of values). These sensors can easily be found in electronics stores or on the Internet. Examples include pressure sensors, bend sensors, potentiometers, thermistors (for sensing temperature), photocells (for sensing light), simple switches, and many others. These sensors come in a variety of styles and configurations, and the appropriate choice is often based on trial and error. This trial-and-error approach is especially important with buttons because buttons and switches come in many different shapes,

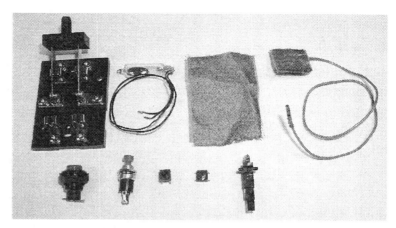

Figure 4.28 *Many different buttons and switches can be used to make homemade input devices. Top row, left to right: a lever switch, a mercury switch, and conductive cloth patches used to make flexible buttons. Bottom row: buttons of different sizes and shapes. (Photograph courtesy of Joseph J. LaViola Jr.)*

sizes, and force thresholds—the amount of force the user needs to activate the button or switch (see Figure 4.28).

In many cases, building the sensors is a feasible option, especially if they are switches or buttons. One powerful approach for building simple switches is to use conductive cloth. Conductive cloth is just fabric with conductive material sewn into it, and it has many advantages for building custom input devices. In fact, the input devices shown in Figures 4.14, 4.15, 4.22, and 4.23 all use conductive cloth as part of their designs. Conductive cloth is inexpensive and a fairly robust material. Because it is cloth, it is flexible, so it can be used just about anywhere, in many different sizes and geometric configurations. Additionally, conductive cloth is easily sewn onto other fabrics so that devices can be constructed on clothing.

Another important consideration when making home-brewed input devices is how the sensors are housed in the physical device. Positioning sensors in the device housing is especially important when they are active components such as buttons, dials, and sliders, because the user must be able to interact with them comfortably to manipulate the device. For example, if a homemade 3D mouse is being constructed with several buttons, these buttons should be placed so that the user does not have to endure any undue strain in order to press any of the buttons at any given time. Sensor placement in homemade input devices is also affected by the geometry of the device itself.

One of the reasons many 3D UI designers do not build homemade devices is that they do not have the ability or equipment to construct the physical housing the sensors are placed in and on. Ideally, a milling machine, vacuform device (a device that heats plastic and stretches it over a mold), or 3D printer would be used to construct the device housing based on a model developed in 3D modeling software. However, these tools are not necessarily household items. One novel approach for constructing device housings is to use Lego bricks. The Lego Interface Toolkit (Ayers and Zeleznik 1996), a rapid prototyping system for creating physical interaction devices, uses this approach. It utilizes Lego bricks along with push buttons and rotational and linear sensors that support a variety of physical configurations. This component-based approach enables the input device developer to quickly snap together different device components. Another approach is to use modeling clay to create input device housings. The advantage of using modeling clay is that it can be molded into any shape the designer wants and can be quickly changed to try out different geometries. Once an appropriate design or designs are found, the clay can be oven fired and used as the device housing.

4.7.2. Connecting the Home-Brewed Input Device to the Computer

The other important part of constructing home-brewed input devices is choosing how to connect them to the computer. In the majority of cases, homemade input devices require some type of logic that the user needs to specify in order for the computer to understand the data the input device produces. The one exception is when existing devices are taken apart so that the sensors in them can be used in different physical configurations. An example of this is the Interaction Slippers shown in Figure 4.22. Because the device uses the rewired components of a wireless mouse, it can use the standard mouse port to transmit information to the computer, thus requiring no additional electronics.

There are two primary approaches for connecting a homemade input device to the computer so it can be used in 3D interfaces. The first approach is to use a microcontroller. A microcontroller is just a small computer that can interface with other electronic components through its pins. There are many different varieties to choose from depending on price, power, ease of programming, and so on. The designer can connect an input device to a microcontroller on a circuit board, which in turn communicates to the computer through a serial or USB port. Typically, the designer first builds the electronics on a prototyping board (breadboard), which is an easy way to establish electrical connections between the device and the microcontroller without the need to solder. Using any of the many software packages (many of them are free and use Basic or C) for writing microcontroller code, the developer can write a program for controlling the input device and download it to the microcontroller. After the prototyping and testing stage, the microcontroller and any associated electronics can be attached to an appropriate circuit board. The homemade input device then has its own electronics unit for sending information from the device to the computer and, with appropriate software such as device drivers, to the 3D UI. Using microcontrollers does require some effort and has a slight learning curve, but the approach gives the input device developer a lot of freedom in choosing how the input device/computer interface is made. A nice introduction to using microcontrollers to build input devices can be found in Forman and Lawson (2003).

One way to still use microcontrollers but sidestep many of the issues involved in using them is to use Phidgets (Greenberg and Fitchett 2001). Phidgets are physical input device widgets that can be combined through a toolkit, which essentially encapsulates the implementation and construction details of connecting input devices to computers. In effect, they provide the ability to create homemade input devices without the need to program microcontrollers and design circuit boards. More details on how Phidgets are used can be found in Greenberg and Boyle (2002).

A second approach to connecting homemade input devices to a computer is to use the Musical Instrument Device Interface (MIDI). MIDI is a protocol that was developed to allow electrical musical instruments to communicate with computers (Rumsey 1994). The important characteristic of MIDI is that it is a protocol for communicating control information, such as if a button was pressed, how hard it was pressed, or how long it was pressed, which means it can be used for connecting input devices to computers. Figure 4.29 shows an example of a MIDI controller and some of the sensors used in developing input devices with it (Figure 4.20 shows an input device that uses this controller). Similar to Phidgets, using MIDI gives the input device developer the advantage of not having to deal with microcontroller programming and circuit design. However, in most cases, the developer still needs to write the device drivers to use the custom-built input devices in 3D applications.

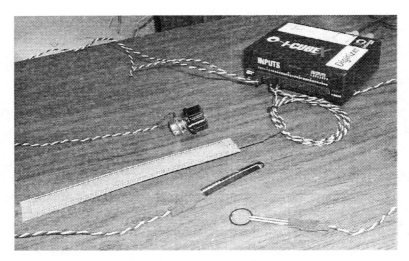

Figure 4.29   *A MIDI controller can be used as the connection between input devices and the computer. The MIDI-compatible sensors attached to the device are, from top to bottom, a turn sensor, a slide sensor, a bend sensor, and a small touch sensor. (Photograph courtesy of Joseph J. LaViola Jr.)*

4.8. Choosing Input Devices for 3D User Interfaces

A key issue in 3D interface design is to choose the appropriate input devices that are best suited to the needs of a particular application. The designer needs to examine the various tasks the 3D UI needs to support, find or develop the appropriate interaction techniques, and ensure that the chosen input devices are mapped to these techniques appropriately. In this section, we first examine some important factors to consider when choosing input devices. We then discuss two important tools, input device taxonomies and empirical evaluations, which can aid the designer in choosing input devices for 3D applications.

4.8.1. Important Considerations

Many factors must be considered when choosing an input device for a particular 3D UI. Device ergonomics, the number and type of input modes, the available technique to device-mapping strategies, and the types of tasks the user will be performing all play a role in choosing suitable input devices. The problem is amplified because of the variety of possible operations the user might perform within the context of a given

3D application. A particular device might be perfect for one task but completely inappropriate for another.

Device ergonomics is clearly an important consideration when choosing an input device for a 3D application. We do not want to put undue strain on the user's body. Such strain can lead to repetitive stress injuries and make it difficult for the user to perform common tasks. Devices should be lightweight, require little training, and provide a significant transfer of information to the computer with minimal effort.

A particular device's input modes must be considered when choosing an input device for a 3D application. The types of input required for the application help to reduce the possible device choices. For example, a conventional 3D modeling system uses a keyboard and other 2D devices such as a mouse or a tablet. However, these devices in an immersive 3D modeler are not appropriate, because they are difficult to use while standing and do not provide the appropriate DOF needed to track the user's head and hands. In contrast, a desktop 3D computer game does not necessarily require a complicated 6-DOF tracking device, because, in most cases, the keyboard and a mouse or a joystick will suffice. To take another example, a simple immersive architectural walkthrough requires the user to be head-tracked and have a way to navigate through the environment. In such an application, although a bend-sensing glove could be used to navigate (using some collection of gestures), it would probably not be appropriate given the complexity of the device. A simpler device such as a Wanda, shown in Figure 4.16, is much easier to use because the application does not need all of the extra DOF that a bend-sensing glove gives the user.

As stated earlier, an input device can handle a variety of interaction techniques depending on the logical mapping of the technique to the device. The major issue is whether that mapping makes the device and the subsequent interaction techniques *usable*. Therefore, an important consideration when choosing an input device in a 3D application is how the device will map to the interaction techniques required to perform application tasks. It is in these mappings where tradeoffs are usually made, because very often a device will have a natural mapping to one or two of the interaction techniques in the application but relatively poor mappings to the others. For example, in the context of an immersive scientific visualization application, a 3D tracker may be attached to the user's hand and used for selection and manipulation of a tool for examining the dataset. The user can simply move the tool within the space of the dataset to explore it, and this represents a natural mapping from device to interaction technique. However, using the 3D tracker to input parameter values to change the rendering style has a less natural mapping from device to interaction technique. If the scientific visualization application were on the desktop, the keyboard would provide a much more natural mapping for changing rendering styles but would make object selection and manipulation much more difficult.

This example makes the point that there is often a tradeoff when choosing an input device for a 3D application. In many cases, input devices have been designed for general use, which means that although they can be used for a variety of interaction techniques, they may not provide the best mapping for any one of them. Thus, several specialized devices may provide better usability than a single general-purpose device.

> It is often better to have a series of specialized devices that work well for a specific group of interaction techniques rather than one or two generic input devices for all of the techniques in a 3D application.

Examples of this type of approach can be found in the work of Hinckley and colleagues (1994); Forsberg, LaViola, and Zeleznik (1998); and Keefe and colleagues (2001).

4.8.2. Input Device Taxonomies

Input device taxonomies can be a useful tool for determining which input devices can be substituted for each other, and they can also help in making decisions about what devices to use for particular tasks. In addition, they are an important part of 3D UI design because they provide a mechanism for understanding and discussing the similarities and differences among input devices. In this section, we briefly review some of these input device taxonomies from a historical perspective to show the evolution of these tools. Additionally, we discuss how they can be used to help make decisions about choosing appropriate devices in 3D UIs.

One of the first input device taxonomies was developed by Foley and Wallace (1974). Their approach was to separate the input device from the interaction technique. They created a set of four virtual devices, which at the time covered most input devices. These virtual devices are the pick, locator, button, and valuator. A *pick* device is used to designate a user-defined object. A *locator* is used to determine position and/or orientation. A *button* is used to designate a system-defined object. Finally, a *valuator* is used to input a single value within a set of numbers. Two additional virtual devices, stroke and string, were added to this set by Enderle, Kansay, and Pfaff (1984). A *stroke* is a sequence of points, and a *string* is a sequence of characters.

This virtual device taxonomy proves useful in many different situations. For example, the 3D UI developer can use this taxonomy as a tool for quickly reducing the number of possible input devices to choose from by simply examining which virtual devices fit the application best and selecting the devices that fit in those categories. If a 3D locator is required in an application, then we can automatically eliminate all of the physical devices that do not map to this virtual device. However, this taxonomy does have a fundamental flaw, because devices that appear to be equivalent in the taxonomy can be dramatically different both physically and practically. For example, a mouse and a trackball are very different devices, yet they are both considered to be 2D locators and stroke devices.

As a result of these limitations, new taxonomies were developed to take other input device characteristics into account. For example, Foley, Wallace, and Chan (1984) improved upon the virtual device taxonomy by mapping elementary interaction tasks (e.g., select, position, orient) to the devices that perform those tasks. Based on task requirements, only a limited set of devices could be used for any particular task. However, because the taxonomy is task-based, an input device can appear for more than one task. Although this taxonomy can help to reduce the set of possible input devices even further than the virtual device taxonomy, it still has the problem that the structure of the device space and any pragmatic differences that distinguish input devices from one another are hidden.

To compensate for the pragmatic deficiencies of earlier taxonomies, Buxton (1983) developed a taxonomy that organizes continuous input devices into a 2D space, the dimensions of which are DOF and properties sensed (i.e., motion, position, pressure). Additionally, a subclassification is used for devices that have a mechanical intermediary between the hand and the sensing mechanism and those that are touch-sensitive. An example of how this taxonomy classifies input devices is shown in Figure 4.30. Two major problems with this taxonomy are that it was not developed to handle discrete input devices and, although it can determine if it is incorrect to substitute one input device for another, it cannot tell us why that substitution is inappropriate.

Property Sensed		Number of Dimensions				
		1		**2**		**6**
	Position	Bend Sensor	Linear Slider	Tablet and Stylus	Isotonic Joystick	Trackers (Position & Orientation)	M
				Touch Tablet			T
	Motion		Treadmill	Mouse	TrackBall		M
	Pressure	Torque Sensor			Isometric Joystick	SpaceBall & SpaceMouse	T

Figure 4.30   *Buxton's input device taxonomy, based on pragmatic attributes of devices, categorizes devices based on DOF, properties sensed, and whether the device uses an intermediary between the user and sensing mechanism (M) or is touch-sensitive (T). (Buxton 1983)*

Mackinlay, Card, and Robertson (1990b) extended Buxton's taxonomy in two ways. First, they distinguished between absolute and relative quantities. Second, they separated translational and rotational movement. In addition, they distinguished between the different translational and rotational axes instead of using DOF. For example, a 6-DOF position-tracking device would be labeled a device for sensing position in *x, y,* and *z* Cartesian coordinates and orientation in *rX, rY,* and *rZ* rotational coordinates with an infinite number of possible values sensed for each axis (see Figure 4.31). Their taxonomy allows for the description of both discrete and continuous devices as well as simple devices that can be combined into complex controls. This taxonomy was one of the first that recognized that human performance issues are important to understanding how devices work for given tasks. It could be used for choosing input devices in a similar manner to previous taxonomies—as a tool to help narrow down device choices by examining device pragmatics and mappings to interaction tasks.

Although the taxonomies we have discussed thus far provide frameworks for characterizing and understanding different input devices, they are limited in that they can reduce the number of possible input device choices but not determine which specific device is preferable. Jacob and

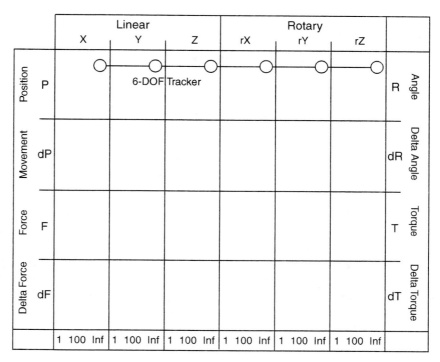

Figure 4.31 *Mackinlay, Card, and Robertson's (1990b) input device taxonomy categorizes a 6-DOF tracker. The circles indicate that the device senses one of the properties shown along the vertical axis. The placement of these circles within a column shows how many values are sensed.*

Sibert (1992) took these flaws into account by realizing that perceptual and cognitive issues were ignored. They developed a taxonomy (actually more of a theoretical model) to address these issues. Their approach is based on the idea that multidimensional spaces have different perceptual structures, and observers perceive multidimensional spaces based on these structures (Garner 1974). The taxonomy breaks these structures into two distinct components. Single composite perceptions are *integrally* related, while distinct perceptions are *separably* related. A multidimensional input device can be considered integral or separable based on whether it is a device that considers DOF together (a single composition) or that treats DOF individually (distinct compositions). The argument for this approach is that two 3D tasks may seem equivalent but have different perceptual spaces, implying that different input devices should be used. This model was not designed for characterizing devices, but rather to indicate when 3D input devices should be used instead of 2D devices for a given task. It has been used in different input device evaluations, such as Hinckley, Tullio, and colleagues (1997) and Balakrishnan and colleagues (1997).

4.8.3. Empirical Evaluations

In general, the taxonomies we discussed in the last section are useful for narrowing down the choice of input device for a particular task or 3D UI. However, in order to get concrete information about which devices are appropriate for given tasks, empirical studies are often required. In contrast to the lack of empirical work done on choosing appropriate output devices for 3D applications (see Chapter 3), there has been a good amount of research evaluating input devices for interacting in 3D. Performing empirical analyses of input devices is somewhat easier than performing comparisons of output devices, because it is easier to obtain quantitative measurements of device performance. Characteristics such as speed, accuracy, and ease of learning are often used to measure how a device will perform in a certain task. In addition, tools such as Fitts's law (Fitts 1954; MacKenzie 1992), a formal relationship between speed and accuracy in aimed movements, and the steering law (Accot and Zhai 1997), a formalization that describes the relationship between steering (i.e., drawing, navigation) time and the integral of the inverse of path width, provide a basis for quantitative analysis.

Studies have been conducted to determine the effectiveness of 3D input devices compared to traditional desktop devices such as the mouse. For example, Hinckley, Tullio, and colleagues (1997) compared the mouse with a 6-DOF tracking device for performing 3D object rotation tasks. Their results showed that the tracking device performed 36% faster than the 2D mouse without any loss of accuracy. In another study, Ware and Jessome (1988) compared the mouse and the bat (see section 4.4) for manipulating 3D objects. These results indicated that 3D object manipulation was easier to perform with the bat than with the mouse. Although these are only two studies, they do suggest that 3D input devices with 3 DOF or more are better than a mouse for handling freeform 3D object manipulation.

Zhai conducted a number of interesting studies specifically on 3D input devices (Zhai 1998) and came up with a number of guidelines for choosing appropriate 3D input devices. For example, in Zhai and Milgram (1998), 6-DOF flying mice were shown to be easy to learn and to outperform many other 3D input devices in terms of speed. However, flying mice, such as the ones described in section 4.4, do have disadvantages in that they cause fatigue easily and lack persistence in position when released. In contrast, desktop 6-DOF devices such as the SpaceBall 5000 and SpaceMouse Plus (see Figure 4.4) were shown to reduce user fatigue, increase device persistence, and provide smoother pointer movement, but with slower performance. This is a specific instance of the classic speed–accuracy tradeoff.

> When speed and a short learning curve are of primary concern (e.g., for video games or location-based entertainment), free moving 6-DOF devices are most suitable. When comfort, trajectory control, and coordination are most important (e.g., for 3D modeling or teleoperation), a desktop-based 6-DOF input device should be used.

Other interesting empirical studies of 3D input devices can be found in Zhai and Woltjer (2003); Balakrishnan and colleagues (1997); Kessler, Hodges, and Walker (1995); and Zhai (1995).

Empirical work for determining appropriate input devices for specific tasks in 3D UIs can be difficult because of the many variables that are involved, but it continues to be an important area of research as 3D UIs continue to evolve. As new devices are developed, scientific studies must be conducted to determine how these devices can be used most effectively.

Recommended Reading

For a more detailed discussion of motion-tracking technology, we recommend the following:

Foxlin, E. (2002). Motion Tracking Requirements and Technologies. *Handbook of Virtual Environments: Design, Implementation, and Applications.* K. Stanney (Ed.), Lawrence Erlbaum Associates, 163–210.

Welch, G., and E. Foxlin (2002). Motion Tracking: No Silver Bullet, but a Respectable Arsenal. *IEEE Computer Graphics & Applications,* special issue on "Tracking" 22(6): 24–38.

Allen, D., G. Bishop, and G. Welch (2001). Tracking: Beyond 15 Minutes of Thought. *SIGGRAPH Course #11.*

A comprehensive discussion of computer vision techniques used in optical tracking can be found in the following:

Forsyth, D., and J. Ponce (2002). *Computer Vision: A Modern Approach,* Prentice Hall.

A thorough discussion of eye tracking can be found in these texts:

Duchowski, A. T. (2003). *Eye Tracking Methodology: Theory and Practice,* Springer-Verlag.

Wilder, J., G. Hung, M. Tremaine, and M. Kaur (2002). Eye Tracking in Virtual Environments. In *Handbook of Virtual Environments: Design, Implementation, and Applications.* K. Stanney (Ed.), Lawrence Erlbaum Associates, 211–222.

Jacob, R. (1995). Eye Tracking in Advanced Interface Design. *Virtual Environments and Advanced Interface Design.* W. Barfield and T. Furness (Eds.), Oxford University Press, 258–288.

A nice survey of data gloves and glove-based input can be found in the following:

LaViola, J. (1999). *Whole-Hand and Speech Input in Virtual Environments.* Master's Thesis, Dept. of Computer Science, Brown University.

Details of two important laws, Fitts's law and the law of steering, used in evaluating input devices, can be found in the following:

Fitts, P. M. (1954). The Information Capacity of the Human Motor System in Controlling the Amplitude of Movement. *Journal of Experimental Psychology* 47: 381–391.

MacKenzie, I. S. (1992). Fitts' Law as a Research and Design Tool in Human Computer Interaction. *Human Computer Interaction* 7: 91–139.

Zhai, S., and R. Woltjer (2003). Human Movement Performance in Relation to Path Constraint: The Law of Steering in Locomotion. *Proceedings of IEEE Virtual Reality 2003,* IEEE Press, 149–158.

Accot, J., and S. Zhai (1997). Beyond Fitts' Law: Models for Trajectory-Based HCI Tasks. *Proceedings of the 1997 ACM Conference on Human Factors in Computing Systems (CHI '97),* ACM Press, 295–302.

Finally, an important starting point for anyone interested in 6-DOF device evaluation is the following:

Zhai, S. (1995). *Human Performance in Six Degree of Freedom Input Control.* PhD Dissertation, Dept. of Computer Science, University of Toronto.

PART III
3D Interaction Techniques

In Part II, we presented information about the input and output device technologies that make 3D interaction possible. However, designing good interaction devices is not sufficient to produce a usable 3D interface. In Part III, we discuss interaction techniques for the most common 3D interaction tasks. Remember that interaction techniques are methods used to accomplish a given task via the interface, and that they include both hardware and software components. The software components of interaction techniques are also known as *control-display mappings* and are responsible for translating information from the input devices into associated system actions that are then displayed to the user (see the introduction to Part II). Many of the techniques we present can be implemented using a variety of different devices; the interaction concept and the implementation details are what make them unique.

We organize Part III by user interaction task. Each chapter describes a task and variations on that task. Techniques that can be used to complete that task, along with guidelines for choosing among the techniques, are discussed. We also provide implementation details for some important techniques.

The implementation issues are described in English in combination with mathematical notation (using the mathematical concepts described in Appendix A). We decided not to provide code or pseudocode for several reasons. Code would have been extremely precise, but we would have had to choose a language and a toolkit or library on which the code would be based. Because there is currently no standard development environment for 3D UIs, this code would have been directly useful to only a small percentage of readers. Pseudocode would have been more general, but even with pseudocode, we would be assuming that your development environment provides a particular set of functionality and uses a particular programming style. Thus, we decided to use both natural and mathematical languages. This choice ensures precision and descriptiveness, and allows each reader to translate the implementation concepts into his or her own development environment.

Chapter 5 covers the closely related tasks of *selection* and *manipulation*. We begin with these tasks because they have been widely studied, they are fundamental aspects of 3D interaction, and techniques for these tasks form the basis for many other 3D interaction techniques.

Chapters 6 and 7 relate to the task of *navigation*, which is movement in and around an environment—a fundamental human task. Navigation includes both *travel* (Chapter 6) and *wayfinding* (Chapter 7). A bit of explanation is needed to distinguish between travel and wayfinding, and to show how we organize these two chapters.

Travel is the motor component of navigation—the low-level actions that the user makes to control the position and orientation of his viewpoint. In the real world, travel is the more physical navigation task, involving moving feet, turning a steering wheel, letting out a throttle, and so on. In the virtual world, travel techniques allow the user to translate and/or rotate the viewpoint and to modify the conditions of movement, such as the velocity.

Wayfinding is the cognitive component of navigation—high-level thinking, planning, and decision making related to user movement. It involves spatial understanding and planning tasks, such as determining the current location within the environment, determining a path from the current location to a goal location, and building a mental map of the environment. Real-world wayfinding has been researched extensively, with studies of aids like maps, directional signs, landmarks, and so on. In virtual worlds, wayfinding can also be crucial—in a large, complex environment, an efficient travel technique is of no use if the traveler has no idea where to go. When we speak of wayfinding techniques, we refer to wayfinding aids included as part of the interface or in the environment. Unlike travel techniques or manipulation techniques, where the computer ultimately performs the action, wayfinding techniques support the performance of the task only in the user's mind.

Is it realistic or even possible to separate the tasks of travel and wayfinding? Clearly, they are both part of the same process and contribute toward achieving the same goals. However, from the standpoint of interaction technique design, we can generally consider these two subtasks to be distinct. A travel technique is necessary to perform navigation tasks, and in some small or simple environments, a good travel technique may be all that is necessary. In more complex environments, wayfinding techniques may also be needed. In some cases, the designer can combine techniques for travel and wayfinding into a single integrated technique, reducing the cognitive load on the user and reinforcing the user's spatial knowledge each time the technique is used. Techniques that make use of miniature environments or maps fit this description, but these techniques are not suitable for all navigation tasks.

Chapter 6 covers the task of travel, while Chapter 7 discusses wayfinding theory and techniques. *System control* tasks are the topic of Chapter 8. This interaction task addresses changing the mode or state of the system, often through commands or menus. Finally, Chapter 9 covers *symbolic input,* the task of entering or editing text, numbers, and other symbols. These two tasks have not been as heavily researched as manipulation, travel, and wayfinding, but they are nonetheless important for many 3D UIs.

One other 3D interaction task deserves mention here: *modeling.* Interactive 3D modeling tasks allow a user to create 3D geometric objects and modify their properties. A wide variety of 3D interaction techniques for modeling have been designed and evaluated by 3D UI researchers, and undoubtedly this is a critical task for some application domains. For this edition of the book, however, we chose not to include a chapter on 3D modeling techniques because of space and time constraints. This should not be taken as a comment on the importance of the task or the quality of existing work in this area, and we hope to include more information on 3D modeling in a future edition.

CHAPTER 5
Selection and Manipulation

The quality of the interaction techniques that allow us to manipulate 3D virtual objects has a profound effect on the quality of the entire 3D UI. Indeed, manipulation is one of the most fundamental tasks for both physical and virtual environments: if the user cannot manipulate virtual objects effectively, many application-specific tasks simply cannot be performed. Furthermore, interaction techniques for travel and system control that are discussed in the following chapters are often based on 3D manipulation techniques. Therefore, we start our discussion of 3D interaction techniques with techniques for selecting and manipulating 3D objects.

5.1. Introduction

The human hand is a remarkable device: it allows us to manipulate physical objects quickly, precisely, and with little conscious attention. Therefore, it is not surprising that the design and investigation of manipulation interfaces are important directions in 3D UIs. The goal of manipulation interface design is the development of new interaction techniques or the reuse of existing techniques that facilitate high levels of user-manipulation performance and comfort while diminishing the impact from inherited human and hardware limitations (Knight 1987).

This chapter is devoted to interaction techniques for 3D manipulation: software components that map user input captured by input devices (Chapter 4), such as the trajectory of the user's hand and button presses, into the desired action in the virtual world (such as selection or rotation of a virtual object). We demonstrate that there is an astonishing variety of 3D interaction techniques for manipulation—the result of the creativity and insight of many researchers and designers. They provide a rich selection of ready-to-use interface components or design ideas that can inspire developers in implementing their own variations of manipulation interfaces.

5.1.1. Chapter Roadmap

We start by answering the question, *What is a 3D manipulation task?* (section 5.2). Understanding the details of manipulation tasks is important, because it does not make sense to design and evaluate interaction techniques for the manipulation task in general. The design, analysis, and deployment of interaction techniques depend heavily on the minute task details for which a technique was developed.

We continue with a discussion of the relation between properties of input devices and interaction techniques in manipulation tasks (section 5.3). Although input devices are discussed in Chapter 4, we mention some of their properties that directly affect the design of manipulation techniques.

Section 5.4.1, Classifications of Manipulation Techniques, provides a general overview of the techniques and is followed by the description of the 3D manipulation techniques themselves. These include a number of pointing and virtual hand techniques, 3D rotation techniques, integrated techniques, and finally techniques for desktop 3D manipulation.

Each section presents only the key ideas behind the technique design. In those cases where the implementation is not obvious, mathematical descriptions of the techniques are provided. We also mention results of empirical evaluations when appropriate. We wrap up this chapter with some general guidelines and conclusions (section 5.5).

5.2. 3D Manipulation Tasks

The effectiveness of 3D manipulation techniques greatly depends on the manipulation tasks to which they are applied. The same technique could be intuitive and easy to use in some task conditions and utterly inadequate in others. For example, the techniques needed for the rapid arrangement of virtual objects in immersive modeling applications could be very different from the manipulation techniques used to handle surgical instruments in a medical simulator. Therefore, before discussing interaction techniques, it is important to define what we actually mean by *manipulation.*

In everyday language, manipulation usually refers to any act of handling physical objects with one or two hands. For the practical purposes of designing and evaluating 3D manipulation techniques, we narrow the definition of the manipulation task to *spatial rigid object manipulation—* that is, manipulations that preserve the shape of objects. This definition is consistent with an earlier definition of the manipulation task in 2D UIs (Foley et al. 1984) as well as earlier human and motion analysis literature (McCormick 1970; Mundel 1978).

However, even within this narrower definition there are still many variations of manipulation tasks characterized by a multitude of variables, such as application goals, object sizes, object shapes, the distance from objects to the user, characteristics of the physical environment (e.g., temperature), as well as the physical and psychological states of the user. Designing and evaluating interaction techniques for every conceivable combination of these variables is not feasible; instead, interaction techniques are usually developed to be used in a *representative subset* of manipulation tasks. There are two basic approaches to choosing this task subset: using a *canonical* set of manipulation tasks or using *application-specific* manipulation tasks.

5.2.1. Canonical Manipulation Tasks

The fundamental assumption of any task analysis is that the entire requisite of human effort in all cases is composed of the same basic tasks, which are building blocks for more complex interaction scenarios (Mundel 1978). Consequently, if we can distill 3D manipulation into a number of such basic tasks, then instead of investigating the entire task space of 3D manipulation, we can design and evaluate interaction techniques only for this small subset. The results can be then extrapolated to the entire space of 3D manipulation activities. This section develops one of the possible sets of canonical manipulation tasks.

Tasks

Virtual 3D manipulation imitates, to some extent, general target acquisition and positioning movements that we perform in the real world—a combination of reaching/grabbing, moving, and orienting of objects.

Therefore, we can designate the following tasks as basic manipulation tasks:

- *Selection* is the task of acquiring or identifying a particular object from the entire set of objects available. Sometimes it is also called a target acquisition task (Zhai et al. 1994). The real-world counterpart of the selection task is picking an object with a hand.
- *Positioning* is the task of changing the 3D position of an object. The real-world counterpart of positioning is moving an object from a starting location to a target location.
- *Rotation* is the task of changing the orientation of an object. The real-world counterpart of rotation is rotating an object from a starting orientation to a target orientation.

This breakdown of the tasks is compatible with a well-known task analysis for 2D GUI (Foley et al. 1984) and several task analyses for VEs (Mine 1995a; Bowman and Hodges 1997; Poupyrev et al. 1997). Although some also include object deformation, such as scaling (Mine 1995a), we do not include it, because 3D object deformations are often accomplished via manipulation of 3D widgets using the three canonical tasks above.

Parameters of Canonical Tasks

For each canonical task, there are many variables that significantly affect user performance and usability (Foley et al. 1984). For example, in the case of a selection task, the user manipulation strategy would differ significantly depending on the distance to the target object, the target size, the density of objects around the target, and many other factors. Some of the task variations are more prominent than others; some are standalone tasks that require specific interaction techniques. For example, object selection within arm's reach and out of arm's reach have been often considered two distinct tasks (Mine 1995a).

Therefore, each canonical task defines a *task space* that includes multiple variations of the same task defined by *task parameters*—variables that influence user performance while accomplishing this task (Poupyrev et al. 1997). Each of these parameters defines a design dimension, for which interaction techniques may or may not provide support. Table 5.1 outlines some of the task parameters for canonical tasks that have been often addressed in the 3D UI literature.

Table 5.1 *Tasks and their parameters.*

Task	Parameters
Selection	Distance and direction to target, target size, density of objects around the target, number of targets to be selected, target occlusion
Positioning	Distance and direction to initial position, distance and direction to target position, translation distance, required precision of positioning
Rotation	Distance to target, initial orientation, final orientation, amount of rotation, required precision of rotation

5.2.2. Application-Specific Manipulation Tasks

The canonical tasks approach simplifies manipulation tasks to their most essential properties. Because of this simplification, however, it may fail to capture some manipulation task aspects that are application-specific. Examples of such application-specific manipulation activities include positioning of a medical probe relative to virtual 3D models of internal organs in a VR medical training application and moving the control stick of the virtual airplane in a flight simulator. Obviously, in these examples, generalization of the manipulation task does not make sense—it is the minute details of the manipulation that are important to capture and replicate. This chapter only briefly considers such application-specific tasks; it concentrates instead on interaction techniques for performing generic manipulation tasks. The design of application-specific techniques is discussed in the special literature related to these applications.

5.3. Manipulation Techniques and Input Devices

There is a close relationship between the properties of input devices that are used to capture user input and the design of interaction techniques for a manipulation task: the choice of devices often restricts which manipulation techniques can be used. We discussed input devices in Chapter 4; here we briefly review some of the important device properties that relate to manipulation techniques.

Just like input devices, visual display devices and their characteristics (supported depth cues, refresh rate, resolution, etc.) can significantly affect the design of 3D manipulation techniques. Haptic displays could also have a pronounced effect on the user performance of manipulation tasks. We restrict our discussion to input devices, however, because they are intimately linked to interaction techniques for manipulation. Some discussion of the effect of display devices on manipulation tasks can be found in Chapter 10.

5.3.1. Control Dimensions and Integrated Control in 3D Manipulation

Two characteristics of input devices that are key in manipulation tasks are, first, the *number of control dimensions* (how many DOF the device can control), and second, the *integration* of the control dimensions (how many DOF can be controlled simultaneously with a single movement). For example, a mouse allows for 2-DOF integrated control, magnetic trackers allow simultaneous control of both 3D position and orientation (i.e., 6-DOF integrated control). Typical game controllers, on the other hand, provide at least 4 DOF, but the control is separated—2 DOF allocated to each of two joysticks, where each has to be controlled separately (see Figure 4.2).

The devices that are usually best for 3D manipulation are multiple DOF devices with integrated control of all input dimensions (Zhai et al. 1997). Integrated control allows the user to control the 3D interface using natural, well-coordinated movements, similar to real-world manipulation, which also results in better user performance (Crowford 1964; Hinckley, Tullio et al. 1997; Zhai and Senders 1997a, 1997b). Although early studies (Ellson 1947; Senders et al. 1955) found that human performance was poor in multidimensional control, recent studies suggest that this conclusion was due mostly to limited input device technology that was available for multiple DOF input at the time when those experiments were conducted. Indeed, the input devices that were used did not allow users to control all degrees of freedom simultaneously (Zhai and Senders 1997a, 1997b). For example, in one experiment, subjects were required to manipulate two separate knobs to control the 2D position of a pointer (Senders et al. 1955).

Most of the techniques discussed in this chapter assume that advanced input devices (such as 6-DOF trackers) are available. The reality of real-world 3D UI development, however, is that the device choice often depends on factors besides user performance, such as cost, device availability, ease of maintenance, and targeted user population. Therefore, even though 6-DOF devices are becoming less expensive and increasingly accessible, a majority of 3D UIs are still designed for input devices with only 2 DOF, such as a mouse, or those that separate degrees of freedom, such as game controllers. Thus, we discuss some 3D interaction techniques for desktop devices later in this chapter.

5.3.2. Force versus Position Control

Another key property of input devices that significantly affects the design of interaction techniques is whether the device measures position of the user's hand, as motion trackers and mice do (isomorphic control), or whether it measures the force applied by the user, as joysticks do (isometric control). Studies by Zhai (Zhai and Milgram 1993) found that in 6-DOF manipulation tasks, position control usually yields better performance than force control. Force control is usually more preferable for controlling rates, such as the speed of navigation. Most 3D manipulation techniques discussed in this chapter assume that devices provide position control.

5.3.3. Device Placement and Form-Factor in 3D Manipulation

The importance of device shape in manual control tasks has been known for a long time. Hand tools, for example, have been perfected over thousands of years, both to allow users to perform intended functions effectively and to minimize human wear and tear (McCormick 1970).

In 3D UIs, these objectives are also highly relevant; furthermore, the shape of the input device strongly influences the choice of 3D manipulation interaction techniques. Two popular device configurations used in 3D UIs are presented in Figure 5.1: on the left, the device is attached to the hand (e.g., with a glove), and on the right, the device is held in the fingers, a so-called *precision grasp*. The choice of approach influences the choice of interaction techniques, as they involve different muscle groups in manipulation (Zhai et al. 1996). When the device is directly attached to the hand, all translation and rotation operations are carried out by larger muscle groups of the user's shoulder, elbow, and wrist. In contrast, with the precision grasp, the user can use smaller and faster muscle groups in the fingers. The results of experimental studies demonstrate that precision grasp usually results in better user performance, particularly in 3D rotation tasks.

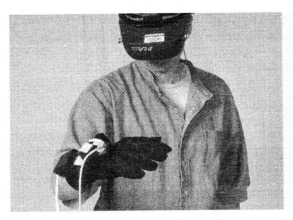 

Figure 5.1   *Two strategies of handling the input device: attached to the hand and rolled in the fingers (precision grasp). (Photograph courtesy of Ivan Poupyrev)*

Precision-grasp devices also decrease the effect of "clutching" on user manipulation (Zhai et al. 1996). Clutching occurs when a manipulation cannot be achieved in a single motion—the object must be released and then regrasped in order to complete the task. A familiar real-world example of clutching is using a traditional wrench to tighten a bolt in a small space. The operator must continually remove the wrench from the bolt, rotate it, and then place it back on the bolt, which is inconvenient and frustrating. Precision-grasp devices allow the user to roll the device in his fingers, thus allowing an infinite amount of spatial rotation without the need for clutching. Devices that are attached to the hand require clutching after a small amount of rotation.

So, as long as the design of the device promotes using fingers for 3D manipulation, user performance benefits. Because a spherical shape is easier to rotate in the user's hand, ball-shaped devices (Figure 5.1) are preferable when precise and efficient manipulation is required. It would also be reasonable to think that shaping the device to replicate the shape of virtual objects would also improve user performance (a so-called "physical props" technique). This, however, was not found to be true: shaping the device like a virtual object does not yield a significant benefit for manipulation performance; in fact, devices with generic shapes usually perform better (Hinckley, Tullio et al. 1997; Ware and Rose 1999). The physical props technique can be, however, beneficial in applications when speed of learning, sense of immersion, or user enjoyment is more important than manipulation performance. We discuss the physical props approach in more detail in Chapter 10.

5.4. Interaction Techniques for 3D Manipulation

The design of effective 3D manipulation techniques is an important research problem. The challenge was very well defined by Sheridan (cited in Zhai 1995): "How do the geometrical mappings of body and environmental objects, both within the VE and the true one, and relative to each other, contribute to the sense of presence, training, and performance? . . . In some cases there may be a need to deviate significantly from strict geometric isomorphism because of hardware limits or constraints of the human body. At present we do not have design/operating principles for knowing what mapping . . . is permissible and which degrades performance."

As this section explains, a vast variety of 3D manipulation techniques have been invented in an attempt to meet this challenge. Their variety might be somewhat overwhelming; therefore, we start with basic classifications of interaction techniques followed by the detailed descriptions.

5.4.1. Classifications of Manipulation Techniques

Many 3D manipulation techniques relate to one another, and many share common properties. Classifying them according to common features is useful in understanding the relations between different groups of techniques and can help us to grasp a larger picture of the technique design space. Certainly, there is more than one way to group techniques together; here we discuss only some that have been proposed in the literature.

Isomorphism in Manipulation Techniques

The design of 3D manipulation interfaces has been strongly influenced by two opposing views. The *isomorphic view* suggests a strict, geometrical, one-to-one correspondence between hand motions in the physical and virtual worlds on the grounds that it is the most natural and therefore is better for users. The results of early human factors studies indicate that although isomorphism is, indeed, often more natural (overview in Knight 1987), it also has important shortcomings. First, these mappings are often impractical because of constraints in the input devices. For example, the tracking range may be restricted, which is one of the most common limitations. Second, isomorphism is often ineffective because of the limitations of humans. For example, our arm length naturally limits our reaching distance. Finally, it has been argued that 3D interfaces can be more effective, intuitive, and rich if, instead of trying to imitate physical reality, we create mappings and interaction techniques that are specifically tailored to 3D environments, providing in some sense a "better" reality (e.g., Stoakley et al. 1995).

Hence, the *nonisomorphic* approach deviates significantly from strict realism, providing users with "magic" virtual tools such as laser beams, rubber arms, voodoo dolls (Poupyrev et al. 1996; Pierce et al. 1999), and others. These nonisomorphic mappings and techniques can allow users to manipulate objects quite differently than in the physical world, while maintaining usability and performance (Bowman and Hodges 1997; Poupyrev, Weghorst et al. 1998).

The relative advantage of isomorphic versus nonisomorphic techniques depends on the application: when strict realism of manipulation is *not* the major requirement of the application, nonisomorphic mappings might be effective and engaging for the user. In fact, the majority of 3D direct manipulation techniques today are nonisomorphic techniques.

Classification by Task Decomposition

We can also observe that all manipulation techniques consist of the same basic components that serve similar purposes (Bowman, Johnson et al. 1999). For example, in a selection task, the interaction technique should provide the user with a means to indicate an object to select and to confirm the selection; and provide visual, haptic, or audio feedback while performing the task (Figure 5.2). Manipulation and rotation tasks can be decomposed in a similar way.

Hence, we can consider 3D manipulation techniques as being constructed out of several interaction "building blocks" (technique components), where each block allows accomplishing a single suboperation. The entire "construction kit" can include a variety of different components for each suboperation. The advantage of this approach is that we can structure the interaction technique design space so that new techniques can be constructed out of basic elements simply by picking the appropriate components and putting them together. More on the use of task decomposition classifications for interaction technique design and evaluation can be found in Chapter 11.

Classification by Metaphor

Most current VE manipulation techniques are based on a few basic interaction metaphors or a combination of metaphors. Each of these metaphors forms the fundamental mental model of a technique—a perceptual manifestation of what users can do by using the techniques (*affordances*),

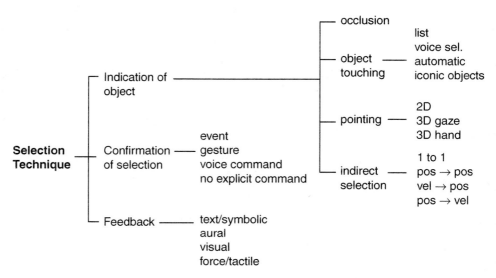

Figure 5.2 *Classification of selection techniques by task decomposition.*

and what they cannot do (*constraints*). Particular techniques can be considered as different implementations of these basic metaphors.

Figure 5.3 presents one possible metaphor-based taxonomy of 3D manipulation techniques for immersive VEs (Poupyrev, Weghorst et al. 1998; Poupyrev and Ichikawa, 1999). The techniques first are classified as *exocentric* or *egocentric* techniques. In exocentric interaction, also known as the god's-eye viewpoint, users interact with the 3D environment from outside of it. For example, in the world-in-miniature (WIM) technique, the user interacts with a small, handheld copy of the environment (Stoakley et al. 1995). In egocentric interaction, the user interacts from inside the environment. In other words, the VE surrounds the user, who has a first-person view of the environment. The classification further subdivides metaphors for egocentric manipulation into *virtual hand* and *virtual pointer.* With techniques based on the virtual hand metaphor, users reach and grab objects by "touching" and "picking" them with a virtual hand. With techniques based on the virtual pointer metaphor, the user interacts with objects by pointing at them.

The classification of techniques by metaphor provides an easy-to-understand way to organize interaction techniques, and we loosely follow this classification when discussing interaction techniques in the rest of this section. Specifically, we examine the metaphors of pointing (section 5.4.2), virtual hand (5.4.3), and WIM (5.4.4). We also include special

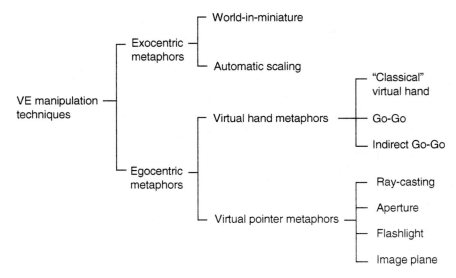

Figure 5.3　*Classification of manipulation techniques by metaphor. (Poupyrev, Weghorst et al. 1998, © 1998 Blackwell Publishing; reprinted by permission)*

sections on combination techniques (5.4.5), nonisomorphic 3D rotation (5.4.6), and desktop techniques for 3D manipulation (5.4.7).

5.4.2.　Interacting by Pointing

This section presents one of the most fundamental classes of 3D manipulation techniques—*pointing* techniques. The motivation behind the pointing technique is to allow the user to easily select and manipulate objects located beyond the area of reach by simply pointing at them. When the vector defined by the direction of pointing intersects a virtual object, the user can select it by issuing a *trigger* event that confirms the selection. Examples of triggers are buttons and voice commands. After the object is selected, it can be attached to the end of a pointing vector for manipulation (Figure 5.4).

One of the earliest instances of a pointing technique was described in the "put-that-there" interface, developed by Bolt at MIT in the early 1980s (Bolt 1980). The put-that-there system allowed users to select and manipulate objects by pointing at them, with voice commands used as a trigger. Since then, a number of pointing techniques have been reported (Jacoby et al. 1994; Mine 1995a; Bowman and Hodges 1997). The difference between them is defined mostly by two design variables: first, how the *pointing direction* is defined (i.e., how the input device position and orientation is mapped onto the direction of the ray), and second, by the *shape of the selection volume,* which defines the visual feedback provided and how many objects are selected when users point at them.

Pointing is a powerful selection technique. A number of experimental evaluations have demonstrated that it results in better selection performance than virtual hand–based techniques (see section 5.4.3), because pointing requires significantly less physical hand movement from the user (Poupyrev, Weghorst et al. 1998; Bowman, Johnson et al. 1999). Pointing, however, is generally a very poor positioning technique: object manipulation can be efficiently accomplished only in radial movements around the user (perpendicular to the pointing direction), and when the task does not require changing the distance between the user and objects. Rotations can be effectively accomplished only about one axis: the axis defined by the pointing vector. Expressive 6-DOF manipulation with these techniques is therefore impossible.

In this section we discuss the following pointing-based interaction techniques:

- simple ray-casting technique
- two-handed pointing
- flashlight technique
- aperture techniques
- image-plane techniques
- fishing-reel technique

Ray-Casting

With ray-casting, the user points at objects with a virtual ray that defines the direction of pointing, and a virtual line segment attached to the hand visualizes the pointing direction (Figure 5.4). In immersive environments, the virtual ray can be attached directly to the virtual hand controlled by a 6-DOF sensor. In a desktop 3D environment, the ray can be attached to a 3D widget that can in turn be controlled by a mouse, though clicking with the mouse directly on 3D objects is an easier and more effective method that is used in most desktop 3D UIs.

The *pointing direction* in the case of the simple ray-casting technique is estimated from the direction of the virtual ray that is attached to the user's virtual hand (vector $\vec{p}$) and the 3D position of the virtual hand $\mathbf{h}$. To define virtual objects that can be selected with the ray, we calculate which objects can be defined in affine space as follows:

Eq. 5.1
$$p(\alpha) = \mathbf{h} + \alpha\,\vec{p},$$

where $0 < \alpha < +\infty$.

More than one object can be intersected by the line $\mathbf{p}(\alpha)$, and only the one closest to the user should be selected; hence, the interaction technique should traverse all possible candidates for selection.

In the simplest case of the ray-casting technique, the *shape* of the ray can be a short line segment attached to the user's hand (Figure 5.4). This, however, could be difficult to use when selecting small objects located far away, as it does not provide the user with sufficient visual feedback on whether the ray is actually intersecting the virtual object. An infinitely long virtual ray provides the user with better visual feedback, as it allows the user to select objects simply by touching them with the ray (Bowman and Hodges 1997).

Virtual ray-casting is a very powerful selection technique, except when a very high precision of selection is required, such as when selecting small or faraway objects (Poupyrev, Weghorst et al. 1998; Bowman, Johnson et al. 1999). In such task scenarios, ray-casting selection perfor-

Figure 5.4   *Ray-casting technique. (Poupyrev, Weghorst et al. 1998, © 1998 Blackwell Publishing; reprinted by permission)*

mance erodes significantly because of the high angular accuracy required and the amplification of hand and tracker jitter with increased distance. This has been observed by a number of researchers (Liang and Green 1994; Forsberg et al. 1996) and supported by results of experimental studies (Poupyrev, Weghorst et al. 1998). At close range, ray-casting is perhaps the most simple and efficient selection technique.

Two-Handed Pointing

Ray-casting uses a virtual hand position and the direction of the virtual ray to define the pointing direction. In cases where both of the user's hands are tracked, the pointing direction can be specified using a two-handed technique: one hand (usually closer to the user) specifies the origin of the virtual ray, while the other hand specifies where the ray is pointing to (Mine et al. 1997). Given 3D positions of the left and right hands in virtual space, the selection line can be defined in affine space as follows:

Eq. 5.2
$$\mathbf{p}(\alpha) = \mathbf{h}_l + \alpha \left(\mathbf{h}_r - \mathbf{h}_l \right),$$

where $0 < \alpha < +\infty$.

Here, $\mathbf{h}_r$ and $\mathbf{h}_l$ are the 3D coordinates of the right and left virtual hands respectively; the direction parameter α should be chosen so that the virtual ray points away from the user.

The disadvantage of two-handed pointing is that both hands must be tracked; however, it allows for richer and more effective pointing interaction. For example, the distance between the hands can be used to control the length of the virtual pointer, while by twisting the hands slightly the user can curve the virtual pointer (Olwal and Feiner 2003). This can provide a simple mechanism to disambiguate among several objects arranged in the depth direction (Figure 5.5, left) and simplifies pointing to fully or partially obscured objects (Figure 5.5, right).

Flashlight and Aperture Techniques

The spotlight or flashlight technique was developed to provide a "soft" selection technique that does not require precision and accuracy of pointing to virtual objects with the ray (Liang and Green 1994). The technique imitates pointing at objects with a flashlight, which can illuminate an object even when the user does not point precisely at it.

Figure 5.5   *A flexible pointer can be used to point to partially obscured objects. (Olwal and Feiner 2003; reprinted by permission of the authors)*

In the flashlight technique, the pointing direction is defined in the same way as in the simple ray-casting technique, but it replaces the virtual ray with a conic selection volume, with the apex of the cone at the input device. Objects that fall within this selection cone can be selected. The technique therefore allows easy selection of small objects even when they are located far from the user.

The obvious problem with the flashlight technique is disambiguation of the desired object when more than one object falls into the spotlight. Two basic rules are usually used for disambiguation (Liang and Green 1994). First, if two objects fall into the selection volume, then the object that is closer to the center line of the selection cone is selected. Second, if the angle between the center line of the selection cone is the same for both objects, then the object closer to the device is selected.

The flashlight technique does not require that an entire object fall into the spotlight: even if an object is touched by the side of the selection volume ("illuminated" by the flashlight), it can be considered a selection candidate. Although this makes it very easy to select virtual objects, this ease of selection becomes a disadvantage when selection of small objects or tightly grouped objects is required. In these situations (as well as some others), it is desirable to directly specify the spread angle of the selection cone.

The *aperture* technique makes this possible. The aperture technique (Forsberg et al. 1996) is a modification of the flashlight technique that allows the user to interactively control the spread of the selection volume. The pointing direction is defined by the 3D position of the user's

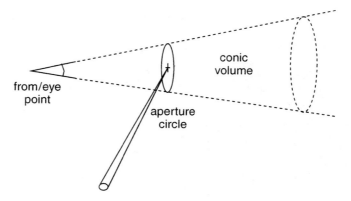

Figure 5.6 *Aperture selection technique. (Forsberg et al. 1996, © 1996 ACM; reprinted by permission)*

viewpoint in virtual space, which is estimated from the tracked head location, and the position of a hand sensor, represented as an aperture cursor within the VE (Figure 5.6, Figure 5.7a).

Given these two points in 3D virtual space, we can define the selection line in affine space as follows:

Eq. 5.3

$$\mathbf{p}(\alpha) = \mathbf{e} + \alpha\left(\mathbf{h} - \mathbf{e}\right),$$

where $0 < \alpha < \infty$.

Here, **e** and **h** are 3D coordinates of the virtual viewpoint and hand respectively.

The user can interactively control the spread angle of the selection volume simply by bringing the hand sensor closer or moving it farther away. The aperture technique thus improves the spotlight technique by providing an efficient interactive mechanism of object disambiguation by interactive control of the selection volume (Figure 5.6).

The aperture technique further simplifies selection of virtual objects by using the orientation of the pointer around a central axis (i.e., its twist) as an additional disambiguation metric. Two small virtual plates are mounted in parallel at the end of the pointer. In a case of selection ambiguity, the user twists the pointer to align the orientation of the plates with the orientation of the object to be selected. This informs the interface which 3D object the user intends to pick up. For example, on

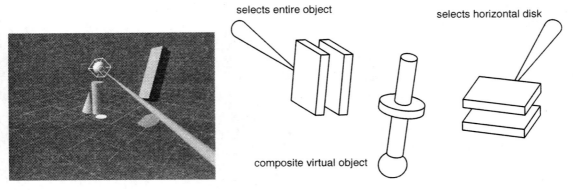

Figure 5.7   *Aperture technique: (a) an example of use; (b) selection sensitivity based on grasp orientation. (Reprinted by permission of Brown University)*

the left side of Figure 5.7b, the orientation of the plates indicates that the user intends to pick up the entire 3D object, because the plate orientation corresponds to the orientation of the object; on the right side of Figure 5.7b, the orientation of the plates indicates that the user would like to select only the horizontal disk located in the middle of the 3D object. Selection sensitivity based on the grasp orientation is directly derived from the real experience of grabbing objects with our hands; we always match our hand orientation with the orientation of the object to make it easy to pick up.

The fundamental design ideas behind the aperture and flashlight techniques can be easily applied to a wide variety of 3D UI configurations, in both desktop and immersive VEs. Of course, the flashlight and aperture techniques are essentially pointing techniques and therefore inherit all the limitations of ray-casting for object manipulation. This means that the flashlight and aperture techniques would not be effective for freeform 6-DOF manipulations of virtual objects. Nevertheless, these are effective and useful techniques. The choice between them depends on the application requirements. In general, if objects are not tightly grouped together, the flashlight is a simple and effective technique. When a higher degree of control is needed, an aperture technique can be effective.

Image-Plane Techniques

The image-plane family of techniques (Pierce et al. 1997) simplifies the object selection task by requiring the user to control only 2 DOF. With this technique, the user selects and manipulates 3D objects by touching and

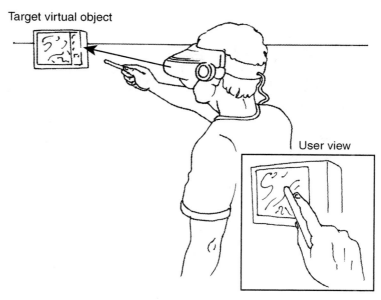

Figure 5.8 *The image-plane technique.*

manipulating their 2D projections on a virtual image plane located in front of the user (Figure 5.8).

There are several variations of the image-plane interaction techniques; Figure 5.8 presents the so-called sticky-finger variation of the image-plane technique. The object underneath the user's finger (or handheld input device) is selected by first casting a vector from the user's eyepoint through the finger and then finding an object intersecting with this vector, in the same manner as the aperture technique. Alternatively, if provided with a data glove device (see Chapter 4), the user can select objects with two fingers by positioning his hand so that his thumb and index finger are directly positioned on the image plane below and above the target object (the head-crusher technique). After selection, the 3D object can be manipulated: the object is scaled down and brought within the user's reach for manipulation.

The implementation of image-plane techniques, particularly headcrusher, is similar to the aperture technique that we discussed above. These techniques, however, have some important differences. With the head-crusher technique, the object is selected only if it is framed between the user's virtual fingers. This is the basic metaphor of the technique and provides a natural disambiguation method. With the aperture technique, however, it is not necessary that the entire object fall into the selection volume; the object can be selected even if it is only touching the side of the selection volume.

Image-plane techniques simulate direct touch and are therefore intuitive and easy to use for selection. Though this technique allows the user to modify the orientation of 3D objects, their distance from the user cannot be directly controlled, because objects are scaled down for manipulation. Mine's scaled-world grab technique (Mine et al. 1997) and Pierce's Voodoo Dolls technique (Pierce et al. 1999) tackle this problem (both are discussed in section 5.4.5).

Fishing-Reel Technique

The difficulty of controlling the distance to the virtual objects being manipulated is a problem for all pointing techniques. One possible solution is to supply the user with an additional input device dedicated to controlling the length of the virtual ray. Similar to the way a fishing reel works, this technique allows the user to select an object with a ray-casting technique, then reel it back and forth using the dedicated input device, which could be, for example, a simple mechanical slider or a pair of buttons added to the tracking device (Bowman and Hodges 1997). Although the fishing reel lets the user control the distance to the object, it separates the manipulation's degrees of freedom—the ray direction is controlled by the spatial movements of the user's hand, while distance is controlled by other means. As we discussed earlier in this chapter, separation of control in a manipulation task usually decreases user performance.

5.4.3. Direct Manipulation: Virtual Hand Techniques

This section presents another fundamental class of 3D manipulation techniques: *virtual hand* techniques by which the user can select and directly manipulate virtual objects with her hands. Typically, a 3D cursor is used to visualize the current locus of user input; for example, the cursor can be a 3D model of a human hand (Figure 5.9). Semitransparent volumetric cursors have also been investigated: their advantage is that transparency adds an additional depth cue, aiding selection of the 3D virtual objects (Zhai et al. 1994). The position and orientation of the input device are mapped onto the position and orientation of the virtual hand. To select an object, the user simply intersects the 3D cursor with the target of selection and then uses a trigger technique (e.g., button press, voice command, or hand gesture) to pick it up. The object is then attached to the virtual hand

Figure 5.9 *Virtual hand. (Poupyrev et al. 1996, © 1996 ACM; reprinted by permission)*

and can be easily translated and rotated within the VE until the user releases it with another trigger.

We discuss the following virtual hand interaction techniques:

- simple virtual hand technique
- Go-Go technique

Simple Virtual Hand

The simple virtual hand technique is a direct mapping of the user's hand
motion to a virtual hand's motion in a VE, typically linearly scaled to establish a direct correspondence between the device and VE coordinate
systems:

Eq. 5.4
$$\mathbf{p}_v = \alpha\mathbf{p}_r, \mathbf{R}_v = \mathbf{R}_r,$$

where $\mathbf{p}_r$ and $\mathbf{R}_r$ are the position (a 3D point) and orientation (a 3×3 matrix or quaternion) of the user's real hand measured using input devices;
$\mathbf{p}_v$ and $\mathbf{R}_v$ are the corresponding position and orientation of the virtual
hand in the VE, and α is a scaling ratio to match the scales of the real and
virtual coordinate systems.

Direct mappings such as this are also called transfer functions or
control-display gain functions. They are often classified by the number of
integrations applied to the measured user input (Knight 1987; Zhai 1995).
For example, in zero-order mappings, displacement of the input device

results in displacement of the controlled element, while in first-order mappings, it results in a change of the velocity. Equation 5.4 shows examples of zero-order transfer functions, also called linear mappings (MacKenzie 1995). Note that although in most cases the orientation $\mathbf{R}_r$ of the input device is mapped directly to the orientation $\mathbf{R}_v$ of the virtual hand, in some cases it is useful to "scale" 3D device rotations similar to the way we scale translations. Scaling rotations is not a trivial problem, and we discuss how this can be done in section 5.4.6.

Virtual hand techniques are isomorphic interaction techniques. They are rather intuitive because they directly simulate our interaction with everyday objects. The fundamental problem with such techniques is that only objects within the area of the user's reach can be selected and manipulated. In order to select objects located further away, the user must employ a travel technique (Chapter 6) to move to the object, which in many cases is inconvenient and increases the complexity of the 3D UI. In fact, the difficulty of selecting objects located outside of the user's reach has been reported as one of the major problems in 3D UIs (Durlach and Mavor 1995), and this has prompted the development of a number of manipulation techniques that attempt to overcome this problem.

Go-Go Interaction Technique

The Go-Go technique (Poupyrev et al. 1996) attempts to improve on the virtual hand by providing a simple and unobtrusive technique that allows the user to interactively change the length of the virtual arm.

To implement the Go-Go technique, the coordinates of the tracked user hand are calculated in the user-centered egocentric coordinate system (i.e., a polar coordinate system) as the triple $\{r_r, \phi, \theta\}$, where r_r is the length of the vector $\bar{\mathbf{r}}_r$, pointing from the user to the hand, and ϕ and θ are angles defining the direction of vector $\bar{\mathbf{r}}_r$ (Figure 5.10). The virtual hand is rendered in position $\{r_v, \phi, \theta\}$, where r_v is the *length* of the "virtual arm" calculated using the nonlinear mapping function F, as seen in Eq. 5.5 and Figure 5.11.

Eq. 5.5
$$r_v = F(r_r) = \begin{cases} r_r & \text{if } r_r \leq D \\ r_r + \alpha(r_r - D)^2 & \text{otherwise} \end{cases},$$

where D and α are constants. Hence, while the user's real hand is close to the user (the distance to the hand is smaller than threshold D), the mapping is one to one, and the movements of the virtual hand correspond to the real hand movements. As the user extends her hand beyond D, the

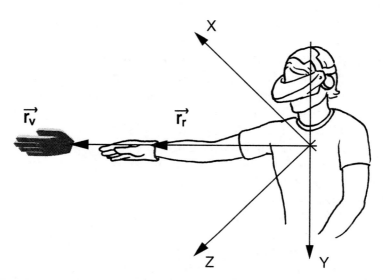

Figure 5.10 *Go-Go interaction technique: egocentric coordinate system. (Poupyrev et al. 1996, © 1996 ACM; reprinted by permission)*

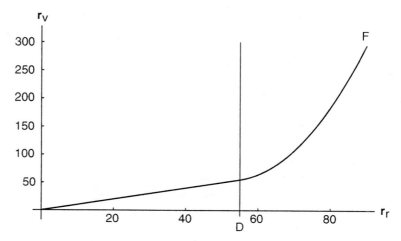

Figure 5.11 *Go-Go interaction technique: mapping function **F**. (Poupyrev et al. 1996, © 1996 ACM; reprinted by permission)*

mapping becomes nonlinear and the virtual arm "grows," thus permitting the user to access and manipulate remote objects. The C^1 continuity of the function F at point D ensures a smooth transition between the linear and nonlinear parts.

The Go-Go technique therefore provides a simple way to interactively control the length of the virtual arm—simply by stretching the real hand out or bringing it closer. A small cube is also rendered in the position of the real hand to provide a visual reference for the user's hand position. Different mapping functions can be used to achieve a different control-display gain between the real and virtual hands (Bowman and Hodges 1997), which allows designers to adjust the mapping for the needs of a particular application.

The Go-Go technique provides direct, *seamless,* 6-DOF object manipulation both close to the user and at a distance. It allows users to both bring faraway objects near and move near objects farther away. The maximum afforded reaching distance, however, is still finite. Furthermore, as the distance increases, the technique maps small movements of the user's hand into large movements of the virtual hand, which complicates precise positioning at a distance. A number of experimental studies (Bowman and Hodges 1997; Poupyrev, Weghorst et al. 1998) have evaluated the Go-Go technique in a subset of manipulation tasks, and all found that users did not have any difficulties understanding it. Although in selection tasks Go-Go is usually less effective than ray-casting (Go-Go requires 3-DOF control as opposed to 2-DOF control), the unique quality of Go-Go is that it allows a uniform interaction within the entire manipulation area.

5.4.4. World-in-Miniature

An alternative to extending the length of the user's arm is to scale the entire world and bring it within the user's reach. The WIM technique (Stoakley et al. 1995) provides the user with a miniature handheld model of the VE, which is an exact copy of the VE at a smaller scale (Figure 5.12). The user can indirectly manipulate virtual objects by interacting with their representations in the WIM.

When implementing the WIM technique, it is important to perform the proper transformations between the WIM coordinate system and the global coordinate system of the full-scale VE. WIM also requires the careful use of backface culling techniques. For example, only the "inside" of the walls of the room model in Figure 5.12 should be rendered, which allows the user to easily see the interior of the WIM from any angle or position.

The WIM is a powerful technique that allows easy object manipulation both within and outside of the area of user reach. It can also combine navigation with manipulation, because the user can also move his or her virtual representation in the WIM (see Chapter 6). There is, however, a downside

Figure 5.12   *WIM technique. (Stoakley et al. 1995, © 1995 ACM; reprinted by permission)*

to this technique: it does not scale well. Although WIM works relatively well for small and medium-sized environments, such as the interior of a virtual building or rooms, using WIM in a very large environment would require an extreme scale factor, resulting in very small object copies in the WIM. This would make accurate selection and manipulation extremely difficult. A technique allowing the user to choose the parts of the environment to be represented within the WIM may overcome this problem.

In spite of this shortcoming, WIM can be effectively used in many different classes of 3D UIs. In particular, it has been successfully used in 3D interfaces for augmented reality (see Chapter 12). WIM can also be used in desktop 3D UIs; in fact, WIM can be considered a 3D generalization of the traditional overview maps that are often used in 3D games.

5.4.5. Combining Techniques

It is difficult, perhaps impossible, to design a single best 3D manipulation technique that fits all possible interaction scenarios. Indeed, just as in the real world there is no tool that can do every possible task, in 3D UIs, no interaction technique can be effective in every manipulation situation. Therefore, combining manipulation techniques has been an active research direction that attempts to bring together the best properties of different interaction techniques. Two basic approaches have emerged: technique aggregation and technique integration.

Aggregation of techniques is the simplest method to combine several techniques together: the user is provided with an explicit mechanism for choosing the desired manipulation technique from a limited set of possible options. This mechanism can be, for example, a 3D menu system that can be displayed on command—a sort of virtual toolbox from which the user can choose manipulation techniques (Mine et al. 1997). Various system control techniques that can be used for this purpose are discussed in Chapter 8.

Technique integration is another approach to combining techniques in which the interface switches transparently between interaction techniques depending on the current *task context*. This approach is based on the simple observation that all manipulations are based on a repeating task sequence: an object must be selected before it can be manipulated (section 5.4.1). Hence, different stages of the manipulation sequence can be completed using different techniques. In the simplest case, the interface can simply switch from the selection technique to the manipulation technique after the user selects an object, and switch back to the selection mode after the user releases the manipulated object. Theoretically, these techniques can be optimized to achieve the best performance in each mode. The techniques discussed in this section implement various versions of this idea.

HOMER

HOMER (Bowman and Hodges 1997) stands for hand-centered object manipulation extending ray-casting. The user selects an object using a ray-casting technique, and instead of the object being attached to the ray, the user's virtual hand instantly moves to the object and attaches to it. The technique then switches to the manipulation mode, allowing the user to position and rotate the virtual object.

To allow the user to position virtual objects within a large manipulation range, the technique linearly scales the user-reaching distance within the user-centered coordinate system introduced in section 5.4.3. The tracked distance between the user and real hand r_r is linearly scaled using constant α_h and then applied to the distance between the user and virtual hand r_v:

Eq. 5.6
$$r_v = \alpha_h r_r$$

The value of scaling constant α_h is defined at the moment of selection. It depends on the distance D_o from the user to the object at the moment of its selection and the distance D_h between the user and real hand at the moment of selection. The value of scaling is defined by Equation 5.7.

Eq. 5.7
$$\alpha_h = \frac{D_o}{D_h}$$

As in the Go-Go technique, the virtual hand (and thus the object) is placed along a line defined by the user's body and the user's real hand, at distance r_v. The rotations of the object are controlled independently using an isomorphic mapping between the real and virtual hands.

As we can see from Equations 5.6 and 5.7, HOMER allows a user to easily reposition an object within the area between the virtual object and himself, no matter how far away the object is at the moment of selection. However, the maximum distance at which the user can reposition an object is limited—it depends on the relation in Equation 5.7 at the moment of selection. For example, if the user picks a virtual object that is located far away, brings it close, and releases it, then returning the object to its original position would be difficult. Indeed, in this case, according to Equation 5.7, the scaling coefficient will be very small ($\alpha_h \approx 1$) because the object is located within the user's reach. Hence, the user would have to move away from the object, use another interaction technique, or perform many consecutive manipulations of the object (clutching) to move it back to its original position.

Scaled-World Grab

The *scaled-world grab* (Mine et al. 1997) technique is based on principles similar to HOMER. The user starts by selecting an object using some selection technique. In scaled-world grab, an image-plane selection technique is used (see section 5.4.2). After successful selection, the interface switches into manipulation mode, and the user can position and rotate the virtual object in space. However, instead of scaling the user's hand motion, as in HOMER, the scaled-world grab technique scales down the *entire VE* around the user's virtual viewpoint. The scaling coefficient α_s is calculated so that that manipulated object is brought within the user's area of reach and, therefore, can be manipulated using the simple virtual hand technique

Eq. 5.8
$$\alpha_s = \frac{D_v}{D_o},$$

where D_v is the distance from the virtual viewpoint to the virtual hand, and D_o is the distance from the virtual viewpoint to the selected object at the moment of selection. An interesting property of this technique is that as long as the center of the scaling operation is the point midway between the user's eyes, the user will often not even notice that scaling actually took place, because the world does not change visually.

Similar to the HOMER technique, the scaled-world grab technique performs well for operations at a distance, but it may not be effective when the user wants to pick up an object located within arm's reach and move it farther away.

Voodoo Dolls

Both HOMER and scaled-world grab are based on the idea of scaling to allow the user to manipulate selected objects at a wide range of distances. The scaling approach, while useful, has one important shortcoming: it works in only one direction. Although it can be effective for manipulation at a distance and for bringing remote objects closer, this approach is less useful when the user needs to move local objects farther away. The Voodoo Dolls technique provides one possible solution to overcome this problem at the expense of adding additional input devices.

Voodoo Dolls (Pierce et al. 1999) is a two-handed interaction technique that combines and builds upon the image-plane and WIM techniques discussed earlier in this chapter. Voodoo Dolls uses a pair of pinch gloves to allow the user to seamlessly switch between different frames of references for a manipulation task, allowing object manipulation of widely varying sizes and at different distances.

The technique is based on several key ideas. First, it proposes to manipulate virtual objects *indirectly*, using temporary, miniature, handheld copies of objects called *dolls* (Figure 5.13). Similar to the WIM, the user manipulates these dolls instead of the virtual objects, which therefore can be at any distance, any size, and any state of occlusion and can still be manipulated.

Unlike the WIM technique, however, the Voodoo Dolls technique allows the user to decide which objects in the VE will be used in interaction. The user starts the manipulation sequence by selecting the target object (or group of objects) with an image-plane technique, which creates the dolls representing the target objects and places them in the user's hand, as shown in Figure 5.14. Because only a subset of the virtual objects is used in manipulation, Voodoo Dolls can scale their copies to a convenient size to interact with, overcoming one of the limitations of the WIM technique, which lacks a mechanism for setting the scale of the world-in-miniature.

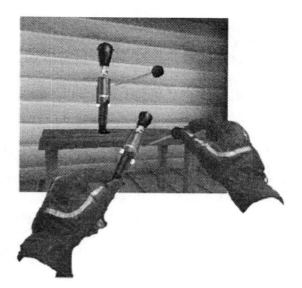

Figure 5.13 *Voodoo Dolls interaction technique. (Pierce et al. 1999, © 1999 ACM; reprinted by permission)*

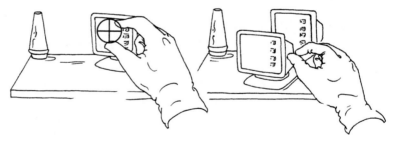

Figure 5.14 *Creating a doll in the Voodoo Dolls technique.*

Second, the technique allows the user to explicitly and interactively specify a frame of reference for manipulation. The doll that the user holds in her nondominant hand represents a *stationary frame* of reference, and the corresponding virtual object does not move when the user moves this doll. The doll that the user holds in her dominant hand *defines the position and orientation* of the corresponding object relative to the stationary frame of reference (Figure 5.13). Because the user can explicitly define the manipulation frame of reference, manipulation can be more convenient. While the user is holding a doll in the nondominant hand, she can easily shift her hands into a more convenient position without affecting the "real" objects. To start manipulation, the user simply passes the doll into the dominant hand.

Voodoo Dolls is an interesting and powerful interaction technique that allows users to perform some sophisticated tasks, such as the manipulation of moving, animated objects—which is difficult to accomplish with other interaction techniques. The technique, however, requires the use of two 6-DOF devices, which increases the hardware demands on the application. Therefore, direct application of this technique to a desktop 3D environment might be difficult. Nevertheless, the key design ideas behind Voodoo Dolls, such as separating functionality depending on the dominant and nondominant hands and defining an explicit interaction frame of reference, are quite universal and can provide an interesting starting point and important insight for developing new interaction techniques for a variety of platforms.

5.4.6. Nonisomorphic 3D Rotation

The 3D interaction techniques discussed above deal only with object selection and translation—rotations are mapped directly from the input device to the virtual object. In some applications, it might be also useful to design and implement other mappings between the rotations of the device and the object—*nonisomorphic 3D rotation techniques.*

For example, by amplifying rotations of the 6-DOF device, we can allow the user to control large ranges of 3D rotations with small rotations of the 3D device. This allows for more effective use of 3D input devices that have an inherently limited rotation range, such as camera-tracked devices (Poupyrev et al. 1999), and can also be used to develop interfaces for users with disabilities. Amplifying virtual rotations also minimizes the need for clutching (see section 5.3.3). It has been demonstrated that clutching significantly hinders user performance in rotation tasks (Zhai et al. 1996).

Alternatively, rotation techniques can also be used to slow down rotation of the device. Such techniques would map large device rotations to smaller rotations of the manipulated object. This allows for very precise 3D rotation control, which can be useful, for example, in teleoperation applications, such as robotic surgery.

The challenge of designing 3D rotation techniques is the nonintuitive mathematics behind 3D rotations—they do not follow the familiar laws of Euclidean geometry, and they often use quaternions, an alternative to matrices as a representation of 3D rotations (Shoemake 1985). In this section, we discuss how 3D rotation techniques can be designed and implemented; for the basic properties of quaternions and how they are related to 3D rotations, please refer to Appendix A and to the recommended readings listed at the end of the chapter.

Designing 3D Rotation Mappings

Given an orientation of the 6-DOF input device, we can linearly amplify or scale its orientation as follows:

Eq. 5.9
$$q_d = q_c^k,$$

where q_c is the quaternion representing the device orientation, q_d is the controlled orientation of the virtual object, and k is the amplification coefficient: when $k > 1$, rotations are scaled up, and when $0 < k < 1$, rotations are scaled down. This equation can be intuitively understood by observing that rotations are combined by multiplying their corresponding quaternions. Therefore, to double a rotation, we simply multiply a quaternion by itself (i.e., raise it to the power of 2, or square it). Equation 5.9 is a generalization of this intuitive observation; for a more formal derivation, please refer to Poupyrev, Weghorst et al. (2000).

Quaternion q_c represents the device orientation as a single rotation from some *initial* or *zero* orientation. Equation 5.10 allows us to amplify device rotations relative to *any* explicit reference orientation q_0:

Eq. 5.10
$$q_d = \left(q_c q_0^{-1}\right)^k q_0$$

This can be interpreted as calculating the rotation that connects q_0 and q_c, amplifying it, and then combining it with initial reference orientation q_0.

These two equations are the most basic zero-order control-display gain functions for 3D rotations, equivalent to the control-display gain equation (Equation 5.4) for translations. They represent the basic form of any linear mapping between rotations of a device and rotations in a 3D space. Therefore, their use is not limited to VEs or 6-DOF input devices; rather, they can be used wherever careful design of 3D rotation mappings is required. For example, they can easily be applied to design mappings for joysticks. They can also be used to design nonlinear rotational mappings; see Poupyrev, Weghorst et al. (1999) for information on how this can be accomplished.

Absolute and Relative 3D Rotation Mappings

Some interesting and nontrivial properties of 3D rotation mappings must be taken into account when designing 3D rotation techniques. These properties follow from the fundamental difference between the absolute and relative amplifications of 3D device rotations.

Absolute amplification simply means that on each cycle of the simulation loop, we scale the absolute orientation of the 3D device (i.e., its rotation relative to the initial zero orientation). This is simply a version of Equation 5.9:

Eq. 5.11
$$q_{d_i} = q_{c_i}^k ,$$

where q_{c_i} is the absolute orientation of the input device measured in the ith cycle of the simulation loop, and q_{d_i} is the orientation that we apply to the virtual object in that cycle of the simulation loop.

Alternatively, we can amplify only *relative* changes in the device orientation. This means that we calculate how much the device orientation has changed from the orientation that we measured in the previous cycle of the simulation loop. We amplify this difference between the current and previous orientation. The virtual object is then rotated from its current orientation by the amplified difference (a specific version of Equation 5.10):

Eq. 5.12
$$q_{d_i} = \left(q_{c_i} q_{c_{i-1}}^{-1} \right)^k q_{d_{i-1}} ,$$

where q_{c_i} and $q_{c_{i-1}}$ are the orientations of the device measured in the current (i^{th}) and previous ($i - 1^{th}$) cycles of the simulation loop respectively; $q_{d_{i-1}}$ is the orientation of the virtual object from the previous cycle of the simulation loop ($i - 1^{th}$ cycle).

Usability Properties of 3D Rotation Mappings

Unlike translations, relative and absolute mappings of 3D rotations produce completely different rotation paths from the *same* 6-DOF device rotation. More importantly, they also produce an entirely different *feel* of the 3D interface (Poupyrev, Weghorst et al. 2000). First, absolute mappings do not always *preserve the direction of 3D rotations*. In some cases, the device and virtual object would rotate in different directions, which violates the principle of *directional compliance* (for more information on feedback compliances, see Chapter 10). Relative mappings, on the other hand, *always* preserve the directional correspondence between rotations of the device and virtual object. Directional compliance in 3D rotations is important, as it allows the user to predict and plan the manipulation sequence to bring a virtual object into the desired orientation. Therefore, absolute mappings have only limited applications in 3D interaction.

Although absolute rotations do not provide directional correspondence, they do preserve *nulling correspondence.* In other words, rotating the device into an initial zero orientation will also bring the virtual object into its initial zero orientation. Relative mappings, however, do not preserve nulling correspondence: nulling the device brings a virtual object into some unpredictable orientation.

Nulling preserves a consistent correspondence between the origins of the coordinate systems in both the physical and virtual spaces. Whether or not it is important for *usability,* however, depends on the input device shape and the tactile cues that the device provides. For devices that provide strong kinesthetic cues so that the user can *feel* the device's orientation, any inconsistency between the zero orientations of the device and virtual object will be easily noticed and may pose a problem. Examples include devices that mount a tracker on a hand, such as a data glove, and other devices that have an easily recognizable shape. If the device does not provide strong kinesthetic cues, such as a ball-shaped device that can be freely rotated in the user's fingers, it is impossible for the user to feel the zero device orientation—in a sense, zero orientation would not exist for such devices. Therefore, the nulling correspondence is not essential, and relative 3D rotation techniques would be effective and usable.

Empirical evaluations (Poupyrev, Weghorst et al. 2000) showed that a relative rotation technique that amplified 6-DOF device rotation was 13% faster than a conventional one-to-one mapping in a 3D orientation matching task, while no effect on accuracy was found. These results demonstrate that linear relative amplification can be an effective tool in designing 3D rotation interfaces.

5.4.7. Desktop 3D Manipulation

The 3D manipulation techniques discussed above share a common assumption that the user is provided with 6-DOF input devices. However, in many real-world applications of interactive 3D computer graphics, this requirement cannot be met. Six-DOF devices are still very expensive, and their operation often requires a highly controlled working environment. Furthermore, the majority of interactive computer graphics systems and applications still exist on conventional desktop computers and are used in office and home environments (e.g., commercial 3D modeling and animation packages, CAD systems, 3D information visualization software, computer games, and many others). Therefore, designing interaction techniques that allow the user to control the 3D position and orientation of virtual objects using conventional desktop input devices, such as a mouse and keyboard, is an important consideration when designing 3D UIs.

The difficulty in designing efficient 3D manipulation techniques for desktop devices is obvious: with a mouse we can capture only 2 DOF simultaneously. Obviously, direct mappings that were possible with 6-DOF input devices cannot be used with 2D devices. Therefore, the most basic approach to designing 3D interaction techniques for the desktop is *separating degrees of control*: the user switches between controlling different degrees of freedom (e.g., switching between rotating and positioning 3D objects).

This section discusses some of the most common 3D manipulation techniques that can be used with 2D input devices. Many of them might be familiar, as they have been implemented and used in 3D UIs in popular 3D applications. Here we discuss

- 2D interface controls for 3D manipulation
- 3D widgets in desktop interaction
- Virtual sphere and ARCBALL techniques for 3D rotation

2D Interface Controls for 3D Manipulation

The simplest method to specify the 3D position or orientation of virtual objects in desktop environments is simply to ask the user to *directly type* the values of coordinates and angles for the desired position and orientation of 3D objects using a keyboard. This method is provided in most 3D modeling and CAD packages when precise and unambiguous specification of 3D position and orientation is essential. This technique is particularly useful because it allows precise incremental adjustment of object position and orientation. In many other interactive scenarios, however, this technique may not be effective, because people have difficulty performing the required mental calculations. In particular, specifying 3D orientation has been proven to be a difficult task (Shepard and Metzler 1971). Usually, it is much easier for users to specify object position and orientation as part of an iterative process: the user repeatedly changes the position of an object, visually evaluates it, readjusts it, and repeats this process until the desired position is achieved. Such a process, although less precise, creates a tight feedback loop between the user input and the result and can significantly speed up the "finding" of the desired position and orientation of an object.

One of the most commonly used methods to separate degrees of control in desktop 3D interfaces is to use separate orthographic views such as a plan or elevation (Figure 5.15). Within each view, the user can manipulate 2 DOF simultaneously, either by direct interaction with the mouse or by using 2D widgets for specific operations such as zooming in, zooming out, rotation, and so on. Conventional GUI sliders can also be used to specify position or orientation: each slider can control one degree of freedom (Chen et al. 1988). Additional tools can be added to perform application-specific tasks such as editing the 3D model and object creation. This approach to 3D interaction has become fundamental in 3D modeling and CAD applications.

Separating DOF and using separate GUI widgets for each DOF may not be effective in all interaction scenarios. Chen and colleagues (1988), for example, studied sliders for a 3D rotation task. Three sliders were

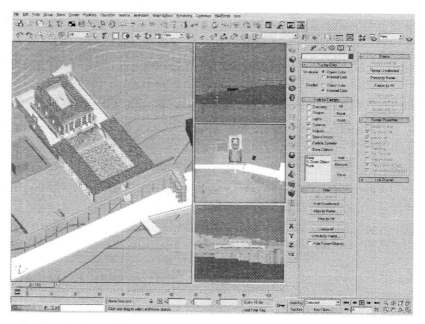

Figure 5.15 *Orthographic view manipulation and 2D interface tools in desktop 3D interaction.*

used to separately control each of the three angles representing object orientation. They found that using sliders allowed easy control of rotations only when single-axis rotations were required. For complex 3D rotations, sliders were significantly less effective, because the user had to decompose a 3D orientation into a sequence of single rotations around each of the principal axes, which is not a trivial task. A number of interaction techniques have been proposed to overcome this difficulty, such as widgets or integrated rotation techniques. These techniques, discussed next, have become standard features of today's desktop 3D UIs.

3D Widgets

Widgets have been used extensively for desktop 3D manipulation. One of the first examples of using widgets to provide a simple way to rotate and position objects in desktop 3D UIs was reported by Houde (1992), and although there have been further developments and expansions (e.g., Conner et al. 1992), the key ideas behind these techniques have not changed significantly.

The basic approach of using widgets and handles is to put controls directly in the 3D scene with the objects that are being manipulated. When an object is selected, a number of 3D graphical objects (widgets) become visible, and they can be clicked and dragged around (Figure 5.16). Each widget is responsible for only a small set of manipulation DOF. For example, some widgets allow users to translate objects only in a horizontal

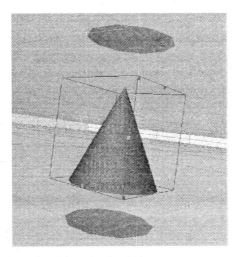

Figure 5.16   *3D widgets for object manipulation.*

plane, others allow translations in the vertical direction, and others enable rotation around a central axis. As the user interacts with a widget, the motion of the mouse is "captured" by the widget, and only a subset of the object's total DOF is affected by the mouse. Hence, widgets work as visual *manipulation constraints.*

The main advantage of widgets is an easy and seamless transition between different manipulation sequences—the user simply selects another widget to perform another manipulation. The disadvantage of widgets is visual clutter: adding manipulation controls increases the number of graphical interface elements in the 3D scene. In addition, the user needs to learn how each of the widgets responds to mouse input, though through intelligent placement of widgets and careful design of affordances, their functionality can become self-explanatory.

3D widgets have become a standard technique to interact with virtual objects, for both desktop and immersive 3D environments, and they have become a standard part of many 3D computer graphics toolkits and applications as well. See Chapter 8 for more detail on 3D widgets.

Virtual Sphere: Integrated Control of 3D Rotations

A number of interaction techniques have proposed *integrated* methods of using 2-DOF mouse movement to control three-axis rotation of 3D objects. Several variations have been reported, such as the Virtual Sphere (Chen et al. 1988), Rolling Ball (Hanson 1992), and Virtual Trackball (Hultquits 1990) techniques. The fundamental approach behind these techniques is similar, and we refer to all of them as Virtual Sphere techniques.

The basic idea for these techniques is simple: Imagine that the 3D object that we wish to rotate is enclosed inside of a glass ball that can be freely rotated around its center point. Then, instead of rotating the object directly, we rotate this glass sphere by nudging it with the mouse cursor as if the cursor were the user's finger, stuck to a location on the surface of the sphere. The sphere rotates in the direction that the user "pushes" it about the axis perpendicular to the direction of cursor movement. To visualize this virtual sphere metaphor, a circle or sphere is often drawn around the virtual object. Because this technique does not allow rotating the object around the axis pointing out of the screen (depth or z-axis), usually mouse movements along the edge of the circle or outside of it produce rotations around this axis.

There are several slightly different implementations of this technique; however, all of them are based on three main steps. First, we determine

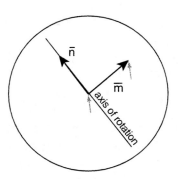

Figure 5.17   *Virtual Sphere technique.*

the rotation axis $\bar{\mathbf{n}}$. When the user moves the mouse outside of the virtual sphere, the axis of rotation is a unit vector pointing out of the screen—that is, $\bar{\mathbf{n}} = (0,0,1)$. If the user clicks inside of the virtual sphere, then the axis of rotation is a 2D vector that lies in the plane of the screen and is perpendicular to the incremental mouse motion vector $\bar{\mathbf{m}} = (m_x, m_y)$. In this case, the axis of rotation can be calculated by rotating the mouse vector by 90 degrees and normalizing it (Figure 5.17):

Eq. 5.13
$$\vec{\mathbf{n}} = \left(\frac{-m_x}{d}, \frac{+m_y}{d}, 0 \right), \text{ where } d = \sqrt{m_x^2 + m_y^2}$$

Second, we have to calculate an angle of rotation. This depends on the rotational sensitivity that we desire from the movement of the mouse; one simple technique is to introduce an effective rolling ball radius R that defines the sensitivity of rotations. Then the rotation angle θ can be defined, for example, as follows (Hanson 1992):

Eq. 5.14
$$\theta = \arctan\left(\frac{d}{R}\right)$$

We can see from Equation 5.14 that small movements of the mouse will result in small angles of rotation, and increasing the mouse motion increases the rotation angle.

Finally, using the calculated axis of rotation $\bar{\mathbf{n}}$ and rotation angle θ, we can easily calculate the resulting rotation of the 3D object.

Note that Equation 5.14 provides only one of many methods to specify rotation angle; other techniques can be used as well. For example, linking the object's size with the effective radius of rotation R would allow for adjusting the sensitivity of rotations depending on the size of the 3D object.

ARCBALL Technique

ARCBALL (Shoemake 1992) is a "mathematically correct" 3D rotation technique designed for the mouse. It is based on the observation that there is a close connection between 3D rotations and spherical geometry. This can be illustrated using a simple physical example. Imagine rotating a pencil fixed at one end. Obviously, the other end would travel on the surface of a sphere, and each orientation of the pencil could be then identified as a *point* on this sphere. *Rotation* of the pencil would draw an *arc* on the sphere. If the pencil has unit length, then the length of the arc is equal to the rotation angle. Thus, in general, the orientation of a body can be represented as a point on a unit sphere, while rotation can be represented as an arc connecting the starting and final body orientations. This example is illustrative, albeit not quite correct: each point on a 3D sphere actually specifies a *family of rotations,* because twisting the pencil would not draw an arc. Therefore, the correct geometric representation of 3D rotations involves using a 4D unit quaternion sphere. Appendix A presents the details of the quaternion representation of rotations.

The implementation of ARCBALL follows from this spherical representation of 3D rotations. Similar to the Virtual Sphere technique, a 3D object is enclosed within a virtual sphere of radius R. The user rotates the object by clicking and dragging the mouse on the circle that represents the projection of the sphere on the screen surface (Figure 5.18). The ARCBALL uses a circle of radius R only to provide a visual reference for the user; all computations are made using a normalized unit sphere.

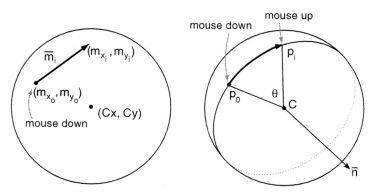

Figure 5.18   *ARCBALL technique. (Shoemake 1992)*

As the user drags the mouse, the ARCBALL technique computes an arc on a *unit* sphere with starting point p_0, corresponding to the 2D mouse position when the user starts rotating (m_{x_0}, m_{y_0}); and current point p_i corresponding to the current mouse position (m_{x_1}, m_{y_1}); see Figure 5.18. The following equations compute the coordinates of point p_i on the unit sphere from the given 2D mouse coordinates; p_0 is calculated in the same way:

Eq. 5.15
$$p_{x_i} = \left(m_{x_i} - C_x\right)/R;$$

Eq. 5.16
$$p_{y_i} = \left(m_{y_i} - C_y\right)/R;$$

Eq. 5.17
$$p_i = \left\{p_{x_i}, p_{y_i}, \sqrt{1 - p_{x_i}^2 - p_{y_i}^2}\right\}$$

C_x and C_y are the 2D coordinates of the center point of the circle. The third (z) component is calculated from the equation of the unit 3D sphere: $x^2 + y^2 + z^2 = 1$. Note that points p_i and p_0 are not quaternions but points on a sphere in 3D space.

Having obtained the initial and final points of the arc on the sphere, we can now calculate the rotation corresponding to this arc. There are several techniques to do this; here we present the one provided by Shoemake (1992), which uses quaternion notation. In the unit quaternion form, the rotation from p_0 to p_i can be calculated as a quaternion product of the final point times the conjugate of the initial point:

Eq. 5.18
$$q(\vec{\mathbf{v}}, w) = p_i p_0^* = p_0 \times p_i, p_0 \cdot p_i$$

Equation 5.18 follows from the quaternion product formula that can be found in the appendix; here, $p_0 \cdot p_i$ denotes the dot product, and $p_0 \times p_i$ is a vector cross product. Note that every unit vector can be represented as a quaternion with a zero scalar part, so it is valid to use points p_0 and p_i in Equation 5.18.

The resulting quaternion q denotes the rotation of the virtual object relative to orientation q_0 (the object orientation when the mouse button was pressed). The actual orientation of the object at the ith cycle of the simulation loop can be calculated as a product qq_0, which can be then applied to the 3D object. Given the quaternion that defines the absolute orientation of the virtual object, it is easy to either build a rotation matrix or extract the angle and axis of rotation from the quaternion. Please refer to Appendix A for details.

5.5. Design Guidelines

The interaction techniques presented in this chapter can form the basis for a wide variety of 3D UIs for manipulation. Many of these techniques can be used in combination with interaction techniques for other tasks not directly related to manipulation, such as travel (Chapter 6) and system control (Chapter 8).

We wrap up this chapter with a set of general design guidelines, highlighting some of the important points discussed earlier in the chapter.

> **Use existing manipulation techniques unless a large amount of benefit might be derived from designing a new, application-specific technique.**

Although designing new interaction techniques is important, there is no need to reinvent the wheel. The requirements of many 3D applications can be met by applying and creatively modifying the interaction techniques presented in this chapter.

> **Use task analysis when choosing a 3D manipulation technique.**

Manipulation is a rich user activity, and some interaction techniques are better for certain conditions of manipulation than for others. The choice and design of manipulation techniques should provide high levels of usability and performance for the most common manipulation tasks in an application. Ask yourself, How precise is the manipulation required to be? Do I need positioning, or is selection sufficient? How far away do users need to manipulate virtual objects? How large are the objects to be manipulated?

> **Match the interaction technique to the device.**

It is important to consider device properties when choosing manipulation techniques. When 6-DOF devices are used, interaction techniques that allow for integrated manipulation control will perhaps be more intuitive and effective than those that separate control dimensions. Carefully consider the shape of the device. When a high level of manipulation precision is required, it might be preferable to use devices that permit a precision grasp and can be manipulated by the fingers.

Use techniques that can help to reduce clutching.

Clutching is wasted motion: by using techniques that amplify the user hand motion in rotation and positioning tasks, we can decrease the need for clutching and therefore can increase comfort and user performance.

Nonisomorphic techniques are useful and intuitive.

The early notion that interaction in VEs should be an exact imitation of our interaction in the real world does not hold—nonisomorphic techniques are useful and intuitive. In fact, most manipulation techniques depart from real-world interaction to a greater or lesser degree by allowing "magic" interactions with virtual objects.

Use pointing techniques for selection and virtual hand techniques for manipulation.

Ray-casting and other pointing techniques provide notably better performance in selection tasks, but they are not as useful in manipulation. Use virtual hand–based techniques for manipulation tasks.

Use grasp-sensitive object selection.

Grasp-sensitive object selection, where the user matches the orientation of the device to the orientation of the desired object, is a powerful technique to simplify and improve user selection.

Reduce degrees of freedom when possible.

Manipulation techniques do not necessarily have to manipulate all 6 DOF. In fact, some very effective selection techniques, such as the image-plane techniques, provide very effective interaction by restricting DOF—making 3D selection an essentially 2D task. In addition, many applications do not require 6-DOF manipulation. Adding constraints (see Chapter 10) to generic 3D manipulation techniques can help the user be more efficient and precise.

> Consider the tradeoff between technique design and environment design.

Two strategies can be used in designing manipulation interfaces. First, you can tune interaction techniques so that they maximize user performance in the target task conditions. Second, you can design your environment so that existing techniques can be used effectively. If the application does not require an environment that matches a real-world environment exactly, this second approach might be extremely useful.

> There is no single best manipulation technique.

The ideal 3D manipulation technique has not yet been designed. Each technique has its strengths and weaknesses. The best technique for one application is not necessarily the best for another. In almost all cases, any choice of technique will result in tradeoffs. Managing these tradeoffs is one of the keys to good 3D UI design.

Recommended Reading

For an excellent overview of the basic human factors principles behind manual control, we recommend the following:

Knight, J. (1987). Manual Control and Tracking. *Handbook of Human Factors.* G. Salvendy (Ed.), John Wiley and Sons, 182–218.

One of the most comprehensive reviews of the physiology and psychology of human grasp and manipulation can be found in this text:

MacKenzie, C., and T. Iberall (1994). *The Grasping Hand.* North-Holland.

An interesting study that discusses the effect of muscle groups and device shapes on manipulation performance can be found in the following:

Zhai, S., and P. Milgram (1993). Human Performance Evaluation of Manipulation Schemes in Virtual Environments. *Proceedings of the 1993 IEEE Virtual Reality Annual International Symposium (VRAIS '93),* IEEE Press, 155–161.

Readers interested in more details on the usability properties of rotation mapping might wish to take a look at this text:

Poupyrev, I., S. Weghorst, and S. Fels (2000). Non-isomorphic 3D Rotational Interaction Techniques. *Proceedings of the 2000 ACM Conference on Human Factors in Computing Systems (CHI 2000),* ACM Press, 540–547.

Finally, classifications, overviews, and empirical evaluations of interaction techniques for 3D manipulation can be found in the following two papers:

Poupyrev, I., and T. Ichikawa (1999). Manipulating Objects in Virtual Worlds: Categorization and Empirical Evaluation of Interaction Techniques. *Journal of Visual Languages and Computing* 10(1): 19–35.

Bowman, D., and L. Hodges (1999). Formalizing the Design, Evaluation, and Application of Interaction Techniques for Immersive Virtual Environments. *The Journal of Visual Languages and Computing* 10(1): 37–53.

CHAPTER 6
Travel

As we described in the introduction to Part III, navigation is a fundamental human task in our physical environment. We are also increasingly faced with navigation tasks in synthetic environments: navigating the World Wide Web via a browser, navigating a complex document in a word processor, navigating through many layers of information in a spreadsheet, or navigating the virtual world of a computer game. Navigation in 3D UIs is the subject of Chapters 6 and 7.

6.1. Introduction

Travel is the motor component of navigation—the task of performing the actions that move us from our current location to a new target location or in the desired direction. In the physical environment, travel is often a no-brainer, or to be more precise, it involves unconscious cognition. Once we formulate the goal to walk across the room and through the door, our brain can instruct our muscles to perform the correct movements to achieve that goal. However, when our travel goal cannot be achieved effectively with simple body movements (we want to travel a great distance, or we want to travel very quickly, or we want to fly), then we use vehicles (bicycles, cars, planes, etc.). All vehicles contain some interface that maps various physical movements (turning a wheel, depressing a pedal, flipping a switch) to travel. In VEs, the situation is similar: In some

VEs, simple physical motions can be used for travel (when head and/or body trackers are used), but this is only effective within a very limited space at a very limited speed. For most travel in VEs (and all travel in desktop VEs), our actions must be mapped in some more or less natural way to travel. A major difference between real-world travel in vehicles and virtual travel, however, is that VEs normally provide only visual motion cues, disregarding vestibular cues.

Interaction techniques for the task of travel are especially important for two major reasons. First, travel is easily the most common and universal interaction task in 3D interfaces. Although there are some 3D applications in which the user's viewpoint is always stationary, those are the exception rather than the rule. Second, travel (and navigation in general) often supports another task rather than being an end unto itself. Consider most 3D games: travel is used to reach locations where the user can pick up treasure, fight with enemies, or obtain critical information. Surprisingly, the secondary nature of the travel task in these instances actually increases the need for usability of travel techniques. That is, if the user has to think about how to turn left or move forward, then he has been distracted from his primary task. Therefore, travel techniques must be intuitive—capable of becoming "second nature" to users.

6.1.1. Chapter Roadmap

In this chapter, we discuss the task of travel and interaction techniques for travel tasks. We begin by describing specific types of travel tasks (section 6.2), and then discuss a wide variety of travel techniques (section 6.3), classified by the metaphors they use. The final section presents design guidelines for travel interfaces (section 6.4).

6.2. 3D Travel Tasks

There are many different reasons why a user might need to perform a 3D travel task. Understanding the various types of travel tasks is important because, as noted above, the usability of a particular technique often depends on the task for which it is used. As we describe various techniques in the next section, we provide guidance (as often as possible) on the task types for which a particular technique is appropriate. Currently, only a small number of "testbed" experiments (Bowman, Johnson et al. 1999; Lampton et al. 1994) have attempted to empirically relate task type to technique usability. The tasks we have identified include *exploration, search,* and *maneuvering.*

6.2.1. Exploration

In an exploration task, the user has no explicit goal for her movement. Rather, she is browsing the environment, obtaining information about the objects and locations within the world, and building up knowledge of the space. For example, the client of an architecture firm may explore the latest building design in a 3D environment. Exploration is typically used at the beginning of an interaction with an environment, serving to orient the user to the world and its features, but it may also be important in later stages. Because a user's path during exploration may be based on serendipity (seeing something in the world may cause the user to deviate from the current path), techniques to support exploration should allow continuous and direct control of viewpoint movement or at least the ability to interrupt a movement that has begun. Forcing the user to continue along the chosen path until its completion would detract from the discovery process. Of course, this must be balanced, in some applications, with the need to provide an enjoyable experience in a short amount of time (Pausch et al. 1996). Techniques should also impose little cognitive load on the user so that the user can focus cognitive resources on spatial knowledge acquisition and information gathering (wayfinding, see Chapter 7).

To what extent should 3D interfaces support exploration tasks? The answer depends on the goals of the application. In some cases, exploration is an integral component of the interaction. For example, in a 3D visualization of network traffic data, the structure and content of the environment is unknown in advance, making it difficult to provide detailed wayfinding aids. The benefits of the visualization depend on how well the interface supports exploration of the data. Also, in many 3D gaming environments, exploration of unknown spaces is an important part of the entertainment value of the game. On the other hand, in a 3D interface where the focus is on performing tasks within a well-known 3D environment, the interface designer should provide more support for search tasks via goal-directed travel techniques.

6.2.2. Search

Search tasks involve travel to a specific goal or target location within the environment. In other words, the user in a search task knows the final location to which he wants to navigate. Whether the user has knowledge of where that location is or how to get there from the current location is another matter. This leads to the distinction between a *naïve search* task, where the user does not know the position of the target or a path to it in advance, and a *primed search* task, where the user has visited the target before or has some other knowledge of its position.

In the extreme, naïve search is simply exploration, although it is exploration with a specific goal in mind. A naïve search may start out as simple exploration, but clues or wayfinding aids may direct the search so that it is much more limited and focused than exploration. Primed search tasks also exist on a continuum, depending on the amount of knowledge the user has of the target and the surrounding environment. A user may have visited a location before but may have to explore the environment around his starting location before he understands how to begin traveling toward the goal. On the other hand, a user with complete survey knowledge of the environment can start at any location and immediately begin navigating directly to the target. Thus, the lines between these tasks are often blurry, but it is still useful to make the distinction.

Many 3D interfaces involve search via travel. For example, the user in our architectural walkthrough application may wish to travel to the front door to check sight lines. Techniques for this task may be more goal-oriented than techniques for exploration. For example, the user may specify the final location directly on a map rather than through incremental movements. Such techniques do not apply to all situations, however. Bowman, Johnson, and Hodges (1999) found that a map-based technique was quite inefficient, even for primed search tasks, when the goal locations were not explicitly represented on the map. It may be useful to combine a target-based technique with a more general technique to allow for the continuum of tasks discussed above.

6.2.3. Maneuvering

Maneuvering is an often overlooked subtask of travel. Maneuvering tasks take place in a local area and involve small, precise movements. The most common use of maneuvering is to position the viewpoint more precisely within a limited local area to perform a specific task. For example, the user may need to read some written information in the 3D environment but must position herself directly in front of the information in order to make it legible. In another scenario, the user wishes to check the positioning of an object she has been manipulating in a 3D modeling system and needs to examine it from many different angles. This task may seem trivial compared to large-scale movements through the environment, but it is precisely these small-scale movements that can cost the user precious time and cause frustration if not supported by the interface.

A designer might consider maneuvering tasks to be search tasks, because the destination is known, and therefore use the same type of travel techniques for maneuvering as for search, but this would ignore the unique requirements of maneuvering tasks. In fact, some applications may require special travel techniques solely for maneuvering. In general, travel techniques for this task should allow great precision of motion but not at the expense of speed. The best solution for maneuvering tasks may be physical motion of the user's head and body because this is efficient, precise, and natural, but not all applications include head and body tracking, and even those that do often have limited range and precision. Therefore, if close and precise work is important in an application, other techniques for maneuvering, such as the object-focused travel techniques in section 6.3.6, must be considered.

6.2.4. Additional Travel Task Characteristics

In the classification of tasks above, tasks are distinguished by the user's goal for the travel task. Remember that many other characteristics of the task should be considered when choosing or designing travel techniques:

- *Distance to be traveled:* In a VE using head or body tracking, it may be possible to accomplish very short-range travel tasks using natural physical motion only. Medium-range travel requires a virtual travel technique but may not require velocity control. Long-range travel tasks should use techniques with velocity control or the ability to jump quickly between widely scattered locations.

- *Amount of curvature or number of turns in the path:* Travel techniques should take into account the amount of turning required in the travel task. For example, steering based on torso direction (section 6.3.3) may be appropriate when turning is infrequent, but a less strenuous method such as pointing (section 6.3.3) would be more comfortable when the path involves many turns.

- *Visibility of the target from the starting location:* Many target-based techniques (section 6.3.5) depend on the availability of a target for selection. Gaze-directed steering (section 6.3.3) works well when the target is visible, but not when the user needs to search for the target visually while traveling.

- *Number of DOF required for the movement:* If the travel task requires motion only in a horizontal plane, the travel technique should not force the user to also control vertical motion. In general, terrain-following is a useful constraint in many applications.

- *Required accuracy of the movement:* Some travel tasks require strict adherence to a path or accurate arrival at a target location. In such cases, it's important to choose a travel technique that allows for fine control and adjustment of direction, speed, or target location. For example, map-based target selection (section 6.3.5) is usually inaccurate because of the scale of the map, imprecision of hand tracking, or other factors. Travel techniques should also allow for easy error recovery (e.g., backing up if the target was overshot) if accuracy is important.

- *Other primary tasks that take place during travel:* Often, travel is a secondary task performed during another more important task. For example, a user may be traveling through a building model in order to count the number of windows in each room. It is especially important in such situations that the travel technique be unobtrusive, intuitive, and easily controlled.

6.3. Travel Techniques

With the various types of travel tasks in mind, let us examine interaction techniques for travel. Before discussing the techniques themselves, we present a number of ways to classify travel techniques.

6.3.1. Technique Classifications

A common theme of 3D interaction research has been the attempt to classify and categorize interaction techniques into structures. This is not a pointless academic exercise, but rather an attempt to gain a more complete understanding of the tasks and techniques involved. For the task of travel, at least four different classification schemes have been proposed. None of these should be considered the "correct" taxonomy; they each provide different views of the same space.

Active versus Passive Techniques

One way to classify travel techniques is to distinguish between *active* travel techniques, in which the user directly controls the movement of the viewpoint, and *passive* travel techniques, in which the viewpoint's movement is controlled by the system. Most of the techniques we present in this chapter are active, but in some cases it may be useful to consider a technique that is automated or semiautomated by the system (Galyean 1995; Mackinlay et al. 1990a). This is especially useful if the user has another primary task, such as gathering information about the environment while traveling. Bowman, Davis, and colleagues (1999) studied active and passive techniques and also included a third category called route planning. Route planning is both active *and* passive—users actively plan their path through the environment, then the system executes this path (section 6.3.4).

Physical versus Virtual Techniques

We can also classify travel techniques into those that use *physical* travel, in which the user's body physically translates or rotates in order to translate or rotate the viewpoint, and *virtual* travel, in which the user's body remains stationary even though the virtual viewpoint moves. Many VEs use a combination of physical rotation (via head tracking) and virtual translation. Desktop 3D systems utilize virtual translation and rotation, while some VEs use physical translation and rotation via a locomotion device (section 6.3.2). The active/passive and physical/virtual classifications are orthogonal, so they can be combined to define a 2 × 2 design space.

Classifications Using Task Decomposition

Bowman, Koller, and Hodges (1997) decomposed the task of travel into three subtasks: direction or target selection, velocity/acceleration selection, and conditions of input (Figure 6.1). Each subtask can be performed using a variety of technique components.

- *Direction or target selection* refers to the primary subtask in which the user specifies *how to move* or *where to move*.
- *Velocity/acceleration selection* describes how users control their speed.
- *Conditions of input* refers to how travel is initiated, continued, and terminated.

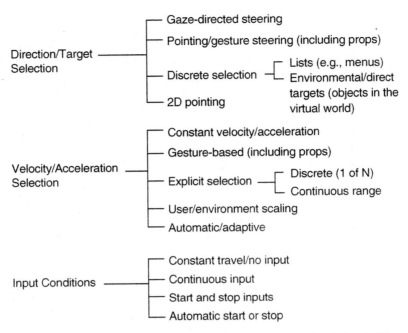

Figure 6.1 *Taxonomy of travel techniques focusing on subtasks of travel. (Bowman et al. 1997, © 1997 IEEE)*

This taxonomy covers a large portion of the design space for travel techniques (only a few representative technique components are shown in the figure), and allows us to view the task of travel in more fine-grained chunks (subtasks) that are separable. By choosing a technique component for each of the three subtasks, we can define a complete travel technique. For example, the most common implementation of the pointing technique (see section 6.3.3) uses pointing steering, constant velocity/acceleration, and continuous input (a button is held down while traveling).

A second task decomposition (Bowman, Davis et al. 1999) subdivides the task of travel in a different, more chronological way (Figure 6.2). In order to complete a travel task, the user first starts to move, then indicates position and orientation, and then stops moving. Of course, this order does not always strictly hold: in some target-based techniques, the user first indicates the target position and then starts to move. One feature of this taxonomy that distinguishes it from the first is the explicit mention of specifying viewpoint orientation, which is an important consideration for desktop 3D environments without head tracking. As shown in the figure, the taxonomy further decomposes the position specification subtask

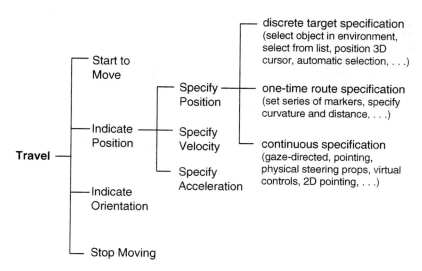

Figure 6.2 *Taxonomy of travel techniques focusing on level of user control. (Bowman, Davis et al. 1999; reprinted by permission of MIT Press and Presence: Teleoperators and Virtual Environments)*

into position (*xyz* coordinates), velocity, and acceleration subtasks. Finally, it lists three possible metaphors for the subtask of specifying position: discrete target specification, one-time route specification, and continuous specification of position. These metaphors differ in the amount of control they give the user over the exact path (the active/passive distinction).

Classification by Metaphor

Finally, we can classify travel techniques by the overall interaction metaphor. In one way, such a classification is not as useful because it does not allow us to look at subtasks of travel separately. However, classification by metaphor is also easier to understand, especially from the user's point of view. If someone tells you that a particular travel technique uses the "flying carpet" metaphor, for example, you can infer that it allows you to move in all three dimensions and to steer using hand motions. In addition, if new metaphors are developed, they can be added to such an informal classification easily. Thus, classification by metaphor is a useful way to think about the design space for interaction techniques. Sections 6.3.2 through 6.3.7 organize travel techniques by six common metaphors: physical locomotion, steering, route-planning, target-based, manual manipulation, and scaling. These sections consider only the task of controlling the position of the viewpoint. In section 6.3.8, we discuss techniques for controlling viewpoint orientation—a crucial issue in desktop 3D applications. Section 6.3.9 introduces techniques for velocity control. Finally, we discuss several systems that tightly integrate position, orientation, and velocity controls in section 6.3.10.

6.3.2. Physical Locomotion Techniques

Physical locomotion techniques use the user's physical exertion to transport her through the virtual world. Thus, most of these techniques are intended for immersive VEs. They mimic, to a greater or lesser degree, a natural method of locomotion in the physical world. Many such techniques have been investigated, and physical locomotion is beginning to be a common technique for travel in high-end video game and location-based entertainment systems. We discuss

- walking
- walking in place
- devices simulating walking
- cycles

Walking

The most direct and obvious technique for traveling in a 3D world is to physically walk through it. This technique is natural, provides vestibular cues (which help the user understand the size of the environment), and promotes spatial understanding. However, because of technological and space limitations, real walking is not always practical or feasible. Real walking can work only when the size of the environment is less than the range of the tracking system (although a scaling technique in which one physical step equals several virtual steps can be used to allow for a slightly larger environment). Even if a large-area tracking system is available, the physical space must also be available and free of obstacles.

Real walking also raises issues with cabling: cables for trackers, input devices, and/or displays may not be long enough to allow complete freedom of movement in the tracked area, and unless carefully handled by another person, walking users can easily become tangled in cables as they move about the space. Wireless devices should alleviate most of these concerns.

Researchers have experimented with ways to overcome these problems in order to use real walking as a travel technique for immersive VEs. The tracker project at the University of North Carolina has a long history of research on various methods for large-area tracking. This research has culminated in the HiBall tracking system (Welch et al. 1999; 2001), an optical tracking system that allows tracking of a wide area by using a scalable tracking grid on the ceiling (also see Chapter 4, section 4.3.1). This allows for an effective physical walking technique with a small 3D environment. In general, two main approaches, shown in Figure 6.3, have been investigated (Meyer and Applewhite 1992). In the *outside-in* approach, optical or ultrasonic sensors are mounted at fixed, well-known locations in the environment and sense locations on the user (Foxlin 2002). These locations can be marked by active beacons (e.g., LEDs) or with passive fiducials (markers that are easy to pick out of an image using image-processing techniques). The *inside-out* approach places the sensors on the user and the emitters/markers in the world (Welch et al. 2001). Both approaches have the potential to be wireless, thus solving the cabling problem. For readers interested in more technical detail, we suggest an older but quite complete survey of tracking technologies (Meyer and Applewhite 1992) and a bibliography for VE tracking from the University of North Carolina (Welch 2004).

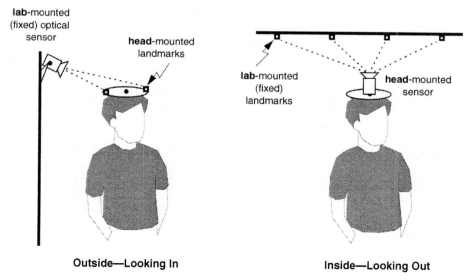

lab-mounted
(fixed) optical
sensor

head-mounted
landmarks

lab-mounted
(fixed)
landmarks

head-mounted
sensor

Outside—Looking In

Inside—Looking Out

Figure 6.3 *Two approaches to wide-area tracking. (Welch et al. 2001; reprinted by permission of MIT Press and Presence: Teleoperators and Virtual Environments)*

Usoh and his colleagues (1999) used the HiBall system to determine the effect of a physical walking technique on the sense of presence. They created a small, compelling environment with a virtual pit whose bottom was far below the floor on which the user stood. They found that users who physically walked through the environment felt more present and exhibited greater fear of the virtual pit than users who walked in place (described on the next page) or used a virtual travel technique. Other researchers have found that real walking leads to a higher level of spatial knowledge in a complex environment (Chance et al. 1998).

Real walking is also becoming more important for other types of 3D applications, especially mobile augmented reality (e.g., Höllerer et al. 1999). In these systems, users are free to walk around in very large-area indoor or outdoor environments and have additional graphical information superimposed on their view of the real world (Figure 6.4). Of course, in very large areas, none of the traditional tracking solutions are feasible. Thus, these applications often use Global Positioning System (GPS) data

Figure 6.4   *Mobile augmented reality: (a) prototype system (© 2002 Computer Graphics and User Interfaces Lab, Columbia University); (b) user's view (© 1999 Tobias Höllerer, Steve Feiner, and John Pavlik, Computer Graphics and User Interfaces Lab, Columbia University)*

for tracking, possibly enhanced with orientation information from self-contained inertial trackers.

Real walking can be an effective and compelling travel technique, but it is not sufficient or appropriate for most applications. In most practical VEs, real walking can be used in a small local area, but other techniques are needed to reach other parts of the environment. However, in our experience, when users are allowed to both walk and use a virtual travel technique, they quickly learn to use only the virtual technique because it requires less effort.

Walking in Place

An alternative to real walking is walking in place: users move their feet to simulate walking without actually translating their bodies. This technique seems a good compromise because users still physically exert themselves, which should increase the sense of presence, and the limitation on the size of the environment is removed.

However, there are several caveats to be considered. First, walking in place does not use the same motion or provide the same vestibular cues as real walking, so the sense of presence or real movement is diminished. Second, the size of the environment, while theoretically unlimited, still has a practical limitation because users cannot walk unlimited distances. In fact, many researchers have reported anecdotally that users have a much lower tolerance for physical motion in a VE than they do in the real world.

Several approaches have been used to implement walking in place. Slater, Usoh, and Steed (1995) placed position trackers on the user's feet and used a neural network to analyze the up/down motion of the feet and distinguish walking in place from other types of foot motion. The GAITER system (Templeman et al. 1999) uses multiple sensors and a more sophisticated algorithm to recognize a natural walking motion. Iwata and Fujii (1996) took a different approach. They used special sandals and a low-friction surface to allow the user to "shuffle" his feet back and forth instead of up and down.

Studies have shown that walking in place does increase the sense of presence relative to completely virtual travel, but that it's not as effective as real walking (Usoh et al. 1999). These techniques also sometimes suffer from the problems of recognition errors and user fatigue. This approach applies to systems where high levels of naturalism/realism are needed and where the environment is not too large. For applications in which the focus is on efficiency and task performance, however, a virtual travel technique is often more appropriate.

Devices Simulating Walking

When realism is desired (e.g., in training applications), walking-in-place techniques can be less than satisfactory because they don't capture the same motion and effort as real walking. Real walking techniques are limited by space and technological constraints. Thus, there is a third approach that uses special locomotion devices to provide a real walking motion and feel while not actually translating the user's body. The simplest form is a common treadmill. Of course, the basic treadmill does not allow the user to turn naturally, so some sort of indirect turning mechanism, such as a joystick, is needed (Brooks 1986). This can be implemented easily but is not appropriate for applications requiring high levels of realism.

Researchers have created many different devices to try to solve this problem. One simple idea is to track the user's head and feet on a standard treadmill in order to detect when the user is trying to make a turn. This detection is based on analysis of the direction the feet are pointing, deviation of a foot's motion from the forward direction, and other factors. When the system detects a turn, it rotates the treadmill, which is mounted on a large motion platform (Noma and Miyasato 1998). The motion platform also allows tilting of the treadmill to simulate slopes. Experience with this setup indicates that it works well for slow, smooth turns but has too much latency for sudden or sharp turns. In addition, it does not allow sidestepping.

Another approach uses a treadmill that is specially constructed to allow belt motion in any direction. This can be achieved by using two sets of rollers that move orthogonally to one another. Because any horizontal direction can be achieved by a combination of motions in these two directions, the treadmill surface has the ability to move in any arbitrary horizontal direction. The omnidirectional treadmill, or ODT (Darken et al. 1997), and the Torus treadmill (Iwata 1999) are examples of this type. The ODT was constructed for the military with the hope that it could be used to train infantry naturally in a VE. The device allowed walking or even running in any direction, but also had some serious usability and safety issues that made it less than effective. The most important issue was that the ODT incorporated an active control that continually moved the surface in order to recenter the user on the treadmill. This was necessary to keep the user from walking off the edge of the device. However, in many cases involving turns or sidestepping, the recentering motion caused the user to lose his balance. The ODT was found to support walking at a

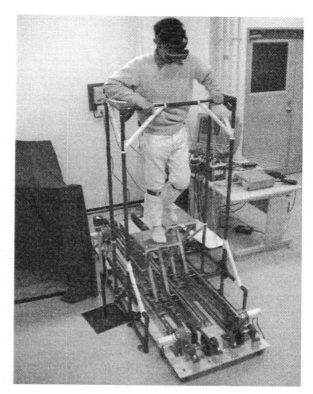

Figure 6.5 *GaitMaster2 locomotion device. (Iwata 2001, © 2003 IEEE; reprinted by permission)*

moderate speed with gradual turns but not many of the other movements that soldiers would need to make. Still, the treadmill approach has shown promise for natural locomotion in large-scale virtual worlds.

The GaitMaster (Iwata 2001) is an approach that does not use a treadmill at all, similar to the earlier Sarcos Biport (Hollerbach 2002). Rather, the user straps her feet onto platforms that rest on top of two small motion bases (Figure 6.5). The system attempts to detect the user's walking motion via force sensors embedded in the platforms and move the platforms appropriately so that a hard "ground" surface is felt at the correct location after each step. This device is technically quite complex and still has serious safety and usability issues because of the powerful hydraulics involved and the latency in detecting foot motion. However, it may be the first of a new generation of locomotion devices.

In general, these specialized walking devices have not been as successful as one might hope. They are still too expensive, too susceptible to mechanical failures, and too slow to respond to the user's movements. Most importantly, the devices do not produce the perception of natural walking for the user. Rather, the user learns to adapt her walking motion to the device's characteristics. Still, such devices may prove useful in certain applications that require physical locomotion via walking. For a more detailed overview of locomotion devices, see Hollerbach (2002).

Cycles

If physical exertion is desired but walking is not necessary, a vehicle-based approach, usually using a bicycle or other pedal-driven device, can be used. A typical exercise bicycle setup (Brogan et al. 1998) is the easiest to implement, because these devices usually already report the speed of pedaling. Some of them also report on handlebar turning or user leaning, allowing natural turning.

Figure 6.6   *Uniport locomotion device. (Photograph courtesy of Sarcos)*

The Uniport is a unicycle-like device that allows travel through virtual worlds seen through an HMD (Figure 6.6); it was designed for infantry training (as one of the precursors to the ODT). It is obviously less effective at producing a believable simulation of walking, and users also have difficulty turning the device. However, it is mechanically much less complex and produces significant exertion in the user.

6.3.3. Steering Techniques

Although a great deal of work has focused on natural locomotion techniques such as those described above, most immersive VE applications and all desktop 3D UIs use some sort of virtual travel technique. Among virtual techniques, by far the most common metaphor is steering. Steering refers to continuous control of the direction of motion by the user. In other words, the user constantly specifies either the absolute ("move along the vector [1,0,0] in world coordinates") or relative ("move to my left") direction of travel. Steering techniques are generally easy to understand and provide the highest level of control to the user. Figure 6.7 shows an abstract representation of a user with several points and vectors defined relative to the user's body. We refer to this figure throughout the section.

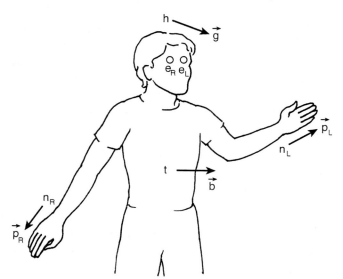

Figure 6.7 *Abstract user with body positions* **h** *(head),* $\mathbf{e}_L$ *(left eye),* $\mathbf{e}_R$ *(right eye),* **t** *(torso),* $\mathbf{n}_L$ *(left hand), and* $\mathbf{n}_R$ *(right hand); and direction vectors* $\vec{\mathbf{g}}$ *(gaze),* $\vec{\mathbf{b}}$ *(body),* $\vec{\mathbf{p}}_L$ *(left-hand pointing), and* $\vec{\mathbf{p}}_R$ *(right-hand pointing).*

The techniques we will describe are

- gaze-directed steering
- pointing
- torso-directed steering
- camera-in-hand technique
- physical steering props
- virtual motion controller
- semiautomated steering

Gaze-Directed Steering

The most common steering technique—and the default travel technique in many 3D toolkits (e.g., Kessler et al. 2000)—is gaze-directed steering (Mine 1995a). Quite simply, this technique allows the user to move in the direction $\bar{g}$ toward which he is looking. In a tracked environment, the gaze direction is obtained from the orientation of a head tracker (although true gaze-directed steering would use an eye tracker); in a desktop environment, the gaze direction is along a ray from the virtual camera position (assumed to be one of the user's eye positions) through the center of the viewing window. Once the gaze direction vector is obtained, it is normalized, and then the user is translated along this vector in the world coordinate system. The vector may also be multiplied by a velocity factor ψ to allow for different rates of travel (see section 6.3.9 for velocity specification techniques). Some discrete event (e.g., button press or initial joystick movement) is needed to start and stop the motion of the user. Thus, between these stop and start events, the user's position s should be modified each frame according to Equation 6.1:

Eq. 6.1
$$s_{new} = s + \psi \frac{\bar{g}}{\|\bar{g}\|}$$

In some graphics systems, a more efficient implementation is to move the user along the viewing vector (often $[0, 0, -1]$) in the camera's coordinate system. The basic concept of gaze-directed steering can be extended by allowing motion along vectors orthogonal to the gaze vector. This gives the user the ability to *strafe*—to move backward, up, down, left, and right. This ability is especially important for desktop systems, where setting the gaze direction may be more cumbersome than in a head-tracked VE.

From the user's point of view, gaze-directed steering is quite easy to understand and control. In a desktop 3D environment, it seems quite natural to move "into" the screen. In an immersive VE with head tracking, this technique also seems intuitive, especially if motion is constrained to the 2D horizontal plane. In addition, the hardware requirements of the technique are quite modest; even in an immersive VE, the user needs only a head tracker and a button. However, if complete 3D motion is needed ("flying"), gaze-directed steering has two problems. First, when users attempt to travel in the horizontal plane, they are likely to travel slightly up or down because it's very difficult to tell whether the head is precisely upright. Second, it's quite awkward to travel vertically up or down by looking straight up or down, especially when wearing an HMD.

But perhaps the most important problem with gaze-directed steering is that it couples gaze direction and travel direction, meaning that users cannot look in one direction while traveling in another. This may seem a small issue, but consider how often you look in a direction other than your travel direction while walking, cycling, or driving in the physical world. In the virtual world, studies have shown that pointing (see below) outperforms gaze-directed steering on tasks requiring motion relative to an object in the environment (Bowman et al. 1997).

Pointing

To avoid the coupling of gaze direction and travel direction, the pointing technique (Mine 1995a) uses a separate vector $\vec{p}$ to specify the direction of travel. The name *pointing* comes from the immersive VE implementation, where $\vec{p}$ is obtained from the orientation of a tracker held in or mounted on the user's hand. The forward vector of the tracker is first transformed into a world coordinate vector (this forward vector depends on the specific tracking system, method of mounting the tracker on the hand, and VE toolkit used). The vector is then normalized and scaled by the velocity, and the user is moved along the resulting vector. The same concept could be implemented on the desktop, for example, by using the keyboard to set the travel direction and the mouse to set the gaze direction. In this case, however, well-designed feedback indicating the direction of travel would be necessary. In the case of an immersive VE, the user's proprioceptive sense (sense of one's own body and its parts) can tell her the direction in which her hand is pointing. Once the travel vector is obtained, the implementation of the pointing technique is identical to that of the gaze-directed technique. Thus, if the right hand is used for pointing, then each frame while movement is taking place,

Eq. 6.2
$$\mathbf{s}_{new} = \mathbf{s} + \psi \frac{\vec{\mathbf{p}}_R}{\|\vec{\mathbf{p}}_R\|}$$

An extension of the pointing concept uses two hands to specify the vector (Mine 1997). Rather than use the orientation of the hand to define the travel direction, the vector between the two hands' positions is used. An issue for this technique is which hand should be considered the "forward" hand. In one implementation (Bowman, Wingrave et al. 2001) using Pinch Gloves, the hand initiating the travel gesture was considered to be forward. This technique makes it easy to specify any 3D direction vector and also allows easy addition of a velocity-control mechanism based on the distance between the hands δ.

In terms of the notation above, then, if the pinch was made on the right hand, then each frame during movement,

Eq. 6.3
$$\mathbf{s}_{new} = \mathbf{s} + \psi \delta \frac{\left(\mathbf{h}_R - \mathbf{h}_L\right)}{\|\mathbf{h}_R - \mathbf{h}_L\|}$$

The pointing technique is more flexible, but also more complex, requiring the user to control two values simultaneously. This can lead to higher levels of cognitive load, which may reduce performance on cognitively complex tasks like information gathering (Bowman, Koller et al. 1998). The pointing technique is excellent for promoting the acquisition of spatial knowledge because it gives the user the freedom to look in any direction while moving and the ability to change the direction of travel easily (Bowman, Davis et al. 1999).

Torso-Directed Steering

Another simple steering technique uses the user's torso to specify the direction of travel. This torso-directed technique is motivated by the fact that people naturally turn their bodies to face the direction in which they are walking. A tracker is attached to the user's torso, somewhere near the waist (for example, the tracker can be mounted on a belt that the user wears). If the tracker is attached much higher than this, undesirable rotations may occur when the user looks away from the direction of travel.

After the travel direction vector is obtained from this tracker, the technique is implemented exactly as gaze-directed steering. The torso-directed technique does not apply to desktop VEs.

The major advantage of the torso-directed technique is that, like pointing, it decouples the user's gaze direction and travel direction. Unlike pointing, it does this in a natural way. The user's cognitive load should be lessened with the torso-directed technique, although this has not been verified experimentally. The torso-directed technique also leaves the user's hands free to perform other tasks. However, the torso-directed technique also has several disadvantages. The most important of these is that the technique applies only to environments where all motion is in the horizontal plane, because it's very difficult to point the torso up or down. The technique also requires an additional tracker beyond the standard head and hand trackers.

Camera-in-Hand Technique

A technique for travel in a desktop VE that still uses position trackers is called the camera-in-hand technique (Ware and Osborne 1990). A tracker is held in the hand, and the absolute position and orientation of that tracker in a defined workspace specifies the position and orientation of the camera from which the 3D scene is drawn. In other words, a miniature version of the world can be imagined in the work area. The tracker is imagined to be a virtual camera looking at this world (see Figure 6.8). Travel then is a simple matter of moving the hand in the workspace.

The camera-in-hand technique is relatively easy to implement. It simply requires a transformation **T** between the tracker coordinate system

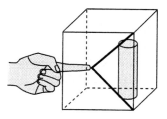
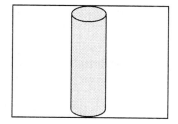

Figure 6.8 *Camera-in-hand technique. The user's hand is at a certain position and orientation within the workspace (left), producing a particular view of the environment (right).*

and the world coordinate system, defining the mapping between the virtual camera position **c** and the tracker position **t**.

Eq. 6.4
$$c = Tt$$

This technique can be effective for desktop 3D UIs (if a tracker is available) because the input is actually 3D in nature, and the user can use her proprioceptive sense to get a feeling for the spatial relationships between objects in the 3D world. However, the technique can also be confusing because the user has an exocentric (third-person) view of the workspace, but the 3D scene is drawn from an egocentric (first-person) point of view.

Physical Steering Props

Steering techniques for travel can also be implemented with a variety of physical props (specialized devices designed for the task of steering). The most obvious of these is a simple steering wheel similar to that found in a car, which of course can be combined with typical accelerator and brake pedals for virtual driving. These devices generally require that the user be seated but can be quite effective to implement a simple vehicle metaphor. They are also usable in either immersive or desktop VEs and are understandable by any user.

Other specialized steering props can be used to simulate real or imaginary vehicles for particular application domains. For example, realistic ship controls can be used to pilot a virtual ship (Brooks 1999), or an actual cockpit from a tractor can be used to control a virtual tractor (Deisinger et al. 2000). Of course, this "near-field haptics" approach (Brooks 1999) has been used in aircraft simulators for years. The Disney company uses steering props in several of its VR-based attractions (Pausch et al. 1996; Schell and Shochet 2001). For example, the virtual jungle cruise ride at DisneyQuest in Orlando allows several guests to collaboratively steer and control the speed of a virtual raft using physical oars, and the Pirates of the Caribbean attraction includes a steering wheel and "throttle" for the virtual ship. In addition, many arcade games use such props—motorcycle handlebars, steering wheels, skateboards, skis, and the like.

In general, physical steering props are useful when a certain type of vehicle is being simulated, when the interface must be usable by anyone without any training, or when the steering is an important part of the overall user experience. Additionally, automobile steering wheels may be a good choice for some general-purpose applications because of their understandability by anyone who has driven a car. Props provide users with appropriate affordances and feedback—telling them what can be done, how to do it, and what has been done. A potential pitfall is that props may create unrealistic expectations of realistic control and response in users accustomed to using the same steering interface in a real vehicle.

Virtual Motion Controller

One particular physical steering device that deserves mention is the Virtual Motion Controller, or VMC (Wells et al. 1996). This general-purpose device aims to allow virtual motion by letting users perform a subset of the walking motion they would perform in the physical world. The VMC consists of a platform with embedded pressure sensors beneath the surface (Figure 6.9). The sensors are distributed along the rim of the platform so that a user standing in the center places no pressure on the sensors and so that the pressure sensed will increase the farther the user steps from the center. By analyzing the pressure sensed at various locations, the device can determine the direction the user stepped from the center. When the user stands at the center of the platform, he remains stationary in the

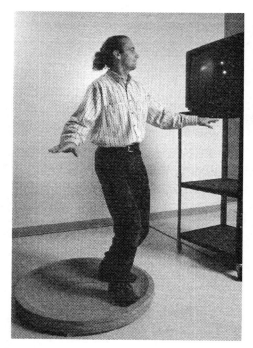

Figure 6.9 *Virtual Motion Controller. (Photograph courtesy of HIT Lab, University of Washington)*

virtual world, but when he steps out from the center, he begins to move in the direction of the step. The farther the user moves from the center, the faster the motion.

This device allows the user to rely on natural proprioceptive and kinesthetic senses to maintain spatial orientation and understanding of movement within the environment. It also integrates direction and speed specification into a single, easy-to-understand movement. The main disadvantage of the VMC is that it is limited to 2D motion unless another technique is added to allow vertical motion.

Semiautomated Steering

In certain applications, particularly in the areas of entertainment, storytelling, and education, the designer wants to give the user the feeling of control while at the same time moving the user toward an eventual goal and keeping her attention focused on important features of the environment. For example, in Disney's Aladdin attraction (Pausch et al. 1996), the user needs to feel as if she is controlling her magic carpet, but the experience must be limited to a certain amount of time, and every user needs to reach the end of the story. In such applications, semiautomated travel techniques are needed.

The basic concept of semiautomated steering is that the system provides general constraints and rules for the user's movement, and the user is allowed to have control of steering within those constraints. This idea is of course applicable to both immersive and desktop 3D UIs. A particular implementation of this concept is Galyean's river analogy (Galyean 1995). He used the metaphor of a boat traveling down a river—the boat will continue to move whether the user is actively steering or not, but the user can affect the movement by using the rudder. In particular, he designed an application in which the designer defined a path through the environment (the river). The user was "attached" to this path by a spring and could move off the path by some amount by looking in that direction (Figure 6.10).

6.3.4. Route-Planning Techniques

A second category of travel techniques, called route planning, allows the user to specify a path or route through the environment, then moves the user along that path. The essential feature of the route-planning metaphor is this two-step process: the user plans, and then the system carries out the plan. This type of technique is much less common than continu-

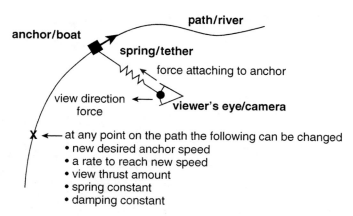

Figure 6.10 *Galyean's (1995) guided navigation technique. (© 1995 ACM; reprinted by permission)*

ous steering but has many uses. The techniques can allow the user to re-view, refine, or edit the path before its execution. For example, the user might want to define a camera path to be followed in an animation. He could do this with a steering technique, but the result would likely be a more erratic and less precise path. Route-planning techniques also allow the user to focus on other tasks, such as information gathering, during the actual period of travel. Route-planning techniques still give users at least some degree of control over their motion, but they move that control to the beginning of the travel task. This section contains information on the following route-planning techniques:

- drawing a path
- marking points along a path
- manipulating a user representation

Drawing a Path

One way to specify a route is to draw the desired path. A continuous path ensures the highest level of user control. One published technique for desktop 3D UIs allows the user to draw directly in the 3D environment using the mouse, by a projection of the 2D mouse path onto the 3D geom-etry in the environment (Figure 6.11; Igarashi et al. 1998). This technique assumes that the camera should always move at a given height above a surface rather than fly through empty space. The technique includes in-telligent mapping of the path: rather than simply projecting the 2D stroke

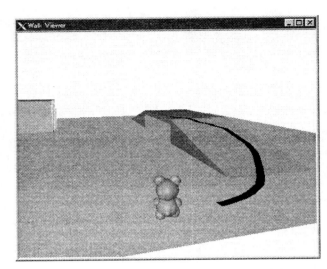

Figure 6.11 *Path-drawing system. (Igarashi et al. 1998, © 1998 ACM; reprinted by permission)*

onto the nearest 3D surface in the scene, the algorithm takes into consideration the continuity of the path and the surface the path has followed up to the current point. Thus, a path can be drawn that goes through a tunnel even if all of the ground within the tunnel is not visible to the user.

In an immersive VE, the user likely cannot reach the entire environment to draw in it directly, so drawing on a 2D or 3D map of the environment could be used to specify the path. This requires a transformation from the map coordinate system to the world coordinate system, and in the case of a 2D map, an inferred height.

Marking Points along a Path

Another method for specifying a path in a 3D environment is to place markers at key locations along the path. Again, these markers could be placed in the environment directly (using a mouse on the desktop or perhaps using a manipulation-at-a-distance technique; see Chapter 5) or on a 2D or 3D map of the environment. The system is then responsible for creating a continuous path that visits all of the marker locations. One simple implementation (Bowman, Davis et al. 1999) used a 3D map of the environment and moved the user along a straight-line path from one marker to the next (Figure 6.12). The path might also be more complex; the markers could be used as control points for a curve, for example. One

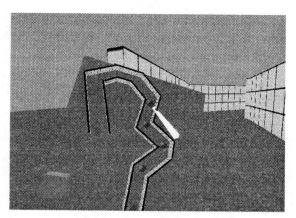

Figure 6.12 *Route-planning technique using markers on a 3D map. (Bowman, Davis et al. 1999; reprinted by permission of MIT Press and Presence: Teleoperators and Virtual Environments)*

advantage of this type of technique is that the user can vary the level of control by placing more (increased user control) or fewer (increased system control) markers. A key issue with marker placement techniques is feedback: how does the user know what path will be traversed? A well-designed technique will include interactive feedback to show the user the path in the environment or on the map.

Manipulating a User Representation

A third route-planning technique involves the user manipulating a virtual representation of himself in order to plan a route. For example, in the world-in-miniature (WIM) technique (see Chapter 5, section 5.4.4), a small human figure represents the user's position and orientation in the miniature world (Figure 6.13). The user selects and manipulates this object in the miniature environment in order to define a path for the viewpoint to move along; then the system executes this motion in the full-scale environment. Pausch and his colleagues (1995) found that this technique is most understandable when the user's view actually flies *into* the miniature world, having it replace the full-scale world and then creating a new miniature. One major advantage of this technique relative to the other route-planning techniques is that the user representation has orientation as well as position so that viewpoint rotations, not just translations, can be defined.

Similarly, a path can be defined by moving a user icon on a 2D map of the environment, a technique that would apply equally well to desktop and

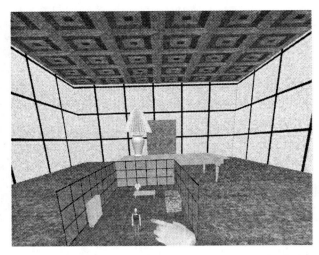

Figure 6.13   *WIM (in foreground) held in front of the corresponding full-scale environment. The user icon is at the bottom of the image. (Image courtesy of Doug A. Bowman)*

immersive 3D UIs. Because this path is only 2D, the system must use rules to determine the height of the user at every point along the path. A common rule would keep the viewpoint at a fixed height above the ground.

6.3.5. Target-Based Techniques

In some cases, the user's only goal for a travel task is to move the viewpoint to a specific position in the environment. The user in these situations is likely willing to give up control of the actual motion to the system and simply specify the endpoint. Target-based travel techniques meet these requirements. Even though the user is concerned only with the target of travel, however, this should not be construed to mean that the system should move the user directly to the target via "teleportation." An empirical study (Bowman et al. 1997) found that teleporting instantly from one location to another in a VE significantly decreases the user's spatial orientation (users find it difficult to get their bearings when instantly transported to the target location). Therefore, continuous movement from the starting point to the endpoint is always recommended.

There are many ways to specify the target of travel. In this section, we describe two techniques:

- map- or WIM-based target specification
- ZoomBack technique

Many other target-based travel techniques specify the target using techniques designed for another task. We call this type of technique a *cross-task* technique because the technique implementation has crossed from one task to another. Cross-task target-specification techniques include

- selecting an object in the environment as the target of travel using a selection technique (Chapter 5)
- placing a target object in the environment using a manipulation technique (Chapter 5)
- selecting a predefined target location from a list or menu (Chapter 8)
- entering 2D or 3D coordinates using a number entry technique, or a location name using a text entry technique (Chapter 9)

Map-Based or WIM-Based Target Specification

A 2D map or 3D WIM can be used to specify a target location within the environment (Figure 6.14). Users manipulate their miniature representation, often using the simple virtual hand technique (Chapter 5, section 5.4.3).

Figure 6.14 *Map-based target specification. The darker dot on the lower right of the map indicates the user's current position and can be dragged to a new location on the map to specify a travel target in the full-scale environment. (Bowman, Johnson et al. 1999; reprinted by permission of MIT Press and Presence: Teleoperators and Virtual Environments)*

When the user releases the representation, the release point in the miniature environment corresponds to the target point in the full-scale environment. Of course, the manipulation of the user representation here is the same as in the techniques described above. The main difference is that the system must generate a path from the current position to the target rather than simply using the path defined by the movement of the user representation on the map or in the WIM.

A typical map-based implementation of this technique (Bowman, Wineman et al. 1998) uses a pointer of some sort (a tracker in an immersive VE, a mouse on the desktop) to manipulate the user icon and simply creates a linear path from the current location to the target, then moves the user along this path with a constant velocity. The height of the viewpoint along this path is defined to be a fixed height above the ground.

To implement this technique, you need to know two things about the way the map relates to the world. First, you need to know the scale factor σ that relates the map coordinate system to the world coordinate system. Second, you need to know the point $\mathbf{o} = (x_o, y_o, z_o)$ in the map coordinate system that represents the origin $(0, 0, 0)$ of the world coordinate system. We assume here that the map model is originally aligned with the world (i.e., the x direction on the map, in its local coordinate system, represents the x direction in the world coordinate system).

When the stylus button is pressed, if the stylus is touching the user icon, then manipulation of the icon begins. The icon should follow the stylus position in the map coordinate system. The only caveat is that the vertical component of the icon's position should be fixed at 0 so that it remains on the map.

When the button is released, the user icon is moved one last time to the stylus's position. Next, the target point in the world coordinate system is calculated based on the stylus's position in the map coordinate system, the position of the world origin in the map coordinate system, and the scale factor σ. Remember that the height (y-coordinate) of the target is inferred by the system using some function h, because it can't be determined from the user's 2D input.

Eq. 6.5

$$x_{target} = \left(x_{pointer} - x_o\right)/\sigma$$

Eq. 6.6

$$z_{target} = \left(z_{pointer} - z_o\right)/\sigma$$

Eq. 6.7

$$y_{target} = h\left(x_{target}, z_{target}\right)$$

Finally, a movement vector $\vec{m}$ is created from the current user position to the target point. This vector is divided by the distance δ between the two points in order to normalize it, and then multiplied by the desired velocity ψ (note: velocity here is specified in units of distance per frame rather than units of distance per second, for simplicity).

Eq. 6.8

$$\vec{m} = \frac{\psi}{\delta}\left[x_{target} - x, y_{target} - y, z_{target} - z\right]$$

Now all that remains is to translate the user by $\vec{m}$ in the world coordinate system each frame until the target is reached. Given our assumptions, it will take $\frac{\delta}{\psi}$ frames to reach the target.

ZoomBack Technique

The ZoomBack technique (Zeleznik et al. 2002) uses a typical ray-casting metaphor (see Chapter 5) to select an object in the environment, and then moves the user to a position directly in front of this object. Ray-casting has been used in other 3D interfaces for target-based travel as well (e.g., Bowman, Johnson et al. 2001). The novel feature of the ZoomBack technique, however, is that it retains information about the previous position of the user and allows users to return to that position after inspecting the target object.

Zeleznik and colleagues used this technique in the context of a virtual museum. The technique allowed users to select a painting on the wall, examine that painting up close, and then return to the original location where multiple paintings could be viewed. Their implementation used a specialized pop-through button device (see Chapter 4, section 4.4.2); users moved to the target object with light pressure on the button and could choose either to remain there by pressing the button firmly or to return to their previous location by releasing the button.

This technique could also be implemented using two standard buttons, but the pop-through buttons provide a convenient and intuitive way to specify a temporary action that can then be either confirmed or canceled. This general strategy could be applied to other route-planning and target-based techniques as well.

6.3.6. Manual Manipulation Techniques

Manual manipulation travel techniques are another type of cross-task technique that can be quite effective in some situations. These techniques use hand-based object manipulation metaphors, such as HOMER, Go-Go, and so on (Chapter 5), to manipulate the *viewpoint* instead of a virtual object.

Manual manipulation techniques for travel should be used in situations where both travel and object manipulation tasks are frequent and interspersed. For example, consider an interior layout application, where the user's goal is to place furniture, carpets, paintings, and other items in a virtual room. This task involves frequent object manipulation tasks to place or move virtual objects and frequent travel tasks to view the room from different viewpoints. Moreover, the designer will likely move an object until it looks right from the current viewpoint and then travel to a new viewpoint to verify the object's placement. If the same metaphor can be used for both travel and object manipulation, then the interaction with this environment will be seamless and simple from the user's point of view.

Examples of manual manipulation techniques described below are

- grabbing the air
- fixed-object manipulation

Grabbing the Air

One method for using manipulation techniques for travel tasks is to allow the user to "grab the air" (Mapes and Moshell 1995; Ware and Osborne 1990). In this concept, the entire world is viewed as an object to be manipulated. When the user makes a grabbing gesture at any point in the world and then moves her hand, the entire world moves while the viewpoint remains stationary. Of course, to the user this appears exactly the same as if the viewpoint had moved and the world had remained stationary.

Although this technique is easy to implement, developers should not fall into the trap of simply attaching the world object to the virtual hand, because this will cause the world to follow the virtual hand's rotations as well as translations, which can be quite disorienting. Rather, while the grab gesture is maintained (or the button held down), the system should measure the displacement of the virtual hand each frame and translate the world origin **w** by that vector (or translate the viewpoint by the negation of that vector). If the left hand ($\mathbf{n_L}$) is used, then each frame while the manipulation is active,

Eq. 6.9

$$\mathbf{w}_{new} = \mathbf{w} + \left(\mathbf{n}_L - \mathbf{n}_{L_{past}} \right)$$

In its simplest form, this technique requires a lot of arm motion on the part of the user. Enhancements to the basic technique can reduce this. First, the technique can be implemented using two hands instead of one (Mapes and Moshell 1995), which makes for an action similar to pulling oneself along a rope, and also allows view rotation based on defining a pivot point with one hand and rotation with the other.

Second, the virtual hand can be allowed to cover much more distance using an arm-extension technique (see Chapter 5) such as Go-Go (Poupyrev et al. 1996).

In order to integrate this travel technique with an object manipulation technique, the system must simply determine whether or not the user is grabbing a moveable object at the time the grab gesture is initiated. If an object is being grabbed, then standard object manipulation should be performed; otherwise, the grab gesture is interpreted as the start of a travel interaction. In this way, the same technique can be used for both tasks.

Fixed-Object Manipulation

You can also use a manipulation technique for travel by letting a selected object serve as a focus for viewpoint movement. In other words, the user selects an object in the environment and then makes hand movements, just as he would to manipulate that object. However, the object remains stationary and the viewpoint is moved *relative* to that object. This is called fixed-object manipulation. Although this is hard to understand without trying it yourself, a real-world analogy may help. Imagine grabbing a flagpole. The pole is fixed firmly to the ground, so when you move your hand toward your body, the flagpole doesn't move; rather, *you* move closer to it. Similarly, you might try to rotate the flagpole by turning your hand, but the effect instead will be to rotate your body in the opposite direction around the pole.

Let us consider a specific example of fixed-object manipulation in 3D UIs. Pierce and colleagues (1997) designed a set of manipulation techniques called image-plane techniques (see Chapter 5, section 5.4.2). Normally, an object is selected in the image plane, then hand movements cause that object to move within the environment. For example, moving the hand back toward the body would cause the selected object to move toward the user as well. When used in travel mode, however, the same hand motion would cause the viewpoint to move *toward the selected object.* Hand rotations can also be used to move the viewpoint *around the selected object.* The scaled-world grab technique (Mine, Brooks, and Séquin 1997; see Figure 6.15) and the LaserGrab technique (Zeleznik et al. 2002) work in a similar way.

Fixed-object manipulation techniques provide a seamless interaction experience in combined travel/manipulation task scenarios, such as the one described above. The user must simply be aware of which interaction mode is active (travel or manipulation). Usually, the two modes are assigned to different buttons on the input device. The two modes can also be intermingled using the same selected object. The user would select an object in manipulation mode, move that object, then hold down the button for travel mode, allowing viewpoint movement relative to that selected object, then release the button to return to manipulation mode, and so on.

6.3.7. Travel-by-Scaling Techniques

In section 6.3.2, we noted that the most natural and intuitive method for traveling in a 3D virtual world is physical walking, but physical walking is limited by available tracking range and space. One way to alleviate this problem is to allow the user to change the scale of the world so that a physical step of one meter can represent one nanometer, one kilometer, or any other distance. This allows your available tracking range and physical space to represent a space of any size.

There are several challenges when designing a technique for travel by scaling. One is that the user needs to understand the scale of the world so that he can determine how far to move and can understand the visual feedback he gets when he moves. Use of a virtual body (hands, feet, legs, etc.) with fixed scale is one way to help the user understand the relative scale of the environment. Another issue is that continual scaling and rescaling may hasten the onset of cybersickness or discomfort (Bowman, Johnson et al. 2001). In addition, scaling the world down so that a movement in the physical space corresponds to a much larger movement in the virtual space will make the user's movements much less precise. Finally, travel-by-scaling techniques often need an additional interface component that allows the user to change the amount of scaling.

Several research projects and applications have used the concept of travel by scaling. One of the earliest was the 3DM immersive modeler (Butterworth et al. 1992). The commercial product SmartScene, which evolved from a graduate research project (Mapes and Moshell 1995), al-

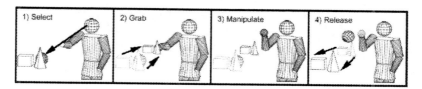

Figure 6.15 *Scaling in the scaled-world grab technique. (Mine et al. 1997, © 1997 ACM; reprinted by permission)*

lowed the user to set an arbitrary scale for the environment in order to allow rapid travel and manipulation of objects of various sizes. The interface for changing the environment's scale was simple—users wore Pinch Gloves, made a simple pinch gesture, and either brought the hands together to signify scaling the world down or moved the hands apart to scale the world up (the same gesture with different hand movements could be used to rotate the scene or travel by grabbing the air). The scaled-world grab technique (Mine, Brooks, and Séquin 1997) scales the user in an imperceptible way when an object is selected (Figure 6.15). The user sees the same scene (disregarding stereo) before and after the selection, although the world has actually been scaled down. Although this technique is meant for object manipulation, the scaling also allows the user to travel larger distances using physical movements.

6.3.8. Viewpoint Orientation Techniques

Thus far, we have focused almost exclusively on techniques for changing the position (*xyz* coordinates) of the viewpoint. Travel also includes, however, the task of setting the viewpoint orientation (heading, pitch, and roll). Here we discuss techniques specifically designed to specify the orientation of the viewpoint, including

- head tracking
- orbital viewing
- nonisomorphic rotation
- virtual sphere techniques

Head Tracking

For immersive VEs, there is usually no need to define an explicit viewpoint orientation technique, because the viewpoint orientation is taken by default from the user's head tracker. This is the most natural and direct way to specify viewpoint orientation, and it has been shown that physical turning leads to higher levels of spatial orientation than virtual turning (Bakker et al. 1998; Chance et al. 1998).

Orbital Viewing

A slight twist on the use of head tracking for viewpoint orientation is orbital viewing (Koller et al. 1996). This technique is used to view a single virtual object from all sides. In order to view the bottom of the object, the user looks up; in order to view the left side, the user looks right; and so on.

Nonisomorphic Rotation

There are certain situations in immersive VEs when some other viewpoint orientation technique is needed. The most common example comes from projected displays in which the display surfaces do not completely surround the user, as in a four-walled surround-screen display. Here, in order to see what is directly behind or above, the user must be able to rotate the viewpoint (in surround-screen displays, this is usually done using a joystick on the "wand" input device). The redirected walking technique (Razzaque et al. 2002) slowly rotates the environment so that the user can turn naturally but avoid facing the missing back wall. Research on nonisomorphic rotation techniques (LaViola et al. 2001) allows the user in such a display to view the entire surrounding environment based on amplified head rotations (for an introduction to nonisomorphic mappings, see Chapter 5).

A number of different nonisomorphic mappings could be used for setting the virtual viewpoint orientation. For a CAVE-like display, LaViola and colleagues (2001) used a nonlinear mapping function, which kicks in only after the user has rotated beyond a certain threshold, dependent on the user's waist orientation vector and position within the CAVE. A scaled 2D Gaussian function has been shown to work well. This function takes θ, the user's waist angle, and d, the distance of the user from the back of the CAVE, and is defined by

Eq. 6.10
$$\phi = f(\theta, d) = \frac{1}{\sqrt{2\pi}\sigma_1} e^{-\frac{(|\theta| - \pi(1 - d/L))^2}{2\sigma_2^2}}$$

where σ_1 is a Gaussian height parameter, σ_2 is a Gaussian steepness parameter, and L is a normalization constant used to lessen the effect of d. Note that the function's μ value is set to π in this case. Using ϕ, the new viewing angle would simply be

Eq. 6.11
$$\theta_{new} = \theta(1-\phi)$$

LaViola and colleagues (2001) offer more details on CAVE-based Auto-Rotation.

Virtual Sphere Techniques

For desktop VEs, setting viewpoint orientation is usually a much more explicit task. The most common techniques are the Virtual Sphere (Chen et al. 1988) and a related technique called the ARCBALL (Shoemake 1992). Both of these techniques were originally intended to be used for rotating individual virtual objects from an exocentric point of view and are described in detail in Chapter 5, section 5.4.7. For egocentric points of view, the same concept can be used from the inside out. That is, the viewpoint is considered to be the center of an imaginary sphere, and mouse clicks/drags rotate that sphere around the viewpoint.

6.3.9. Velocity Specification Techniques

Next, we need to consider techniques for changing the speed of travel. Many 3D UIs ignore this aspect of travel and simply set what seems to be a reasonable constant velocity. However, this can lead to a variety of problems, because a constant velocity will always be too slow in some situations and too fast in others. When the user wishes to travel from one side of the environment to another, frustration quickly sets in if he perceives the speed to be too slow. On the other hand, if he desires to move only slightly to one side, the same constant velocity will probably be too fast to allow precise movement. Therefore, considering how the user or system might control velocity is an important part of designing a travel technique.

The user can control velocity in many different ways. Often, velocity control can be integrated with the direction control technique being used. For example, in gaze-directed steering, the orientation of the head is used to specify travel direction, so the position of the head (relative to the body) can be used to specify velocity. This is called *lean-based* velocity (Fairchild et al. 1993; LaViola et al. 2001; Song and Norman 1993). In LaViola's implementation, this involves looking at the absolute horizontal distance between the head and the waist. Once this distance exceeds a threshold, then the user begins to translate in the direction of leaning, and the velocity is some multiple of the leaning magnitude.

Similarly, a technique that bases velocity on hand position relative to the body (Mine 1995a) integrates well with a pointing technique. A discrete technique for velocity control might use two buttons, one to increase the speed by a predefined amount and the other to decrease the speed. The user might also select the current velocity from a menu or enter a numeric value for the velocity. Finally, physical props such as accelerator/brake pedals or a throttle might be used.

The main drawback to allowing the user to control velocity is that it adds complexity to the interface. In cases where velocity control would be overly distracting to the user, a system-controlled velocity technique may be appropriate. For example, to allow both short, precise movements with a small velocity and larger movements with a high velocity, the system could automatically change the velocity depending on the amount of time the user had been moving. Travel would start slowly, then gradually get faster until it reached some maximum speed. The shape of the velocity curve and the maximum velocity would depend on the size of the environment, the need for precise travel, and other factors. Of course, this technique would decrease the precision of longer movements. Another potential technique uses the concept of "slow-in, slow-out" from animation (Mackinlay et al. 1990a), meaning that travel begins slowly, gets faster, and then slows again as the destination comes near. This implies that the destination is known, so this can be fully automated only with a target-based travel technique (section 6.3.5).

Velocity may also be controlled with the use of physical force–based devices, such as a force-feedback joystick. For more information on such techniques, see MacKenzie (1995).

6.3.10. Integrated Camera Controls for Desktop 3D Environments

Many of the travel techniques we have seen so far can be used effectively in desktop 3D environments. In some cases, however, a desktop application requires an integrated set of interaction techniques designed specifically for desktop use. These techniques usually assume that the user has a standard mouse and keyboard for input, and therefore they must provide a mapping between 2D input and 6-DOF camera movement.

One typical approach is to break up the 6 DOF into several components and provide separate virtual controls for each of them. For example, many VRML browsers have several navigation modes that allow the user to control one or two of the six camera DOF at a time. This approach is

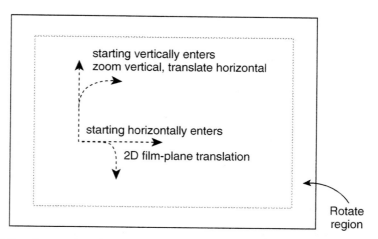

Figure 6.16   *Gesture-based controls for camera translation and rotation. (Zeleznik and Forsberg 1999; © 1999 ACM; reprinted by permission)*

also prominent in 3D modeling and animation software. For greater precision, many applications also allow the entry of numeric coordinates for the camera position and orientation.

A more novel approach to controlling a 3D camera on the desktop is Zeleznik and Forsberg's (1999) UniCam, a 2D gestural camera-control mechanism (Figure 6.16). Originally derived from the SKETCH camera-control metaphor (Zeleznik et al. 1996), the user can control travel through the 3D scene using gestural commands to manipulate the virtual camera, using a mouse or stylus with a button. To facilitate camera translation and orbiting, the viewing window is broken up into two regions, a rectangular center region and a rectangular border region. If the user clicks within the border region, a virtual sphere rotation technique is used to orbit the viewer about the center of the screen. If the user clicks within the center region, either image-plane translation or camera zoom is invoked depending on the mouse's initial movements. The mouse pointer trajectory is compared against a vertical and horizontal line. If the initial mouse pointer trajectory indicates a horizontal line, image-plane translation is invoked. If the trajectory indicates a vertical line, a camera zooming technique is invoked.

If the user makes a quick click with the mouse button, a focus dot is placed under the mouse cursor. The focus dot enables other types of camera motion controls. For example, if the user clicks a second time on any location except the focus dot, orbital viewing is invoked about the specified dot. Depending on the next interaction after the focus dot is created, other camera-control techniques, such as automatic region zooming and camera position saving and restoration, can be instantiated. See Zeleznik and Forsberg (1999) for more detail on these techniques.

Zhai and colleagues (1999) developed a two-joystick technique for 3D navigation on the desktop called the bulldozer technique. Using combinations of movements of the two joysticks similar to those that would be used to control the separate treads of a bulldozer or tank, users can translate and rotate the camera in a wide variety of ways with no mode switching. Not surprisingly, they found this technique to be far superior in terms of task performance when compared to typical mode-based 3D navigation techniques. The lesson to be learned from this work is that when navigation performance is at a premium, a small investment in more flexible input devices may be worthwhile.

6.4. Design Guidelines

This chapter has provided a large number of potential techniques for travel in 3D environments. One reason there are so many techniques for this and other 3D interaction tasks is that no single technique is best for all applications and situations. Therefore, as in the other chapters in Part III, we present some general guidelines to help the designer choose an appropriate travel technique for a given application.

> Match the travel technique to the application.

The authors are of the opinion that there is no set of 3D interaction techniques that is perfect for all applications. Designers must carefully consider the travel tasks that will be performed in the application (section 6.2), what performance is required for travel tasks, in what environment travel will take place, and who will be using the application.

Example: A visualization of a molecular structure uses an exocentric point of view and has a single object as its focus. Therefore, an object inspection technique such as orbital viewing is appropriate.

> Consider both natural and magic techniques.

Many designers start with the assumption that the 3D interface should be as natural as possible. This may be true for certain applications that require high levels of realism, such as military training, but many other applications have no such requirement. "Magic" travel techniques may prove much more efficient and usable. See Chapter 10 for more on the use of magic in 3D UIs.

> **Example:** The task of furniture layout for an interior design application requires multiple viewpoints, but not natural travel. A magic technique such as fixed-object manipulation will be efficient and will also integrate well with the object manipulation task.

> **Use an appropriate combination of travel technique, display devices, and input devices.**

The travel technique cannot be chosen separately from the hardware used in the system.

> **Example:** If a personal dome display is used, a vehicle-steering metaphor for travel fits the physical characteristics of this display. If a pointing technique is chosen, then an input device with clear shape and tactile orientation cues, such as a stylus, should be used instead of a symmetric device, such as a ball.

> **Choose travel techniques that can be easily integrated with other interaction techniques in the application.**

Similarly, the travel technique cannot be isolated from the rest of the 3D interface. The travel technique chosen for an application must integrate well with techniques for selection, manipulation, system control, and symbolic input if applicable.

> **Example:** A travel technique involving manipulation of a user representation on a 2D map suggests that virtual objects could be manipulated in the same way, providing consistency in the interface.

> **Provide multiple travel techniques to support different travel tasks in the same application.**

Many applications include a range of travel tasks. It is tempting to design one complex technique that meets the requirements for all these tasks, but including multiple simple travel techniques is often less confusing to the user. Most VE applications already do this implicitly, because the user can physically walk in a small local area but must use a virtual travel technique to move larger distances. It will also be appropriate in some cases to include both steering and target-based techniques in the same application. We should note, however, that users will not automatically know which technique to use in a given situation, so some small amount of user training may be required.

> **Example:** An immersive design application in which the user verifies and modifies the design of a large building requires both large-scale search and small-scale maneuvering. A target-based technique to move the user quickly to different floors of the building plus a low-speed steering technique for maneuvering might be appropriate.

Make simple travel tasks easier by using target-based techniques for goal-oriented travel and steering techniques for exploration and search.

If the user's goal for travel is not complex, then the travel technique providing the solution to that goal should not be complex either. If most travel in the environment is from one object or well-known location to another, then a target-based travel technique is most appropriate. If the goal is exploration or search, a steering technique should be used.

> **Example:** In a virtual tour of a historical environment, the important areas are well known, and exploration is not required, so a target-based technique such as choosing a location from a menu would be appropriate. In a visualization of weather patterns, the interesting views are unknown, so exploration should be supported with a steering technique such as pointing.

Use a physical locomotion technique if physical user exertion or naturalism is required.

Physical locomotion devices are currently costly, unreliable, and barely usable. However, for some applications, especially training, where the physical motion and exertion of the user is an integral part of the task, such a device is required. First, however, consider whether your application might make do with something simpler, like walking in place or the VMC.

Example: A sports training application will be effective only if the user physically exerts himself, so a locomotion device should be used.

> **Use graceful transitional motions if overall environment context is important.**

Simply providing a smooth path from one location to another will increase the user's spatial knowledge and keep her oriented to the environment (Bowman et al. 1997). This approach complements the use of wayfinding aids. Only in cases where knowledge of the surrounding environment is irrelevant should teleportation be used.

Example: Unstructured environments such as undeveloped terrain or information visualizations can be quite confusing. Give users spatial context by always animating their travel smoothly.

> **Train users in sophisticated strategies to help them acquire survey knowledge.**

If spatial orientation is especially important in an application, there are some simple strategies that will help users obtain spatial knowledge (Bowman, Davis et al. 1999). These include flying up to get a bird's-eye view of the environment, traversing the environment in a structured fashion (see Chapter 7, section 7.3.5), retracing paths to see the same part of the environment from the opposite perspective, and stopping to look around during travel. Users can easily be trained to perform these strategies in unfamiliar environments.

Example: Training soldiers on a virtual mockup of an actual battlefield location should result in increased spatial knowledge of that location. If the soldiers are trained to use specific spatial orientation strategies, their spatial knowledge in the physical location should improve.

> **Consider integrated (cross-task) interaction techniques if travel is used in the context of manipulation.**

The manual manipulation techniques in section 6.3.6 allow the same basic technique to be used for both travel and object manipulation. Certain applications benefit greatly from these integrated techniques.

Example: A furniture layout environment for interior designers could use manual manipulation techniques to allow integrated furniture manipulation and visual verification of the layout.

> Desktop 3D navigation techniques should allow the user to accomplish the most common travel tasks with a minimum of effort.

Depending on the application, environment, and user goals, particular types of travel are likely to be common in a specific system, while others will be used only infrequently. The default navigation mode or controls should focus on the most common tasks.

Example: In a desktop 3D game in an indoor environment, most travel will be parallel to the floor, and users very rarely need to roll the camera. Therefore, a navigation technique that uses left and right mouse movement for camera yaw, up and down movement for camera pitch, and arrow keys to move the viewpoint forward, backward, left, and right would be appropriate for this application.

Recommended Reading

For an excellent overview of locomotion devices, we recommend the following:

Hollerbach, J. (2002). Locomotion Interfaces. *Handbook of Virtual Environments: Design, Implementation, and Applications.* K. Stanney (Ed.), Lawrence Erlbaum Associates, 239–254.

An informative presentation on the implementation of travel techniques for desktop 3D interfaces can be found in this text:

Barrilleaux, J. (2000). *3D User Interfaces with Java 3D,* Manning Publications Company.

Readers interested in more details on the empirical performance of common travel techniques should take a look at the following:

Bowman, D., D. Johnson, and L. Hodges (2001). Testbed Evaluation of VE Interaction Techniques. *Presence: Teleoperators and Virtual Environments* 10(1): 75–95.

CHAPTER 7
Wayfinding

In this chapter, we discuss the 3D interaction task called wayfinding. As we saw in the introduction to Part III, wayfinding is the cognitive component of navigation. Here, we look at the psychological foundations of wayfinding, techniques and principles for supporting users' wayfinding in 3D environments, and the connection between wayfinding and travel techniques.

7.1. Introduction

We can define wayfinding as follows: Wayfinding is the cognitive process of defining a path through an environment, using and acquiring spatial knowledge, aided by both natural and artificial cues.

Wayfinding is a common activity in our daily lives. We move through real-world environments, such as cities, buildings, and roadways, for the purpose of reaching a destination or perhaps simply to explore. Wayfinding tasks can be as easy as visiting the bakery around the corner or as difficult as finding a specific address on a back road in an unknown neighborhood.

Wayfinding is often an unconscious activity—we move from one point to another without actively considering that we are finding our way through an environment. When we get lost, however, wayfinding may come to the forefront of our attention.

Many different types of information help us to perform wayfinding tasks. Landmarks such as a church, or specific items in a building such as the soda machine, may help us decide which way to travel. Routes that we have traveled before provide familiar surroundings. Signs, maps, and other directional information can help in unfamiliar situations.

It is important to provide as many different types of spatial information as possible when 3D virtual worlds are used for wayfinding-related purposes. These purposes can roughly be subdivided into two categories:

1. *Transferring spatial knowledge to the real world*: We can use a VE to obtain knowledge of the layout of an environment so we can use this knowledge in the real world. For example, firefighters have used VEs to quickly get an impression of the layout of a burning building to reduce the potentially hazardous effects of getting lost (Bliss et al. 1997; Waller et al. 1998).

2. *Navigation through complex environments in support of other tasks:* Large-scale, complex virtual worlds used for real-world work may require wayfinding support. For example, this may happen when someone is evaluating a large building and needs to relate structural information from different building locations to a colleague. With regards to complexity, an environment becomes increasingly difficult for us to comprehend when we cannot overview the complete environment at once, from one location.

Wayfinding in 3D UIs is difficult to support because of the differences between wayfinding in a real environment and in a virtual environment. We are used to having solid ground under our feet, but in a VE, we may have to work without these natural constraints. Unconstrained movement can disorient people easily, and the absence of physical constraints may increase this feeling of disorientation. The lack of realistic motion cues due to virtual movement instead of physical walking also makes wayfinding more difficult and may even lead to cybersickness (LaViola 2000a).

On the other hand, 3D UIs provide a wealth of opportunities for both natural and artificial wayfinding aids. We can classify these wayfinding aids in two groups: user-centered and environment-centered aids. *User-centered* aids make use of the characteristics of human perception and can draw upon multiple human senses. Many of these aids relate to the topic of *presence,* the feeling of being in an environment. A detailed discussion of presence is beyond the scope of this text, but we provide some useful references in the recommended reading list at the end of the chapter. *Environment-centered* wayfinding aids refer to the conscious design of the virtual world to support wayfinding. The fields of visual communication sciences and urban planning are excellent sources of information on real-world environment-centered aids.

7.1.1. Chapter Roadmap

The aim of this chapter is to describe the activity of wayfinding as a decision-making process and to identify techniques to support this process. This requires some background in psychology, so the first part of this chapter introduces some basic cognitive principles on which wayfinding is built (section 7.2).

In the second part of the chapter, we explain how to apply the cognitive foundations to support wayfinding in VEs. Wayfinding aids are described in sections on user-centered support (section 7.3) and environment-centered support (section 7.4). Finally, we describe how aids can be evaluated (section 7.5) and provide some general guidelines for their use in 3D UIs (section 7.6).

7.2. Theoretical Foundations

Wayfinding is a decision-making process (Figure 7.1). This means that a user makes decisions (where am I? which direction should I go?) by mentally processing "input" (information obtained from the environment) and producing "output" (movement along a trajectory). Decision making is a very general cognitive process, and it can be represented in many ways. Golledge (1999) provides a good overview of cognitive processes and specific cognitive factors that affect wayfinding. Readers unfamiliar with cognitive psychology will find this and the other recommended readings (found at the end of the chapter) to be helpful.

Navigation in a 3D environment involves the processing of multiple sources of sensory information that we receive from the environment and the use of this information to execute a suitable travel trajectory. The environmental information is stored in our long-term memory and is

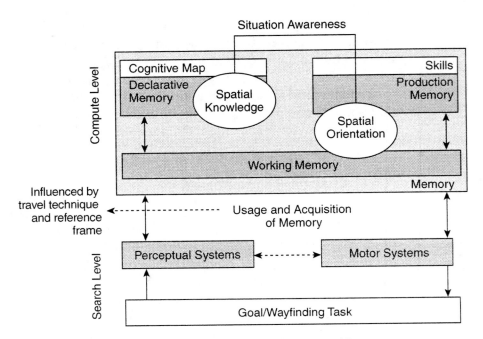

Figure 7.1   *A representation of wayfinding as a decision-making process.*

generally referred to as the *cognitive map*, the corpus of spatial knowledge we obtain from our environment. To be more precise, the cognitive map is a mental, hierarchical structure of information that represents spatial knowledge (Stevens and Coupe 1978; Downs and Stea 1977).

When we perform a wayfinding task, we make use of existing spatial knowledge, acquire new spatial knowledge, or use a combination of the two. The process of accessing, using, and building the treelike structures in the cognitive map is also called *cognitive mapping*.

Navigation is based on a tight feedback loop that continuously defines the relationship between the information we receive and our cognitive map of the environment, which enables us to understand our position and orientation. The knowledge of our location and viewing direction is called *spatial orientation*, while the combination of spatial orientation and spatial knowledge (cognitive map) is called *situation awareness* (a term generally used in aviation).

7.2.1. Wayfinding Tasks

In Chapter 6, we introduced three types of travel tasks. Wayfinding tasks are similar, but we present them here in the wayfinding context. We also consider a fourth wayfinding task with no analogous travel task.

Exploration involves browsing the environment. The user has no particular goal in mind, and perhaps a less structured movement pattern. However, exploration may be very effective in helping to build the cognitive map.

The second type of wayfinding task is *search*. Naturally, during search tasks, spatial knowledge is not only acquired, but also used. Naïve search is a task that is target-based, but in which the user does not know the exact location of the target. This means that the cognitive map does not contain enough information to allow direct movement toward the target. A primed search is also a target-based search task, but with a known target location. Therefore, the user's ability to use the cognitive map to understand the relationship between his present location and the target's location will define the success of finding the target.

In *maneuvering* tasks, a user performs many small-scale movements to reach a very specific position. During wayfinding, maneuvering may happen occasionally as a subtask of the search tasks mentioned above. It may, for example, be needed to identify a landmark from a specific point of view or to find a very small target. Maneuvering may also occur when the user is lost and needs to obtain more information from a specific location in order to decide which way to go.

The final wayfinding task is *specified trajectory movement*. In this task, the user is guided automatically through an environment along a predefined path in order to obtain a broad overview of the environment. This type of movement allows her to build a basic cognitive map in a short time, as long as the trajectory is defined effectively (with regards to movement pattern and viewpoints). Allowing the user to control viewpoint orientation during the movement provides for more effective gathering of spatial knowledge. This task was not identified as a travel task because it does not involve active user motion through an environment.

7.2.2. Types of Spatial Knowledge

Search strategies and movement parameters influence the effectiveness of spatial knowledge acquisition. These factors affect not only the efficiency of building a cognitive map but also which of the qualitatively different kinds of spatial knowledge are acquired.

During wayfinding, people obtain at least three different kinds of spatial knowledge (Thorndyke and Hayes-Roth 1982):

- *Landmark knowledge* consists of the visual characteristics of the environment. Visually prominent objects ("landmarks") form part of this information, but other visual features such as shape, size, and texture also play a role. In London, for example, Big Ben, the river Thames, and Heathrow airport are locations that many visitors immediately add to their landmark knowledge.

- *Procedural knowledge* (or *route knowledge*) describes the sequence of actions required to follow a certain path or traverse paths between different locations. Only sparse visual information is needed for procedural knowledge to be used properly (Gale et al. 1990). For example, a visitor to London will quickly memorize the route between her hotel and the nearest underground station.

- *Survey knowledge* can be described as the configurational or topological knowledge of an environment, consisting of object locations, interobject distances, and object orientations. This kind of knowledge is maplike and can therefore also be obtained from a map, even though the acquired knowledge from the map tends to be orientation-specific (Darken and Cevik 1999). Of the three kinds of spatial knowledge, survey knowledge represents the (qualitatively) highest level of knowledge and normally also takes the longest to mentally construct. Our fictitious visitor to London may attempt to obtain survey knowledge by studying the map of the underground (although she may not be successful!).

Building spatial knowledge requires visual, vestibular, and other motion information. For more information, refer to Henry and Furness (1993) and Steck and Mallot (2000).

7.2.3. Egocentric and Exocentric Reference Frames

During real-life motion, we feel as if we are in the center of space, a phenomenon that is called *egomotion*. During such motion, we need to match *egocentric* (first-person) information to the cognitive map, which typically stores *exocentric* (third-person) information (Thorndyke and Hayes-Roth 1982). The differences between the egocentric and exocentric reference frames play a crucial role in wayfinding.

But what are these differences? Basically, an egocentric reference frame is defined relative to a certain part of the human body, whereas an exocentric reference frame is object- or world-relative.

During egocentric tasks, judgments are made according to the egocentric reference frame, which consists of the stationpoint (nodal point of the eye), retinocentric (the retina), headcentric (focused solely on the head), bodycentric (the torso), and proprioceptive subsystems (visual and nonvisual cues from our body parts, such as hands and legs), as shown in Figure 7.2. Details on these reference frames can be found in Howard (1991).

The egocentric reference frame provides us with important information such as distance (obtained from physical feedback like a number of strides or an arm's length) and orientation (obtained from the direction of the eyes, head, and torso). An object's position, orientation, and movement are related to the position and orientation of the eyes, head, and body.

During exocentric tasks, the position, orientation, and movement of objects are defined in coordinates external to the body. Namely, they are

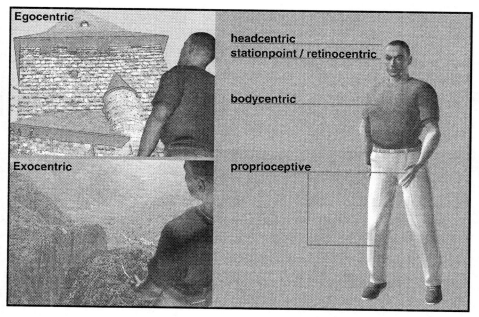

Figure 7.2 *Human reference frames (right) and associated views (left). In an egocentric view (top left), the user is inside the environment, while in an exocentric view (bottom left), the user is outside the environment, looking in. (Image courtesy of Ernst Kruijff)*

defined by an object's shape, orientation, and motion. Exocentric attributes are not affected by our orientation or position.

The reference frame is directly dependent on our viewpoint. The egocentric reference frame corresponds to first-person viewpoints, while exocentric reference frames are related to third-person (bird's-eye or outside-in) viewpoints. For example, in many video games, the user typically sees a first-person (egocentric) view of the environment as he navigates through it, but can also access an overview map of the environment showing his current location (exocentric).

When we find our way through an environment, we build up an exocentric representation (survey knowledge). However, when we enter an environment for the first time, we basically depend on egocentric information (landmark and procedural knowledge). Therefore, we often depend on landmarks at first, then develop routes between them, and eventually we generalize that egocentric spatial information into exocentric survey knowledge. It remains unclear, however, how the human brain determines the relationship between egocentric and exocentric spatial knowledge.

7.3. User-Centered Wayfinding Support

With the psychological foundations of wayfinding in mind, we now illustrate how to support wayfinding in a 3D environment. In general, the effectiveness of wayfinding depends on the number and quality of wayfinding *cues* or *aids* provided to users. This section (on user-centered cues) and the next (on environment-centered cues) present a number of different wayfinding aids and address questions such as, When and how should I include cues? and How does the design of my environment affect wayfinding?

Recall that user-centered wayfinding aids are targeted to human sensory systems. Thus, most user-centered support is technology-oriented. Because output devices still cannot deliver information that fully matches the capabilities of the human perceptual system (see Chapter 3), they can have a negative impact on wayfinding. There are certain strategies that developers can use, however, to lessen these negative effects. In this section we discuss

- field of view
- motion cues

- multisensory output
- presence
- search strategies

All of these wayfinding cues can be employed to some degree in desktop 3D UIs, but wide fields of view, physical motion cueing, and presence are typically associated with more immersive systems.

7.3.1. Field of View

A small field of view (FOV) may inhibit wayfinding. Because a smaller portion of the environment is visible at any given time, the user requires repetitive head movements to comprehend the spatial information obtained from the viewpoint. Using a larger FOV reduces the amount of head movement and allows the user to understand spatial relationships more easily. Some studies, such as Péruch, May, and Wartenburg (1997) and Ruddle, Payne, and Jones (1998), do not fully support these claims, showing little difference in the orientation capabilities of a user between several small FOVs (40, 60, and 80 degrees, or in desktop environments). However, they have demonstrated the usefulness of larger FOVs when environments become more detailed and complex. Furthermore, wide FOVs closer to the FOV of the human visual system (like those in some surround-screen displays) were not considered in these studies.

Another negative side effect of a small FOV is the lack of optical-flow fields in users' peripheral vision. Peripheral vision provides strong motion cues, delivering information about the user's direction, velocity, and orientation during movement. In addition, it has been shown that small FOVs may lead to cybersickness (Stanney et al. 1998).

7.3.2. Motion Cues

Supplying motion cues enables the user to judge both the depth and direction of movement and provides the information necessary for dead reckoning (backtracking of the user's own movement). Motion cues can be obtained from peripheral vision, as discussed above, but motion cues are not purely visual—it is important to supply the user with additional vestibular (real motion) cues if possible. A lack of vestibular cues causes an intersensory conflict between visual and physical information. This may cause cybersickness and can affect judgments of egomotion, thus negatively impacting the formation of the cognitive map.

The effect of real motion cues on the orientation abilities of users in VEs has been the subject of a range of studies. Usoh and his colleagues (1999) compared a virtual travel technique based on pointing (Chapter 6, section 6.3.3) against walking in place and natural walking (using wide-area tracking; Chapter 6, section 6.3.2). Walking techniques (physical motion) performed better than pointing techniques (purely virtual motion), even though some users preferred pointing because of ease of use. Although there were no large differences between walking in place and - natural walking for the spatial orientation of the user, natural walking increased the sense of presence considerably (see section 7.3.4). Other studies of virtual and real travel have shown positive effects of real motion on spatial orientation (Klatzky et al. 1998; Chance et al. 1998).

Our understanding of the proper balance between visual and vestibular input is still being formed. Harris (Harris et al. 1999) performed tests matching visual and passive vestibular input, and concluded that developers should add vestibular information corresponding to at least one-quarter of the amount of visual motion.

Motion cues are difficult to implement for desktop 3D UIs. Peripheral vision cues cannot be provided because of the size of the display screen, and physical motion cues are limited for a seated user. The use of vestibular cue devices (see Chapter 3, section 3.4.3) can provide some motion cues directly to the brain, but their effects are not well understood.

7.3.3. Multisensory Output

In addition to the visual and vestibular systems, developers might want to experiment with other sensory systems to deliver wayfinding cues. Audio (see Chapter 3, section 3.3) can provide the user with useful directional and distance information (Davis et al. 1999). For example, the sound of trains can indicate the direction to the station, whereas the volume allows the user to estimate the distance to the train station. Audio for wayfinding support is still a largely open question.

Another form of multisensory support is the tactile map—a map whose contours are raised so they can be sensed by touch as well as sight. Initial experiments used tactile maps to fill in gaps in the spatial knowledge of visually impaired people. The tactile map was used as an additional cue, not as a substitute for another cue type (Jacobson 1996). Tan and colleagues (2002) showed that tactile cues can aid in the formation and usage of spatial memory, so tactile wayfinding aids are another area of great potential.

7.3.4. Presence

The sense of presence (the feeling of "being there") is a much explored but still not well-understood phenomenon that is assumed to have an impact on spatial knowledge. Briefly, the idea is that if the user feels more present in a virtual world, then real-world wayfinding cues will be more effective. Many factors influence the sense of presence, including sensory immersion, proprioception, and the immersive tendency of the user. The inclusion of a *virtual body*—that is, the user's own virtual representation—may enhance the sense of presence, which in turn has a positive effect on spatial knowledge acquisition and usage (Draper 1995; Usoh et al. 1999). You can find recommended reading on this topic at the end of the chapter.

7.3.5. Search Strategies

A final user-centered wayfinding technique is to teach the user to employ an effective search strategy. Using a search strategy often depends on user skill. More skilled users, like professional aviators, use different strategies than users with limited navigation experience. Not only do skilled users depend on other kinds of spatial knowledge, and therefore on other cues in the environment, but they often use different search patterns as well. Whereas novice users depend largely on landmarks, skilled users make use of cues like paths (e.g., a coastline).

Using a search strategy inspired by navigation experts can increase its effectiveness. For example, search patterns used during aviation search-and-rescue missions may aid a user during wayfinding (Wiseman 1995).

Figure 7.3 shows several possible effective search patterns. The basic line search follows a pattern of parallel lines along a specific line. The pattern search starts at a specific central point and moves further away from it, using quadratic or radial patterns. The contour search is designed to follow contours in a landscape, like a river or a mountain. Finally, the fan search starts from a center point and fans out in all directions until the target is found. Of course, the use of these search strategies is dependent on the content of the environment—they might work well in a large outdoor environment, but would not make sense in a virtual building.

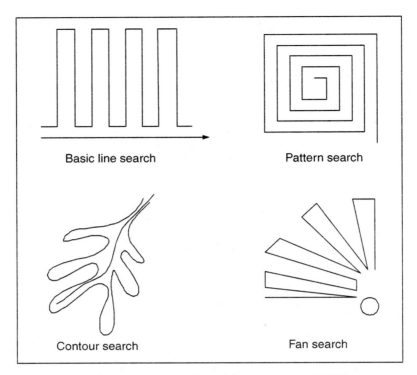

Figure 7.3   *Search patterns. (Figure adapted from Wiseman [1995])*

Another important search strategy is to obtain a bird's-eye view of the environment rather than performing all navigation on the ground. Users can be trained to employ this strategy quite easily, and it results in significantly better spatial orientation (Bowman, Davis et al. 1999). This can even be automated for the user. In the "pop-up" technique (Darken and Goerger 1999), users can press a button to temporarily move to a significant height above the ground, then press the button again to go back to their original location on the ground.

We assume that novice users can learn search techniques, even if the described pattern search strategies are seen primarily in expert navigators. Placing a rectangular or radial grid directly in the environment provides a visual path along which users can search. Although these grids may supply directional and depth cues, they do not necessarily force the user to maximize search effectiveness.

7.4. Environment-Centered Wayfinding Support

Beyond the technology and training support described above, most wayfinding aids for virtual worlds can be directly related to aids from the real world. These range from natural environmental cues like a high mountain to artificial cues such as a map. We discuss both *environment design* (the structure and visual aspects of an environment) and *artificial aids* (cues that can be added to an environment either as an environmental element or as a tool) as effective approaches to environment-centered wayfinding support.

7.4.1. Environment Design

The first type of environment-centered support relates to the construction of the environment itself. The world's structure and form can provide strong wayfinding cues without the need for cluttering the environment with added wayfinding aids. Of course, when the virtual world must accurately reflect a real-world location, such explicit environment design may not be possible. But in cases where the designer has some freedom, these techniques can be invaluable. Our discussion focuses on two types of environment design principles:

- legibility techniques
- real-world wayfinding principles drawn from the natural environment and from architectural design

Legibility Techniques

Many of the structural rules applied to VEs are obtained from urban design principles. A book that has been the basis for many of those rules is *The Image of the City* (Lynch 1960). In this book, Lynch describes so-called *legibility techniques.* These techniques allow the user to quickly obtain an understanding of an environment by understanding its basic structural elements. For 3D environment design, we can summarize Lynch's theory as follows (Darken and Sibert 1996; Ingram et al. 1996):

- Divide large-scale environments into parts with a distinct character.
- Create a simple spatial organization in which the relationships between the parts are clear.
- Support the matching process between egocentric and exocentric reference frames by including directional cues.

Lynch identifies several basic building blocks that can be applied to achieve a legible environment: paths, edges, districts, nodes, and landmarks. *Paths* are elements or channels for linear movement, like streets or railways. People often view a city from the perspective of such paths. *Edges* are related to paths, but are focused on bordering spaces rather than on movement. These edges can be natural, like a river, or artificial, like a walled structure. *Districts* are areas that are uniquely identifiable because of their style (e.g., building style), color, or lighting. *Nodes* are gathering points, such as a major intersection of streets, or the "entrance" to a certain district. Finally, *landmarks* are objects that are easily distinguished and are often placed near a node (Darken and Sibert 1996).

A legible environment often has a repetitive structure; for example, think about how cities like New York are structured—they have a strong, regular pattern (see Figure 7.4). Most such structures deliberately make use of right angles. Research has shown that structures containing irregular corners (smaller or larger than 90 degrees) can lead to severe disorientation, even to the degree that survey knowledge can hardly be obtained. Users may then only be able to build the cognitive map to the level of route knowledge (Moeser 1988). Continuous change of the angles used in

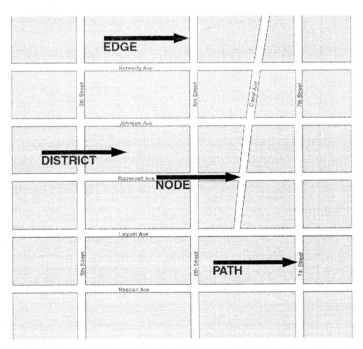

Figure 7.4 *Legibility techniques illustrated by a typical American city structure.*

corners (as in many European medieval towns) may also lead to disorientation (Ruddle et al. 1998).

These principles can be applied to virtual cities, buildings, and landscapes as easily as they can be applied to the real-world counterparts, and the virtual world provides even more flexibility in this regard. For example, Darken and Sibert (1996) placed large artificial landmarks in an environment that could be seen from any location in the environment, and also found that the lines of a grid overlaid on the environment functioned effectively as edges or paths during search tasks. Even abstract information visualizations can be organized around these rules to improve users' spatial orientation. For example, data points can be clustered to create "districts" or visually linked to create "paths" (Ingram et al. 1996).

Real-World Design Principles

Many of the real-world design principles that can be applied to VE design are directly related to perceptual issues, like depth or distance estimation or visual communication. These techniques are often used to help us distinguish between structural elements.

Natural environment principles We may draw upon the natural environment to supply the user with some basic wayfinding aids. A *horizon* gives us basic directional orientation information; *atmospheric* color methods or *fog* may provide better depth cues and help us to estimate distances more exactly.

Architectural design principles Related to city planning techniques, architectural design principles can help in the acquisition and usage of spatial knowledge or in leading the user deliberately to specific parts of the environment. For example, correct *lighting* not only provides *shadows* as depth cues, but can also be used as a directional cue. Illuminating certain objects in an environment (like a doorway), may make them more recognizable as landmarks. We often tend to move toward a light source, so lighting a target may also help users to find it more easily. In addition, the careful design of *closed and open spaces* can be used to direct a user to certain locations because we tend to move toward openings (e.g., a door in the wall).

Color and texture The useful application of *colors* is probably one of the most powerful real-world design techniques. Color provides us with landmark knowledge but can also be used to identify certain types of objects. Structure can be communicated by making color groups. Specific objects (like landmarks) can be made more identifiable by giving them a contrasting color. Well-chosen *textures* not only provide us with depth cues, but can also provide landmark knowledge. In some cases, textures can also be used to visually lay out a path through an environment in order to support the formation of procedural knowledge. For example, a ribbon of colored carpet in a building can lead users along a path to important locations.

7.4.2. Artificial Cues

A second major way to support wayfinding in the environment is the addition of artificial wayfinding aids. With this approach, we enhance an existing environment rather than design the environment itself to support wayfinding. Artificial cues can be either placed directly in the environment or provided to the user as tools. Some of the artificial cues that have been used in 3D environments include:

- maps
- compasses
- signs
- reference objects
- artificial landmarks
- trails
- audio and olfactory cues

Maps

A map is a powerful tool for the acquisition of spatial knowledge. Because a map normally provides an exocentric representation of an environment, it can aid the formation of survey knowledge by a user. The knowledge obtained from traditional maps, however, tends to be orientation-specific (Tlauka and Wilson 1996; Darken and Cevik 1999). Looking south in the environment while trying to use a map with north at the top can lessen our wayfinding abilities. We need to be able to match the exocentric information from the map with the egocentric information from a first-person perspective.

Directional problems are just one example of difficulties with implementing a map in a 3D UI. Here are some other design guidelines for including maps in virtual worlds.

> ## Use you-are-here maps.

You-are-here (YAH) maps combine a map with a YAH marker. Such a marker helps the user to gain spatial awareness by providing her viewpoint position and/or orientation dynamically on the map. This means that the marker needs to be continuously updated to help the user match her egocentric viewpoint with the exocentric one of the map.

> ## Consider multiple maps at different scales.

In some large-scale environments, a single map might not be sufficient. Ruddle, Payne, and Jones (1999) experimented with a combination of local and global maps. Global maps provide the world-reference positions of objects for easy location, whereas local maps communicate the direct surroundings of the user, allowing him to easily detect important objects in a scene. This is an application of the well-known "focus plus context" principle from information visualization (Ware 2000). Figure 7.5 shows the global and local map combination, with a YAH marker in the local map.

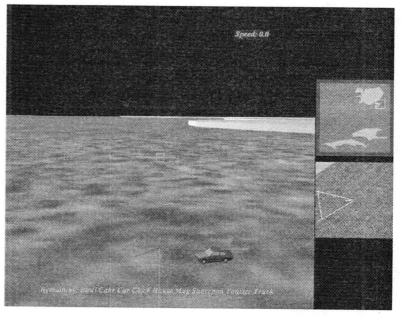

Figure 7.5 *Local (bottom right) and global (upper right) maps. (Image courtesy of Roy Ruddle)*

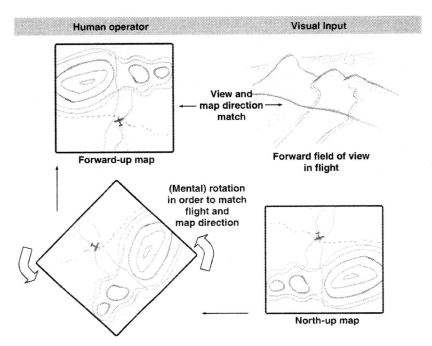

Figure 7.6   *Rotation of a map to align viewpoint direction and map direction. (Figure adapted from Wickens and Carswell [1997])*

Carefully choose the orientation of the map.

When a map is not aligned with the environment, users must mentally rotate the map information (Figure 7.6). Mental rotations can cause high cognitive load for a user.

One of the most famous studies on mental rotation (Shepard and Metzler 1971) shows that every 60 degrees of mental rotation will take a person approximately one second. Therefore, carefully choosing the orientation of a map may save the user time. Darken and Cevik (1999) compared a standard "north-up" map to a "forward-up" map (which rotates so that the map is always aligned with the environment; see Figure 7.7). He found that a forward-up map is preferable in egocentric search tasks (e.g., searching for an intersection in a city), whereas in exocentric search tasks (e.g., searching for an airport from the air) a north-up map provides better performance.

Figure 7.7 *North-up map versus forward-up. (Image courtesy of the MOVES Institute, Naval Postgraduate School)*

Make the map legible.

It is important for a map to communicate its contents clearly. The details of choosing a graphical representation for the environment is beyond the scope of this text, but other books on the design of graphical information (Tufte 1990) provide an excellent reference on the subject. A map should clearly show the organizational structure of the environment, for example, by combining a map with a grid. The grid may also support search strategies such as those described in section 7.3.5.

Use appropriate map size and placement to reduce occlusion of the environment.

Maps can fill a large portion of the display and thus occlude (block) the environment. A map must be large enough to communicate its details to the user. The size is dependent on the size of the environment, the resolution, and even the contrast of the display.

In an HMD-based system, for example, the resolution is typically quite low, meaning that a legible map might take up a quarter to a half of the display area! One solution is to allow the user to hide or show the map when needed, although this may lead to orientation difficulties. Another way to quickly access a map and reduce occlusion is to place the map on a tracked physical surface, such as a tablet (Figure 7.8), so that

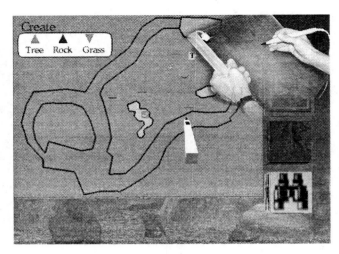

Figure 7.8   *Tablet-based map from the Virtual Habitat application. (Bowman, Wineman et al. 1999)*

users can look at the map when needed and drop it out of their field of view at other times (Bowman, Wineman et al. 1998). In a surround-screen display, the map could be placed on the floor, as in Figure 7.9.

Compasses

A *compass* (Figure 7.10) can also provide directional cues. For a trained navigator, a compass in combination with a map is an invaluable way-

Figure 7.9   *A floor-based map called the Step WIM. (LaViola et al. 2001; © 2001 ACM; reprinted by permission)*

Figure 7.10 *Compasses in virtual and real-world scenarios. (Images courtesy of the MOVES Institute, Naval Postgraduate School)*

finding tool. Most users of 3D UIs, however, will not be familiar with effective methods for using compass information. As a VE wayfinding aid, compasses are typically found in navigation training tools, such as those used in the military.

Signs

Signs are used extensively in real-world environments to provide spatial knowledge and directions (Figure 7.11), but surprisingly there is little research on the use of signs as a wayfinding cue in VEs. Signs can be

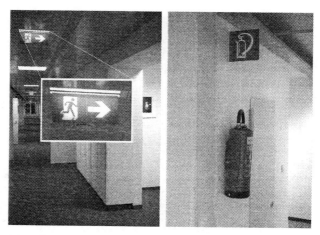

Figure 7.11 *Use of signs to direct wayfinders. (Photograph courtesy of Ernst Kruijff)*

extremely effective because of their directness, but signs can also become confusing in complex environments (think about badly designed airports). Signs should be placed in an easily observable location, should supply clear directions, and should be spaced far enough apart that multiple signs do not confuse the user.

Reference Objects

Reference objects are objects that have a well-known size, such as a chair or a human figure, and aid in size and distance estimation. Users often have difficulty judging distances in large, mostly empty environments. Because there are often no reference objects in these large spaces with which to compare the size of the room, distances are highly under- or overestimated. As soon as reference objects are placed in such a space, estimation of sizes and distances becomes easier.

Artificial Landmarks

Artificial landmarks are another group of cues that are similar to reference objects. These are easily distinguishable objects that can be used to maintain spatial orientation, develop landmark and/or route knowledge, and serve as foundations for distance or direction estimation. Although landmarks are naturally part of a legible environment design, artificial landmarks may be added to any environment to support users' wayfinding tasks.

Landmarks are most often implemented in the environment itself, although they can be used as tools. For example, in Worldlets (Elvins et al. 1997), a desktop-based landmark application, the landmark becomes a tool like a compass. It is held in the hand or displayed on a surface (Figure 7.12). The user can turn the landmark and look at it from different sides to obtain knowledge of the environment around it and possibly use it to find the landmark's location in the full-scale environment.

We can identify two different sorts of landmarks: the *local* and the *global landmark*. Global landmarks are visible from practically any location, so they provide directional cues similar to a compass. Local landmarks help users in the decision-making process—when a decision point is reached, the available local landmarks provide useful information (Steck and Mallot 2000).

Several studies have investigated the use of landmarks in VEs (e.g., Vinson 1999), leading to two design guidelines.

Figure 7.12   *Spherical and frustum Worldlets, which can be viewed from within the Viewpoint Guidebook Window. (Image courtesy of T. Todd Elvins and David R. Nadeau, San Diego Supercomputer Center)*

> Use clearly distinguishable visual characteristics.

It is important that a user be able to distinguish the landmark from other surrounding objects within the environment. Therefore, we should make it stand out by using a contrasting color, different lighting, a contrasting form, or a different size.

> Carefully pick the location of the landmark.

When placing the landmark, we can use the requirement of legibility to place it so it can easily be spotted, like a corner in a city structure, instead of placing it within a city block. Use the structure of the environment to support the detection of the landmark.

Trails

In order to help the user "retrace his steps" in an environment, or to show which parts of the world have been visited, *trails* can be included as an artificial wayfinding aid. A trail can be made up of a simple line or by using markers that include directional information, just like footprints in the real world. A trail can be placed directly into the environment, but can also be shown on a map (Darken and Peterson 2002; Grammenos et al. 2002).

Audio and Olfactory Cues

Audio is another artificial wayfinding cue. For example, speech can be used to explain the route to a user, as in modern car navigation systems. As noted earlier, audio can also be coupled to objects to provide distance and directional cues or to uniquely identify an object. Imagine a dripping faucet to lead you to the virtual kitchen! Similarly, olfactory cues could be implemented—some objects have a distinct smell (a nasty smell like a factory or a pleasant one like a garden). Even though direction and distance can hardly be communicated via current olfactory interfaces, they, just like audio, can become a unique identifier.

7.5. Evaluating Wayfinding Aids

The performance of wayfinding aids and the usefulness of a VE for transferring spatial knowledge to the real world can be tested by a variety of methods (Darken and Peterson 2002). Figure 7.13 shows one setup that has been used to evaluate wayfinding performance. Although we discuss 3D UI evaluation in general in Chapter 11, here we discuss a few evaluation metrics that apply specifically to the evaluation of wayfinding.

Figure 7.13   *Wayfinding test environment. Using chroma keying, the pilot sees the real map and the cockpit as well as the VE. On the left is an image of a map study's results. (Images courtesy of the MOVES Institute, Naval Postgraduate School)*

First, *time-to-target* tests have been performed to analyze the user's movement time between two arbitrary points in a VE. This is a measure of the efficiency gains (or losses) provided by a wayfinding aid. Second, *path analysis* (see Figure 7.13, left) can be used to analyze the way the user moves through an environment. An ideal path should be predefined to which the comparison can be made. If a user turns around and retraces his movements several times, for example, then obviously the existing wayfinding aids are not sufficient.

Asking the user to draw *layout sketches* (simple maps) of an environment can be a powerful method of defining the quality of the spatial knowledge acquired during movement through the environment. These sketches are also an indication of the likelihood of transferring spatial knowledge from the VE to the real world. The sketches can be analyzed for the user's perception of the overall structure of the environment, including relative and absolute sizes of objects and spaces, the location of objects like landmarks, and directional information.

Most evaluations of the performance of wayfinding aids have focused on visual cues. Research on the performance of cues using other sensory channels and on the relationships between sensory channels are fruitful areas for future work.

7.6. Design Guidelines

Although guidelines specific to certain types of wayfinding aids have appeared throughout the chapter, here we collect some general guidelines. One particular area of focus is the relationship between travel techniques and wayfinding—how travel techniques affect wayfinding and how travel techniques can be improved to support wayfinding tasks.

> **Match the cue to the task.**

It is important that the characteristics of a wayfinding cue match the task requirements. For example, a map can be very powerful in a real-world setting like a landscape or building environment, but might simply be confusing in a more abstract environment.

> **Match the cue to users' skill.**

Experience influences the way that people find their way through an environment. Therefore, it also influences the way that we need to use wayfinding aids in a VE. For example, implementing landmarks can be an effective way of supporting novice users, while experts may choose not to use such cues.

> **Don't make cues dominant features.**

Subtlety is important, especially in environment design. When wayfinding cues become the dominant features in an environment, they may also turn out to be counterproductive. A cue should be seen as a tool to ease the user's navigation through an environment without being the sole point of information retrieval. For example, Darken and Sibert (1996) stated that the accentuated artificial landmarks in their environments led partly to users moving through the environment from one landmark to another. This may actually discourage the acquisition of spatial knowledge: a user may stick to a basic mental representation of the environment depending heavily on the dominant cue and missing other important spatial information about the environment.

> **Choose input devices providing real motion cues if possible.**

The choice of the input device used for travel can affect wayfinding performance to a considerable extent. Vestibular cues (real motion cues) support the egocentric reference frame—real motion cues deliver important distance information. When users can walk naturally by using a wide-area-tracking system or a locomotion device such as a treadmill (Chapter 6, section 6.3.2), vestibular cues are present. However, when purely virtual travel techniques are used, real motion cues are limited to physical rotation, or they are missing altogether. The lack of real-motion cues may lead to false distance perception and therefore more difficulty in wayfinding tasks.

> **Avoid teleportation.**

Travel techniques that teleport the user directly from one location to another are not recommended when applications require effective wayfinding. Users are often disoriented after teleportation because they need to rebuild their spatial awareness (Bowman et al. 1997). Even with target-based travel techniques, smooth motion from one location to another is preferred. The same study, however, found that velocity does not have a noticeable effect on spatial orientation. Thus, the intermediate motion can be at high speed as long as the environment remains recognizable.

> Integrate travel and wayfinding components.

Because travel and wayfinding are intimately linked, techniques for these two tasks should be integrated if possible. In some cases, devices like a treadmill allow this directly by coupling a method of travel with a vestibular-feedback component. Other techniques have inherent proprioceptive cues. Gaze-directed steering, for example, supplies directional information via headcentric cues. Wayfinding aids may actually be part of the travel technique. For example, the world-in-miniature technique combines a 3D map with a route-planning travel metaphor (Chapter 6, section 6.3.4). Finally, wayfinding aids can be placed in the environment near the focus of the user's attention during travel. For example, a small compass can be attached to the (real or virtual) tip of a stylus when the pointing technique (Chapter 6, section 6.3.3) is used.

7.7. Conclusion

Wayfinding is a complex issue. Because of the wide variety of different environments, with regard to both hardware and content, it can be challenging to support effective wayfinding. In this chapter, we looked at a variety of wayfinding aids, cues, and techniques, including solutions based on technology, training, environment design, and tools. 3D wayfinding research is still relatively immature. We encourage readers to experiment with different combinations of aids that may yield superior wayfinding performance.

Recommended Reading

For further information on perception and cognition, we recommend the following reading:

Anderson, J. (1983). *The Architecture of Cognition*, Harvard University Press.

Newell, A., P. Rosenbloom, and J. Laird (1989). Symbolic Architectures for Cognition. *Foundations in Cognitive Science*. M. Posner (Ed.), MIT Press, 93–131.

Kosslyn, S. (1993). *Image and Brain*, MIT Press.

Marr, D. (1982). *Vision*, W. H. Freeman.

Johnson-Laird, P. (1993). *The Computer and the Mind: An Introduction to Cognitive Science*, Fontana Press.

Winston, P. (1993). *Artificial Intelligence*, 3rd ed., Addison-Wesley.

For an introduction to the effects of the sense of presence on wayfinding, we recommend the following:

Usoh, M., K. Arthur, M. Whitton, R. Bastos, A. Steed, M. Slater, and F. Brooks Jr. (1999). Walking > Walking-in-Place > Flying in Virtual Environments. *Proceedings of SIGGRAPH '99*, ACM Press, 359–364.

Regenbrecht, H., T. Schubert, and F. Friedman (1998). Measuring the Sense of Presence and Its Relations to Fear of Heights in Virtual Environments. *International Journal of Human-Computer Interaction* 10(3): 233–250.

For an example of a study on the effects of wayfinding in training transfer, we recommend the following:

Darken, R., and W. Banker (1998). Navigating in Natural Environments: A Virtual Environment Training Transfer Study. *Proceedings of the 1998 IEEE Virtual Reality Annual International Symposium (VRAIS '98)*, IEEE Press, 12–19.

CHAPTER 8
System Control

In 2D interfaces, UI elements such as pull-down menus, pop-up menus, toolboxes, palettes, toggles, radio buttons, and checkboxes are everywhere. These elements are examples of *system control* techniques—they allow us to send commands to an application, change a mode, or modify a parameter. Although we don't think much about the design of such techniques in 2D UIs, system control interfaces for 3D UIs are not trivial. Simply adapting 2D desktop-based widgets is not the ultimate solution. In this chapter, we discuss and compare various system control solutions for 3D UIs.

8.1. Introduction

The issuing of *commands* is a critical way to access any computer system's functionality. For example, with traditional desktop computers, we may want to save a document or change from a brush tool to an eraser tool in a painting application. In order to perform such tasks, we use graphical user interface (GUI) system control techniques like menus or function keys on a keyboard. Research in desktop system control has provided us with a wealth of techniques, such as those used in the WIMP (Windows, Icons, Menus, and Pointers) metaphor (Preece et al. 2002).

Although much of the "real work" in a computer application consists of interaction tasks like selection, manipulation, and symbolic input, system control is critical because it is the "glue" that allows the user to control the interaction flow between the other key tasks in an application. For example, in writing this book with a word processor, the core activity is symbolic input, accomplished by typing on a keyboard. But this activity is interspersed with many small system control tasks—saving the current document by clicking on a button, inserting a picture by choosing an item from a menu, or underlining a piece of text by using a keyboard shortcut, just to name a few.

We can more precisely define system control as follows: System control is the user task in which a command is issued to

1. request the system to perform a particular function,
2. change the mode of interaction, or
3. change the system state.

The key word in this definition is *command*. In selection, manipulation, and travel tasks, the user typically specifies not only *what* should be done, but also *how* it should be done, more or less directly controlling the action. In system control tasks, the user typically specifies only *what* should be done and leaves it up to the system to determine the details. In part 1 of the definition, the system has a self-contained piece of functionality (e.g., for making plain text bold), and the user simply requests (commands) this function to be executed. Part 2 indicates a task such as choosing a new tool from a toolbox—nothing has changed besides the interaction mode. Changing the system state, part 3 of the definition, is exemplified by tasks such as clicking on a window to bring it to the front—that window becomes the "current window" in the system state, and subsequent actions are applied to it.

How can system control tasks be performed in 3D UIs? In 2D interfaces, system control is supported by the use of a specific *interaction style*, such as pull-down menus, text-based command lines, or tool palettes (Preece et al. 2002). Many of these interaction styles have also been adapted to 3D UIs (see section 8.3), which is certainly appropriate for desktop-based 3D UIs. In immersive and semi-immersive environments, however, WIMP-style interaction may not be effective in all situations. We cannot assume that simply transferring conventional interaction styles will lead to usability. In immersive VEs, users have to deal with 6-DOF input as opposed to 2 DOF on the desktop, and the input and output devices used in VEs differ considerably from the keyboard and mouse.

These differences create both new problems and new possibilities for system control. Therefore, in 3D UIs, it may be more appropriate to use *nonconventional* system control techniques (Bullinger et al. 1997).

What determines the success (usability and performance) of a system control technique in a 3D UI? Before describing specific techniques, let's consider three sets of factors that influence the effectiveness of all techniques: human factors, input devices, and system- and application-level factors.

8.1.1. Human Factors of System Control

When designing system controls, we can learn much from the design of mechanical systems (Bullinger et al. 1997). In mechanical systems, control refers to the transfer of mechanical energy or information to a system for performing control actions. The interaction between the control device and the human's body is called the *control-body linkage.* As with all other interaction techniques, the user's physical characteristics, training, and experience level affect the operating effectiveness of the control-body linkage. Other factors that often affect user performance in traditional mechanical control systems include the shape and size of controls, their visual representation and labeling, methods of selection, and underlying control structures.

Many of these factors can be applied directly to the design of system control techniques for 3D UIs. For example, think about a menu in which the user rotates her hand to select an item (a "1-DOF menu," see section 8.3.1). When designing this menu technique, we need to consider how the user can rotate her wrist, and the placement and size of the menu items that will lead to comfortable and efficient selection. When we design the menu poorly (e.g., when the user needs to turn her wrist to an uncomfortable position to select the items at the edges of the menu), the menu will not be very usable.

8.1.2. Input Devices

Many of the system control techniques described in this chapter are connected to particular input devices; for example, voice commands require use of a microphone. Hence, the properties of input devices influence the design of many system control interaction techniques. Some techniques, however, are device-independent.

The input devices used for system control techniques in 3D UIs can also have an effect on user performance and comfort. For example, a menu can be placed on a tracked physical surface, and the menu items can be selected with a tracked physical pen (the pen-and-tablet technique). The constraint provided by the physical surface will increase efficiency and accuracy. On the other hand, the user may tire more quickly when holding two physical devices.

The number and placement of buttons on input devices is a third factor that may influence the usability of system control techniques in 3D UIs. Multiple buttons allow "lightweight" mode switching and more flexibility of expression. The common context-sensitive menu in desktop interfaces, for example, is usually accessed via the right mouse button. However, multiple buttons can also lead to user confusion and error, especially if the mapping between buttons and functionality is inconsistent or unclear.

8.1.3. System- and Application-Level Factors

Factors related to the system's implementation can also influence the effectiveness of system control in a 3D UI. For example, recognition errors in speech or gesture interfaces can significantly reduce user performance and perceived usability.

The complexity of the application also plays an important role. With an increase in functionality, issuing commands becomes more difficult because the user needs to know how to access all the functionality of the system. The system can be structured to help the user in this task. In addition, system control techniques that work well for accessing 10 commands may be completely unusable if the number of commands swells to 100.

8.1.4. Chapter Roadmap

We begin this chapter with a classification of system control techniques for 3D UIs (section 8.2). Next, we describe each of the major categories in this classification (sections 8.3–8.6). In each of these sections, we describe representative techniques, discuss the relevant design and implementation issues, and provide guidance on the practical application of the techniques. In section 8.7, we cover multimodal system control techniques, which combine multiple methods of input to improve usability and performance. Section 8.8 describes some important design guidelines and the specific interrelationships between system control and other interaction techniques. Finally, a case study (section 8.9) serves as a real-world example of system control design in a 3D UI.

Note that the techniques described in this chapter come mostly from work in immersive VEs. In many cases, however, the techniques or the principles they represent might also be used in augmented reality or desktop 3D UIs.

8.2. Classification

Although there is a broad diversity of system control techniques for 3D UIs, many of them draw upon a small number of basic metaphors or their combination. Figure 8.1 presents a classification of techniques organized around these metaphors. This classification was also influenced by the description of nonconventional control techniques in McMillan et al. (1997). As was the case in the other chapters on 3D interaction techniques, this classification is only one of many possibilities, and alternatives have been proposed (e.g., Lindeman et al. 1999). However, we find this classification useful in understanding and discussing 3D system control techniques, and we use it as the organizing structure for the next four sections.

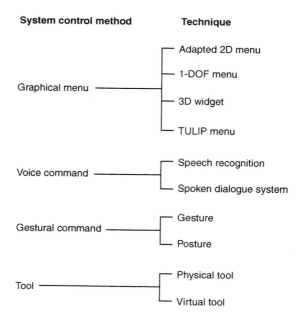

Figure 8.1 *Classification of system control techniques.*

8.3. Graphical Menus

Graphical menus for 3D UIs are the 3D equivalent of the 2D menus that have proven to be a successful system control technique in desktop UIs. Because of their success and familiarity to users, many developers have chosen to experiment with graphical menus for 3D UIs.

8.3.1. Techniques

In this section, we describe four techniques:

- adapted 2D menus
- 1-DOF menus
- TULIP menus
- 3D widgets

Adapted 2D Menus

Menus that are simple adaptations of their 2D counterparts have, for obvious reasons, been the most popular group of 3D system control techniques. These menus basically function in the same way as they do on the desktop. Some examples of adapted 2D menus are pull-down menus, pop-up menus, floating menus, and toolbars. Figure 8.2 shows an example of an adapted 2D menu used in a Virtual Museum application in a

Figure 8.2   *A floating menu in the Virtual Museum application. (Photograph courtesy of Gerhard Eckel, Fraunhofer IMK)*

surround-screen display. It allows a user to plan an exhibition by finding and selecting images of artwork. The menu is semitransparent to reduce occlusion of the 3D environment.

One adaptation of 2D menus that has been successful in 3D UIs is to attach the menus to the user's head—this way, the menu is always available, no matter where the user is looking. Another powerful technique is to attach the menu to a tracked physical surface (a tablet). Finding the menu is then as easy as bringing the physical tablet into view. The physical surface of the tablet also helps the user to select the menu items, and the menu can easily be put away as well.

The main advantage of adapted 2D menus is their familiar interaction style. Almost all users will instantly recognize these elements as menus and will understand how to use them. On the other hand, these menus can occlude the environment, and users may have trouble finding the menu or selecting items within it using a 3D selection technique (see section 8.3.2 for more on placement issues).

1-DOF Menus

Selection of an item from a menu is essentially a one-dimensional operation. This observation led to the development of *1-DOF menus*. A 1-DOF menu is often attached to the user's hand, with the menu items arranged in a circular pattern around it (Figure 8.3); this design led to the name *ring menu* (Liang and Green 1994; Shaw and Green 1994). With this design, the

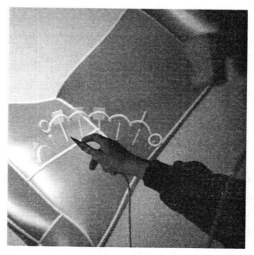

Figure 8.3   *A 1-DOF menu. (Photograph courtesy of Gerold Wesche, Fraunhofer IMK)*

user rotates his hand until the desired item falls within a "selection bas-ket." Of course, the hand rotation or movement can also be mapped onto a linear menu; it does not have to be circular. The performance of a ring menu depends on the physical movement of the hand and wrist, and the primary axis of rotation should be carefully chosen. Of course, hand rota-tion is only one possible way to select an item in a 1-DOF ring menu. For example, the user could rotate the desired item into position with the use of a button or buttons on the input device.

Handheld widgets are another type of 1-DOF menu. These do not use rotation, but instead relative hand position (Mine et al. 1997). By moving the hands closer together or further apart, different items in the menu can be selected.

In general, 1-DOF menus are quite easy to use. Menu items can be se-lected quickly, as long as the number of items is relatively small. Because of the strong placement cue, 1-DOF menus also afford rapid access and use—the user does not have to find the menu if it is attached to his hand and does not have to switch his focus away from the area in which he is performing actions.

TULIP Menus

Another method of attaching a menu to the user's hand in a 3D UI is to assign menu items to different fingers. Using Pinch Gloves (see Chap-ter 4, section 4.3.3), the system can interpret a pinch between a finger and the thumb on the same hand as a menu selection. If there are no more than eight menu items, this technique works very well. Up to 16 menu items can be accommodated if the items are organized into four menus with four items each—the nondominant hand can be used to select a menu, and the dominant hand to select an item within the menu.

In many applications, however, there will be many more than 16 menu items. The TULIP (Three-Up, Labels In Palm) technique was de-signed to address this problem (Bowman and Wingrave 2001). In TULIP (Figure 8.4), when there are more than four items in a menu, the first three items are displayed, attached to the user's index, middle, and ring fin-gers. The pinky finger is labeled "more," and selecting this item moves the next three items in the menu onto the user's fingers. All of the inactive items are displayed, in groups of three, on the palm of the virtual hand. In this way, the selection of items is still direct, and users can see all of the items and how to access them. An empirical study has shown that this technique is moderately efficient, comfortable, and easy to use (Bowman and Wingrave 2001).

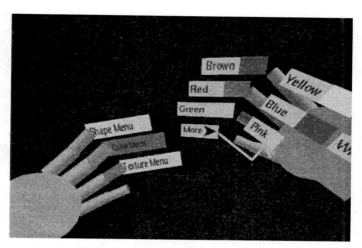

Figure 8.4 *TULIP menus. (Bowman and Wingrave 2001, © 2001 IEEE)*

3D Widgets

The most exotic group of graphical menu techniques for system control are 3D widgets. They take advantage of the extra DOF available in a 3D environment to enable more complex menu structures or better visual affordances for menu entries. We distinguish between two kinds of 3D widgets: colocated (context-sensitive) widgets and non-context-sensitive widgets.

With colocated widgets, the functionality of a menu is moved onto an object in the 3D environment, and geometry and functionality are strongly coupled. Conner and colleagues (1992) refer to widgets as "the combination of geometry and behavior." For example, suppose a user wishes to manipulate a simple geometric object like a box. We could design an interface in which the user first chooses a manipulation mode (e.g., translation, scaling, rotation) from a menu, and then manipulates the box directly. With colocated 3D widgets, however, we can place the menu items directly on the box—menu functionality is directly connected to the object (Figure 8.5). To scale the box, the user simply selects and moves the scaling widget, thus combining the mode selection and the manipulation into a single step. The widgets are context-sensitive; only those widgets that apply to an object appear when the object is selected. As in the example, colocated widgets are typically used for changing geometric parameters.

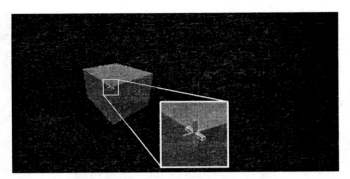

Figure 8.5 *A 3D colocated widget for scaling an object. (Image courtesy of Andrew Forsberg, Brown University Computer Graphics Group)*

A variety of colocated 3D widgets are shown in the context of a scientific visualization application in Figure 8.6: the widget near the front of the space shuttle is used to change the number of streamlines used to examine the flow field, as well as their location in 3D space. The widget near the rear of the space shuttle is used to adjust the size and location of a color plane.

The command and control cube, or C^3 (Grosjean et al. 2002), is a more general-purpose type of 3D widget (non-context-sensitive). The C^3 (Figure 8.7) is a $3 \times 3 \times 3$ cubic grid, where each of the 27 grid cubes is a menu

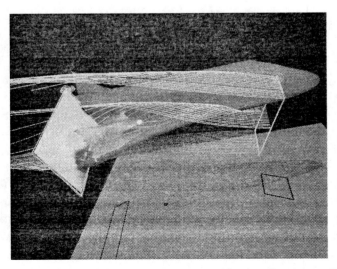

Figure 8.6 *A variety of 3D widgets used in a scientific visualization application. (Image courtesy of Andrew Forsberg, Brown University Computer Graphics Group)*

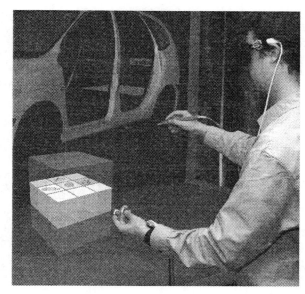

Figure 8.7   *The command and control cube. (i3D-INRIA. Data © Renault. Photograph courtesy of Jerome Grosjean)*

item. The user brings up the menu by pressing a button or making a pinch on a Pinch Glove; the menu appears, centered on the user's hand. Then the user moves his hand in the direction of the desired menu item cube relative to the center position, and releases the button or the pinch. This is similar in concept to the "marking menus" (Kurtenbach and Buxton 1991) used in software such as Maya from Alias.

8.3.2. Design and Implementation Issues

There are many considerations when designing or implementing graphical menus as system control techniques in a 3D UI. We discuss the issues of placement, selection, representation, and structure.

Placement

The placement of the menu influences the user's ability to access the menu (good placement provides a spatial reference) and the amount of occlusion of the environment. We can consider menus that are *world-referenced, object-referenced, head-referenced, body-referenced,* or *device-referenced* (adapted from the classification in Feiner et al. [1993]).

World-referenced menus are placed at a fixed location in the virtual world, while object-referenced menus are attached to an object in the 3D scene. Although not useful for most general-purpose menus, these may be useful as colocated 3D widgets.

Head-referenced or body-referenced menus, such as TULIP menus (attached to the hand), provide a strong spatial reference frame: the user can easily find the menu. Mine, Brooks, and Séquin (1997) explored body-referenced menus and found that the user's proprioceptive sense (sense of the relative locations of the parts of the body in space) can significantly enhance menu retrieval and usage. Body-referenced menus may even enable eyes-off usage, allowing users to perform system control tasks without having to look at the menu.

The last reference frame is the group of device-referenced menus. For example, on a workbench display, menus may be placed on the border of the display device. The display screen provides a physical surface for menu selection as well as a strong spatial reference.

Selection

Traditionally, desktop menus make use of a 2D selection method (mouse-based). In a 3D UI, we encounter the problem of using a 3D selection method with these 2D (or 1D) menus. This makes interaction with the system control interface particularly difficult. In order to address this problem, several alternative selection methods have been developed that simply constrain the DOF of the system control interface, considerably improving performance. For example, when an adapted 2D menu is shown, one can discard all tracker data except the 2D projection of the tracker on the plane of the menu. Two-DOF selection techniques such as ray-casting or image-plane selection also address this issue (see Chapter 5). Finally, the menu can be placed on a physical 2D surface such as a screen or a tracked tablet in order to reduce the DOF of the selection task (see Chapter 10).

Representation and Structure

Another important issue in developing a graphical menu is its representation: how are the items represented visually, and if there are many items, how are they structured?

Because of the technology used in VEs, the size of items and the space between them is very important. Do not make items and inter-item distances too small, or the user might have problems selecting the items. The more complex the application gets, the more functions will be available. Make sure to structure the interface by using either functional grouping (items with similar function are clustered) or sequential grouping (using the natural sequence of operations to structure items), or by using context-sensitive menus so that only the applicable functions are displayed when the user accesses the menu. Finally, control coding, which uses different colors, shapes, surfaces, textures, dimensions, positions, text, and symbols to differentiate items, can give an extra cue about the relations between different items and therefore make the structure and the hierarchy of the items more clear (Bullinger et al. 1997).

8.3.3. Practical Application

Menu techniques can be very powerful in 3D UIs when their limitations can be overcome. Selection of menu items should be easy, and the menu should not overlap too much with the workspace in which the user is working. Especially with applications that have a large number of functions, a menu is probably the best choice of all the system control techniques for 3D UIs. Finally, if the 3D graphical menus presented here are simply not usable enough for a particular application, developers may choose to use *remote menus* on a dedicated 2D device like a PDA or tablet PC (Figure 8.8). This approach works only when users can see the physical world (i.e., not in an HMD-based system), but it helps to ensure usability.

Figure 8.8 *User in the iCone display system using a remote interface. (Photograph courtesy of Fraunhofer IMK)*

Of course, this type of setup is also more expensive, more cumbersome, and perhaps more difficult to implement.

8.4. Voice Commands

The issuing of voice commands can be performed via simple speech recognition or by means of spoken dialogue techniques. Speech recognition techniques are typically used for issuing single commands to the system, while a spoken dialogue technique is focused on promoting discourse between the user and the system.

8.4.1. Techniques

A spoken dialogue system provides an interface between a user and a computer-based application that permits spoken interaction with the application in a relatively natural manner (McTear 2002). The most critical component of a spoken dialogue system (and of simple speech recognition techniques) is the *speech recognition engine.* A wide range of factors influences the speech recognition rate, such as variability among speakers and background noise. The recognition engine can be speaker-dependent, requiring initial training of the system, or speaker-independent, which normally does not require training. Systems also differ in the size of their vocabulary. The response generated as output to the user can confirm that an action has been performed or inform the user that more input is needed so as to complete a control command. In a spoken dialogue system, the response should be adapted to the flow of discourse (requiring a dialogue control mechanism) and generated as artificial speech.

Current speech recognition packages include IBM ViaVoice and BBN HARK, while current spoken dialogue systems include CSLU toolkit, IBM Voice Server SDK, Speechworks, and Unisys Natural Language Speech Assistant. More information on these systems, including references to academic work, can be found in McTear (2002).

Many 3D UIs that use speech recognition also include other complementary input methods (e.g., Billinghurst 1998). These techniques are labeled *multimodal* and are discussed in section 8.7.

8.4.2. Design and Implementation Issues

The development of a 3D UI using simplified speech recognition or the more complex spoken dialogue systems involves many factors. A developer should start by defining which tasks need to be performed via voice interfaces. For an application with a limited number of functions, a normal speech recognition system will probably work well. The task will define the vocabulary size of the speech engine—the more complex the task and the domain in which it is performed, the more likely it is that the vocabulary size will increase. Highly complex applications may need conversational UIs via a spoken dialogue system in order to ensure that the full functionality of voice input is accessible. In the case of a spoken dialogue system, it should also be considered what vocal information the user needs to provide in order for the system to determine the user's intentions.

Developers should be aware that voice interfaces are *invisible to the user.* The user is normally not presented with an overview of the functions that can be performed via a speech interface. Therefore, in order to grasp the actual intentions of the user, one of the key factors is verification. Either by error correction via semantic and syntactic filtering (prediction methods that use the semantics or syntax of a sentence to limit the possible interpretation) or by a formal discourse model (question-and-answer mechanism), the system must ensure that it understands what the user wants.

Unlike other system control techniques, speech-based techniques initialize, select, and issue a command "all at once." Sometimes, another input stream (like a button press) or a specific voice command should be used to initialize the speech system. This disambiguates the start of a voice input and is called a push-to-talk system (also see Chapter 4, section 4.6.1). Error rates will increase when the application involves direct communication between multiple participants. For instance, a comment to a colleague can easily be misunderstood as a voice command to a system. Therefore, one should separate human–human and human–computer interaction when designing speech interfaces. Syntactic differences between personal communication and system interaction might be used to distinguish between voice streams (Shneiderman 2000).

8.4.3. Practical Application

Speech input as a system control technique in a 3D UI can be very powerful—it is hands-free and natural. Still, continuous voice input is tiring and cannot be used in every environment.

Unless a spoken dialogue system is used, the user first needs to learn the voice commands before they can be issued. A user can easily learn simple commands for a limited number of functions. However, voice commands are probably not very useful in applications that allow only short learning times or no learning at all.

Finally, we note that similar interface issues have been studied in many different contexts. For example, speech commands for controlling a system via a telephone poses many of the same problems as using voice commands in a 3D UI. Please refer to Brewster (1998) for further discussion of issues involved in such communication streams.

8.5. Gestural Commands

Gestures were one of the first system control techniques for VEs and other 3D environments. Ever since early projects like Krueger's Videoplace (Krueger et al. 1985), developers have been fascinated by using the hands as direct input, almost as if one is not using an input device at all. Gestural commands can be classified as either *postures* or *gestures*. A posture is a static configuration of the hand (Figure 8.9), whereas a gesture is a dynamic movement. An example of a posture is holding the fingers in a V-like configuration (the "peace" sign), whereas waving and drawing are examples of gestures. The usability of gestures and postures for system

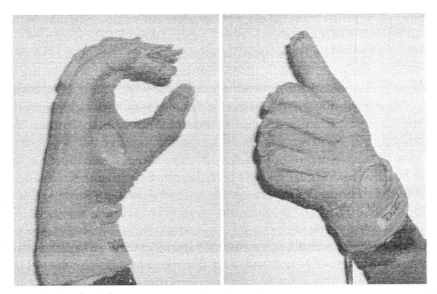

Figure 8.9   *Examples of postures using a DataGlove. (Photograph courtesy of Joseph J. LaViola Jr.)*

control depends on the number and complexity of the gestural commands—more gestures imply more learning for the user.

8.5.1. Techniques

One of the best examples to illustrate the diversity of gestural commands is Polyshop (later Multigen's SmartScene; Mapes and Moshell 1995). In this VE application, all interaction was specified by postures and gestures, from navigation to the use of menus. For example, the user could move forward by pinching an imaginary rope and pulling herself along it (the "grabbing the air" technique—see Chapter 6). As this example shows, system control overlaps with manipulation and navigation in such a 3D UI. Consider the definition of system control as being the "change of mode of interaction." In Polyshop, the switch to navigation mode is lightweight and effective because no "active" change of mode is performed.

In everyday life, we use many different types of gestures (Mulder 1996; Kendon 1988), and these categories also apply to the use of gestures in 3D UIs:

- *Speech-connected hand gestures:* Spontaneous gesticulation performed unintentionally during speech or language-like gestures that are integrated in the speech performance. Speech-connected gestures have been studied intensely in HCI and applied to multimodal interfaces (e.g., Bolt 1980).

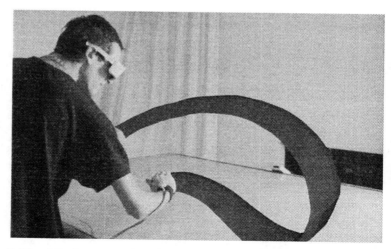

Figure 8.10   *Mimic gesture. (Schkolne et al. 2001; © 2001 ACM; reprinted by permission)*

- *Mimic gestures:* Gestures that are not connected to speech but are directly used to "describe" a concept. For example, Figure 8.10 shows a sweeping gesture in 3D space that defines a curved surface (Schkolne et al. 2001).
- *Symbolic gestures:* Gestures as used in daily life to express things like insults or praise (e.g., "thumbs up")
- *Sign language:* The use of a specified set of postures and gestures in communicating with hearing-impaired people. At least one 3D UI project has used sign language–like gestures for communication (Fels 1994).

8.5.2. Design and Implementation Issues

The implementation of gestural input is usually tied to the input device used. Here are the major types of gesture input techniques:

- *Glove-based recognition:* The raw data coming from glove devices (see Chapter 4, section 4.4.3) is analyzed by recognition algorithms such as hidden Markov models and neural networks. The hand has been used as button, valuator, locator, and pick device (Zimmerman et al. 1987; Sturman et al. 1989). Pinch Gloves can be used for limited postures, while DataGloves provide both postures and gestures using joint-angle measurements.
- *Camera-based recognition:* Video images of hand or finger gestures can be analyzed by using computer vision methods to recognize specific configurations of the hand (Starner et al. 1998).
- *Surface-based recognition:* Display screens, touch screens, or other flat surfaces can be used for gestures (Rekimoto 2002). Typically, a penlike device is used to make gestures on the flat surface. Here, the gestures do not involve the whole hand at all, but rather the strokes created by the pen (Figure 8.11).

Gesture-based system control shares many of the characteristics of speech input discussed in the previous section. Like speech, a gestural command combines initialization, selection, and issuing of the command. In addition, the available gestures in the system are typically invisible to the user. Finally, the user may have trouble remembering a large number of gestures. Thus, as with push-to-talk in speech inter-

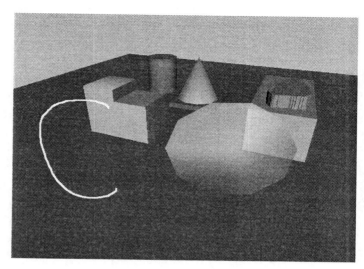

Figure 8.11 *A C-gesture used to select the color picker in the SKETCH application. (Zeleznik et al. 1996; image courtesy of Brown University Computer Graphics Group)*

faces, the UI designer should ensure that the user really intends to issue a gestural command via some implicit or explicit mechanism (this could be called a "push-to-gesture" technique). The number of gestures should be limited, and they should be highly learnable. The system should also provide adequate feedback to the user when a gesture is recognized.

8.5.3. Practical Application

Gestural commands have significant appeal for system control in 3D UIs because of their important role in our day-to-day lives. However, with a few notable exceptions, such as the surface-based gestural interfaces of Teddy (Igarashi et al. 1999) and SKETCH (Zeleznik 1996), purely gestural system control interfaces have not been extremely successful. Choose gestural commands if the application domain already has a set of well-defined, natural, easy-to-understand, and easy-to-recognize gestures. In addition, gestures may be more useful in combination with another type of input (see section 8.7). For further reading on gestural interaction, please refer to Bordegoni and Hemmje (1993), Mapes and Moshell (1995), and LaViola (1999a).

8.6. Tools

In many 3D applications, the use of familiar (real-world) devices for 3D interaction can lead to increased usability. These devices, often called *tools*, provide directness of interaction because of their real-world correspondence. Although individual tools may be used for selection, manipulation, travel, or other 3D interaction tasks, we consider a set of tools in a single application to be a system control technique. Like the tool palettes in many popular 2D drawing applications, tools in 3D UIs provide a simple and intuitive technique for changing the mode of interaction: simply select an appropriate tool.

We distinguish between two kinds of tools: physical tools and virtual tools. Physical tools are a collection of real physical objects (with corresponding virtual representations) that are also sometimes called *props*. A physical tool might be space-multiplexed (the tool performs only one function) or time-multiplexed (the tool performs multiple functions over time). A user accesses a physical tool by simply picking it up and using it.

Virtual tools have no physical instantiation. This can best be exemplified with a "tool belt" technique (Figure 8.12).

Figure 8.12   *Tool belt menu. Note that the tool belt appears larger than normal because the photograph was not taken from the user's perspective. (Photograph reprinted from Forsberg et al. [2000], © 2000 IEEE)*

8.6.1. Techniques

A wide range of purely virtual tool belts exists, but they are largely undocumented in the literature. Therefore, we focus on the use of physical tools, as used for system control in 3D UIs, in this section. A more general discussion of prop-based interaction can be found in Chapter 10.

Based on the idea of props, a whole range of tangible user interfaces (TUIs) has appeared. TUIs make use of real-world objects to perform actions in a VE (Ullmer and Ishii 2001; Fitzmaurice et al. 1995). A TUI uses physical elements that represent a specific kind of action in order to interact with an application. For example, the user could use a real eraser to delete virtual objects or a real pencil to draw in the virtual space.

Figure 8.13 shows a TUI for 3D interaction. Here, Ethernet-linked "interaction pads" representing different operations are used together with radio frequency identification (RFID) tagged physical cards, blocks, and wheels, which represent network-based data, parameters, tools, people,

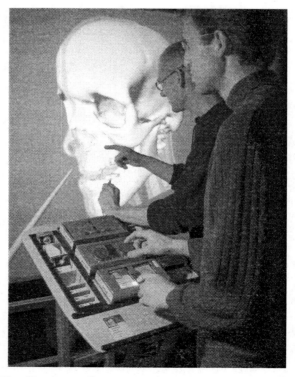

Figure 8.13 *Visualization artifacts—physical tools for mediating interaction with 3D UIs. (Image courtesy of Brygg Ullmer and Stefan Zachow, Zuse Institute Berlin)*

and applications. Designed for use in immersive 3D environments as well as on the desktop, these physical devices ease access to key information and operations. When used with immersive VEs, they allow one hand to continuously manipulate a tracking wand or stylus, while the second hand can be used in parallel to load and save data, steer parameters, activate teleconference links, and perform other operations. Functioning prototypes of this sort are beginning to be used by physicians and astrophysicists.

A TUI takes the approach of combining representation and control. This implies the combination of both physical representations and digital representations, or the fusion of input and output in one mediator. TUIs have the following key characteristics (from Ullmer and Ishii 2001):

- Physical representations are computationally coupled to underlying digital information.
- Physical representations embody mechanisms for interactive control.
- Physical representations are perceptually coupled to actively mediated digital representation.

These ideas can be applied to develop prop-based "physical menus." In HMD-based VEs, for example, a tracked pen can be used to select from a virtual menu placed on a tracked tablet (Bowman and Wingrave 2001). In a projection-based VE, a transparent physical tablet can be used to achieve the same effect—the menu is displayed on the visual output device (projection screen) but is correctly aligned with the tablet so that the user sees the menu appear on the tablet. An example of this approach is the Personal Interaction Panel (Schmalsteig et al. 1999).

The principal advantage of displaying a menu on a tablet is the direct haptic feedback to the user who interacts with the menu. This results in far fewer selection problems compared to a menu that simply floats in the VE space.

An example of a slightly more sophisticated approach to using props and tools is the Virtual Tricorder (Wloka and Greenfield 1995). In this technique, a real physical 3D mouse is registered to its virtual copy inside the VE (Figure 8.14). By pressing buttons on the mouse, the user can access the menu and choose the desired tool from it. The functionality and virtual 3D appearance of the mouse then changes according to the selected tool. The strength of this approach is that it produces a single multipurpose tool for 3D interaction.

Figure 8.14 *The Virtual Tricorder. (Image reprinted with permission from van Dam et al. [2000]; © 2000 IEEE)*

8.6.2. Design and Implementation Issues

The form of the tool communicates the function the user can perform with the tool, so carefully consider the form when developing props. A general approach is to imitate a traditional control design, for example, in machinery design. Another approach is to duplicate everyday tools in the VE. The user makes use of either the real tool or something closely resembling the tool in order to manipulate objects in a VE.

Another important issue is the *compliance* between the real and virtual worlds (Hinckley et al. 1994). Some prop-based interfaces, like the Cubic Mouse (Fröhlich and Plate 2000), have demonstrated a need for a *clutching* mechanism. See Chapter 5 for more information on compliance and clutching in manipulation techniques.

The use of props naturally affords blind operation (the user can operate the device by touch), which may have significant advantages, especially when the user needs to focus visual attention on another task. On the other hand, it also means that the prop must be designed to allow tactile interaction. A simple tracked tablet, for example, does not indicate the locations of menu items with haptic cues; it only indicates the general location of the menu.

A specific issue for physical menus is that the user may want to place the menu out of sight when it is not in use. The designer may choose to put a clip on the tablet so that the user can attach it to his clothing, may reserve a special place in the display environment for it, or may simply provide a handle on the tablet so it can be held comfortably at the user's side.

8.6.3. Practical Application

Physical tools are very specific devices. In many cases, they perform only one function. In applications with a great deal of functionality, tools can still be useful, but they may not apply to all the user tasks. There is a trade-off between the specificity of the tool (a good affordance for its function) and the amount of tool switching the user will have to do. Performing a simple user study will quickly reveal any problems with device switching.

Public installations of VEs (e.g., in museums) can greatly benefit from the use of tools. Users of public installations by definition must be able to use the interface immediately. Tools tend to allow exactly this. A well-designed tool has a strong affordance, and users may draw from personal experience with a similar device in real life. Many theme park installations make use of props to allow the user to begin playing right away. For example, the Pirates of the Caribbean ride at DisneyQuest uses a physical steering wheel and cannons. This application has almost no learning curve—including the vocal introduction, users can start interacting with the environment in less than a minute.

8.7. Multimodal System Control Techniques

The classification of system control techniques presented in Figure 8.1 does not contain the last group of system control techniques: *multimodal techniques,* which combine multiple input streams. In certain situations, the use of multimodal system control techniques can significantly increase the effectiveness of system control tasks.

Multimodal interaction is the use of multiple input channels (e.g., speech and gesture) to control a system. Following are some of the advantages for using multimodal system control in VEs:

- *Decoupling:* Using an input channel that differs from the main input channel used for interaction with the environment, can decrease user cognitive load. If users do not have to switch between manipulation and system control actions, they can keep their attention focused on their main activity.

- *Error reduction and correction:* The use of multiple input channels can be very effective when the input is ambiguous or noisy, especially with recognition-based input like speech or gestures. The combination of input from several channels can significantly increase recognition rate (Oviatt 1999; Oviatt and Cohen 2000).

- *Flexibility and complementary behavior:* Control is more flexible when users can use multiple input channels to perform the same task. In addition, different modalities can be used in a complementary way based on the perceptual structure of the task (Grasso et al. 1998; Jacob and Sibert 1992).

- *Control of mental resources:* Multimodal interaction can be used to reduce cognitive load (Rosenfeld et al. 2001); on the other hand, it may also lead to less effective interaction because multiple mental resources need to be accessed simultaneously. For example, as Shneiderman (2000) observes, the part of the human brain used for speaking and listening is the same one as used for problem solving—speaking consumes precious cognitive resources.

Probably the best-known multimodal technique is the famous "put-that-there" technique (Bolt 1980). Using this technique, users can perform actions by combining pointing with speech. Many others have used the same combination of gesture and speech (e.g., Figures 8.15 and 8.16). In some cases speech can be used to disambiguate a gesture, and vice versa.

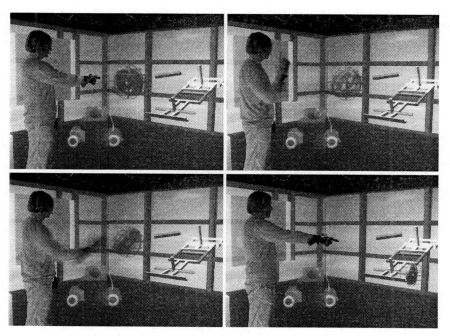

Figure 8.15 *A car wheel is selected, rotated, and moved to its correct position using voice and gestures. (Photographs courtesy of Marc Eric Latoschik, AI & VR Lab, University of Bielefeld; Latoschik 2001)*

Figure 8.16 *A multimodal interface that combines hand gestures and speech used for scientific visualization. (Photograph reprinted from van Dam et al. [2000]; © 2000 IEEE)*

Another possible technique is to combine gesture-based techniques with traditional menus, as in the "marking menus" technique. This means that novice users can select a command from a menu, while more experienced users can access commands directly via gestural input. This redundancy is similar to the use of keyboard shortcuts in desktop interfaces.

8.8. Design Guidelines

Throughout this chapter, we have presented many design guidelines for specific 3D system control techniques. In this section, we summarize some overall guidelines. Because of the relative lack of empirical evaluations of system control techniques for 3D UIs, however, these guidelines are primarily based on anecdotal evidence and personal experience. For now, therefore, most of the guidelines should be regarded as rules of thumb.

> Avoid disturbing the flow of action of an interaction task.

System control is often integrated with another 3D interaction task. Such a task structure forms a "chain of actions." Because of this integration, system control techniques should be designed to avoid disturbing the flow of action of an interaction task. Lightweight mode switching, physical tools, and multimodal techniques can all be used to maintain the flow of action.

> **Prevent unnecessary changes of the focus of attention.**

One of the major interruptions to a flow of action is a change of attentional focus. This may occur when users have to cognitively and/or physically switch between the actual working area and a system control technique, or even when they must look away to switch devices.

> **Avoid mode errors.**

Always provide clear feedback to the user so that she knows which interaction mode is currently active.

> **Use an appropriate spatial reference frame.**

Placing your system control technique in the "right position" can make a big difference in its usability. Users often get distracted when searching for a way to change the mode of interaction or issue a command. If the controls are not visible at all, placed far away from the actual focal area, or not oriented toward the user, the result will be wasted time. On the other hand, system controls attached to the user's hand, body, or a device are always available.

> **Structure the functions in an application.**

There are several good techniques for structuring the functionality of an application, including hierarchical menu structures and context-sensitive system control. In cases where the number of functions is so large that these techniques are not effective, it can make sense to place some of the system control functionality on another device, such as a PDA, where resolution and selection accuracy are less of an issue.

> Consider using multimodal input.

Using multimodal input can provide more fluid and efficient system control but can also have its drawbacks.

8.9. Case Study: Mixing System Control Methods

System control in 3D UIs is a complex topic, and the techniques for it are wide-ranging. Thus, it is useful to examine a case study of system control techniques in a complex 3D application in order to illuminate some of the important issues involved in system control design for 3D UIs.

8.9.1. The ProViT Application

The case study examines a VE application called ProViT (Kruijff et al. 2003). This application is a distributed engineering environment in which several remote collaborators cooperate on complex design review tasks. The application allows users to run simulations, manipulate 3D objects, access data from other applications, and communicate with one another via videoconferencing, all within the context of an immersive VE.

ProViT uses two display devices: a large stereoscopic L-shaped workbench (Figure 8.17) and a 12-inch tablet PC (Figure 8.18). It also uses three

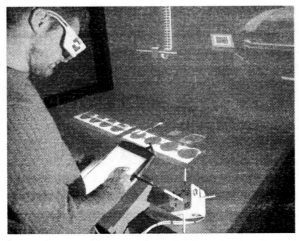

Figure 8.17   *A user controlling the distributed engineering application. (Photograph courtesy of Ernst Kruijff)*

Figure 8.18 *Remote user interface. (Photograph courtesy of Stefan Conrad, Fraunhofer IMK)*

input devices: a tracked stylus, a Cubic Mouse (see Chapter 4, section 4.4), and the tablet PC.

8.9.2. System Control Design Approach for ProViT

The high-level approach used in designing the 3D UI for this application was to separate the 3D and 2D interaction. Predictably, the inherently 3D actions are performed with the stylus or the Cubic Mouse, whereas 2D actions (like numeric input) are done via the tablet PC. This use of multiple devices to control the application could result in increased performance, but also creates a more complex input structure, which needs to be supported by techniques for maintaining the flow of action.

8.9.3. Mapping of Tasks to Devices

Considering the functions that this application must support, a 3D UI could have been designed that supported all of the functionality with a single device. In fact, this would have been similar to most other complex VE applications. The designers felt, however, that efficiency and usability could be improved with the use of multiple devices, even if users sometimes had to stop what they were doing to switch devices.

The mapping of tasks to devices has a direct effect on the usability of system control tasks. In this application, the three devices have different inherent features and limitations for system control. The tablet PC brings with it a wide range of highly optimized 2D system control techniques. The Cubic Mouse has a large number of physical buttons, but these buttons have few natural mappings to functions. The stylus must make use of virtual system control techniques because it has only a single button. In this application, the designers decided to use a hand-referenced 1-DOF menu (section 8.3.1) with the stylus.

Two of the devices can be used together: the stylus can be used to interact directly with the tablet PC. This eliminates the need to put down the stylus or pick up another device to access the 2D GUI.

Some functions, like navigation, were explicitly mapped to multiple devices to avoid device switching. For example, the user often needs to change the viewpoint in between manipulation actions. If the navigation function were mapped only to one device, this would automatically result in frequent device switching. In the current design, the user can use either the Cubic Mouse or the stylus for 3D navigation.

8.9.4. Placement of System Control

The second main issue in this application is the placement of its visible elements. The main working area and main focus of attention is the center of the workbench. In general, the designers wanted the user to be able to maintain focus on this area. In addition, this area should not be highly occluded by system control elements or widgets. These two goals are somewhat in conflict.

The hand-referenced 1-DOF menu addresses the first goal. It appears attached to the stylus, which is usually located in or near the working area. The user can always find the menu—no visual search is required—but this menu might occlude the VE content.

The GUI elements on the tablet PC meet the second goal. It places menus and complex information in one place (a display attached to the front of the workbench), and this information does not occlude the VE content. However, to use the tablet PC, the user must shift focus from one area to another, requiring significant head movements as the user performs an action in the GUI and then verifies that action in the 3D environment.

8.9.5. **System Control Feedback**

Finally, it is of utmost importance that feedback to the user is robust and understandable. Because of the multiple input devices used in this application, the designers provide feedback that does not depend on the input device in use. Instead, the feedback is attached to one of the displays and is consistent no matter what device or function the user happens to be using.

One very simple solution is a mode cue that is displayed in a small text bar in a corner of the workbench. The text bar shows the current interaction mode and is placed close to the user's working area. The second approach is to use the GUI on the tablet PC as a feedback method. Because the GUI is constantly synchronized with the VE application, the user can always look at the GUI in order to obtain a direct and detailed overview of the state of the system.

8.10. **Conclusion**

System control for 3D UIs is only in its infancy as a research topic. Although we have discussed a wide range of techniques, the design space for such techniques is virtually limitless. We expect to see many new and interesting 3D system control techniques, not only within the categories described here, but also in new categories that have not yet been invented. There is also a lack of good empirical evidence for the usability of various system control techniques at the present time—usability evaluations are desperately needed in order to validate current design guidelines and develop new ones. Nevertheless, this chapter has served to demonstrate the importance and complexity of system control interfaces and has presented a wide range of existing system control techniques for 3D UIs.

Recommended Reading

A general introduction to system control issues from a human factors background can be found in the following:

Bullinger, H., P. Kern, and M. Braun (1997). Controls. *Handbook of Human Factors and Ergonomics*. G. Salvendy (Ed.), John Wiley & Sons, 697–728.

CHAPTER 9
Symbolic Input

We turn our attention in this chapter to the task of symbolic input, a 3D interaction task that has been studied relatively little compared to travel, wayfinding, selection, manipulation, and system control. Symbolic input is the task in which users communicate symbolic information (text, numbers, and other symbols or marks) to the system. Everyone who uses computers performs symbolic input tasks constantly—writing email messages, entering numbers into a spreadsheet, composing documents, and so on. The importance of symbolic input in 2D interfaces is clear, but why is symbolic input an important task in 3D UIs?

9.1. Introduction

Symbolic communication—the use of abstract symbols to represent objects, ideas, concepts, quantities, and the like—is one of the crowning achievements of human civilization. It allows us to provide and obtain information precisely and concisely; it allows information to be persistent; it provides for methods of thought not possible without symbols. Imagine what it would be like to live in a world without language or mathematics! Symbolic communication pervades everything we do.

It is strange, then, that symbolic communication in most 3D interfaces is either nonexistent or limited to one-way communication. Many 3D applications, such as architectural walkthroughs, neither present nor accept symbolic information; rather, they present a purely geometric and visual world for the user to perceive. Of the 3D applications that do include symbolic information, most provide symbolic output only. That is, text, numbers, or speech are embedded in the environment. This might take the form of labels on virtual buttons, a legend on a map, a numeric display of the user's coordinates, or audio help, to name a few examples. Symbolic input, however, is rarely present.

9.1.1. Why Is Symbolic Input Important?

We claim that a lack of symbolic input in 3D interfaces does not mean that the task is unimportant for 3D applications, but rather that usable and efficient techniques for this task are difficult to design and implement, which has caused developers to largely avoid the issue. We posed the question, Is text/number entry an important task for VEs? on the 3D UI mailing list, an online community whose membership includes many of the key researchers in the field of 3D interaction worldwide. This question sparked the longest discussion thread ever on the mailing list. Although no one envisioned word processing systems in a VE, all of the respondents agreed that text input for immersive VEs was an important research area. Many of them also suggested novel techniques that might be attempted, including split, wearable keyboards and hand gestures.

9.1.2. Scenarios of Use

In order to further demonstrate the potential importance of symbolic input for 3D UIs, we discuss several realistic scenarios of use. The scenarios involve immersive VEs or augmented environments where a general text/number-input technique would be needed and where speech input alone would likely not suffice. The list of scenarios includes the following:

- *Design annotation:* Suppose an architect develops a new design for the atrium of a building. He sends the 3D model to his clients, who walk through the new design in a VE. During the walkthrough, clients wish to annotate the design with questions, suggestions, or change orders. Speech could be used for this application, but a text/number-entry technique would allow for greater precision, the ability to edit the annotation, the ability to use nonspeech elements such as URLs or numeric measurements, and better understanding of the annotation when it is read.

- *Filename entry:* Many immersive systems that allow the user to add new elements to the environment or modify objects in the environment need the ability to open and save files, similar to text editors or other 2D applications. Because filenames are often nonwords, a general symbolic input technique is needed for this task.

- *Labeling:* Another type of annotation is the task of adding labels to objects in virtual or augmented environments. For example, the user of a mobile augmented reality system might be able to provide further augmentation by adding labels to objects she sees in the world.

- *Precise object manipulation:* In certain situations, the typical freeform object manipulation techniques (Chapter 5) may not provide enough precision. For example, if the user is designing an engineering model that will be used to produce a physical part, precise position, thickness, length, and other dimensions will be needed. Rough manipulation could be performed with a direct technique, but the final values may need to be entered numerically. This scenario is analogous to current desktop 3D modeling and CAD software, which typically includes both direct manipulation and numeric field entry for specifying object properties.

- *Parameter setting:* Many applications require a numeric entry technique to set some parameter needed by the system. For example, in a visualization of airflow around an airplane fuselage, the user might need to specify the aircraft velocity or the angle of the flaps. An immersive game might allow the user to set the maximum number of virtual opponents. Specifying RGB color values might be necessary to match two colors in a 3D design environment.

- *Communication between users:* When multiple users share a 3D environment, they usually require some method of communication. In collaborative VEs (CVEs), speech is most often used for this task, but some CVEs would benefit from a nonspeech text/ number-entry technique. For example, if two engineers are collaborating to assess the structural integrity of a proposed bridge design, they could use a shared "whiteboard" to work out equations or note possible design alternatives. Unlike speech, this communication would be precise and persistent. The popularity of text-based chat systems also illustrates that people accept textual as well as spoken communication.

- *Markup:* Many of the scenarios above would provide further benefit if users could augment their textual input with markup features, such as underlining, italics, and highlighting. For example, the architectural annotations described earlier might carry more force if the client could highlight or use bold text to emphasize important points.

9.1.3. Brief History of Symbolic Input

The canonical symbolic input device for computing systems is, of course, the keyboard. In particular, the so-called QWERTY layout (named after the first six keys on the second row of the keyboard) is the accepted keyboard for almost all typewriters, computers, and other text-entry systems. The history of the QWERTY keyboard is complex and interesting, and a complete treatment of it is beyond the scope of this book, but we summarize it below (see the following references for more thorough surveys: Cooper [1983]; Dvorak et al. [1936]; Yamada [1980]).

The QWERTY layout was first devised by Christopher Sholes in 1873. Sholes had been working to find a typewriter keyboard layout that would minimize mechanical jams caused by the arms that strike the paper to print a character. Because of this, it is often assumed today that Sholes designed the QWERTY layout intentionally to slow typists down, but this is not the case. Rather, the layout places letters that commonly appear consecutively on opposite sides of the keyboard. Because the corresponding arms would also be on opposite sides, there would be fewer jams, but because typists could also use fingers on different hands to type the two consecutive letters, there would be an increase in typing speed as well. Nevertheless, the layout is based on only rough statistics about the frequency of letters and their tendency to appear consecutively.

Since the development of the QWERTY layout, numerous layouts have been devised that are statistically much more optimal in terms of letter frequency and the use of the two hands in rapid sequence. The most famous of these is the Dvorak layout. It has even been claimed that a random ordering of the letters on the keyboard would almost always be better than QWERTY. Despite intense effort in this area, however, only minimal gains in efficiency have been found, and then only when typists practice the layouts over a long period of time. Thus, the QWERTY layout became a standard that was so entrenched that it has never been displaced.

Of course, the QWERTY layout applies only to keyboards meant to produce text using a Latin alphabet (for languages such as English). There are other keyboard layouts for other alphabets, such as Cyrillic, Japanese kanji, and Mandarin. However, because of the limited scope of this book, we limit our discussion of text input for 3D interfaces to the Latin alphabet.

Because computing devices have become smaller, more portable, and more ubiquitous, research in keyboard design in particular and text-input techniques in general has once again become prominent. We now have keyboards used for text input on personal organizers (PDAs), cell phones, automatic teller machines, and palmtop computers. Many of these still default to the QWERTY layout because everyone is familiar with it. Most were not designed for 10-finger touch typing, but rather assume a single finger or pen will be used. However, some of these devices use alternate keyboard layouts or form factors, and some use a virtual ("soft") keyboard or no keyboard at all. We draw heavily from these domains in our discussion of symbolic input techniques for 3D UIs.

9.1.4. Distinctive Features of Symbolic Input in 3D UIs

Symbolic input techniques for 3D UIs will be necessarily different from traditional techniques (keyboards) because of the inherent differences between 3D (non-desktop) and 2D UIs. Put simply, traditional keyboards don't work in non-desktop 3D UIs because

- Users are often standing.
- Users may physically move about.
- There is usually no surface on which to place a keyboard.
- It may be difficult or impossible to see a keyboard in low-light environments (e.g., in a surround-screen display) or when the user's vision is occluded (e.g., in an HMD).

These constraints don't apply to all 3D UIs, and there are potential workarounds (e.g., a keyboard can be strapped to the user's waist in such a way that it can be used while the user is standing and walking around), but in general, we need to consider different methods of symbolic input in VEs and augmented environments.

Given these constraints, if symbolic input tasks in 3D UIs were exactly the same as those in 2D UIs, then the 3D symbolic input problem would be a very difficult one to solve. Looking at the list of scenarios in section 9.1.2, however, we see that symbolic input in 3D UIs may be much less frequent than symbolic input in other interfaces. Furthermore, each instance of symbolic input in a 3D UI may be relatively short in terms of the number of symbols entered—as we have said, we do not foresee document or email composition in an immersive VE.

Another aid to the designer is the wealth of information that already exists on symbolic input in nontraditional computing environments. Designers of wearable computers, palmtop computers, PDAs, and even cell phones have had to tackle these issues. Although the usability of some of the symbolic input techniques for these devices is questionable, these domains are an important source of ideas for 3D UI symbolic input.

9.1.5. Chapter Roadmap

In section 9.2, we look closely at the general categories of symbolic input tasks for 3D UIs. The heart of the chapter, in section 9.3, is a presentation of techniques, both implemented and proposed, for 3D UI symbolic input. A list of design guidelines is presented in section 9.4.

The chapter focuses solely on symbolic input and ignores the issue of symbolic *output* in 3D UIs. We chose not to include output for two reasons. First, our aim in this book is to present methods of 3D interaction, and symbolic output is not strictly an interaction task, because it involves no action on the part of the user. Second, the design of symbolic output in 3D UIs is simply a special application of well-known principles of information presentation and layout. For further information, refer to the literature in this area (e.g., Tufte 1990; Zwaga et al. 1999).

This chapter is also different from the other chapters in Part III in two ways. First, we focus almost exclusively on non-desktop interfaces (VEs and AR) because symbolic input on the desktop is standardized and well studied. Second, there is less information in this chapter on empirical evaluation and performance of the techniques because there have been very few formal experiments on 3D UI symbolic input techniques.

9.2. Symbolic Input Tasks

As we have stated, the task of symbolic input in general involves the entry of letters, numbers, and other marks and symbols. However, tasks related to the actual entry of the symbols should also be considered, including editing and markup. We discuss the following tasks in this section:

- alphanumeric input
- editing alphanumeric symbols
- markup input

9.2.1. Alphanumeric Input

We use the term *alphanumeric* to denote all of the possible types of symbols users can enter. These include, but are not limited to, alphabetic characters (e.g., a, R), numeric characters (e.g., 2, 6), punctuation (e.g., comma, quotation marks), white space (e.g., space, tab, carriage return), accent marks (e.g., é, ö), and other symbols (e.g., *, %, >, @, #). In 3D UIs, alphabetic and numeric characters, white space, and perhaps a limited subset of punctuation marks, will most often be sufficient. Certain specific applications may require the entry of other symbols as well (e.g., symbols used in mathematical notation). In addition, there are many other alphabets (e.g., Cyrillic, Japanese kanji) that need to be considered for international applications.

9.2.2. Editing Alphanumeric Symbols

Users may make errors in the entry of symbols; they may decide that another word would be more appropriate; or they may want to suggest a change to some symbols input previously. All of these scenarios require the ability to edit existing symbols. Editing subtasks include specifying an insertion point, deleting the previous character, selecting a character or string of characters, changing a character or string to some other character or string, and so on. At a minimum, users must be able to delete the last symbol entered. This alone is sufficient to perform all the editing subtasks mentioned above, but of course this is hardly desirable if you have just finished a paragraph and realize that the first word is misspelled.

9.2.3. Markup Input

Finally, users may wish to enhance their symbolic input by applying additional formatting, styles, or emphasis, which we call *markup* input. Examples of markup input include underlining, italics, bold characters, highlighting, font specification, color specification, line-spacing specification, editing marks, and the like. In typical 2D interfaces, markup is specified either through the use of special tags embedded in the text (as in HTML) or via a GUI (as in most word processors). Markup input is certainly the least studied, and probably the least important, symbolic input task for 3D UIs.

9.3. Symbolic Input Techniques

In this section, we present a wide range of possible techniques for symbolic input in 3D UIs. We classify the techniques as keyboard-based, pen-based, gesture-based, or speech-based.

9.3.1. Keyboard-Based Techniques

The techniques that fall into the keyboard-based category either use a physical keyboard or are based on a keyboard metaphor. Although it may be possible to use a standard, full-sized keyboard in some 3D UIs, we do not explicitly consider them here. The keyboard-based techniques we will cover are

- miniature keyboards
- low key-count keyboards
- chord keyboards
- Pinch Keyboard
- soft keyboards

Miniature Keyboards

Perhaps the easiest way to bring a keyboard into a 3D UI is to miniaturize it so it can be carried or worn. This technique also has the advantage that it can retain the familiar QWERTY layout so that users do not have to relearn the keys' positions. For this reason, miniature keyboards are popular on many consumer-level mobile devices such as PDAs. However, miniature keyboards are not generally large enough to allow touch typing (or 10-finger typing), so users must type with one or two fingers and cannot use the muscle memory built up from years of keyboard usage.

In a 3D UI, a miniature keyboard may be held in one hand while the other hand types (similar to a palmtop computer), or the keyboard may be worn by the user or attached to the user. An experiment comparing several text-input devices for wearable computers found that a miniature keyboard strapped to the forearm of the nondominant hand produced the best performance and user satisfaction (Thomas et al. 1998).

Low Key-Count Keyboards

A second way to make the keyboard small enough to be held in one hand is to reduce the number of physical keys. For example, the keypads on mobile phones can easily be used with one hand by pressing the 12 to 15 keys with the thumb. Because today's mobile phones contain so many features requiring text input (e.g., entering names into a list of contacts), many different symbolic input mechanisms have been developed for them, some of which could be applied in 3D UIs.

The most common phone-based text-input technique uses the standard layout of letters on the numeric phone keypad (a, b, and c are mapped to the 2 key; d, e, and f to the 3 key; and so on). Users press the key with the desired letter and disambiguate the letter by pressing the key multiple times. In other words, pressing 2 once produces the letter a, while pressing 2 twice produces the letter b. This technique is precise and easy to learn, but can be quite inefficient. Speed with this technique can be especially slow when two letters mapped to the same key need to be entered in sequence. For example, pressing the 2 key three times could be interpreted as aaa, ab, ba, or c. In order to make the meaning clear, the system forces the user to wait for a certain amount of time before another letter can be entered using the same key.

Another phone-based technique, typified by the T9 text-input system, only requires that each key be hit once. In order to determine which letter is meant by each key, the system uses a dictionary and tries to match the set of keystrokes to known words. When the system has a guess for the current word, the word is displayed and the user can either accept the word or continue typing. This technique can be quite efficient if the guessing works well, but typing names, rare words, or nonwords can be difficult. The method of word completion, however, can be applied to any text-input technique.

Chord Keyboards

A *chord keyboard* is a physical input device that aims to provide all the functionality of a full-sized keyboard, but using many fewer keys. In order to provide more symbols than there are keys on the device, the user presses multiple keys simultaneously to produce some symbols. The set of keys that are pressed together is called a chord, a name taken from the method of producing a musical chord on the piano by striking multiple keys at once. Figure 9.1 shows a chord keyboard (the Twiddler2) that has 12 keys and requires no more than two keys to be pressed at once to produce any letter, number, or standard punctuation symbol.

Chord keyboards have been studied extensively in other contexts (Noyes 1983), particularly mobile and wearable computing, and many different layouts and form factors have been tried. In general, users need a great deal of training to become proficient with chord keyboards because the layout is not related to the standard QWERTY keyboard, but the advantage of one-handed symbolic input may make this training worthwhile in some situations.

In an experiment comparing several symbolic input techniques (chord keyboard, speech, Pinch Keyboard, and pen-and-tablet keyboard) in an immersive VE, a chord keyboard had the slowest performance, the largest number of errors, and the lowest user preference ratings (Bowman, Rhoton

Figure 9.1   *A 12-key chord keyboard. (Photograph courtesy of Doug Bowman)*

et al. 2002). However, this study did not allow a large amount of training time, and the chord keyboard's performance may have improved over a longer set of trials.

Pinch Keyboard

Bowman and colleagues developed a technique for text input in VEs called the Pinch Keyboard (Bowman, Wingrave et al. 2001). It uses Pinch Gloves, lightweight gloves with conductive cloth on each fingertip that sense when two or more fingers are touching (see Chapter 4, section 4.3.3). The gloves are comfortable to wear, and because of their on/off nature, there is no ambiguity to user actions. This technique also uses a standard QWERTY keyboard layout so that users can take advantage of the typing skill they already have.

The basic concept of the Pinch Keyboard is that a simple pinch between a thumb and finger on the same hand represents a key press by that finger. Thus, on the home row of the keyboard, left pinky represents a, left ring represents s, and so on. In order to use the "inner" keys such as g and h, and to change rows of the keyboard, 6-DOF trackers are mounted on the gloves. Inner keys are selected by rotating the hand inward (Figure 9.2). The user changes the active row by moving the hands closer to the body (bottom row) or farther away (top row). Users calibrate the location of the rows before using the system by indicating the middle of the top and bottom rows while holding the hands palm down. Still, because the trackers have limited accuracy, fairly large-scale motions are required to change rows or select the inner keys, reducing efficiency.

Graphical feedback is extremely important to make up for the lack of visual and haptic feedback provided by a physical keyboard. Two feedback objects are attached to the view. These show the location of each character and the currently active characters (based on hand position and orientation) via highlighting (Figure 9.2). The text entered by the user is also attached to the user's view. In addition, the technique provides audio feedback that lets the user know when a key has been pressed or when calibration is complete.

Finally, the technique includes special gestures for space (thumb to thumb), backspace (ring to ring), delete all (pinky to pinky), and enter (index to index). This set of arbitrary gestures is small enough to be memorized by the user.

In our experience with the Pinch Keyboard technique, novice users type very slowly and deliberately, even though many of them are speedy touch typists. This might suggest that typing skill does not transfer to our

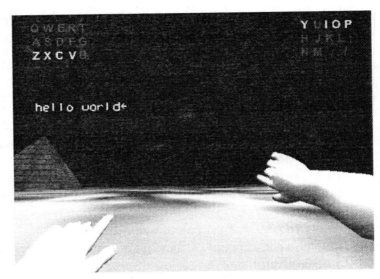

Figure 9.2   *User's view of the Pinch Keyboard. (Bowman, Wingrave et al. 2001, © 2001 by Springer-Verlag; reprinted with permission)*

technique and that training is required. However, all users immediately understand the technique. Expertise is gained not through cognitive training, but rather through motor training, because the movements are different from those used with a standard keyboard. Therefore, novice users can immediately begin typing, although their performance might be poor. Early experimental results (Bowman, Rhoton et al. 2002) indicate that the Pinch Keyboard is slower than speech or soft keyboard techniques, but also that users find the technique easy to learn, satisfying, and comfortable to use.

Soft Keyboards

A "soft" keyboard is a virtual device implemented entirely in software. In other words, users press virtual keys instead of physical ones to enter symbols. Some PDAs that lack a physical keyboard include a soft keyboard that is displayed on the screen. Users tap the virtual keys with a stylus or finger to simulate pressing the key. Soft keyboards have the advantages that they can easily be reconfigured for different layouts or alphabets and that they don't require a specialized input device. However, the major disadvantages of soft keyboards are the limitation of single-point input (one finger or pen at a time) and their lack of active and passive haptic feedback. Even if the virtual keyboard lies on a physical surface, the user cannot feel the contours of the keys to help her find a key without looking or the "click" of the key being depressed to help her know a symbol was entered.

Many types of soft keyboards have been designed that could be used in 3D UIs. For example, the pen-and-tablet metaphor that we have previously seen used for map-based travel (Chapter 6), object manipulation (Chapter 5), and menus (Chapter 8) can also provide a soft keyboard. In Bowman, Rhoton, and Pinho's experiment (2002), this technique was second only to speech in speed and had the fewest errors. Soft keyboards on other devices, such as PDAs, could also be used in 3D UIs, provided that the user was able see the device (this technique would not work in HMDs, for example).

A novel virtual keyboard device called the Senseboard (Figure 9.3) may hold some promise for 3D UIs. The concept is that a full-sized QWERTY keyboard can exist virtually on any surface, and users can type with all 10 fingers on this virtual keyboard. This is accomplished by the use of muscle sensors to determine finger movement plus pattern recognition to determine the probable word in ambiguous situations.

Note that virtual keyboards need not be limited to the standard QWERTY layout. In fact, for tapping of a soft keyboard by a pen or single finger, the QWERTY layout is certainly suboptimal (although it will allow better performance by novices). For example, Zhai and colleagues (2000) developed the Metropolis keyboard, a layout for soft keyboards based on quantitative analysis of letter frequency, distance between keys, and so on.

Figure 9.3 *Senseboard virtual keyboard prototype. (Photograph courtesy of Senseboard Technologies AB)*

9.3.2. Pen-Based Techniques

Mobile computing platforms, such as PDAs, often use neither a physical keyboard nor a soft keyboard for symbolic input. Rather, they use pen-based input in which the user writes characters, symbols, or other gestures with a pen/stylus on the device. For example, the Apple Newton allowed users to write in natural cursive handwriting and attempted to recognize entire words. More commonly, single characters are recognized for increased accuracy using either natural characters or modified single-stroke characters, as in the Graffiti alphabet used in the PalmOS. Some such techniques have been applied to 3D UIs, and others may also be appropriate.

We divide pen-based techniques into two categories: *pen-stroke gesture recognition* and *unrecognized pen input,* also called *digital ink.*

Pen-Stroke Gesture Recognition

Recognition of written input is in many ways similar to gesture recognition (section 9.3.3). In pen-based input, the basic unit of recognition is the *stroke*—a pen movement that starts when the pen touches the input surface and ends when the pen is lifted. A complete review of stroke recognition is beyond the scope of this book, but suffice it to say that the same recognition algorithms used in PDAs and other pen-based devices apply equally well to pen-based input in 3D UIs.

A large number of pen-based symbolic input schemes have been developed. Graffiti, mentioned earlier, is a *character-level* technique, using one stroke per character. Allegro from Fonix Corporation is another technique of this type. *Word-level* techniques, such as Cirrin (Mankoff and Abowd 1998) and Quikwriting (Perlin 1998), allow the input of multiple characters with a single stroke. For example, in Cirrin, a stroke begins in the central area of a circle and moves through regions around the circle representing each character in the word (Figure 9.4).

Another interesting word-level technique, incorporating dynamic rearrangement of letters, is Dasher (Ward et al. 2002). In this technique, the user moves the pen to the first letter in the word or phrase, choosing from all possible letters oriented in a vertical menu. When the first letter has been chosen, the software computes the probability that each letter is the next letter in the word or phrase. The most probable letters appear near the pen and have a larger area than other letters (Figure 9.5). The user continues to move the pen to successive letters until he is finished.

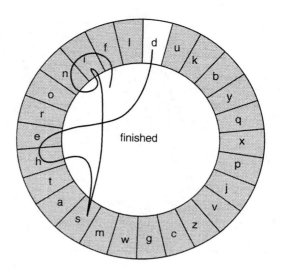

Figure 9.4 *Layout of the Cirrin soft keyboard for pen-based input. (Mankoff and Abowd 1998, © 1998 ACM; reprinted by permission)*

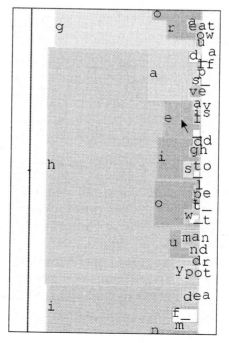

Figure 9.5 *Dasher text-input technique. (Ward et al. 2002; image courtesy of David Ward, Inference Group, University of Cambridge, UK)*

Figure 9.6   *The Virtual Notepad system allowing handwriting in an immersive VE.
(Poupyrev, Tomokazu et al. 1998, © 1998 IEEE)*

The Virtual Notepad system (Poupyrev, Tomokazu et al. 1998) used a pen-and-tablet metaphor and simple stroke recognition to provide symbolic input in an immersive VE (Figure 9.6). Handwritten input was also used to command the system. High tracker latency made writing in the original Virtual Notepad system somewhat tedious, but current tracking technology would allow for relatively precise and speedy symbolic input.

Unrecognized Pen Input (Digital Ink)

Another method of symbolic input using pen-based input is to simply draw the actual strokes of the pen, as if the pen were writing with "digital ink." This technique is available on many PDAs as well and allows users to easily and naturally input text, symbols, numbers, drawings, and so on. Of course, the disadvantages of digital ink are that it is readable only by other humans, not by computers, and it is very difficult to edit. Therefore, it may be appropriate for tasks like leaving annotations, but not for tasks like specifying filenames or numeric parameters.

The Virtual Notepad system (Poupyrev, Tomokazu et al. 1998) mentioned above also allowed users to write with digital ink (Figure 9.6). This mode was envisioned for use in medical environments, for example, allowing a physician to make annotations on a patient's x-ray. Annotations in this system could even be edited by using the opposite end of the pen to erase existing strokes.

9.3.3. Gesture-Based Techniques

As we have seen, a great deal of 3D interaction is done with the hands. Thus, it is natural to consider symbolic input techniques that take advantage of hand posture, position, orientation, and motion—in other words, based on *gestures* (see Chapter 8, section 8.5). Although gesture-based interaction has fallen somewhat out of favor in the 3D interaction community because of difficulty with gesture recognition, calibration of data gloves, and similar drawbacks, it can still be a powerful method of input requiring only the user's hands. We consider three types of gesture-based symbolic input:

- sign language gestures
- numeric gestures
- instantaneous gestures

Sign Language Gestures

One method of symbolic communication based on gestures is already used by millions of people around the world—sign language. Sign language is incredibly descriptive and can allow its users to "speak" very rapidly. Fels and Hinton (1998) have developed the GloveTalk systems to allow signing to be used as a speech synthesizer. Although such a system has not been used in a 3D UI for symbolic input, its use of a data glove as an input device certainly indicates that it might be useful for 3D applications. The main drawbacks of such a technique are that only a small percentage of the population knows sign language and that even for experienced signers, the neural-network-recognition system must be trained.

Numeric Gestures

For numeric entry, gestures offer an obvious interaction technique—the use of fingers to represent numbers (e.g., one index finger raised to represent the number 1). Such gestures are practically universal and can be performed with either one hand or two. However, we know of no 3D UI research or application that has used this technique.

Instantaneous Gestures

Both of the techniques described above require continuous gesture recognition using a data glove or similar device that continuously reports the angles of the joints on the hand. However, instantaneous devices such as

Pinch Gloves can also provide limited "gestures," especially when a tracker is added to the glove.

The Pinch Keyboard (section 9.3.1) is one example of such a technique, although most of the gestures in that case are meant to emulate the use of a standard keyboard. Certainly, other types of pinch gestures could be used to represent letters, symbols, numbers, editing, or markup. Again, however, there has been little research in this area.

One exception is some unpublished research by Bowman and colleagues that explored various schemes for numeric input using Pinch Gloves. Ideas included "counting" techniques in which simple gestures on one hand represented the numbers 0 to 4 and simple gestures on the other hand represented the numbers 5 to 9, and "keyboard" techniques in which the hand's position and the pinch gesture were combined to form a virtual numeric keypad layout, similar to the Pinch Keyboard technique. Initial studies indicated that keyboard-based techniques were easier to learn and use, and offered reasonable performance.

A technology called Thumbscript, intended for mobile/phone-based text entry, is another possible instantaneous gesture technique for 3D UIs. Thumbscript is similar to Cirrin and Quikwriting (see section 9.3.2) in that it maps letters to gestures going from one region of the device to another. Instead of pen-based input, however, it uses nine buttons. Users press the button corresponding to the beginning of the gesture and then the button corresponding to the end of the gesture.

9.3.4. Speech-Based Techniques

Finally, we turn to the use of speech for symbolic input in 3D UIs. Speech has a large number of desirable characteristics: it leaves the user's hands free; it utilizes an untapped input modality; it allows the efficient and precise entry of large amounts of text; and it is completely natural and familiar. Nevertheless, speech is rarely used for symbolic input in 3D UIs (or 2D UIs, for that matter). If speech is used at all, it is almost always for system control (see Chapter 8, section 8.4).

The old argument in UI circles was that speech was rarely used because speech recognition systems were slow, inaccurate, and required training, but today's speech recognition technology, while still flawed, certainly seems good enough to do the job. Thus, lack of user acceptance must be due to other issues, such as privacy, the perception of bothering others, the awkwardness of speaking to a machine, and so on. Zhai, Hunter, and Smith (2000) also note the interesting findings that "users

[find] it 'harder to talk and think than type and think' and [consider] the keyboard to be more 'natural' than speech for text entry."

Still, because it offers so many potential advantages for 3D UIs, no section on symbolic input techniques would be complete without considering speech input. We also point the reader to the sections on general speech input in Chapter 4 and speech input for system control in Chapter 8. For symbolic input, we can consider three types of speech input:

- single-character speech recognition
- whole-word speech recognition
- unrecognized speech input

Single-Character Speech Recognition

One technique for symbolic input using speech is to have the user utter each character or symbol explicitly. In the case of phrase or sentence composition, this single-character approach would be unwieldy, but in many situations involving the entry of nonword text and symbols (such as filenames), this "spelling" technique makes sense. Furthermore, recognition accuracy may near 100% with single-character speech because the set of possible utterances is so small.

This type of speech input was tested in Bowman, Rhoton, and Pinho's experiment (2002) using an idealized "Wizard of Oz" recognition system (a human listened to the user's speech and pressed the appropriate key on a keyboard, but users were led to believe that their speech was being recognized by the system). Of the four techniques tested, this speech technique was clearly the most efficient. However, users made significant errors with this technique and had trouble correcting their errors. Furthermore, users perceived their performance to be slower with the speech technique because it was "boring" to spell out the words. Subjects were also observed modifying their speech rate to match their perception of the system's speed.

Whole-Word Speech Recognition

Most common speech recognition software will also recognize a lexicon of words or phrases in addition to single characters. This of course allows speech input to proceed even faster, but perhaps at the cost of increased errors. Such a system would be appropriate when significant amounts of plain text needed to be entered (annotations, descriptions, etc.). We are not aware of any 3D UIs that have used whole-word speech recognition for symbolic input.

Unrecognized Speech Input

We can also consider "digital voice," the speech analogue of digital ink. This is speech input that is simply saved as an audio stream rather than interpreted as symbols or words. Like digital ink, unrecognized speech input applies only to symbolic input tasks where another human is the intended recipient of the message. The Virtual Annotation system (Harmon et al. 1996) is an example of a 3D UI that used this technique. It allowed a user (e.g., a teacher) to select an object in a visualization and attach an audio annotation to that object. The annotation was persistent so that later users of the visualization (e.g., students) could listen to the annotation.

9.4. Design Guidelines

We are aware of only three major experiments on user performance in symbolic input tasks in 3D UIs. Bowman and colleagues compared speech, a soft keyboard using a pen and tablet, the Pinch Keyboard, and a chord keyboard in an immersive VE (Bowman et al. 2002). Figure 9.7 shows the

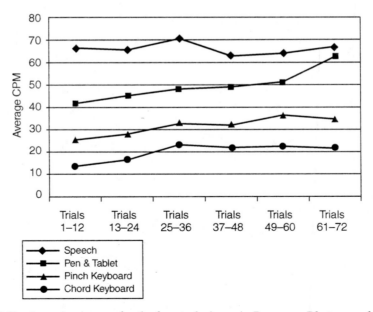

Figure 9.7   *Learning curves for the four techniques in Bowman, Rhoton, and Pinho's (2002) experiment. (Reprinted with permission from Proceedings of the Human Factors and Ergonomics Society Annual Meeting, 2002, © 2002 by the Human Factors and Ergonomics Society. All rights reserved)*

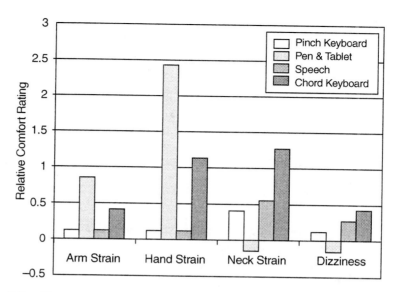

Figure 9.8 *Change in comfort rating from the beginning to the end of the experiment for the four techniques in Bowman, Rhoton, and Pinho's (2002) study. (Reprinted with permission from Proceedings of the Human Factors and Ergonomics Society Annual Meeting, 2002, © 2002 by the Human Factors and Ergonomics Society. All rights reserved)*

average characters per minute (CPM) achieved by subjects in this study with each of the techniques. Based on pure performance, speech and the soft keyboard technique are clearly superior. Other factors were also important in this study, however. Figure 9.8 shows the average change in user comfort (four categories) over the course of the experiment. The pen-and-tablet technique and the chord keyboard caused discomfort in a large number of users after about 45 minutes of use. Users preferred the pen-and-tablet and Pinch Keyboard techniques, and also found these to be quite natural because they were based on the QWERTY layout.

The second experiment compared five techniques in a wearable computing setting (Thomas et al. 1998). Techniques included a miniature keyboard mounted on the user's forearm, a soft keyboard, a chord keyboard, speech, and a standard QWERTY keyboard (used as a baseline). Unlike the previous experiment, this study included six lengthy sessions so that subjects would have time to develop expertise with each of the techniques. Table 9.1 shows the performance of each of the techniques in each of the sessions, given in seconds per character (lower numbers are better). As the table indicates, the forearm-mounted keyboard had the best performance of the four novel techniques—even better than speech. The

Table 9.1   *Performance results for five text input devices (in seconds per character).*

	Session 1	Session 2	Session 3	Session 4	Session 5	Session 6
Forearm	1.03	1.09	0.97	0.87	0.90	0.81
Virtual (soft)	3.29	2.63	2.64	2.27	2.11	2.04
Kordic (chord)	4.75	3.65	3.43	2.63	2.64	2.54
Voice	1.09	1.04	1.03	0.90	1.58	0.90
QWERTY	0.65	0.73	0.44	0.45	0.62	0.45

Source: Thomas, B., S. Tyerman, and K. Grimmer (1998). Evaluation of Text Input Mechanisms for Wearable Computers. *Virtual Reality: Research, Development, and Applications* 3: 187–199.

chord keyboard had the worst performance, but also showed significant gains in speed as users became familiar with the device.

Finally, Osawa, Ren, and Suzuki (2003) examined the use of four mobile-computing text-entry techniques that could be used in a CAVE-like immersive VE. Subjects entered short phrases (in Japanese) using handwriting recognition, digital ink, and a soft keyboard on a PDA, and button input on a mobile phone. They found digital ink (unrecognized handwritten notes) to be the most efficient, followed by button input on the mobile phone, the soft keyboard, and finally recognized handwriting. Subjects preferred the mobile phone technique, however, and found digital ink to be the least preferable method.

Based on these results, we can posit some preliminary guidelines for the use of symbolic input techniques in 3D UIs.

> Use the QWERTY layout if symbolic input will be infrequent or if most users will be novices.

The familiarity of almost all users with the QWERTY layout more than makes up for its deficiencies. Alphabetic layouts, although more understandable at a conceptual level, still force users to search for each character. Other layouts, optimized for pen-based input, two-finger input, and so on may prove much better than QWERTY with extended use, but for "walk-up-and-use" 3D UIs, QWERTY can't be beat.

> Haptic feedback is an important component of keyboard use, so use keyboards with physical buttons if practical. If using virtual keyboards, place the virtual keys on a physical surface.

You don't realize how much you depend on touch when typing until you use a soft keyboard with no haptic cues. The physical outlines of the keys help users find them without looking; raised dots on certain keys orient users to their finger position on the keyboard; and the passive force feedback helps users understand when a key is actually considered to be pressed. Although soft keyboards can't duplicate these cues, they should at least be grounded on a physical surface rather than floating in the air.

> **Don't neglect user comfort.**

Avoid heavy devices and those that force the user to hold the hand in a single posture for long periods of time. Consider the other tasks that users will be performing and whether the symbolic input devices will get in the way of these tasks.

> **Don't assume that speech will always be the best technique.**

Speech can be quite useful for short utterances, annotations, and the like, but it can also lead to error-correction problems, user frustration, and user self-consciousness.

> **Consider specialized, nonstandard devices and techniques only if users will be entering symbols very frequently.**

Chord keyboards, gesture-recognition techniques, and special-purpose pen-based techniques can all provide reasonably good levels of performance after users have worked with them for some length of time. If your application involves users who can be expected to approach expert performance, these devices and techniques might be appropriate. On the other hand, these techniques will not work when the application is designed for first-time or infrequent users.

> **Use unrecognized digital ink when speed is the most important aspect of usability.**

Osawa's (2003) study showed that unrecognized handwritten input could be more efficient than other techniques. Digital ink also allows users to produce sketches and certain forms of markup. But beware of the limitations of digital ink—it can be read only by other users, not by the system; it is difficult to edit; and it may encourage users to write more quickly, decreasing readability even by other humans.

9.5. Beyond Text and Number Entry

Much more research is needed in this area to enable more complex 3D UIs for future applications. In particular, there has been no work that we are aware of on symbolic input tasks for 3D UIs other than text and number entry. If 3D UIs are going to support complex symbolic input scenarios such as those in section 9.1.2, the challenges of text editing and markup, symbol (e.g., punctuation) entry, and multilanguage support will have to be addressed. Although existing work from other types of interfaces will also inform these efforts, there are sure to be unique challenges when the techniques are applied to a 3D UI.

Recommended Reading

A special double issue of the journal *Human-Computer Interaction* focused on "Text Entry for Mobile Computing." The articles in this special issue, while not specifically aimed at symbolic input for 3D UIs, provide good insights into the issues involved in off-the-desktop symbolic input. In particular, the article by MacKenzie and Soukoreff provides an excellent overview.

MacKenzie, I. S., and R. Soukoreff (2002). Text Entry for Mobile Computing: Models and Methods, Theory and Practice. *Human-Computer Interaction* 17(2/3): 147–198.

PART IV
Designing and Developing 3D User Interfaces

Thus far, we have focused on the low-level components of 3D UIs—input/output devices and interaction techniques. Through the guidelines presented in each chapter, we have shown you how to choose devices and techniques for your application that match its requirements and that will result in high levels of usability.

But how do you put all of these components together? What do complete 3D UIs look like? How do you verify that your system is easy to use and efficient? The answers to these questions are the focus of Part IV.

We recommend a *usability engineering* process (Gabbard et al. 1999) when constructing 3D UIs. This type of process begins with *requirements gathering*—an analysis of the existing situation, the problems users are having, the tasks users need to perform, and the characteristics of the users themselves. Next, you develop the *design* of the system and its UI, and build one or more *prototypes* that represent the system. Finally, you *evaluate* the prototype to find usability problems and to assess the quality of your design. In addition, usability engineering uses an *iterative* process, with multiple design-prototype-evaluate cycles.

In this part of the book, we address parts of this process that are *unique to 3D UIs*. (For a good overall introduction to usability engineering, we recommend books by Rosson and Carroll [2001] or Hix and Hartson

[1993].) Chapter 10 deals with the *design* phase. It presents general design approaches and specific UI strategies that have been proven to work well in 3D UIs—these approaches and strategies can serve as the foundation for a 3D UI design. In Chapter 11, we look at the *evaluation* of 3D UIs, surveying the distinctive characteristics of 3D UI evaluation and various approaches to assessing usability.

We do not explicitly cover the requirements analysis phase, because 3D UI requirements analysis is very similar to generic requirements analysis processes. We also do not discuss the details of 3D UI prototyping or implementation. The current state of development tools for 3D UIs is extremely dynamic and uncertain—there are hosts of 3D modeling tools, programming languages, integrated development environments, toolkits, and libraries for 3D applications. We have chosen to keep our discussion on a high level and focus on 3D UI design because any specific development information we might present could quickly become obsolete.

CHAPTER **10**

Strategies in Designing and Developing 3D User Interfaces

This chapter discusses some general strategies and principles for designing 3D UIs. Unlike the design of 3D interaction techniques (Part III), which is motivated by the requirements of particular tasks, the design strategies that we discuss in this chapter are high-level and can be used in a wide variety of 3D tasks and applications. Some of these strategies are designed to match 3D UIs to the basic properties of human psychology and physiology; others are based on common sense, rules of thumb, or cultural metaphors.

10.1. Introduction

The previous chapters have focused on the basic building blocks common to many 3D UIs: input devices, displays, and interaction techniques for performing basic interaction tasks, such as manipulation and navigation. Although these techniques are essential in designing a variety of 3D interfaces, their simple mechanical combination does not necessarily guarantee an intuitive, easy-to-use, and enjoyable interactive experience.

On a microlevel, the devil is in the details, meaning that the effectiveness and usability of a 3D UI depends on the minute implementation details of interaction techniques, such as the careful choice of parameters and the match between the properties of interaction techniques and input/output devices.

On a macrolevel, there are many high-level, general design strategies driven not by the requirements of an interaction task but derived from more general principles, such as the strengths and limitations of human psychology and physiology, common sense, rules of thumb, cultural metaphors, and so on. For example, the basic principles for designing two-handed interaction techniques were developed independently of any interaction task. Rather, they were motivated by the simple observation that people naturally use two hands in real-world activities, so using two hands in a 3D UI might improve usability or performance. Similarly, many of the principles that we discuss in this section are general enough to be applicable to a wide range of interaction tasks.

The strategies and principles discussed in this chapter can be roughly divided into two large groups: *designing for humans* (i.e., strategies to match the design of interaction techniques and applications to human strengths, limitations, and individual differences), and *inventing 3D interaction techniques* (i.e., designing techniques based on commonsense approaches, creative exploration of 3D UI design, rules of thumb, etc.).

10.1.1. Designing for Humans

Many of the interface design principles from the human factors (Salvendy 1997) and general UI literature (Shneiderman 1998) can be applied to the design of 3D UIs. Reduction of short-term memory load, consistency of interface syntax and semantics, feedback, error prevention, and aesthetic appeal are as important in 3D interaction as in any other human–machine interface. Expanding to the third dimension, however, brings new challenges, such as designing for user comfort, that require different design strategies that are usually not explored in traditional UI literature. In addition, different strategies can be applied to UI design for different user groups, such as children, disabled individuals, or novices.

10.1.2. Inventing 3D User Interfaces

There are numerous application domains for 3D UIs, and even though the interaction techniques discussed earlier in this book can provide a starting point for UI design, it is not realistic to propose that they can cover all possible applications. Therefore, it's often necessary to invent new 3D interaction techniques and design new interaction experiences. While human factors–based principles can offer valuable insight into how 3D interfaces should be designed, they may not necessarily help designers to invent new and enjoyable interaction techniques. In this chapter, therefore, we also survey some of the informal, rule-of-thumb approaches that have often been used in creating new 3D UIs; they can trigger a designer's imagination and provide a starting point for creating new and compelling 3D interaction experiences.

10.1.3. Chapter Roadmap

The chapter begins with a discussion of strategies and principles to match the design of 3D UIs with human characteristics, including issues of feedback, constraints, two-handed interaction, user populations, and user comfort (section 10.2). Section 10.3 is focused on strategies for inventing 3D UIs, such as those that are based on replicating the real world, adapting techniques from 2D interaction, and using magic and aesthetics in 3D UI design. A final section of guidelines (section 10.4) summarizes some important ideas discussed in this chapter, as well as some practical tips and techniques for designing interactive 3D applications.

10.2. Designing for Humans

All UIs must be designed in accordance with the most basic characteristics of human physiology and psychology. These *human factors* principles of interface design can be found throughout the literature, which can be very informative, though somewhat overwhelming. In this section, we do not attempt to discuss all of the human factors issues that might be relevant to 3D user interaction. Instead, we focus on some of the most basic topics that apply directly to 3D UIs. The recommended reading list at the end of the chapter provides some references for those who might want more information.

10.2.1. Feedback in 3D User Interfaces

Providing effective feedback is crucial in the design of any interface, whether it is a 3D VR system, a desktop 2D GUI, or a simple knob on a stereo system. Feedback refers to any information conveyed to the user that helps the user understand the state of the system, the results of an operation, or the status of a task. This information may come from the system, from the environment, or from the user's own body.

It has long been understood that our ability to self-regulate body movements, such as manipulating objects or walking through the environment, is mediated by feedback-control mechanisms (Wiener 1948). In human–machine interaction, the user controls his movements by integrating various kinds of feedback provided by external sources (e.g., the UI) and self-produced by the human body (e.g., kinesthetic feedback). When interacting with a 3D UI, the user's physical input, such as hand movements, is captured by devices and translated into visual, auditory, and haptic feedback displayed to the user via display devices. At the same time, feedback is generated by the user's own body; this includes kinesthetic and proprioceptive feedback, which allow the user to "feel" the position and motion of his limbs and body.

Therefore, the goal of a 3D UI designer is to create an interactive system that provides sufficient levels of feedback to the user and ensures compliance (agreement) between different levels and types of feedback.

Multiple Dimensions in Feedback

Several different dimensions of feedback can be sensed by the user and provided by the interface. We consider two basic classifications of the feedback dimensions: sense-based and system-based.

The *sensory dimensions* of feedback include visual, auditory, tactile, and olfactory feedback from sources external to the user's body; and proprioceptive and kinesthetic feedback generated by the user's body in response to limb and body movements. The 3D UI designer has direct control of the external visual feedback provided to the user. Given the appropriate devices, the 3D UI can provide feedback to most other sensory feedback channels, except for the kinesthetic and proprioceptive senses. Providing compliant feedback to multiple sensory channels, such as combining haptic and visual feedback, improves user performance and satisfaction in 3D UIs.

Some types of sensory feedback are still difficult to provide effectively in 3D UIs. For example, force and tactile feedback devices are still bulky and difficult to use; consequently, VE applications are often criticized for the absence of haptic feedback. The idea of *sensory feedback substitution* has often been used in designing VE systems—visual or audio cues can be provided to compensate for missing haptic feedback. See Chapter 3 for further discussion of sensory feedback.

From a *systems* point of view, feedback can be split into three categories: reactive, instrumental, and operational feedback (Smith and Smith 1987). *Reactive feedback* combines all the self-generated visual, auditory, haptic, and proprioceptive information that results from operating the user interface. *Instrumental feedback* is generated by the interface controls and tools operated by the human user, such as the vibration of a pen when writing. Finally, *operational feedback* is feedback that the user receives from the system as the results of his or her actions. For example, when a user manipulates a 3D virtual object with a 6-DOF device, the user gets reactive feedback from moving the device with her arm (in the form of kinesthetic feedback), instrumental feedback from observing the movement of the 6-DOF device and feeling its shape, and operational feedback from observing the motion of the virtual object.

The boundaries of the categories in this classification are a bit fuzzy, but they are still important in analyzing the different techniques for providing feedback to the user and particularly in discussing the main principle in designing feedback—*compliance.*

Feedback Compliance in 3D UIs

The key principle in designing effective feedback for interactive systems is the principle of compliance between different dimensions of the feedback provided to the user. It suggests that for efficient interaction, the 3D UI should *maintain spatial and temporal correspondence between multiple feedback dimensions* that the user receives. For the sensory dimensions, for example, if the visual feedback conflicts with the kinesthetic or proprioceptive feedback generated by the body, then user performance rapidly degrades (Smith and Smith 1987). This would happen, for example, if virtual objects moved in the opposite direction from the hand movement, a condition often called *feedback displacement.*

Because 3D UIs may tend to involve and engage users more than other UIs, a lack of compliance between the sensory dimensions may result not only in decreased performance, but also in much more dramatic effects such as headaches, blurred vision, dizziness, disorientation, or even severe vomiting (*cybersickness*). The most basic explanation for cybersickness is a conflict between the feedback from the visual sense and other intrinsic feedback systems, such as the vestibular and proprioceptive systems (LaViola 2000a).

A number of specific compliances have been discussed in the human factors and 3D UI literature, and we discuss them in this section.

Spatial compliances Spatial feedback compliances include directional compliance, also called stimulus-response (S-R) compatibility (Fitts and Jones 1953); nulling compliance; and others. *Directional compliance* suggests that a virtual object should move in the same direction as the manipulated input device. For example, when the user rotates a virtual object using a 6-DOF input device, both the device and the virtual object should rotate in the same direction; that is, they should rotate around the same axis of rotation (Poupyrev, Weghorst et al. 2000). Directional compliance preserves the correspondence between the motions of virtual objects and the observed or felt motion of the physical input device. This allows the user to effectively anticipate the motion of the virtual objects in response to input and therefore plan and execute the desired trajectory of motion. Ensuring directional feedback compliance is important, although it has been shown that humans are extremely adaptable and can compensate for disparities between stimulus and response. However, a significant breakdown in directional feedback compliance might result in a decrease in user performance and even in cybersickness such as in the case of navigation without directional compliance.

Another category of spatial compliances is *nulling compliance.* Nulling compliance means that when the user returns the device to the initial position or orientation, the virtual objects also return to the corresponding initial position or orientation (Buxton 1986). The importance of preserving nulling compliance depends on the application. It has been shown, for example, that if the device is attached to the user's body, the nulling compliance might be important, as it allows the user to use "muscle memory" to remember the initial, neutral position of the device and object.

On the system level it is also desirable that instrumental and operational feedbacks are spatially compliant: for example, a virtual hand should be aligned as closely as possible with the user's real hand.

Temporal compliances and latency The most typical example of temporal *in*compliance is latency—the temporal delay between user input and sensory feedback generated by the system in response to it. The investigation of latency was particularly relevant in the early days of VEs, when it was a critical problem because of slower computers and computer graphics rendering hardware. A large number of user studies have investigated the negative effects of latency on performance (e.g., Ellis et al. 1999; Allison et al. 2001).

From the sensorimotor point of view, the reason that latency affects user performance is the incompliance between internal feedback (e.g., proprioceptive and kinesthetic feedback) and external sensory feedback received by the user (e.g., visual feedback from the system). This incompliance can significantly decrease user performance. For example, studies of flight simulators have shown that viewpoint control lags as short as 50 ms have a significant impact on user performance, while latencies that are much longer can lead to oscillations and loss of control (Wickens 1986).

Not only absolute latency but also its variability may affect user performance. Indeed, in most complex computer graphics applications, latency is not constant. Experimental studies have found that at 20 frames per second (fps) update rate, latency fluctuations as large as 40% do not significantly affect user performance on a manipulation task. At 17 fps, their effect becomes noticeable, and fluctuations become a significant problem at 10 fps, which is normally considered a lower bound for acceptable frame rate in 3D computer graphics applications (Watson et al. 1997).

With the rapid improvements in computer graphics hardware and software, the problem of latency may become less critical. On the other hand, as rendering performance increases, the requirements for visual realism and environment complexity also increase, so latency may remain an issue for some time to come.

The simplest technique for dealing with latency is to increase the update rate by reducing the environment's complexity, using more sophisticated culling algorithms, or rendering the scene progressively (simple rendering during interaction and high-quality rendering during breaks in interaction (Airey et al. 1990). However, note that simply increasing the update rate does not eliminate all the sources of latency. For example, tracking devices have an inherent latency that is not tied to the update rate. Predictive filtering of the user input stream (e.g., tracking data) has also been investigated and has resulted in some success in reducing latency (Liang, Shaw 1991; Azuma and Bishop 1994).

Feedback Substitution

In designing and developing 3D UIs, it is often difficult to allow for all possible types of feedback. In particular, haptic feedback often requires devices that are expensive and difficult to operate. In the absence of haptic feedback, a feedback substitution principle has been often used. Instead of

Figure 10.1   *Feedback substitution: a visual cue substitutes for haptic feedback when a user touches a virtual object. (Reprinted with permission of HIT Lab, University of Washington)*

haptic feedback, additional audio or visual cues can be provided. For example, in a selection task, the action of touching the virtual object can be indicated with a visual highlight (e.g., drawing a frame around the object or changing its color [Figure 10.1]). An enhancement of this technique, predictive highlighting (Butterworth et al. 1992), shows the user the 3D object that is likely to be selected if the user continues the operation. This was found to be particularly useful in model editing mode, where the most probable vertex would highlight when the 3D cursor approached it.

Passive Haptic Feedback

Another method of providing simple haptic feedback is to match the shape and appearance of a virtual object with the shape and appearance of a physical object so that the user can both see and "feel" the virtual object. This approach is called *passive haptic feedback,* or *props.* Passive feedback is a type of instrumental feedback: it provides users with a tactile sense of the virtual tools they are using. Although this approach is significantly less flexible than "real" force-feedback devices, it has been quite successful for real-world 3D UIs (see also Chapters 3 and 8).

One of the first uses of props in a 3D UI was a two-handed interface for interactive visualization of 3D neurological data (Hinckley et al. 1994). A 6-DOF magnetic tracker was embedded into in a doll's head (Figure 10.2), and by manipulating the toy head, the user was able to quickly and reliably relate the orientation of the input device to the orientation of

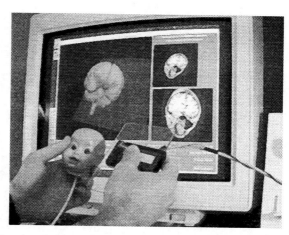

Figure 10.2 *Two-handed interface with passive haptic feedback provided by the doll's head and cutting plane tool held by the user. (Hinckley et al. 1994, © 1994 IEEE)*

the volumetric brain data on the screen. This resulted in efficient and enjoyable interaction, because from the user perspective, the interaction was analogous to holding a miniature "real" head in one hand. The tactile properties of the prop allowed the user to know its orientation without looking at the device, so the focus of attention could be kept entirely on the task. Although this interface was nonimmersive, in immersive VEs, passive props can be even more effective. By spatially registering tracked physical objects with virtual objects of the same shape, the designer can provide the user with inexpensive yet very realistic haptic feedback. Hoffman refers to this technique as *tactile augmentation* (Hoffman et al. 1998).

Using passive physical props is an extremely useful design technique for 3D UIs. Props provide inexpensive physical and tactile feedback, significantly increasing the sense of presence and ease of interaction in immersive and nonimmersive environments (Hoffman et al. 1998). They establish a common perceptual frame of reference between the device and the virtual objects, which in addition to ease of use may make it easier to learn the 3D UI (Hinckley et al. 1994). The introduction of tactile augmentation also allows designers to explicitly control the realism of VEs, which can be useful in such applications as the treatment of phobias (Carlin et al. 1997).

There are also several disadvantages of using passive haptic feedback. First is the issue of scalability: using multiple physical props requires multiple trackers, which might be expensive and difficult to implement. Second, experimental studies have not yet shown any quantitative improvement in user performance when using props (Hinckley, Tullio et al. 1997; Ware and Rose 1999). However, the studies did show that users preferred physical props.

10.2.2. Constraints

In 3D UIs, constraints are usually very narrowly understood as relations between 3D virtual objects in a scene. The theory of constraints, however, is more general and does not necessarily consider the type of objects involved in constraint specification. Constraints are generally defined as a *relation* between variables that must be satisfied (Marriott and Stuckey 1998). Examples of such relations could be that a line should stay horizontal, that values in spreadsheet cells are always related through a formula, or that pressure in a closed volume should stay below a specified critical level. The objective of constraint theory is the development of algorithms that can find the values of variables satisfying the specified constraints.

For interactive computer graphics, constraints can be defined as relations that define some sort of *geometrical coherence* of the virtual scene during the user's interaction with it. Although the implementation of constraints in interactive 3D computer graphics can use the theory and algorithms developed in constraint theory, from the user interaction point of view, the way constraints are *applied* is more important than the details of their implementation. The main reason that constraints are used in 3D UIs is that they can significantly simplify interaction while improving accuracy and user efficiency. Several types of constraints can be used in 3D UIs.

Physically realistic constraints are an often used type of constraints. One of the best examples of such constraints is collision detection and avoidance. When collision detection is enabled, the user's freedom of movement is constrained by the boundaries of the virtual objects—the user's virtual viewpoint or virtual hand is not allowed to pass through them. Another typical constraint is gravity—objects fall to the virtual ground when the user releases them. Physical constraints should be used with caution: in some applications, such as training or games, satisfying physical constraints is important because it is a critical part of the experience. However, in other applications, introducing such constraints may make interaction more difficult and frustrating. For example, in modeling applications, it might be convenient to leave objects "hanging in the air" when the user releases them (Smith 1987). The flexibility of 3D UIs allows us to selectively choose which physical properties of the physical environment are implemented in the virtual world, and the choice should be based on the requirements of the application.

Constraints also are used to *reduce the number of DOF of the user input* so as to make interaction simpler. For example, a virtual object can be constrained to move only on the surface of a virtual plane, which makes positioning it easier because the user has to control only 2 DOF instead of 3 DOF. Such constrained manipulation has often been used in desktop 3D UIs to allow effective manipulation of 3D models using a mouse (e.g., Bier 1990). Another example is constraining travel to the ground or terrain of the virtual scene. This allows a user to effectively manipulate the viewpoint using only 2D input devices (e.g., Igarashi et al. 1998), and it may help users with 3D input devices to maintain spatial orientation.

Dynamic alignment tools, such as snap grids, guiding lines, and guiding surfaces, are a more complex way to reduce the required DOF. In this approach, the position and orientation of objects are automatically modified to align them with a particular guiding object, which can be as simple as a grid in space or as complex as a 3D surface (e.g., Bier 1986; 1990). With this type of constraint, objects "snap" to alignment with these guides. For example, objects can snap to an equally spaced 3D grid in space in order to make the alignment of several objects easier, or an object can automatically rotate so that it lies exactly on the guiding surface when the user brings it near to that surface.

Intelligent constraints take into account the *semantics* of objects and attempts to constrain their interaction in order to enforce meaningful relations. For example, a virtual lamp can be constrained to stand only on horizontal surfaces such as tables, while a picture frame only "hangs" on vertical walls (Bukowski and Séquin 1995).

The disadvantage of all constraints is that they reduce user control over the interaction, which might not be appropriate for all applications. In many applications, therefore, it is important to allow the user to easily turn constraints on and off. However, when the user requirements are clearly understood and interaction flow carefully designed, constraints can be a very effective design tool for 3D UIs.

10.2.3. Two-Handed Control

Using both hands for 3D interaction allows users to transfer their everyday manipulation experiences and skills to interaction with 3D computer-generated environments. Furthermore, two-handed interaction can significantly increase user performance on certain tasks both in real and virtual interaction. For example, it has been shown that a writing task using both hands resulted in 20% more efficient performance than when only one hand was used (Guiard 1987).

Therefore, two-handed or *bimanual* input has been an active topic of investigation in UIs since the early 1980s (Buxton and Myers 1986). The benefits of two-handed input have been demonstrated in various tasks and applications, including both 2D interfaces (Bier et al. 1993) and 3D interfaces (Sachs et al. 1991; Hinckley et al. 1994; Mapes and Moshell 1995; Zeleznik et al. 1997). In this section, we briefly overview some of the important principles that have been proposed for designing bimanual 3D UIs.

Guiard's Framework of Bimanual Manipulation

The theoretical foundation behind most of the current research on bimanual 3D interaction was proposed by Guiard, who studied the underlying mechanisms controlling the distribution of work between the dominant and nondominant hands of humans (Guiard 1987). He observed that some tasks are inherently *unimanual,* such as throwing darts. Other tasks are *bimanual symmetric,* where each hand performs identical actions either *synchronously,* such as pulling a rope or weightlifting, or *asynchronously,* such as milking a cow or typing on the keyboard. A third class of bimanual actions is *bimanual asymmetric* tasks (sometimes called *cooperative* manipulation) in which the actions of both hands are different but closely coordinated to accomplish the same task (Figure 10.3). A familiar

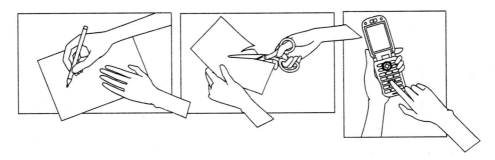

Figure 10.3   *Examples of the asymmetric separation of work between hands in bimanual manipulation: the nondominant hand defines a spatial framework for the actions of the preferred hand. (Illustrations by Keiko Nakao)*

example of such an asymmetric bimanual task is writing: the nondominant hand controls the orientation of the page for more convenient and efficient writing by the dominant hand.

Guiard proposed three principles that characterize the roles of the hands in tasks involving an asymmetric division of labor (Guiard 1987):

1. The nondominant hand dynamically adjusts the spatial frame of reference for the actions of the dominant hand.

2. The dominant hand produces fine-grained precision movements, while the nondominant hand performs gross manipulation.

3. The manipulation is initiated by the nondominant hand.

We should note, however, that the separation of labor between hands is a fluid, dynamic process, and in complex tasks, hands rapidly switch between symmetric and asymmetric manipulation modes.

Guiard's principles provide an important theoretical framework for investigating and designing two-handed 3D UIs. In the rest of this section, we discuss some examples of such interfaces, classifying them according to the asymmetric and symmetric division of labor.

Asymmetric Bimanual 3D Interaction Techniques

The bimanual 3D interface for neurological visualization that we've already seen in section 10.2.1 (Hinckley et al. 1994) was one of the earliest attempts to develop bimanual interaction techniques based on Guiard's principles. In Hinckley's interface, the nondominant hand controlled the orientation of the 3D volumetric neurological data (using a doll's head prop), while the dominant hand controlled a virtual cutting plane that "sliced" the data and presented slices on the screen for analysis (Figure 10.2). According to the principles of asymmetric separation of labor, the nondominant hand controlled the gross position and orientation of a 3D virtual workspace, and the dominant hand performed fine operations in that workspace.

The basic method presented above has been explored in a number of 3D interaction systems and for a variety of tasks. A two-handed interface for an immersive workbench display (Cutler et al. 1997), for example, provides tools for two-handed *object manipulation and rotation* using 6-DOF input devices. The nondominant hand controls the position of a virtual object and the orientation of its rotation axis, while the dominant hand controls rotation around the axis. Zeleznik and colleagues (1997)

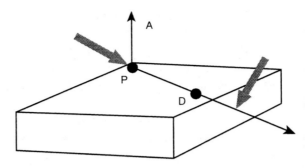

Figure 10.4   *Bimanual positioning and rotation of 3D objects: objects are constrained to move only on the plane. (Zeleznik et al. 1997, © 1997 ACM; reprinted by permission)*

propose a similar 3D position and rotation technique using two mice as input devices (Figure 10.4). With the nondominant hand, the user positions a point on a 2D ground plane, creating a vertical axis (left cursor in Figure 10.4), while the dominant hand allows the user to rotate an object around that axis (right cursor in Figure 10.4). Scaling and zooming were implemented in a similar way.

Virtual menus have often been implemented using bimanual manipulation in which the virtual menu is held in the nondominant hand while the dominant hand is used to select an item in the menu (Mapes and Moshell 1995; Cutler et al. 1997). Virtual writing techniques (Poupyrev, Tomokazu et al. 1998) use the nondominant hand to hold a tracked tablet input device, while the user writes on the tablet with the dominant hand. Similar two-handed, prop-based interfaces are quite common (Coquillart and Wesche 1999; Schmalstieg et al. 1999). The Voodoo Dolls interaction technique that we discussed in Chapter 5 (section 5.4.5) is yet another example of using asymmetric bimanual control for object manipulation (Pierce et al. 1999).

A somewhat different two-handed interface has been implemented for desktop 3D viewpoint control (Balakrishnan and Kurtenbach 1999). The nondominant hand controls the 3D position of the virtual viewpoint, while the dominant hand performs application-specific tasks, such as selection, docking, and 3D painting.

A number of user studies have shown that carefully designed asymmetric bimanual interfaces have a significant performance advantage and are strongly preferred by users (Hinckley et al. 1997). A study by Balakrishan and Kurtenbach (1999), for example, found that in a selection task, user performance was 20% faster than a one-handed interface when the user controlled the viewpoint using the nondominant hand and used the dominant hand to perform another task.

Symmetric Bimanual 3D Interaction Techniques

Symmetric two-handed manipulation has received somewhat less attention. A typical task that has been implemented using symmetric bimanual manipulation is *scaling,* where the user can scale objects by picking up two sides of the object and moving the hands apart or together simultaneously (Zeleznik et al. 1997). A bimanual rotation technique implemented on a workbench display (Cutler et al. 1997) allowed the user to rotate the virtual scene with a "steering-wheel" gesture. Both of these techniques are examples of synchronous bimanual interaction.

Asynchronous, symmetric, two-handed manipulation can also be implemented for interaction with 3D environments. For example, the Polyshop system implemented a rope-pulling gesture for 3D travel (see Chapter 6, section 6.3.6): the user pulled himself through the environment by pulling on an invisible rope with both hands (Mapes and Moshell 1995).

10.2.4. Designing for Different User Groups

Another important part of 3D UI design is to determine the characteristics of the target user population. These user characteristics can have a significant effect on the design of a usable 3D UI. Here, we briefly overview some of the key user characteristics and their influence on 3D UI design.

Age

The methods of both information presentation and interaction depend on the age of the user. Children often require a different interface design than adults because they are physically smaller, they have a shorter attention span, and the mental model they form about the interaction differs from that of adults. Older users may need text presented in a larger font size, or they may not be able to make movements quickly. More research is needed to determine the effects of age on the usability and performance of 3D UIs.

Prior Experience with 3D UIs

Targeting a user population that is already proficient with 3D input and output devices allows us to design more complex 3D UIs. Also, observations indicate that experience with console games or desktop 3D computer games can be positively correlated with performance in 3D UIs. On the other hand, 3D UIs for novice users need to be simplified and easily learnable.

Physical Characteristics

Simple things like a user's height can affect the usability of a 3D UI. For example, a basic implementation of the Go-Go technique (see Chapter 5, section 5.4.3) has a fixed threshold at which the nonlinear arm extension begins. Users with shorter arms, therefore, will not be able to reach nearly as far into the environment as other users. In this case, an adaptive threshold based on arm length would be appropriate. The user's handedness (i.e., his dominant hand) is another example: many input devices are designed only for right-handers. Asymmetric bimanual interfaces must be adaptable for both left- and right-handed users.

Perceptual, Cognitive, and Motor Abilities

People's color recognition and stereo vision abilities are different, and this of course affects the choice of a display system. A specific cognitive characteristic affecting 3D UI design is the user's spatial ability (ability to think, plan, and act in a 3D space). If the user population is known to have lower-than-average spatial abilities, a simplified interface for 3D travel and manipulation may be needed (e.g., the use of additional constraints). People with cognitive or motor disabilities may require a simplified interface as well as the use of special-purpose devices.

10.2.5. Designing for User Comfort

In the design of 2D UIs, a great deal of effort is spent in designing a system that is understandable, intuitive, and well organized, but very rarely do designers have to consider the physical actions users will be performing (although issues such as repetitive stress injuries have made these actions more prominent). In 3D UIs, however, users are often interacting while standing, while wearing or holding heavy or bulky devices, and while moving the whole body. Thus, issues of user comfort and safety are extremely relevant. We offer several practical guidelines for designing comfortable 3D UIs, with a particular emphasis on *public installations* as an example of 3D UIs for real-world use.

> **Move wires and cables out of the way; reduce weight of the equipment.**

HMDs, trackers, and other input/output devices are typically tethered to the host computer or to an interface box (although wireless devices are becoming more common). One of the most common complaints of VE users is that wires and cables get in the way during system use. If the wires are near the floor, users can trip over them or get them wrapped around their legs when they turn. Hanging wires can get in the way during arm movements. Such situations are annoying, can interrupt the user's interaction, and can reduce the sense of presence. Especially for public systems, it is important to find a cable-management solution, such as hanging cables from the ceiling, to minimize these problems. Care should be taken to leave enough length in the cables to allow users free physical movement.

Hanging wires from the ceiling can also reduce the weight of the equipment worn by the user. Weight is an important problem, especially in immersive VE installations; many 3D input and display devices are heavy. The weight of some HMDs is especially troublesome—even short periods of use can result in user fatigue. In mobile AR systems, the user must also carry the computer and other peripherals (such as a GPS receiver), so total weight may be even more important. Every effort should be made to reduce the overall weight the user must bear.

> **Provide physical barriers to keep the user and the equipment safe.**

With HMD-based systems, the user cannot see the physical world and thus is prone to walk into walls, chairs, tables, or other physical objects. In surround-screen systems, the screens seem to disappear when the virtual world is projected on them, so users tend to walk into the screens, which may damage them. The most common approach to addressing these issues is to establish a "safe zone" around the user by making a physical barrier, such as a railing, that the user can hold on to. The safe zone should be large enough to allow sufficient physical movement, but small enough to keep the user away from any potentially dangerous areas.

> **Limit interaction in free space; provide a device resting place.**

The interface design should limit free-space interaction in which the user hand is not physically supported. For example, the image-plane interaction technique (Chapter 5, section 5.4.2) requires the user to hold her hand in free space to select an object, which over a long period of time is very tiresome. Thus, interaction sequences should be designed so that free-space interaction occurs in short chunks of time with resting periods in between. The user should be allowed to rest her hands or arms without breaking the flow of interaction. Also, consider providing a resting place for a device if it is not attached to the user—this could be a stand, a hook, a tool belt, or some other method for putting a device away when it is not needed.

> **Design public systems to be sanitary.**

When a large number of users wear, hold, or touch the same devices, hygiene and health issues are important (Stanney et al. 1998). The designer might consider a routine schedule for cleaning the devices. Another approach is to use removable parts that can be disposed of after a single use, such as thin glove liners for glove-based input devices or HMD liners—light plastic disposable caps that users put on before using the HMD.

> **Design for relatively short sessions.**

Cybersickness and fatigue can be a significant problem when using immersive VE systems. Even though graphics, optics, and tracking have greatly improved, many users may still feel some symptoms of sickness or fatigue after 30 to 45 minutes of use. In public VR installations, the time that the user spends in the system can be explicitly limited (Davies and Harrison 1996). In other applications, the interface designer can mitigate these problems by allowing the work to be done in short blocks of time.

10.3. Inventing 3D User Interfaces

This section surveys some of the informal approaches that have often been used in creating 3D UIs and interaction techniques. These approaches lie in a continuum between strict *imitations of reality* (naturalism or isomorphism) and *magic* (nonisomorphism, things that can't be found in the real world). The approaches presented here should be taken as illustrative examples to help designers and developers to ask the "right questions" that will lead to the development of compelling 3D UIs. Of course, the process of creating something new is difficult to formalize and explain; that is perhaps the most magical, or artistic, part of designing 3D UIs.

10.3.1. Borrowing from the Real World

The most basic, tried-and-true approach is to attempt to simulate, or adapt from, the real, physical world. In some cases the goal is to replicate the real world as closely as possible; in other cases, only elements of the real world are brought into the VE and creatively adapted to the needs of 3D interaction. In this section, we discuss some of the basic approaches and techniques that have been reported in the literature.

Simulating Reality

Simulating reality is key in all simulation applications, such as flight simulators, medical training, treatment of phobias, some entertainment applications, and human factors evaluations of human-controlled mechanisms such as vehicles (e.g., Loftin and Kenney 1995; Carlin et al. 1997; Burdea et al. 1998; Cruz-Neira and Lutz 1999).

The advantage of using this approach is that the user already knows how to use the interface from everyday experience, so the time spent learning how to use the system can be kept to a minimum. Furthermore, the interface often can be implemented based either on the designer's intuition and common sense or on the clearly specified technical design requirements of the application. Advanced and special-purpose 3D interaction techniques, such as some of those presented earlier in this book, might not be necessary in such applications. Interaction with virtual space in this type of interface might be frustrating and difficult, but if the real-world interaction is also frustrating and difficult, then this is actually a feature!

Designers may, however, need to compromise on how realistic the simulation needs to be. Because of the limitations of current technology,

Figure 10.5   *Immersive entertainment environment simulating a dinosaur habitat focuses on the fluidity of interaction, but not on visual realism. (Reprinted with permission of HIT Lab, University of Washington)*

the simulations that we can create are either far from real-life experiences or prohibitively expensive (e.g., professional flight simulators). The realism of simulation that the developer should aim for thus depends heavily on the requirements of the application. The virtual interaction should attempt to reproduce real-world interaction in those details that are essential for the application.

For example, in a VE for entertainment, the goal might be to provide visitors with a first-person immersive experience in an environment that cannot be normally experienced in the real world (Figure 10.5). Exact visual realism might be less important than responsiveness and ease of learning for this application, and thus interaction can be limited to a very simple flying technique that allows the user to fully experience the environment. As another example, in a medical training simulator designed to teach medical students palpation skills in diagnosing prostate cancer, a realistic visual simulation is not required at all, so only a primitive 3D visual model is needed. A realistic and precise simulation of haptic sensation, however, is a key issue, because learning the "feel" of human tissue is the main goal of the system (Burdea et al. 1998). On the other hand, in a system developed for treatment of spider phobia, a simple toy spider was used to provide the patients with a passive haptic sensation of the virtual spider that they observed in the VE (Carlin et al. 1997). It was found that this haptic feedback combined with the graphical representation of the spider was realistic enough to trigger a strong reaction from the patient.

These examples demonstrate that the importance of realism is dependent on the application; 3D UIs should deliver only as much realism as is needed for the application. The effect of realism, or level of detail, on user performance, learning, and training transfer is an important topic of research but is outside the scope of this book. For further reading on this subject, see Luebke and colleagues (2002).

Adapting from the Real World

Instead of attempting to replicate the real world, 3D UIs can also adapt artifacts, ideas, and philosophies from the real world.

The use of *real-world metaphors*—adapting everyday or special-purpose tools as metaphors for 3D interaction—has been a very effective technique for the design of 3D widgets and interaction techniques. For example, a virtual vehicle metaphor has been one of the most often used metaphors for 3D navigation. A virtual flashlight has been used to set viewpoint or lighting directions, and shadows have been used not only to add realism to the rendering, but also to provide simple interaction techniques—the user can manipulate objects in a 3D environment by dragging their shadows (Figure 10.6; Herndon et al. 1992).

As these examples show, the metaphors are only a starting point, and interaction techniques based on them should be carefully designed to match the requirements of the applications and limitations of the

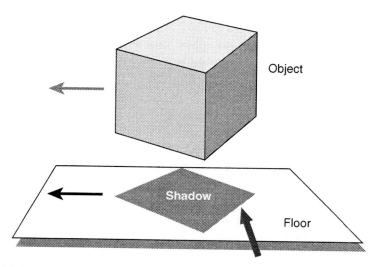

Figure 10.6 *Shadows can be used for constrained 3D manipulation. (Herndon et al. 1992, © 1992 ACM; reprinted by permission)*

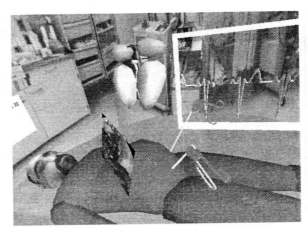

Figure 10.7   *ECG monitor widget designed for VR experience. (Reprinted with permission of HIT Lab, University of Washington)*

technology used. For example, the ECG monitor widget used in the VR emergency room project (Kaufman et al. 1997) had to be larger and less detailed than a real ECG monitor because of the lower resolution of VE displays. At the same time, it was made transparent so that it did not occlude large parts of the VE (Figure 10.7).

Not only single tools, objects, and their features but also entire domains of human activity can inspire and guide the design of 3D UIs. *Architecture* and *movies* have been an important source of inspiration. The objective is not simply to replicate, but instead to creatively adapt the basic principles and ideas in designing 3D UIs and virtual spaces. For example, games have been heavily influenced by the movie culture, exploring transition and storytelling techniques fundamental to film. It has also been observed that both architecture and virtual worlds are based on ordering and organizing shapes and forms in space (Alexander et al. 1977); the design principles from architecture therefore can be transferred to the design of 3D UIs.

Campbell (1996), for example, attempted to design VEs using basic architectural principles (Figure 10.8), suggesting that this would allow users to rely on their familiarity with real-world architectural spaces in helping them to quickly understand and navigate through 3D virtual worlds. At the same time, designers of VEs are not limited by the fundamental physical restrictions that are encountered in traditional architecture, giving them new creative freedom in designing 3D interactive

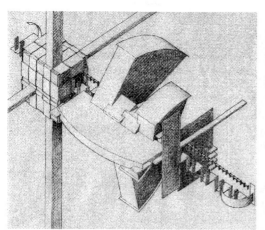 

Figure 10.8 *Virtual architecture design from architectural sketch (left) to VE (right). (Campbell 1996; reprinted by permission of the author)*

spaces. See the discussion of architectural wayfinding cues in Chapter 7 (section 7.4.1) for more on this topic.

Another common technique for adapting elements from the real world to the design of a 3D UI is to borrow natural physical actions that we use in real life. For example, in the Osmose interactive VE, the user navigated by using breathing and balance control, a technique inspired by the scuba diving technique of buoyancy control (Davies and Harrison 1996). The user was able to float upward by breathing in, to fall by breathing out, and to change direction by altering the body's center of balance. The intention was to create an illusion of floating rather than flying or driving in the environment.

Numerous real-world artifacts and concepts can be used in designing 3D UIs, providing an unlimited source of ideas for the creativity of designers and developers. Because users are already familiar with real-world artifacts, it is easy for them to understand the purpose and method of using 3D interaction techniques based on them. Metaphors, however, are never complete, and an important goal is to creatively adapt and change the real-world artifacts and interactions. It is also difficult to find real-world analogies and metaphors for abstract operations. For example, in an early VR authoring system, an "egg" widget was used to create new objects—a metaphor that is not very easy to grasp without prior explanation. In such cases, a symbolic representation might be much more appropriate.

10.3.2. Adapting from 2D User Interfaces

Adapting interaction techniques from traditional 2D UIs has been another common 3D UI design technique. Two-dimensional interaction techniques have many attractive properties. First, 2D UIs and interaction have been thoroughly studied, and interaction paradigms in 2D interfaces are well established, which makes it relatively easy for 3D interface designers to find an appropriate interaction technique. Second, users of 3D UIs are already fluent with 2D interaction, so learning can be kept to a minimum. Third, interaction in two dimensions is significantly easier than interaction in three dimensions—the user has to manipulate only 2 DOF rather than 6 DOF. Consequently, 2D interaction may allow users to perform some tasks, such as selection and manipulation, with a higher degree of precision. Finally, some common tasks that the user may need to perform do not scale well into three dimensions. For example, writing and sketching is significantly easier to perform in 2D than in 3D. These considerations have prompted researchers to design 3D UIs that attempt to take advantage of both 2D and 3D interaction techniques, trying to combine these two input styles in a seamless and intuitive manner (see Chapter 8 for the use of 2D interaction for system control).

Literal Approach: Overlaying a 2D GUI on a 3D World

With little or no modification, 2D UI elements can be embedded directly into a 3D environment. Certainly, for desktop-based 3D applications, this is a natural technique—the 3D scene is rendered in a window, and traditional 2D GUI elements (menus, sliders, etc.) can be attached to this window outside of the 3D environment. A similar approach has been used quite often in immersive VEs, particularly for system control tasks and when interacting with inherently 2D information. Figure 10.9 presents an example of one such system, which simply provides familiar cascading 2D menus overlaid on the 3D world (Bolter et al. 1995).

The shortcoming with this approach is that the GUI interaction elements are introduced as a separate layer on top of the 3D world, so it introduces an additional mode of interaction: the user has to switch into the menu mode and then switch back to 3D UI mode. The approach also does not scale well to other 2D tasks.

2D GUI as an Element of the 3D Environment

An alternative way to place a 2D GUI into a 3D environment is to render the interface as a first-class object in the 3D world. For example, menus

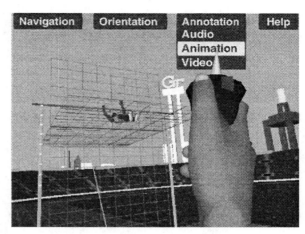

Figure 10.9 *Overlaid 2D interface elements in a 3D VE. (Bolter et al. 1995, © 1995 IEEE)*

and other interface elements can be rendered on some planar surface within the VR, either as 3D buttons and menus arranged on a plane or as a dynamic 2D texture attached to a polygon (Angus and Sowizral 1996). The user can interact with these 2D UI elements in the same way we interact with them in desktop environments—by touching and dragging them on a 2D virtual surface using virtual hand or ray-casting interaction techniques (e.g., Mine 1995b). The difficulty with this approach is that there is no haptic feedback, so interacting with the 2D interface might be difficult and frustrating. To overcome this problem, a physical prop— such as a clipboard—can be tracked and registered with the 2D interface so that it appears on top of the clipboard. The user, holding the physical clipboard in one hand, can touch and interact with 2D interface elements using a pen held in the other hand, which is also tracked. This design technique is sometimes called the *pen-and-tablet* technique.

One of the first systems that used this approach was implemented by Angus and Sowizral (1996); it provided the immersed user (who was inspecting a virtual model of an aircraft) with a hyperlinked document that included 2D plans, drawings, and other information (Figure 10.10). A similar technique was developed for the semi-immersive workbench environment by Coquillart and Wesche (1999), where instead of using an everyday clipboard, 2D data was spatially registered with a tracked, transparent plastic pad. When the user looked through the pad, he perceived the illusion that the 2D information appeared on the pad (see also the transparent prop discussion below).

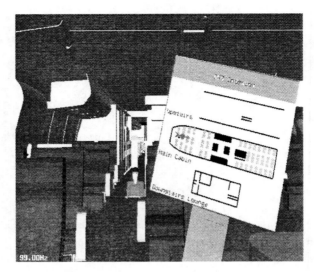

Figure 10.10   *Embedding an interactive 2D interface into a 3D VE. (Angus and Sowizral 1996, © 1996 IEEE)*

The pen-and-tablet technique can be extended by using a touch-sensitive tablet instead of a passive prop. With this active prop, the user can perform significantly more advanced interaction than simply pressing 2D buttons. The Virtual Notepad, for example, allows users not only to view 2D information while immersed in a VE, but also to annotate it with 2D drawings (Figure 10.11; Poupyrev, Tomokazu et al. 1998).

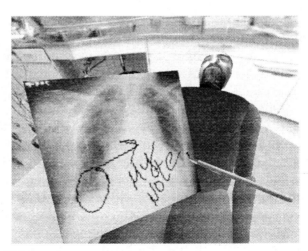

Figure 10.11   *The Virtual Notepad. (Poupyrev, Tomokazu et al. 1998, © 1998 IEEE)*

You have probably noticed that we have already discussed the pen and tablet idea several times in the context of different tasks. That's because it's a rather generic approach in designing 3D UIs that also incorporates many of the strategies we have discussed before. To summarize, the pen and tablet makes use of

- two-handed, asymmetric interaction
- physical props (passive haptic feedback)
- 2D interaction, reducing the DOF of input
- a surface constraint to aid input
- body-referenced interaction

2D Interaction with 3D Objects

It has been often noted that 3D interaction is difficult: the coordinated control of 6 DOF requires significantly more effort than manipulation of only 2 DOF. Reducing the number of degrees of control is especially crucial when high-precision interaction is needed, such as when creating 3D models or performing virtual surgery. Using constraints (section 10.2.2) is one technique to reduce the number of controlled DOF and simplify interaction. A particular instance of this technique that has been successful is based on constraining input with physical 2D surfaces and using gesture-based interaction.

Schmalstieg and his colleagues (1999), for example, developed an effective 2D gestural interface for 3D interaction by using tracked, transparent, passive props with a workbench display (Figure 10.12). The user looks at the 3D environment through the transparent prop (e.g., a simple, transparent Plexiglas plate) and interacts with objects by drawing 2D gestures on the prop. The transparent plate acts as a physical constraint for the user input, making drawing relatively easy.

The system determines the objects that the user interacts with by casting a ray from the user's viewpoint through the pen and transparent pad. For example, Schmalstieg and his colleagues (1999) demonstrated how a group of 3D objects can be selected by drawing a lasso around them on the prop.

Transparent props allow the development of very generic techniques that can be used to interact with any 3D objects in the scene. Furthermore, when the position of objects can be constrained to lie on a virtual ground plane, the user can draw 2D gestures directly on the surface of the

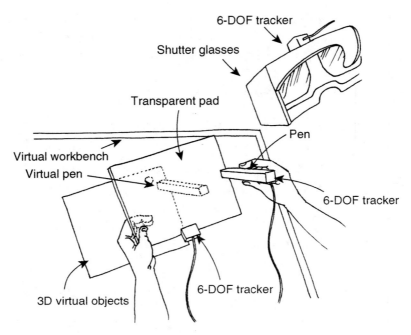

Figure 10.12   *Using transparent props for 2D interaction in a VE.*

display, as long as the pen-tracking technology is provided. For example, in Ergodesk, the user interacts in 2D by drawing directly on the display surface (Figure 10.13), sketching 3D models using a three-button stylus (Forsberg et al. 1997). The system is based on the SKETCH modeling system (Zeleznik et al. 1996) that interprets lines as operations and parameters for 3D modeling commands. Creating a cube, for example, requires the user to draw three gesture lines, one for each of the principal axes, meeting at a single point.

The sketching interface is simple to learn and allows the user to easily create 3D objects by sketching them on a 2D physical surface. This is significantly easier then manipulating or sculpting 3D objects directly using all 6 DOF of input. Furthermore, the user can use another hand for performing traditional 3D input tasks, such as navigating or manipulating 3D objects.

10.3.3. Magic and Aesthetics

It has long been argued that the real power of 3D UIs lies not only in simulating or adapting real-world features, but also in creating a "better" re-

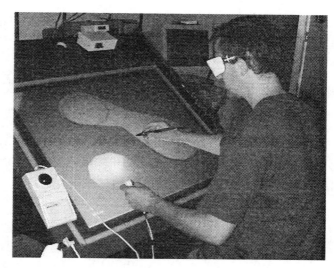

Figure 10.13 *Sketching 3D objects directly on the display surface in Ergodesk. (Forsberg et al. 1997, © 1997 IEEE)*

ality by utilizing magical interaction techniques (e.g., Smith 1987; Stoakley et al. 1995; Shneiderman 2003). One advantage of magical interaction techniques is that they allow users to overcome many human limitations that are so prominent in the real world: limitations of our cognitive, perceptual, physical, and motor capabilities. The second advantage of this approach is that it reduces the effect of technological limitations by compensating for them with enhanced capabilities of the UI. In fact, most of the interaction techniques discussed in Part III of this book are magic techniques to some degree. For example, Go-Go (Chapter 5, section 5.4.3) and flying techniques (Chapter 6, section 6.3.3) enhance our motor capabilities by allowing us to reach further and travel in ways we can't in the real world; the world-in-miniature technique (Chapter 5, section 5.4.4) extends our perceptual capabilities by allowing us to see the entire 3D environment at once; and many system control techniques enhance our cognitive capabilities by visually presenting available choices rather than forcing us to remember them.

There are many approaches that can help to develop new magical techniques. Considering human limitations and looking for solutions that help to overcome them is one possible approach. Cultural clichés and metaphors, such as a flying carpet, can also suggest interesting possibilities for designing magical 3D UIs. For example, the Voodoo Dolls technique (Chapter 5, section 5.4.5) is based on a magical metaphor that suggests that the user can affect remote objects by interacting with their miniature, toylike representations. Because such metaphors are rooted in the popular culture, users may be able to grasp interaction concepts almost immediately. The relationships between techniques and cultural metaphors, however, can also be a source of difficulties. For example, in order to understand the metaphor of flying carpet techniques—a very popular metaphor in VEs (Butterworth et al. 1992; Pausch et al. 1996)—the user needs to know what a magic carpet is and what it can do. Although some metaphors are quite universal, others might be significantly more obscure. For example, the Virtual Tricorder metaphor (Wloka and Greenfield 1995) is based on imaginary devices from the *Star Trek* television series, which may not be well known by users outside of countries where this show is popular. It is not easy to find effective and compelling metaphors for magical interaction techniques; however, the right metaphor can lead to a very enjoyable and effective 3D UI.

The discussion of realism and magic in designing 3D UIs also directly relates to the *aesthetics* of the 3D environment. The traditional focus of interactive 3D computer graphics, strongly influenced by the film and simulation industries, was to strive for photorealistic rendering—attempting to *explicitly* reproduce physical reality. Although this approach is important in specific applications, such as simulation and training, photorealism may be neither necessary nor effective in many other 3D applications. In fact, modern computer graphics are still not powerful enough to reproduce reality so that it is indistinguishable from the real world. Furthermore, humans are amazingly skilled at distinguishing real from fake, particularly when it comes to humans: that is why faces rendered with computer graphics often look artificial and therefore unpleasant.

In many applications, however, photorealism may not be entirely necessary: sketchy, cartoonlike rendering can be effective and compelling in communicating the state of the interaction, while at the same time being enjoyable and effective. One example of such an application is a 3D learning environment for children (Johnson et al. 1998).

Nonphotorealistic cartoon rendering can be particularly effective in drawing humans, because it can suggest similarities using a few strong visual cues while omitting many less relevant visual features. We can observe this effect in political cartoons: even when drawings are grossly distorted, they usually have striking similarities with the subjects of the cartoons, making them immediately recognizable. Simple, cartoonlike rendering of virtual humans is also effective from a system point of view

Figure 10.14 *Cartoon drawing used in 3D online communities. (Reprinted here with permission of There, Inc.)*

because simpler 3D models result in faster rendering. Thus, more computational power can be dedicated to other aspects of human simulation, such as realistic motion. This allows designers to create effective and enjoyable interfaces for such applications as online 3D communities and chat environments (Figure 10.14).

Another advantage of nonphotorealistic aesthetics in 3D interfaces is the ability to create a mood or atmosphere in the 3D environment, as well as to suggest properties of the environment rather then render them explicitly. For example, a rough pencil-style rendering of an architectural model can inform the client that the project is still unfinished (Klein et al. 2000). The possibility to create mood and atmosphere is key in entertainment applications as well as in media art installations. One of the systems that pioneered this broader sense of aesthetics for 3D UIs was Osmose, a VE designed by Char Davies (Davies and Harrison 1996). The aesthetics of Osmose were neither abstract nor photorealistic, but somewhere in between. Implemented using multilayer transparent imagery and heavy

Figure 10.15   *Vertical tree. Digital frame captured in real time through head-mounted display during live performance of immersive virtual environment OSMOSE. (© 1995 Char Davies)*

use of particle animation, Osmose (Figure 10.15) provided the user with the impression of being surrounded by the VE, creating a strong sense of being there (i.e., sense of presence).

The aesthetic aspect of 3D UI design is an interesting and very important part of compelling, immersive, and easy-to-use interfaces. As the rendering power of computer graphics increases, and therefore the range of tools available to artists and designers broadens, the importance of aesthetics in 3D interaction will continue to grow in the future.

10.4. Design Guidelines

We conclude the chapter with a number of specific design guidelines, some of which summarize our previous discussion and others that offer helpful rules of thumb for designing and developing 3D UIs.

> **Ensure temporal and spatial compliance between feedback dimensions.**

It is crucial to ensure the spatial and temporal correspondence between reactive, instrumental, and operational feedback dimensions. In particular, interfaces must be designed to ensure directional compliance between a user's input and the feedback she receives from the system. Reduce latency and use multisensory feedback when appropriate, such as auditory and haptic feedback in combination with visuals.

> **Use constraints.**

Using constraints can greatly increase the speed and accuracy of interaction in many tasks that rely on continuous motor control, such as object manipulation and navigation. However, also consider including functionality that allows the user to switch constraints off when more freedom of input is needed.

> **Consider using props and passive feedback, particularly in highly specialized tasks.**

Using props and passive haptic feedback is an easy and inexpensive way to design a more enjoyable and effective interaction. The drawback of props is that they are highly specialized—the physical shape of props cannot change—therefore, they are particularly effective in very specialized applications.

> **Use Guiard's principles in designing two-handed interfaces.**

Guiard's framework has proven to be a very useful tool for designing effective two-handed interfaces. Use these principles to determine the functions that should be assigned to each hand.

> **Consider real-world tools and practices as a source of inspiration for 3D UI design.**

Adapting everyday or special-purpose tools as metaphors has been a very effective method for designing 3D interaction techniques. Because users are often already familiar with real-world artifacts, it is easy for them to understand the purpose and method of using 3D interaction techniques based on them.

> **Consider designing 3D techniques using principles from 2D interaction.**

Two-dimensional interaction techniques have many attractive properties: they have been thoroughly studied and are well established, most users are already fluent with 2D interaction, and interaction in two dimensions is significantly easier than interaction in a 3D environment.

> **Use and invent magical techniques.**

The real power of 3D UIs is in creating a "better" reality through the use of magical interaction techniques. Magical interaction allows us to overcome the limitations of our cognitive, perceptual, physical, and motor capabilities. It is not easy to find effective and compelling metaphors for magical interaction techniques, but if one is found, it can lead to a very enjoyable and effective 3D UI.

> **Consider alternatives to photorealistic aesthetics.**

In many applications, photorealism may not be entirely necessary; sketchy, cartoonlike rendering can be effective and compelling in communicating the state of the interaction while at the same time being enjoyable. Nonphotorealistic cartoon rendering suggests similarities using a few strong visual cues, which results in simple and more effective rendering. Another advantage of nonphotorealistic aesthetics in 3D interfaces is the ability to create a mood or atmosphere as well as to suggest properties of the environment rather then render them explicitly.

Recommended Reading

For an excellent review of the basics in feedback-control mechanisms and a discussion of early psychological and human factors experiments in this area, consider the following chapter:

Smith, T., and K. Smith (1987). Feedback-Control Mechanisms of Human Behavior. *Handbook of Human Factors.* G. Salvendy (Ed.), John Wiley & Sons, 251–293.

For an in-depth discussion of some of the aspects of realism and level of detail and their effect on user performance, see the following book:

Luebke, D., M. Reddy, J. Cohen, A. Varshney, B. Watson, and R. Huebner (2002). *Level of Detail for 3D Graphics,* Morgan Kaufmann.

Two classic texts on architectural design and philosophy can inspire you to develop new interaction techniques and approaches for planning and developing VEs:

Lynch, K. (1960). *The Image of the City,* MIT Press.

Alexander, C., S. Ishikawa, and M. Silverstein (1977). *A Pattern Language: Towns, Buildings, Construction,* Oxford University Press.

CHAPTER **11**
Evaluation of 3D User Interfaces

Most of this book has covered the various aspects of 3D UI design. We have addressed questions such as, How do I choose an appropriate input device? How do I support wayfinding in large-scale environments? and What object manipulation techniques provide precise positioning? However, one of the central truths of human–computer interaction (HCI) is that even the most careful and well-informed designs can still go wrong in any number of ways. Thus, evaluation of UIs becomes critical. In fact, the reason we can provide answers to questions such as those above is that researchers have performed evaluations addressing those issues. In this chapter, we discuss some of the evaluation methods that can be used for 3D UIs, metrics that help to indicate the usability of 3D UIs, distinctive characteristics of 3D UI evaluation, and guidelines for choosing evaluation methods. We argue that evaluation should not only be performed when a design is complete, but that it should also be used as an integral part of the design process.

11.1. Introduction

Evaluation has often been the missing component of research in 3D interaction. For many years, the fields of VEs and 3D UIs were so novel and the possibilities so limitless that many researchers simply focused on developing new devices, interaction techniques, and UI metaphors—exploring the design space—without taking the time to assess how good the new designs were. As the fields have matured, however, we are taking a closer look at usability. We must critically analyze, assess, and compare devices, interaction techniques, UIs, and applications if 3D UIs are to be used in the real world.

11.1.1. Purposes of Evaluation

Simply stated, evaluation is the analysis, assessment, and testing of an artifact. In UI evaluation, the artifact is the entire UI or part of it, such as a particular input device or interaction technique. The main purpose of UI evaluation is the identification of usability problems or issues, leading to changes in the UI design. In other words, design and evaluation should be performed in an *iterative* fashion, such that design is followed by evaluation, leading to a redesign, which can then be evaluated, and so on. The iteration ends when the UI is "good enough," based on the metrics that have been set (or, more frequently in real-world situations, when the budget runs out or the deadline arrives!).

Although problem identification and redesign are the main goals of evaluation, it may also have secondary purposes. One of these is a more general understanding of the usability of a particular technique, device, or metaphor. This general understanding can lead to *design guidelines* (such as those presented throughout this book), so that each new design can start from an informed position rather than from scratch. For example, we can be reasonably sure that users will not have usability problems with the selection of items from a pull-down menu in a desktop application, because the design of those menus has already gone through many evaluations and iterations.

Another, more ambitious, goal of UI evaluation is the development of *performance models.* These models aim to predict the performance of a user on a particular task within an interface. For example, Fitts's law (Fitts 1954) predicts how quickly a user will be able to position a pointer over a target area based on the distance to the target, the size of the target, and the muscle groups used in moving the pointer. Such performance models must be based on a large number of experimental trials on a wide range of generic tasks, and they are always subject to criticism (e.g., the model doesn't take an important factor into account, or the model doesn't apply to a particular type of task). Nevertheless, if a useful model can be developed, it can provide important guidance for designers.

11.1.2. Terminology

We must define some important terms before continuing with our discussion of 3D UI evaluation. The most important term (which we've already used a couple of times) is *usability*. We define usability in the broadest sense, meaning that it encompasses everything about an artifact and a person that affects the person's use of the artifact. Evaluation, then, measures some aspects of the usability of an interface (it is not likely that we can quantify the usability of an interface with a single score). Usability measures (or metrics) fall into several categories, such as system performance, user task performance, and user preference (see section 11.3).

There are at least two roles that people play in a usability evaluation. A person who designs, implements, administers, or analyzes an evaluation is called an *evaluator*. A person who takes part in an evaluation by using the interface, performing tasks, or answering questions is called a *user*. In formal experimentation, a user is sometimes called a *subject*.

Finally, we distinguish below between *evaluation methods* and *evaluation approaches*. Evaluation methods (or techniques) are particular steps that can be used in an evaluation. An evaluation approach, on the other hand, is a combination of methods, used in a particular sequence, to form a complete usability evaluation.

11.1.3. Chapter Roadmap

We begin by providing some background information on usability evaluation from the field of HCI (section 11.2). We then narrow the focus to the evaluation of 3D UIs (specifically the evaluation of immersive VEs), looking first at evaluation metrics (section 11.3) and then distinctive characteristics of 3D UI evaluation (section 11.4). In section 11.5, we classify 3D UI evaluation methods and follow that with a description and comparison of two comprehensive approaches to 3D UI evaluation—testbed evaluation and sequential evaluation. Finally, we conclude with a set of guidelines for those performing evaluations of 3D UIs (section 11.7).

11.2. Background

In this section, we describe some of the common tools and methods used in 3D UI evaluation. None of these tools or methods is new or unique to 3D UIs. They have all been used and tested in many other usability evaluation contexts. We present them here as an introduction to these topics for the reader who has never studied HCI. For more detailed information, you can consult any one of a large number of introductory books on HCI (see the recommended reading list at the end of the chapter).

11.2.1. Tools for Evaluation Design and Implementation

The tools presented below are useful for designing, organizing, and implementing usability evaluations of 3D UIs.

User Task Analysis

A user task analysis (Hackos and Redish 1998) provides the basis for design in terms of what users need to be able to do with the application. This analysis generates (among other resources) a list of detailed task descriptions, sequences, and relationships, user work, and information flow. Typically, a user task analysis is provided by a design and development team, based on extensive input from representative users. Whenever possible, it is useful for an evaluator to participate in the user task analysis.

Scenarios

The user task analysis also shapes representative user task scenarios by defining, ordering, and ranking user tasks and task flow. The accuracy and completeness of a scenario directly affect the quality of the subsequent formative and summative evaluations because these methods typically do not reveal usability problems associated with a specific interaction within the application unless it is included in the user task scenario (and is therefore performed by users during evaluation sessions). Similarly, in order to evaluate how well an application's interface supports high-level information gathering and processing, representative user task scenarios must include more than simply atomic, mechanical- or physical-level tasking; they should also include high-level cognitive, problem-solving tasking specific to the application domain. This is especially important in 3D UIs, where user tasks generally are inherently more complex, difficult, and unusual than in many GUIs.

Taxonomy

Taxonomy is defined as the science of classification, but it has also come to mean a specific classification scheme. Many different types of taxonomies have been used in 3D UI research, including multidimensional

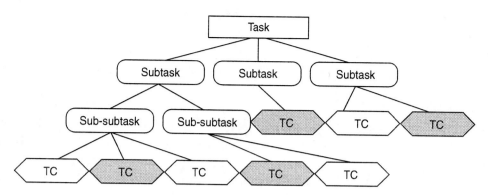

Figure 11.1 *Generic technique-decomposition taxonomy. The shaded technique components can be combined to form a complete interaction technique for the top-level task.*

design spaces (Card et al. 1990) and metaphor-based classifications (Poupyrev, Weghorst et al. 1997). The main goal of all of these types is to organize a particular set of objects so that they can be thought about systematically. Here we focus on a specific type of taxonomy—the technique-decomposition taxonomy.

The concept of technique decomposition is that each interaction task can be partitioned (decomposed) into subtasks. Similarly, we can decompose the techniques for a particular task into subtechniques, which we call *technique components* (Bowman and Hodges 1999). Each technique component addresses a single subtask (Figure 11.1). We can think of each subtask as a question that must be answered by the designer of an interaction technique, and the set of technique components for a subtask as the set of possible answers for that question.

The set of technique components for each subtask may be built in two ways. First, we can decompose existing techniques and list the components for each subtask. Second, we can think of original technique components that could be used to accomplish each subtask in the taxonomy.

Such technique-decomposition taxonomies have several advantages. Most relevant to the topic of this chapter, the taxonomy can be used as a guide for the evaluation of techniques. In other words, we can perform summative evaluations (Hix and Hartson 1993) that compare technique components rather than holistic techniques. This means that the results of our evaluation will be more precise—we will be able to claim, for example, that object-manipulation techniques that use the virtual object as the center of rotation are more precise than those that use the virtual hand as the center of rotation. Of course, this increased precision comes with a cost—we must perform more complex and time-consuming evaluations. The taxonomy can also be used to design new techniques. For example, the four shaded components in Figure 11.1 could be combined to create a complete interaction technique.

Prototyping

In order to perform a usability evaluation, there must be something to evaluate. In some cases, the full-fledged, final application is available to be evaluated, but more often, evaluation is (or should be) performed earlier in the design cycle so that most problems can be caught early. Thus, many evaluations use some form of prototype.

Prototypes are generally classified based on their level of *fidelity*—that is, how closely the prototype resembles and acts like the final product. Somewhat surprisingly, a great deal of useful usability information can be gleaned from the evaluation of a low-fidelity prototype such as a paper-based sketch, a storyboard, or a static mockup of the interface. In general, the fidelity of the prototype will increase with each successive evaluation.

One important prototyping method for 3D UIs is the so-called Wizard of Oz (WOZ) approach. A WOZ prototype appears to have a large amount of functionality, even though that functionality is not actually present. A human controls the prototype (like the wizard behind the curtain), making it appear more intelligent or high-fidelity than it actually is. For 3D UIs, this prototyping method can be quite useful because the actual implementation of many 3D interaction techniques and UI metaphors can be very complex. For example, one may not want to go to the trouble of implementing a full-fledged speech interface if it is only one of the options being considered. By developing a simple keyboard-based interface, an evaluator can mimic the actions that would be taken by the system when a user speaks a particular word or phrase and can thus determine the usability characteristics of the actual speech interface.

For more detailed information on prototyping in general, see Hix and Hartson (1993).

11.2.2. Evaluation Methods Used for 3D Interfaces

From the literature, we have compiled a list of usability evaluation methods that have been applied to 3D UIs (although numerous references could be cited for some of the techniques we present, we have included citations that are most recognized and accessible). Most of these methods were developed for 2D or GUI usability evaluation and have been subsequently extended to support 3D UI evaluation.

Cognitive Walkthrough

The *cognitive walkthrough* (Polson et al. 1992) is an approach to evaluating a UI based on stepping through common tasks that a user would perform and evaluating the interface's ability to support each step. This approach is intended especially to gain an understanding of the usability of a system for first-time or infrequent users, that is, for users in an exploratory learning mode. Steed and Tromp (1998) have used a cognitive walkthrough approach to evaluate a collaborative VE.

Heuristic Evaluation

Heuristic or *guidelines-based expert evaluation* (Nielsen and Molich 1992) is a method in which several usability experts separately evaluate a UI design (probably a prototype) by applying a set of heuristics or design guidelines, that are either general enough to apply to any UI or are tailored for 3D UIs in particular. No representative users are involved. Results from the several experts are then combined and ranked to prioritize iterative design or redesign of each usability issue discovered. The current lack of well-formed guidelines and heuristics for 3D UI design and evaluation make this approach more challenging for 3D UIs. Examples of this approach applied to 3D UIs can be found in Gabbard, Hix, and Swan (1999); Stanney and Reeves (2000); and Steed and Tromp (1998).

Formative Evaluation

Formative evaluation (both formal and informal; Hix and Hartson 1993); is an observational, empirical evaluation method, applied during evolving stages of design, that assesses user interaction by iteratively placing representative users in task-based scenarios in order to identify usability problems, as well as to assess the design's ability to support user exploration, learning, and task performance. Formative evaluations can range from being rather informal, providing mostly qualitative results such as critical incidents, user comments, and general reactions, to being very formal and extensive, producing both qualitative and quantitative (task timing, errors, etc.) results.

Collected data are analyzed to identify UI components that both support and detract from user task performance and user satisfaction. Alternating between formative evaluation and design or redesign efforts ultimately leads to an iteratively refined UI design. Most usability evaluations of 3D UIs fall into the formative evaluation category. The work of Hix and her colleagues (1999) provides a good example.

Summative Evaluation

Summative or *comparative evaluation* (both formal and informal; Hix and Hartson 1993; Scriven 1967) is an evaluation and statistical comparison of two or more configurations of UI designs, UI components, and/or UI techniques. As with formative evaluation, representative users perform task scenarios as evaluators collect both qualitative and quantitative data. As with formative evaluations, summative evaluations can be formally or informally applied.

Summative evaluation is generally performed after UI designs (or components) are complete and as a traditional factorial experimental design with multiple independent variables. Summative evaluation enables evaluators to measure and subsequently compare the productivity and cost benefits associated with different UI designs. Comparing 3D UIs requires a consistent set of user task scenarios (borrowed and/or refined from the formative evaluation effort), resulting in primarily quantitative results that compare (on a task-by-task basis) a design's support for specific user task performance.

Many of the formal experiments discussed in Part III of this book are summative evaluations of 3D interaction techniques. For example, see Bowman, Johnson and Hodges (1999) and Poupyrev, Weghorst, and colleagues (1997).

Questionnaires

A *questionnaire* (Hix and Hartson 1993) is a written set of questions used to obtain information from users before or after they have participated in a usability evaluation session. Questionnaires are good for collecting demographic information (e.g., age, gender, computer experience) and subjective data (e.g., opinions, comments, preferences, ratings) and are often more convenient and more consistent than spoken interviews.

In the context of 3D UIs, questionnaires are used quite frequently, especially to elicit information about subjective phenomena such as presence (Witmer and Singer 1998) or simulator sickness/cybersickness (Kennedy et al. 1993).

Interviews and Demos

The *interview* (Hix and Hartson 1993) is a technique for gathering information about users by talking directly to them. An interview can gather more information than a questionnaire and may go to a deeper level of detail. Interviews are good for getting subjective reactions, opinions, and insights into how people reason about issues. *Structured* interviews have a predefined set of questions and responses. *Open-ended* interviews permit the respondent (interviewee) to provide additional information, and they permit the interviewer to ask broad questions without a fixed set of answers and explore paths of questioning that may occur to him spontaneously during the interview. Demonstrations (typically of a prototype) may be used in conjunction with user interviews to aid a user in talking about the interface.

In 3D UI evaluation, the use of interviews has not been studied explicitly, but informal interviews are often used at the end of formative or summative usability evaluations (e.g., Bowman and Hodges 1997).

11.3. Evaluation Metrics for 3D Interfaces

Now we turn to metrics. That is, how do we measure the characteristics of a 3D UI when evaluating it? We focus on the general metric of usability. A 3D UI is usable when the user can reach her goals; when the important tasks can be done better, easier, or faster than with another system; and when users are not frustrated or uncomfortable. Note that all of these have to do with the user.

We discuss three types of metrics for 3D UIs: system performance metrics, task performance metrics, and user preference metrics.

11.3.1. System Performance Metrics

System performance refers to typical computer or graphics system performance, using metrics such as average frame rate, average latency, network delay, and optical distortion. From the interface point of view, system performance metrics are really not important in and of themselves. Rather, they are important only insofar as they affect the user's experience or tasks. For example, the frame rate probably needs to be at real-time levels before a user will feel present. Also, in a collaborative setting, task performance will likely be negatively affected if there is too much network delay.

11.3.2. Task Performance Metrics

User task performance refers to the quality of performance of specific tasks in the 3D application, such as the time to navigate to a specific location, the accuracy of object placement, or the number of errors a user makes in selecting an object from a set. Task performance metrics may also be domain-specific. For example, evaluators may want to measure student learning in an educational application or spatial awareness in a military training VE.

Typically, speed (efficiency) and accuracy are the most important task performance metrics. The problem with measuring both speed and accuracy is that there is an implicit relationship between them: *I can go faster but be less accurate,* or *I can increase my accuracy by decreasing my speed.* It is assumed that for every task, there is some curve representing this speed/accuracy tradeoff, and users must decide where on the curve they want to be (even if they don't do this consciously). In an evaluation, therefore, if you simply tell your subjects to do a task as quickly and precisely as possible, they will probably end up all over the curve, giving you data with a high level of variability. Therefore, it is very important that you instruct users in a very specific way if you want them to be at one end of the curve or the other. Another way to manage the tradeoff is to tell users to do the task as quickly as possible one time, as accurately as possible the second time, and to balance speed and accuracy the third time. This gives you information about the tradeoff curve for the particular task you're looking at.

11.3.3. User Preference Metrics

User preference refers to the subjective perception of the interface by the user (perceived ease of use, ease of learning, satisfaction, etc.). These preferences are often measured via questionnaires or interviews and may be either qualitative or quantitative. The user preference metrics generally contribute significantly to overall usability. A usable application is one whose interface does not pose any significant barriers to task completion. Often, HCI experts speak of a *transparent* interface—a UI that simply disappears until it feels to the user as if he is working directly on the problem rather than indirectly through an interface. UIs should be intuitive, provide good affordances (indications of their use and how they are to be used), provide good feedback, not be obtrusive, and so on. An application cannot be effective unless users are willing to use it (and this is precisely the problem with some more advanced VE applications—they provide functionality for the user to do a task, but a lack of attention to user preference keeps them from being used).

For 3D UIs in particular, *presence* and *user comfort* can be important metrics that are not usually considered in traditional UI evaluation. Presence is a crucial, but not very well understood metric for VE systems. It is the "feeling of being there"—existing in the virtual world rather than in the physical world. How can we measure presence? One method simply asks users to rate their feeling of being there on a 1 to 100 scale. Questionnaires can also be used and can contain a wide variety of questions, all designed to get at different aspects of presence. Psychophysical measures are used in controlled experiments where stimuli are manipulated and then correlated to users' ratings of presence (for example, how does the rating change when the environment is presented in mono versus stereo modes?). There are also some more objective measures. Some are physiological (how the body responds to the VE). Others might look at users' reactions to events in the VE (e.g., does the user duck when he's about to hit a virtual beam?). Tests of memory for the environment and the objects within it might give an indirect measurement of the level of presence. Finally, if we know a task for which presence is required, we can measure users' performance on that task and infer the level of presence. There is still a great deal of debate about the definition of presence, the best ways to measure presence, and the importance of presence as a metric (e.g., Usoh et al. 2000; Witmer and Singer 1998).

The other novel user preference metric for 3D systems is user comfort. This includes several different things. The most notable and well studied is so-called *simulator sickness* (because it was first noted in flight simulators). This is symptomatically similar to motion sickness and may result from mismatches in sensory information (e.g., your eyes tell your brain that you are moving, but your vestibular system tells your brain that you are not moving). There is also work on the physical aftereffects of being exposed to 3D systems. For example, if a VE misregisters the virtual hand and the real hand (they're not at the same physical location), the user may have trouble doing precise manipulation in the real world after exposure to the virtual world. More seriously, activities like driving or walking may be impaired after extremely long exposures (1 hour or more). Finally, there are simple strains on arms/hands/eyes from the use of 3D devices. User comfort is also usually measured subjectively, using rating scales or questionnaires. The most famous questionnaire is the simulator sickness questionnaire (SSQ) developed by Kennedy and his colleagues (1993). Researchers have used some objective measures in the study of aftereffects—for example by measuring the accuracy of a manipulation task in the real world after exposure to a virtual world (Wann and Mon-Williams 2002).

11.4. Distinctive Characteristics of 3D Interface Evaluation

The approaches we discuss below for usability evaluation of 3D UIs have been developed and used in response to perceived differences between the evaluation of 3D UIs and the evaluation of traditional UIs such as GUIs. Many of the fundamental concepts and goals are similar, but use of these approaches in the context of 3D UIs is distinct. Here, we present some of the issues that differentiate 3D UI usability evaluation, organized into several categories. The categories contain overlapping considerations but provide a rough partitioning of these important issues. Note that many of these issues are not necessarily found in the literature, but instead come from personal experience and extensive discussions with colleagues.

11.4.1. Physical Environment Issues

One of the most obvious differences between 3D UIs and traditional UIs is the *physical* environment in which that interface is used. In many 3D UIs, nontraditional input and output devices are used, which can preclude the use of some types of evaluation. Users may be standing rather than sitting, and they may be moving about a large space, using whole-body movements. These properties give rise to several issues for usability evaluation. Following are some examples:

- In interfaces using non-see-through HMDs, the user cannot see the surrounding physical world. Therefore, the evaluator must ensure that the user will not bump into walls or other physical objects, trip over cables, or move outside the range of the tracking device (Viirre 1994). A related problem in surround-screen VEs (such as the CAVE) is that the physical walls can be difficult to see because of projected graphics. Problems of this sort could contaminate the results of a usability evaluation (e.g., if the user trips while in the midst of a timed task) and more importantly could cause injury to the user. To mitigate risk, the evaluator can ensure that cables are bundled and will not get in the way of the user (e.g., cables may descend from above). Also, the user may be placed in a physical enclosure that limits movement to areas where there are no physical objects to interfere.

- Many 3D displays do not allow multiple simultaneous viewers (e.g., user and evaluator), so equipment must be set up so that an evaluator can see the same image as the user. With an HMD, for example, this can be done by splitting the video signal and sending it to both the HMD and a monitor. In a surround-screen or workbench VE, a monoscopic view of the scene could be rendered to a monitor, or, if performance will not be adversely affected, both the user and the evaluator can be tracked (this can cause other problems, however; see section 11.4.2 on evaluator considerations). If images are viewed on a monitor, then it is difficult to see both the actions of the user and the graphical environment at the same time, meaning that multiple evaluators may be necessary to observe and collect data during an evaluation session.

- A common and very effective technique for generating important qualitative data during usability evaluation sessions is the "think-aloud" protocol (as described in Hix and Hartson [1993]). With this technique, subjects talk about their actions, goals, and thoughts regarding the interface while they are performing specific tasks. In some 3D UIs, however, voice recognition is used as an interaction technique, making the think-aloud protocol much more difficult and perhaps even impossible. Post-session interviews may help to recover some of the information that would have been obtained from the think-aloud protocol.

- Another common technique involves recording video of both the user and the interface (as described in Hix and Hartson [1993]). Because 3D UI users are often mobile, a single, fixed camera may require a very wide shot, which may not allow precise identification of actions. This could be addressed by using a tracking camera (with, unfortunately, additional expense and complexity) or a camera operator (additional personnel). Moreover, views of the user and the graphical environment must be synchronized so that cause and effect can clearly be seen on the videotape. Finally, recording video of a stereoscopic graphics image can be problematic.

- An ever-increasing number of proposed 3D applications are shared among two or more users (Stiles et al. 1996; Normand

et al. 1999). These collaborative 3D UIs become even more difficult to evaluate than single-user 3D UIs due to physical separation of users (i.e., users are in more than one physical location),
the additional information that must be recorded for each user,
the unpredictability of network behavior as a factor influencing
usability, the possibility that each user will have different devices, and the additional complexity of the system, which may
cause more frequent crashes or other problems.

11.4.2. Evaluator Issues

A second set of issues relates to the role of the evaluator in a 3D UI usability evaluation. Because of the complexities and distinctive characteristics of 3D UIs, a usability study may require multiple evaluators,
different evaluator roles and behaviors, or both. Following are some
examples:

- Many VEs attempt to produce a sense of *presence* in the user—
  that is, a feeling of actually being in the virtual world rather than
  the physical one. Evaluators can cause breaks in presence if the
  user can sense them. In VEs using projected graphics, the user
  will see an evaluator if the evaluator moves into the user's field
  of view. This is especially likely in a CAVE environment (Cruz-
  Neira et al. 1993) where it is difficult to see the front of a user
  (e.g., their facial expressions and detailed use of handheld devices) without affecting that user's sense of presence. This may
  break presence, because the evaluator is not part of the virtual
  world. In any type of VE, touching or talking to the user can
  cause such breaks. If the evaluation is assessing presence, or if
  presence is hypothesized to affect performance on the task being
  evaluated, then the evaluator must take care to remain unsensed
  during the evaluation.

- When breaks in presence are deemed very important for a particular VE, an evaluator may not wish to intervene at all during an
  evaluation session. This means that the experimental application/
  interface must be robust and bug-free so that the session does not
  have to be interrupted to fix a problem. Also, instructions given
  to the user must be very detailed, explicit, and precise, and the
  evaluator should make sure the user has a complete understanding of the procedure and tasks before beginning the session.

- 3D UI hardware and software are often more complex and less robust than traditional UI hardware and software. Again, multiple evaluators may be needed to do tasks such as helping the user with display and input hardware, running the software that produces graphics and other output, recording data such as timings and errors, and recording critical incidents and other qualitative observations of a user's actions.

- Traditional UIs typically require only a discrete, single stream of input (e.g., from mouse and keyboard), but many 3D UIs include multimodal input, combining discrete events, gestures, voice, and/or whole-body motion. It is much more difficult for an evaluator to process these multiple input streams simultaneously and record an accurate log of the user's actions. These challenges make multiple evaluators and video even more important.

11.4.3. User Issues

There are also a large number of issues related to the user population used as subjects in 3D UI usability evaluations. In traditional evaluations, subjects are gleaned from the target user population of an application or from a similar representative group of people. Efforts are often made, for example, to preserve gender equity, to have a good distribution of ages, and to test both experts and novices if these differences are representative of the target user population. The nature of 3D UI evaluation, however, does not always allow for such straightforward selection of users. Following are some examples:

- 3D UIs are still often a "solution looking for a problem." Because of this, the target user population for a 3D application or interaction technique to be evaluated may not be known or well understood. For example, a study comparing two virtual travel techniques is not aimed at a particular set of users. Thus, it may be difficult to generalize performance results. The best course of action is to evaluate the most diverse user population possible in terms of age, gender, technical ability, physical characteristics, and so on, and to include these factors in any models of performance.

- It may be impossible to differentiate between novice and expert users because there are very few potential subjects who could be considered experts in 3D UIs. Most users who could be considered experts might be, for example, research staff, whose participation in an evaluation could confound the results. Also, because most users are typically novices, the evaluation itself may need to be framed at a lower cognitive and physical level. Evaluators can make no assumptions about a novice user's ability to understand or use a given interaction technique or device.

- Because 3D UIs will be novel to many potential subjects, the results of an evaluation may exhibit high variability and differences among individuals. This means that the number of subjects needed to obtain a good picture of performance may be larger than for traditional usability evaluations. If statistically significant results are required (depending on the type of usability evaluation being performed), the number of subjects may be even greater.

- Researchers are still studying a large design space for 3D interaction techniques and devices. Because of this, evaluations often compare two or more techniques, devices, or combinations of the two. To perform such evaluations using a within-subjects design, users must be able to adapt to a wide variety of situations. If a between-subjects design is used, a larger number of subjects will again be needed.

- VE evaluations must consider the effects of cybersickness and fatigue on subjects. Although some of the causes of cybersickness are known, there are still no predictive models for it (Kennedy et al. 2000), and little is known regarding acceptable exposure time to VEs. For evaluations, then, a worst-case assumption must be made. A lengthy experiment (anything over 30 minutes, for example, might be considered lengthy, depending on the specific VE) must contain planned rest breaks and contingency plans in case of ill or fatigued subjects. Shortening the experiment is often not an option, especially if statistically significant results are needed.

- Because it is not known exactly what VE situations cause sickness or fatigue, most VE evaluations should include some measurement (e.g., subjective, questionnaire-based [Kennedy et al. 2000], or physiological) of these factors. A result indicating that an interaction technique was 50% faster than any other evaluated technique would be severely misleading if that interaction technique also made 30% of subjects sick! Thus, user comfort measurements should be included in low-level VE evaluations.

- Presence is another example of a measure often required in VE evaluations that has no analogue in traditional UI evaluation. VE evaluations must often take into account subjective reports of perceived presence, perceived fidelity of the virtual world, and so on. Questionnaires (Usoh et al. 2000; Witmer and Singer 1998) have been developed that purportedly obtain reliable and consistent measurements of such factors.

11.4.4. Evaluation Type Issues

Traditional usability evaluation can take many forms. These include informal user studies, formal experiments, task-based usability studies, heuristic evaluations, and the use of predictive models of performance (see section 11.3 for further discussion of these types of evaluations). There are several issues related to the use of various types of usability evaluation in 3D UIs. Following are some examples:

- Evaluations based solely on heuristics (i.e., design guidelines), performed by usability experts, are very difficult in 3D UIs because of a lack of published, verified guidelines for 3D UI design. There are some notable exceptions (Bowman 2002; Conkar et al. 1999; Gabbard 1997; Kaur 1999; Kaur et al. 1999; Mills and Noyes 1999; Stanney and Reeves 2000), but for the most part, it is difficult to predict the usability of a 3D interface without studying real users attempting representative tasks in the 3D UI. It is not likely that a large number of heuristics will appear, at least not until 3D input and output devices become more standardized. Even assuming standardized devices, however, the design space for 3D interaction techniques and interfaces is very large, making it difficult to produce effective and general heuristics to use as the basis for evaluation.

- Another major type of usability evaluation that does not employ users is the application of performance models (e.g., GOMS, Fitts's law). Very few models of this type have been developed for or adapted to 3D UIs. However, the lower cost of both heuristic evaluation and performance model application makes them attractive for evaluation.

- Because of the complexity and novelty of 3D UIs, the applicability or utility of automated, tool-based evaluation may be greater than it is for more traditional UIs. For example, several issues above have noted the need for more than one evaluator in a 3D UI usability evaluation session. Automated usability evaluations could reduce the need for several evaluators in a single session. There are at least two possibilities for automated usability evaluation of 3D UIs: first, to automatically collect and/or analyze data generated by one or more users in a 3D UI, and second, to perform an analysis of an interface design using an interactive tool that embodies design guidelines (similar to heuristics). Some work has been done on automatic collection and analysis of data using specific types of repeating patterns in users' data as indicators of potential usability problems (e.g., Siochi and Hix 1991). However this work was performed on a typical GUI, and there appears to be no research yet conducted that studies automated data collection and evaluation of users' data in 3D UIs. Thus, differences in the kinds of data for 3D UI usability evaluation have not been explored, but they would involve, at a minimum, collating data from multiple users in a single session, possibly at different physical locations and even in different parts of the 3D environment. At least one tool, MAUVE (Multi-Attribute Usability evaluation tool for Virtual Environments) incorporates design guidelines organized around several VE categories: navigation, object manipulation, input, output (e.g., visual, auditory, haptic), and so on (Stanney et al. 2000). Within each of these categories, MAUVE presents a series of questions to an evaluator, who uses the tool to perform a multicriteria, heuristic-style evaluation of a specific 3D UI.

- When performing statistical experiments to quantify and compare the usability of various 3D interaction techniques, input devices, interface elements, and so on, it is often difficult to know which factors have a potential impact on the results. Besides the primary independent variable (e.g., a specific interaction technique), a large number of other potential factors could be included, such as environment, task, system, or user characteristics. One approach is to try to vary as many of these potentially important factors as possible during a single experiment. This "testbed evaluation" approach (Bowman, Johnson et al. 1999; Snow and Williges 1998) has been used with some success (see section 11.6.1). The other extreme would be to simply hold as many of these other factors as possible constant and evaluate only in a particular set of circumstances. Thus, statistical 3D UI experimental evaluations may be either overly simplistic or overly complex—finding the proper balance is difficult.

11.4.5. Miscellaneous Issues

- 3D UI usability evaluations generally focus at a lower level than traditional UI evaluations. In the context of GUIs, a standard look and feel and a standard set of interface elements and interaction techniques exist, so evaluation usually looks at subtle interface nuances or overall interface metaphors. In 3D UIs, however, there are no interface standards, and there is not even a good understanding of the usability of various interface types. Therefore, 3D UI evaluations most often compare lower-level components, such as interaction techniques or input devices.

- It is tempting to overgeneralize the results of evaluations of 3D interaction performed in a generic (nonapplication) context. However, because of the fast-changing and complex nature of 3D UIs, one cannot assume anything (display type, input devices, graphics processing power, tracker accuracy, etc.) about the characteristics of a real 3D application. Everything has the potential to change. Therefore, it is important to include information about the environment in which the evaluation was performed and to evaluate in a range of environments (e.g., using different devices) if possible.

11.5. Classification of 3D Evaluation Methods

A classification space for 3D UI usability evaluation methods can provide a structured means for comparing evaluation methods. One such space classifies methods according to three key characteristics: *involvement of representative users, context of evaluation,* and *types of results produced* (Figure 11.2).

The first characteristic discriminates between those methods that *require* the participation of representative users (to provide design or use-based experiences and options) and those methods that do not (methods not requiring users still require a usability expert). The second characteristic describes the type of context in which the evaluation takes place. In particular, this characteristic identifies those methods that are applied in a generic context and those that are applied in an application-specific

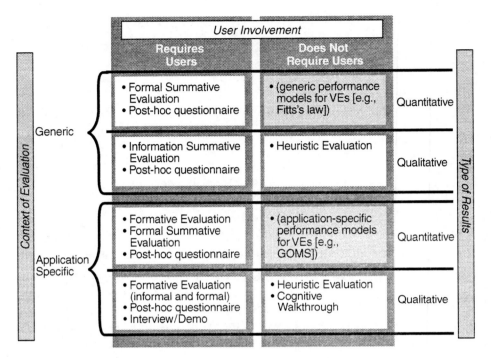

Figure 11.2   *A classification of usability evaluation methods for 3D UIs. (Image reprinted by permission of MIT Press and Presence: Teleoperators and Virtual Environments)*

context. The context of evaluation inherently imposes restrictions on the applicability and generality of results. Thus, conclusions or results of evaluations conducted in a generic context can typically be applied more broadly (i.e., to more types of interfaces) than results of an application-specific evaluation method, which may be best suited for applications that are similar in nature. The third characteristic identifies whether or not a given usability evaluation method produces (primarily) qualitative or quantitative results.

Note that the characteristics described above are not designed to be mutually exclusive, and are instead designed to convey one (of many) usability evaluation method characteristics. For example, a particular usability evaluation method may produce both quantitative and qualitative results. Indeed, many of the identified methods are flexible enough to provide insight at many levels. These three characteristics were chosen (over other potential characteristics) because they are often the most significant (to evaluators) because of their overall effect on the usability process. That is, a researcher interested in undertaking usability evaluation will likely need to know what the evaluation will cost, what the impact of the evaluation will be, and how the results can be applied. Each of the three characteristics addresses these concerns: degree of user involvement directly affects the cost to proctor and analyze the evaluation; results of the process indicate what type of information will be produced (for the given cost); and context of evaluation inherently dictates to what extent results may be applied.

This classification is useful on several levels. It structures the space of evaluation methods and provides a practical vocabulary for discussion of methods in the research community. It also allows researchers to compare two or more methods and understand how they are similar or different on a fundamental level. Finally, it reveals "holes" in the space (Card et al. 1990)—combinations of the three characteristics that have rarely or never been tried in the 3D UI community.

Figure 11.2 shows that there are two such holes in this space (the shaded boxes). More specifically, there is a lack of current 3D UI usability evaluation methods that do not require users and that can be applied in a generic context to produce quantitative results (upper right of the figure). Note that some possible existing 2D and GUI evaluation methods are listed in parentheses, but few, if any, of these methods have been applied to 3D UIs. Similarly, there appears to be no method that provides quantitative results in an application-specific setting that does not require users (third box down on the right of the figure). These areas may be interesting avenues for further research.

11.6. Two Multimethod Approaches

A shortcoming of the classification discussed in section 11.5 is that it does not convey "when" in the software development lifecycle a method is best applied or "how" several methods may be applied. In most cases, answers to these questions cannot be determined without a comprehensive understanding of each of the methods presented, as well as the specific goals and circumstances of the 3D UI research or development effort. In this section, we present two well-developed 3D UI evaluation approaches and compare them in terms of practical usage and results.

11.6.1. Testbed Evaluation Approach

Bowman and Hodges (1999) take the approach of empirically evaluating interaction techniques outside the context of applications (i.e., within a generic context rather than within a specific application) and add the support of a framework for design and evaluation, which we summarize here. Principled, systematic design and evaluation frameworks give formalism and structure to research on interaction; they do not rely solely on experience and intuition. Formal frameworks provide us not only with a greater understanding of the advantages and disadvantages of current techniques, but also with better opportunities to create robust and well-performing new techniques based on knowledge gained through evaluation. Therefore, this approach follows several important evaluation concepts, elucidated in the following sections. Figure 11.3 presents an overview of this approach.

Initial Evaluation

The first step toward formalizing the design, evaluation, and application of interaction techniques is to gain an intuitive understanding of the generic interaction tasks in which one is interested and current techniques available for the tasks (see Figure 11.3, area labeled 1). This is accomplished through experience using interaction techniques and through observation and evaluation of groups of users. These initial evaluation experiences are heavily drawn upon for the processes of building a taxonomy, listing outside influences on performance, and listing performance measures. It is helpful, therefore, to gain as much experience of this type as possible so that good decisions can be made in the next phases of formalization.

Taxonomy

The next step is to establish a taxonomy (Figure 11.3, area 2) of interaction techniques for the interaction task being evaluated. These are technique-decomposition taxonomies, as described in section 11.2.1. For example, the task of changing an object's color might be made up of three subtasks: selecting an object, choosing a color, and applying the color. The subtask for choosing a color might have two possible technique components: changing the values of R, G, and B sliders or touching a point within a 3D color space. The subtasks and their related technique components make up a taxonomy for the object coloring task.

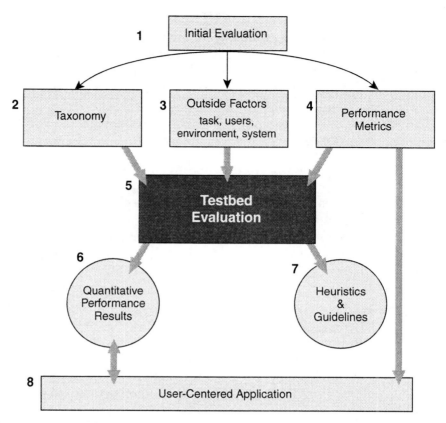

Figure 11.3 *Testbed evaluation approach. (Image reprinted by permission of MIT Press and Presence: Teleoperators and Virtual Environments)*

Ideally, the taxonomies established by this approach need to be correct, complete, and general. Any interaction technique that can be conceived for the task should fit within the taxonomy. Thus, subtasks will necessarily be abstract. The taxonomy will also list several possible technique components for each of the subtasks, but they do not list every conceivable component.

Building taxonomies is a good way to understand the low-level makeup of interaction techniques and to formalize differences between them, but once they are in place, they can also be used in the design process. One can think of a taxonomy not only as a characterization, but also as a design space. Because a taxonomy breaks the task down into separable subtasks, a wide range of designs can be considered quickly, simply by trying different combinations of technique components for each of the subtasks. There is no guarantee that a given combination will make sense as a complete interaction technique, but the systematic nature of the taxonomy makes it easy to generate designs and to reject inappropriate combinations.

Outside Factors

Interaction techniques cannot be evaluated in a vacuum. A user's performance on an interaction task may depend on a variety of factors (Figure 11.3, area 3), of which the interaction technique is but one. In order for the evaluation framework to be complete, such factors must be included explicitly and used as secondary independent variables in evaluations. Bowman and Hodges (1999) identified four categories of outside factors.

First, task characteristics are those attributes of the task that may affect user performance, including distance to be traveled or size of the object being manipulated. Second, the approach considers environment characteristics, such as the number of obstacles and the level of activity or motion in the 3D scene. User characteristics, including cognitive measures such as spatial ability and physical attributes such as arm length, may also contribute to user performance. Finally, system characteristics, such as the lighting model used or the mean frame rate, may be significant.

Performance Metrics

This approach is designed to obtain information about human performance in common 3D interaction tasks—but what is performance? Speed and accuracy are easy to measure, are quantitative, and are clearly important in the evaluation of interaction techniques, but there are also many other performance metrics (Figure 11.3, area 4) to be considered. Thus, this approach also considers more subjective performance values, such as perceived ease of use, ease of learning, and user comfort. The choice of interaction technique could conceivably affect all of these, and they should not be discounted. Also, more than any other current computing paradigm, 3D UIs involve the user's senses and body in the task. Thus, a focus on user-centric performance measures is essential. If an interaction technique does not make good use of human skills, or if it causes fatigue or discomfort, it will not provide overall usability, despite its performance in other areas.

Testbed Evaluation

Bowman and Hodges (1999) use testbed evaluation (Figure 11.3, area 5) as the final stage in the evaluation of interaction techniques for 3D interaction tasks. This approach allows generic, generalizable, and reusable evaluation through the creation of testbeds—environments and tasks that involve all important aspects of a task, that evaluate each component of a technique, that consider outside influences (factors other than the interaction technique) on performance, and that have multiple performance measures. A testbed experiment uses a formal, factorial, experimental design and normally requires a large number of subjects. If many interaction techniques or outside factors are included in the evaluation, the number of trials per subject can become overly large, so interaction techniques are usually a between-subjects variable (each subject uses only a single interaction technique), while other factors are within-subjects variables. See the case studies below for examples of testbed experiments.

Application and Generalization of Results

Testbed evaluation produces a set of results or models (Figure 11.3, area 6) that characterize the usability of an interaction technique for the specified task. Usability is given in terms of multiple performance metrics with respect to various levels of outside factors. These results become part of a performance database for the interaction task, with more information being added to the database each time a new technique is run through the testbed. These results can also be generalized into heuristics or guidelines (Figure 11.3, area 7) that can easily be evaluated and applied by 3D UI developers.

The last step is to apply the performance results to 3D applications (Figure 11.3, area 8) with the goal of making them more useful and usable. In order to choose interaction techniques for applications appropriately, one must understand the interaction requirements of the application. There is no single "best" technique, because the technique that is best for one application may not be optimal for another application with different requirements. Therefore, applications need to specify their interaction requirements before the most appropriate interaction techniques can be chosen. This specification is done in terms of the performance metrics that have already been defined as part of the formal framework. Once the requirements are in place, the performance results from testbed evaluation can be used to recommend interaction techniques that meet those requirements.

Case Studies

Although testbed evaluation could be applied to almost any type of interactive system, it is especially appropriate for 3D UIs because of its focus on low-level interaction techniques. Testbed experiments have been performed comparing techniques for the tasks of travel (Bowman, Davis et al. 1999) and selection/manipulation (Bowman and Hodges 1999).

The travel testbed experiment compared seven different travel techniques for the tasks of naïve search and primed search. In the primed search trials, the initial visibility of the target and the required accuracy of movement were also varied. The dependent variables were time for task completion and subjective user comfort ratings. Forty-four subjects participated in the experiment. The researchers gathered both demographic and spatial ability information for each subject.

The selection/manipulation testbed compared the usability and performance of nine different interaction techniques. For selection tasks, the independent variables were distance from the user to the object, size of the object, and density of distracter objects. For manipulation tasks, the required accuracy of placement, the required degrees of freedom, and the distance through which the object was moved were varied. The dependent variables in this experiment were the time for task completion, the number of selection errors, and subjective user comfort ratings. Forty-eight subjects participated, and the researchers again obtained demographic data and spatial ability scores.

In both instances, the testbed approach produced unexpected and interesting results that would not have been revealed by a simpler experiment. For example, in the selection/manipulation testbed, it was found that selection techniques using an extended virtual hand performed well with larger, nearer objects and more poorly with smaller, farther objects, while selection techniques based on ray-casting performed well regardless of object size or distance. The testbed environments and tasks have also proved to be reusable. The travel testbed was used to evaluate a new travel technique and compare it to existing techniques, while the manipulation testbed has been used to evaluate the usability of common techniques in the context of different VE display devices.

11.6.2. Sequential Evaluation Approach

Gabbard, Hix, and Swan (1999) present a sequential approach to usability evaluation for specific 3D applications. The sequential evaluation approach is a usability engineering approach and addresses both design and evaluation of 3D UIs. However, for the scope of this chapter, we focus on different types of evaluation and address analysis, design, and prototyping only when they have a direct effect on evaluation.

Although some of its components are well suited for evaluation of generic interaction techniques, the complete sequential evaluation approach employs application-specific guidelines, domain-specific representative users, and application-specific user tasks to produce a usable and useful interface for a particular application. In many cases, results or lessons learned may be applied to other, similar applications (for example, 3D applications with similar display or input devices, or with similar types of tasks). In other cases (albeit less often), it is possible to abstract the results for general use.

Sequential evaluation evolved from iteratively adapting and enhancing existing 2D and GUI usability evaluation methods. In particular, it modifies and extends specific methods to account for complex interaction techniques, nonstandard and dynamic UI components, and multimodal tasks inherent in 3D UIs. Moreover, the adapted/extended methods both streamline the usability engineering process and provide sufficient coverage of the usability space. Although the name implies that the various methods are applied in sequence, there is considerable opportunity to iterate both within a particular method as well as among methods. It is important to note that all the pieces of this approach have been used for years in GUI usability evaluations. The unique contribution of Gabbard, Hix, and Swan's (1999) work is the breadth and depth offered by progressive use of these techniques, adapted when necessary for 3D UI evaluation, in an application-specific context. Further, the way in which each step in the progression informs the next step is an important finding: the ordering of the methods guides developers toward a usable application.

Figure 11.4 presents the sequential evaluation approach. It allows developers to improve a 3D UI by a combination of expert-based and user-based techniques. This approach is based on sequentially performing user task analysis (see Figure 11.4, area labeled 1), heuristic (or guideline-based expert) evaluation (Figure 11.4, area 2), formative evaluation (Figure 11.4, area 3), and summative evaluation (Figure 11.4, area 4), with iteration as appropriate within and among each type of evaluation. This

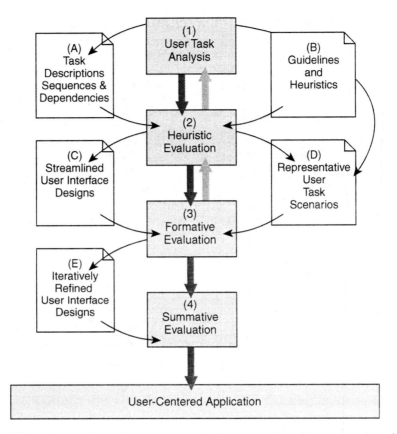

Figure 11.4 *Sequential evaluation approach. (Image reprinted by permission of MIT Press and Presence: Teleoperators and Virtual Environments)*

approach leverages the results of each individual method by systematically defining and refining the 3D UI in a cost-effective progression.

Depending upon the nature of the application, this sequential evaluation approach may be applied in a strictly serial approach (as Figure 11.4's solid black arrows illustrate) or iteratively applied (either as a whole or per-individual method, as Figure 11.4's gray arrows illustrate) many times. For example, when used to evaluate a complex command-and-control battlefield visualization application (Hix et al. 1999), user task analysis was followed by significant iterative use of heuristic and formative evaluation and lastly followed by a single, broad summative evaluation.

From experience, this sequential evaluation approach provides cost-effective assessment and refinement of usability for a specific 3D application. Obviously, the exact cost and benefit of a particular evaluation effort depends largely on the application's complexity and maturity. In some cases, cost can be managed by performing quick and lightweight formative evaluations (which involve users and thus are typically the most time-consuming to plan and perform). Moreover, by using a "hallway methodology," user-based methods can be performed quickly and cost-effectively by simply finding volunteers from within one's own organization. This approach should be used only as a last resort or in cases where the representative user class includes just about anyone. When used, care should be taken to ensure that "hallway" users provide a close representative match to the application's ultimate end users.

The individual methods involved in sequential evaluation are described earlier in the chapter (user task analysis in section 11.2.1 and heuristic, formative, and summative evaluation in section 11.2.2).

Case Studies

The sequential evaluation approach has been applied to several 3D UIs, including the Naval Research Lab's Dragon application: a VE for battlefield visualization (Gabbard et al. 1999). Dragon is presented on a Responsive Workbench that provides a 3D display for observing and managing battlespace information shared among commanders and other battle planners. The researchers performed several evaluations over a nine-month period, using one to three users and two to three evaluators per session. Each evaluation session revealed a set of usability problems and generated a corresponding set of recommendations. The developers would address the recommendations and produce an improved UI for the next iteration of evaluation. The researchers performed four major cycles of iteration during the evaluation of Dragon, each cycle using the progression of usability methods described in this section.

During the expert guideline-based evaluations, various user interaction design experts worked alone or collectively to assess the evolving user interaction design for Dragon. The expert evaluations uncovered several major design problems that are described in detail in Hix et al. (1999). Based on user task analysis and early expert guideline-based evaluations, the researchers created a set of user task scenarios specifically for battlefield visualization. During each formative session, there were at least two and often three evaluators present. Although both the expert guideline-based evaluation sessions and the formative evaluation sessions were personnel-intensive (with two or three evaluators involved), it was found that the quality and amount of data collected by multiple evaluators greatly outweighed the cost of those evaluators.

Finally, the summative evaluation statistically examined the effect of four factors: locomotion metaphor (egocentric versus exocentric), gesture control (controls rate versus controls position), visual presentation device (workbench, desktop, CAVE), and stereopsis (present versus not present). The results of these efforts are described in Hix and Gabbard (2002). This experience with sequential evaluation demonstrated its utility and effectiveness.

11.6.3. Comparison of Approaches

The two major evaluation methods we have presented for 3D UIs—testbed evaluation and sequential evaluation—take quite different approaches to the same problem: how to improve usability in 3D applications. At a high level, these approaches can be characterized in the space defined in section 11.5. Sequential evaluation is done in the context of a particular application and can have both quantitative and qualitative results. Testbed evaluation is done in a generic evaluation context and usually seeks quantitative results. Both approaches employ users in evaluation.

In this section, we take a more detailed look at the similarities of and differences between these two approaches. We organize this comparison by answering several key questions about each of the methods. Many of these questions can be asked of other evaluation methods and perhaps should be asked prior to designing a usability evaluation. Indeed, answers to these questions may help identify appropriate evaluation methods given specific research, design, or development goals. Developers should attempt to find valid answers to these and related questions regarding different usability evaluation methods. Another possibility is to understand the general properties, strengths, and weaknesses of each approach so that the two approaches can be linked in complementary ways.

What Are the Goals of the Approach?

As mentioned above, both approaches ultimately aim to improve usability in 3D applications. However, there are more specific goals that exhibit differences between the two approaches.

Testbed evaluation has the specific goal of finding generic performance characteristics of interaction techniques. This means that one wants to understand interaction technique performance in a high-level, abstract way, not in the context of a particular application. This goal is important because, if achieved, it can lead to wide applicability of the results. In order to do generic evaluation, the testbed approach is limited to general techniques for common, universal tasks (such as navigation, selection, or manipulation). To say this in another way, testbed evaluation is not designed to evaluate special-purpose techniques for specific tasks, such as applying a texture. Rather, it abstracts away from these specifics, using generic properties of the task, user, environment, and system.

Sequential evaluation's immediate goal is to iterate toward a better UI for a particular application, in this case a specific 3D application. It looks very closely at particular user tasks of an application to determine which scenarios and interaction techniques should be incorporated. In general, this approach tends to be quite specific in order to produce the best possible interface design for a particular application under development.

When Should the Approach Be Used?

By its non-application-specific nature, the testbed approach actually falls completely outside the design cycle of a particular application. Ideally, testbed evaluation should be completed before an application is even a glimmer in the eye of a developer. Because it produces general performance/usability results for interaction techniques, these results can be used as a starting point for the design of new 3D UIs.

On the other hand, sequential evaluation should be used early and continually throughout the design cycle of a 3D application. User task analysis is necessary before the first interface prototypes are built. Heuristic and formative evaluations of a prototype produce recommendations that can be applied to subsequent design iterations. Summative evaluations of different design possibilities can be done when the choice of design (e.g., for interaction techniques) is not clear.

The distinct time periods in which testbed evaluation and sequential evaluation are employed suggests that combining the two approaches is possible and even desirable. Testbed evaluation can first produce a set of general results and guidelines that can serve as an advanced and well-informed starting point for a 3D application's UI design. Sequential evaluation can then refine that initial design in a more application-specific fashion.

In What Situations Is the Approach Useful?

Testbed evaluation allows the researcher to understand detailed performance characteristics of common interaction techniques, especially user performance. It provides a wide range of performance data that may be applicable to a variety of situations. In a development effort that requires a suite of applications with common interaction techniques and interface elements, testbed evaluation could provide a quantitative basis for choosing them, because developers could choose interaction techniques that performed well across the range of tasks, environments, and users in the applications; their choices are supported by empirical evidence.

As we have said, the sequential evaluation approach should be used throughout the design cycle of a 3D UI, but it is especially useful in the early stages of interface design. Because sequential evaluation produces results even on very low-fidelity prototypes or design specifications, a 3D application's UI can be refined much earlier, resulting in greater cost savings. Also, the earlier this approach is used in development, the more time remains for producing design iterations, which ultimately results in a better product. This approach also makes the most sense when a user task analysis has been performed. This analysis will suggest task scenarios that make evaluation more meaningful and effective.

What Are the Costs of Using the Approach?

The testbed evaluation approach can be seen as very costly and is definitely not appropriate for every situation. In certain scenarios, however, its benefits can make the extra effort worthwhile. Some of the most important costs associated with testbed evaluation include difficult experimental design (many independent and dependent variables, where some of the combinations of variables are not testable), experiments requiring large numbers of trials to ensure significant results, and large amounts of time spent running experiments because of the number of subjects and trials. Once an experiment has been conducted, the results may not be as detailed as some developers would like. Because testbed evaluation looks at generic situations, information on specific interface details such as labeling, the shape of icons, and so on will not usually be available.

In general, the sequential evaluation approach may be less costly than testbed evaluation because it can focus on a particular 3D application rather than pay the cost of abstraction. However, some important costs are still associated with this method. Multiple evaluators may be needed. Development of useful task scenarios may take a large amount of effort. Conducting the evaluations themselves may be costly in terms of time, depending on the complexity of task scenarios. Most importantly, because this is part of an iterative design effort, time spent by developers to incorporate suggested design changes after each round of evaluation must be considered.

What Are the Benefits of Using the Approach?

Because testbed evaluation is so costly, its benefits must be significant before it becomes a useful evaluation method. One such benefit is generality of the results. Because testbed experiments are conducted in a generalized context, the results may be applied many times in many different types of applications. Of course, there is a cost associated with each use of the results because the developer must decide which results are relevant to a specific 3D UI. Second, testbeds for a particular task may be used multiple times. When a new interaction technique is proposed, that technique can be run through the testbed and compared with techniques already evaluated. The same set of subjects is not necessary, because testbed evaluation usually uses a between-subjects design. Finally, the generality of the experiments lends itself to development of general guidelines and heuristics. It is more difficult to generalize from experience with a single application.

For a particular application, the sequential evaluation approach can be very beneficial. Although it does not produce reusable results or general principles in the same broad sense as testbed evaluation, it is likely to produce a more refined and usable 3D UI than if the results of testbed evaluation were applied alone. Another of the major benefits of this method relates to its involvement of users in the development process. Because members of the representative user group take part in many of the evaluations, the 3D UI is more likely to be tailored to their needs and should result in higher user acceptance and productivity, reduced user errors, and increased user satisfaction. There may be some reuse of results, because other applications may have similar tasks or requirements, or they may be able to use refined interaction techniques produced by the process.

How Are the Approach's Evaluation Results Applied?

The results of testbed evaluation are applicable to any 3D UI that uses the tasks studied with a testbed. Currently, testbed results are available for some of the most common tasks in 3D UIs: travel and selection/manipulation (Bowman, Johnson et al. 2001). The results can be applied in two ways. The first, informal technique is to use the guidelines produced by testbed evaluation in choosing interaction techniques for an application (as in Bowman, Johnson et al. 1999). A more formal technique uses the requirements of the application (specified in terms of the testbed's performance metrics) to choose the interaction technique closest to those requirements. Both of these approaches should produce a set of interaction techniques for the application that makes it more usable than the same application designed using intuition alone. However, because the results are so general, the 3D UI will almost certainly require further refinement.

Application of results of the sequential evaluation approach is much more straightforward. Heuristic and formative evaluations produce specific suggestions for changes to the application's UI or interaction techniques. The result of summative evaluation is an interface or set of interaction techniques that performs the best or is the most usable in a comparative study. In any case, results of the evaluation are tied directly to changes in the interface of the 3D application.

11.7. Guidelines for 3D Interface Evaluation

In this section, we present some guidelines for those wishing to perform usability evaluations of 3D UIs. The first subsection presents general guidelines, and the second subsection focuses specifically on formal experimentation.

11.7.1. General Guidelines

> Begin with informal evaluation.

Informal evaluation is very important, both in the process of developing an application and in doing basic interaction research. In the context of an application, informal evaluation can quickly narrow the design space and point out major flaws in the design. In basic research, informal evaluation helps you understand the task and the techniques on an intuitive level before moving on to more formal classifications and experiments.

> Acknowledge and plan for the differences between traditional UI and 3D UI evaluation.

Section 11.4 detailed a large number of distinctive characteristics of 3D UI evaluation. These differences must be considered when designing a study. For example, you should plan to have multiple evaluators, incorporate rest breaks into your procedure, and assess whether breaks in presence could affect your results.

> **Choose an evaluation approach that meets your requirements.**

Just as we discussed with respect to interaction techniques, there is no optimal usability evaluation method or approach. A range of methods should be considered, and important questions such as those in section 11.6.3 should be asked. For example, if you have designed a new interaction technique and want to refine the usability of the design before any implementation, a heuristic evaluation or cognitive walkthrough fits the bill. On the other hand, if you must choose between two input devices for a task in which a small difference in efficiency may be significant, a formal experiment may be required.

> **Use a wide range of metrics.**

Remember that speed and accuracy alone do not equal usability. Also remember to look at learning, comfort, presence, and other metrics in order to get a complete picture of the usability of the interface.

11.7.2. Guidelines for Formal Experimentation

> **Design experiments with general applicability.**

If you're going to do formal experiments, you will be investing a large amount of time and effort, so you want the results to be as general as possible. Thus, you have to think hard about how to design tasks that are generic, performance measures to which real applications can relate, and a method for applications to easily reuse the results.

> Use pilot studies to determine which variables should be
> tested in the main experiment.

In doing formal experiments, especially testbed evaluations, you often have too many variables to actually test without an infinite supply of time and subjects. Small pilot studies can show trends that may allow you to remove certain variables because they do not appear to affect the task you're doing.

> Look for interactions between variables—rarely will a single
> technique be the best in all situations.

In most formal experiments on the usability of 3D UIs, the most interesting results have been interactions. That is, it's rarely the case that technique A is always better than technique B. Rather, technique A works well when the environment has characteristic X, and technique B works well when the environment has characteristic Y. Statistical analysis should reveal these interactions between variables.

Recommended Reading

Many entry-level HCI textbooks, such as the following, provide an excellent introduction to usability evaluation and usability engineering:

Hix, D., and H. Hartson (1993). *Developing User Interfaces: Ensuring Usability Through Product & Process,* John Wiley & Sons.

Rosson, M., and J. Carroll (2001). *Usability Engineering: Scenario-Based Development of Human Computer Interaction,* Morgan Kaufmann Publishers.

Acknowledgment

Much of the content in this chapter comes from a 2002 article by Doug Bowman, Joseph Gabbard, and Deborah Hix that appeared in the journal *Presence*: "A Survey of Usability Evaluation in Virtual Environments: Classification and Comparison of Methods." (*Presence: Teleoperators and Virtual Environments,* 11[4], 404–424).

We thank the coauthors and the MIT Press for their generous permission to reuse the material here. This content is © 2002 MIT Press.

PART V

The Future of 3D User Interfaces

In this final part of the book, we look toward the future. Chapter 12 describes some new technologies and interface styles that present important new problem areas for 3D UI designers. The focus in this chapter is on augmented reality (AR) and mixed reality (MR), which combine virtual images and objects with real-world images and objects. Chapter 13 concludes the book with a look at some of the most important challenges facing 3D UI researchers.

CHAPTER 12
Beyond Virtual: 3D Interfaces for the Real World

Despite the dramatic developments in the fields of desktop-based and immersive 3D computer-generated environments, we still spend most of our lives in the real world. *Augmented reality* (AR), a relatively new field of interactive computer graphics, proposes to augment real-world and physical spaces with computer-controlled sensory stimuli, such as images, sounds, and smells. These stimuli create, in a sense, an interactive virtual space embedded into the physical world around us. AR environments differ from pure VEs in that we can have access to both real and virtual objects at the same time, so instead of replacing the real environments around us, we can *enhance* them with tools and experiences that are impossible in the real world. In this chapter, we look at the issues involved in designing 3D UIs for AR applications.

12.1. Introduction

Although AR has been proposed as an alternative to VEs (Wellner et al. 1993), recently the two have been viewed as complementary technologies—each has its own advantages and range of applications. Indeed, AR interfaces allow users to access both the real and virtual worlds at the same time, so virtual computer-generated objects can be used in coordination with physical objects to "improve" the physical environment. Therefore, the typical applications of AR are usually focused on enhancing users' real-world activities, such as providing real-time guidance to surgeons by displaying possible paths for needles (State et al. 1996) or evaluating proposed changes to airplane cockpit designs in relation to the real physical cockpit (Poupyrev et al. 2001).

Physical environments, however, are complex, and AR interfaces may further increase their complexity. VEs, on the other hand, provide highly flexible and controlled interaction spaces that exist only inside the computer and are not affected much by the physical world. Therefore, pure VEs are effective in applications that benefit from the immersive qualities of virtual worlds (e.g., simulation, training, and 3D modeling) or that do not require access to physical objects.

Recently, a *mixed reality* (MR) view became prominent; in the MR view, VEs and AR are not separate ideas, but instead two points along a continuum of UIs spread between pure reality and pure virtuality (Milgram, Takemura et al. 1994; Figure 12.1).

From an interaction point of view, however, AR is simply a new, emerging type of 3D UI. This means that, on the one hand, it opens a new and exciting field for future 3D UI research and development and a whole new range of AR-specific 3D interaction techniques and applications.

On the other hand, a large portion of the ideas and principles discussed in this book may be directly applied to the design of AR UIs. At the least, they can inform designers of the fundamental principles of spatial interaction. Many concepts presented in this book, such as design principles for manipulation and system control techniques (Chapters 5 and 8), text input in 3D environments (Chapter 9), two-handed interaction, and constraints (Chapter 10), are quite general and can be useful in designing any type of 3D UI, including an AR UI. Indeed, some 3D interaction techniques, such as world-in-miniature (section 5.4.4), have already been used in designing effective AR interfaces (Bell et al. 2002).

This chapter surveys some of the basic approaches and techniques for designing and developing 3D UIs for the real world. It does not attempt to be a comprehensive review of AR technology and interaction techniques. For more information on topics such as AR tracking and registra-

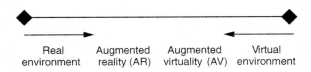

Real   Augmented   Augmented   Virtual
environment   reality (AR)   virtuality (AV)   environment

Figure 12.1   *Reality–virtuality continuum. (Billinghurst et al. 2001, © 2001 IEEE)*

tion, please see the recommended reading list at the end of the chapter. Instead, we forgo technology and focus on interaction, giving a broad overview of AR interface design to provide a starting point for investigating this rapidly growing and exciting field.

12.1.1. What Is Augmented Reality?

AR interfaces have been defined by Azuma as interfaces that

1. superimpose virtual information on the real world (combine virtual and physical objects in the same interaction space),
2. are interactive in real time, and
3. are spatial—the virtual objects are registered and interactive in 3D space (Azuma 1997).

Figure 12.2 shows an example of an early AR application (Feiner et al. 1993) in which the user sees a virtual representation of the interior parts of a copier for the purpose of repair or maintenance.

Azuma's definition is a classical view of AR that is focused on "grafting" 3D virtual objects onto the real world. In this chapter, however, our approach follows the MR philosophy discussed above: we do not necessarily demand that only 3D virtual objects must be used, but we do require that virtual objects are registered in 3D physical space in relation to other physical objects.

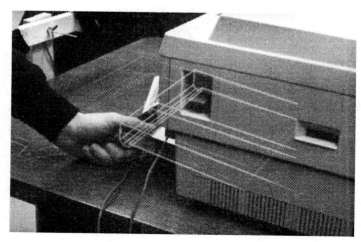

Figure 12.2 *KARMA AR system. (Feiner et al. 1993, © 1993 ACM; reprinted by permission)*

We also discuss only interactive AR systems. For example, although large-scale projection screens are common in public spaces, and the virtual images that they display are sometimes registered to the surrounding environment, they are not interactive.

12.1.2. Bringing Virtual Interfaces into the Real World

The basic technologies required to build AR systems are *tracking, registration,* and *display.* Similar to VEs, the most commonly used tracking technologies are magnetic, optical, acoustic, inertial, and vision-based (see Chapter 4, section 4.3.1). Tracking information is used to register (align) virtual objects with real objects or locations.

The most common AR display technologies are see-through HMDs, which can be either optical or video see-through. *Optical see-through* displays place optical combiners in front of the user's eyes; the combiners are partially transparent so that the user can see the real world through them and partially reflective so that the user can see virtual images reflected from small head-mounted screens. *Video see-through* displays work by streaming real-time video from head-mounted cameras to the graphics subsystem, which renders virtual computer graphics images into the video buffers in real time, blending the virtual and real. The result is displayed to the user in a traditional closed-view HMD (Azuma 1997). Figure 12.3 presents an example of an early AR video see-through display.

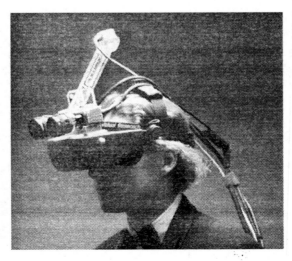

Figure 12.3   *Early video see-through AR. (Included by permission from UNC, Department of Computer Science)*

Similar to VE UI design, the design of AR interfaces is often limited and defined by the properties and limitations of AR display, tracking, and registration technologies. Ideally, the basic AR technologies should allow unobtrusive user interaction with virtual objects superimposed on 3D physical objects everywhere in the physical environment. However, because this is not possible with current technology, there is always a compromise, which leads to several very different interaction styles that are discussed in this chapter.

12.1.3. Chapter Roadmap

In the rest of the chapter, we survey various classes of AR interfaces. We start by discussing AR interfaces for *3D data browsing* (section 12.2), where the user can only observe superimposed virtual objects and little interaction is provided. *3D AR interfaces* (section 12.3) extend this approach by adding interactive capabilities similar to 3D interaction techniques in VE applications. *Augmented surfaces* (section 12.4) make up a class of AR interfaces that does not use HMDs but instead projects data onto the working surfaces where they are registered—an approach that is often called *tangible interfaces.* Considering the shortcomings of all these interaction styles, we introduce *tangible AR interfaces* (section 12.5), which attempt to combine tangible interaction with 3D AR interfaces. We then discuss a number of other interesting directions in AR interaction, such as *agent-based* (section 12.6) and *transitional* (section 12.7) AR interfaces. The chapter concludes by discussing future research directions (section 12.8).

12.2. AR Interfaces as 3D Data Browsers

AR data browsing was one of the very first visions for AR interfaces. The technology was used to superimpose virtual 3D objects on the real world so that the user could see both. The goal was to create an illusion of virtual objects being just as real as physical objects: in a sense, we can call this *real-world VR.*

The main technical challenge and objective for AR 3D data browsers is to correctly register and render 3D virtual objects in relation to the real-world objects and the user's head position, which constantly changes. Many of these AR systems are based on see-through HMDs and 6-DOF optical or magnetic trackers.

One of the very first applications for this style of AR interface was designed to support the decision-making process of a doctor during medical

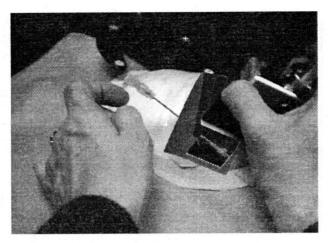

Figure 12.4 *AR data browsers: virtual needle paths are registered to the real patient. (State et al. 1996, © 1996 ACM; reprinted by permission)*

procedures. For example, this can be achieved by superimposing real-time ultrasound images on the patient (Bajura et al. 1992) or by displaying possible needle paths (State et al. 1996), as shown in Figure 12.4. Other proposed applications were aircraft wiring support and training applications (Feiner et al. 1993).

The augmenting data does not necessarily have to be 3D or modeled from real-world objects. Any information, such as text notes, voice, and video annotations, can be superimposed on the real world. This approach was initially proposed by Fitzmaurice (1993) in the Chameleon system and by Rekimoto and Nagao (1995) in the NaviCam system. In both systems, a handheld display is tracked in 3D space; the user looks at the real world through the handheld display and sees virtual data "attached" to real-world objects (Figure 12.5). To implement this system, Rekimoto and Nagao used registration markers attached to the physical objects and a video see-through setup, while Fitzmaurice used magnetic trackers.

This interaction style, also known as *context-aware information displays,* is still an active area of investigation. For example, wearable AR systems have been developed that use global positioning systems (GPS) to track users in a large outdoor environment, such as a university campus, and present a variety of information to the user on a see-through AR display (Höllerer et al. 1999).

The interaction in AR 3D data browsers can go beyond a simple overlay of information. The WIM interaction technique (Chapter 5, section

Figure 12.5 *Augmenting the real world with text annotations: the user interacting with the system (left) and the interface output (right). (Rekimoto and Nagao 1995; reprinted by permission of the authors)*

5.4.4) has been used in AR interfaces to provide a dynamic 3D map of a real environment (Bell et al. 2002). The orientation of the WIM corresponds to the viewpoint orientation of the user in the real world, and annotations that appear on real-world objects can also be transferred and viewed on the WIM (Figure 12.6). This interesting technique provides an example of how VE interaction techniques can inspire the design of AR interfaces.

Figure 12.6 *WIM interaction technique used in AR environments. (Bell et al. 2002, © 2002 ACM; reprinted by permission)*

The interaction in all these systems, however, is limited to navigation within the information space overlaid on the physical world. Obviously, viewing information superimposed on the physical environment does not cover the entire spectrum of human activities. We also need to have an *active impact* on both the physical and virtual worlds—so that we can change them. However, in all these applications, AR interfaces act only as 3D information browsers and do not provide a means to manipulate, modify, or create virtual data in the course of interaction.

12.3. 3D Augmented Reality Interfaces

The simplest and most natural approach to add interactivity to AR information browsers is to use 6-DOF input devices that are commonly used in VE interfaces to allow the user to manipulate virtual objects. Again, virtual objects are presented using either optical or video see-through HMDs.

The typical interaction tasks in these systems are very similar to the 3D interaction tasks described in Part III, such as 3D object manipulation, system control, and others. To support these tasks, many interaction techniques originally developed for VEs can be used. Such interfaces have been investigated by many researchers (Kiyokawa et al. 2000; Ohshima et al. 1998; Schmalstieg et al. 1996; Szalavári et al. 1997).

Although these interaction techniques can be effective for geometric virtual objects in AR, how can we interact with and manipulate information in the context-aware information browsers that we described above? InfoPoint (Khotake et al. 1999) adds 3D interaction to context-aware information browsers, allowing the user to move virtual data from one physical location to another. It's a handheld device with a built-in camera that tracks registration markers that identifying various physical locations. The user points the device with the camera to a marker and "loads" information from the marker into the InfoPoint by pressing the button. This information can then be attached to any other marked location in the physical environment with the same operation: pointing and pressing the button. InfoPoint does not use an HMD, and the visual feedback to the user is therefore limited to the small LCD display attached to the device.

The design of 3D AR interfaces is an important research and development direction, and they have been used successfully in entertainment and design applications (Ohshima et al. 1998). They provide *seamless spa-*

tial interaction: the user can interact with virtual objects anywhere in the physical environment, and they support natural, familiar interaction metaphors, such as the simple virtual hand (Chapter 5, section 5.4.3). There are, however, several disadvantages of this interaction style. This sort of 3D AR interface has insufficient tactile feedback, and usually requires an HMD. Furthermore, the user is required to use *different input modalities* for physical and virtual objects: real hands for physical objects and special-purpose input devices for virtual objects. This introduces an *interaction seam* into the natural workflow.

12.4. Augmented Surfaces and Tangible Interfaces

An alternative approach to the 3D AR interfaces described above is to register virtual 3D objects only to *selected* work surfaces instead of registering objects anywhere in 3D space. In this approach, called *augmented surfaces,* either overhead or back projection is used to superimpose virtual images on the real world. The user can then interact with virtual objects by using traditional and familiar tools, such as a pen, or by using specifically designed physical handles called *phicons* (physical icons). These tools and phicons can be tracked on the augmented surface using a variety of sensing technologies, most often computer vision. This approach was first proposed in the Digital Desk project (Wellner 1993; Figure 12.7) and has been extended by other researchers (Fitzmaurice et al. 1995; Ullmer and Ishii 1997; Rekimoto and Saitoh 1999).

One important example of augmented surfaces is the metaDesk system (Ullmer and Ishii 1997). In the metaDesk interface, the image is back-projected on a semitransparent table that is also back-illuminated with infrared lamps. Physical objects on the table reflect the infrared lights, and their position and orientation on the table can be tracked using a camera with an infrared filter located under the table. Virtual images can be registered relative to physical objects and tools (phicons) so that users can interact with projected virtual images simply by moving the phicons on the table surface (Figure 12.8).

Another way to design augmented surfaces is to use an overhead projection system (Rekimoto and Saitoh 1999; Underkoffler and Ishii 1998). Physical objects can be tracked on the table by using 2D markers attached to the objects. An overhead camera and computer-vision tracking techniques allow the system to estimate the physical objects' 2D positions on the table, and by manipulating these phicons, the user can select

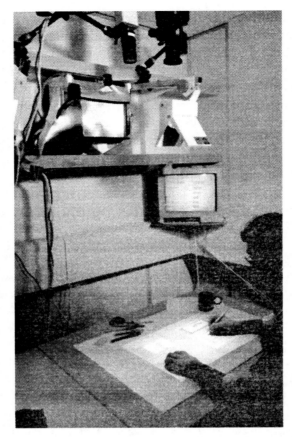

Figure 12.7   *Digital Desk: the first augmented surface interface. (Wellner 1993, © 1993 ACM; reprinted by permission)*

Figure 12.8   *Physical handles can be used to interact with virtual objects on augmented surfaces. (Underkoffler et al. 1998, © 1998 ACM; reprinted by permission)*

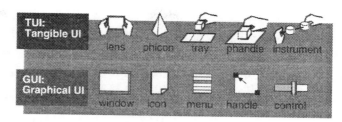

Figure 12.9 *Possible tangible and graphical UI semantics. (Underkoffler et al. 1998, © 1998 ACM; reprinted by permission)*

and move virtual objects. Rekimoto and Saitoh (1999) further extended this idea by linking multiple projection surfaces and using traditional computer devices, such as laptop computers, to interact with virtual objects.

Interaction with physical objects like phicons is known as *tangible interaction,* and the interface in which this interaction takes place is termed a *tangible user interface* (TUI). The interesting property of these interfaces is that different interface functionality can be controlled by physical objects with different form factors; hence, the physical shape of phicons defines the semantics of interaction. This in turn leads to a physical language of tangible interaction, such as the one presented in Figure 12.9.

In TUIs and augmented surfaces, the same input modality is used for interacting with both the physical and virtual worlds: direct manipulation with the human hand. Hence, in contrast to 3D AR interfaces, there is no need to wear special-purpose input devices, which makes interaction significantly easier for the user. Thus, the interaction seam that was present in 3D AR interfaces does not exist in augmented surfaces.

The disadvantage of augmented surfaces is that interaction is limited to the 2D augmented surface, and full 3D interaction is nearly impossible. Therefore, there is a *spatial seam* in the interaction flow—the user cannot interact with 3D virtual content everywhere in physical space.

12.5. Tangible AR Interfaces

The properties of 3D AR interfaces and augmented surfaces are orthogonal (Poupyrev et al. 2001): 3D AR provides users with a spatially continuous interactive environment, where 3D objects can be displayed and accessed from everywhere in space. At the same time, 3D AR introduces a seam into the interaction flow by requiring the use of different devices for physical and virtual interactions.

Augmented surfaces, on the other hand, provide a seamless flow of interaction, as users can interact with virtual and physical objects using only their hands; there is no inherent need to use multiple input devices. However, this does not allow for seamless 3D augmented space: the interaction is limited to the 2D space of the augmented surfaces.

The *tangible AR interface* approach proposes an interface style that bridges the gap between 3D AR and augmented surfaces.

12.5.1. Design of Tangible AR

In tangible AR interfaces, 2D or 3D virtual objects are registered to marked physical objects (i.e., physical handles) and displayed to the user using video see-through AR registration techniques (i.e., the user observes the augmented real-world environment through a camera mounted on an HMD; Figure 12.10). The user can manipulate the virtual objects by physically manipulating the physical, tangible containers that hold them (Rekimoto 1988; Billinghurst et al. 2000). Multiple users can interact with the virtual objects at the same time, which naturally leads to collaborative interfaces.

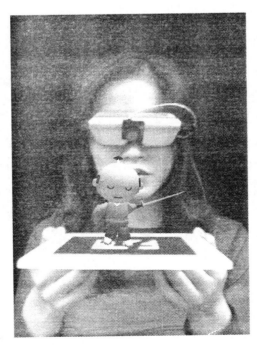

Figure 12.10   *Tangible AR interface. (Billinghurst et al. 2000, © 2000 IEEE)*

Tangible AR interfaces allow us to define generic interface elements and techniques, similar to GUIs and TUIs. For example, the Tiles system (Poupyrev et al. 2002) proposes a simple, yet effective and generic, UI paradigm that can be used for designing a wide range of applications. A designer can use the Tiles system to author interactive AR environments (Poupyrev et al. 2001) that allow the user to add, remove, copy, duplicate, and annotate virtual objects. The generic interface element is a *tile* that acts as a tangible interface control, similar to icons in a GUI. Instead of interacting with digital data by manipulating it with a mouse, the user interacts with digital data by physically manipulating the corresponding tiles (Figure 12.11). There are three classes of tiles: data tiles, operator tiles, and menu tiles. All share a similar physical appearance and common operation. The only difference in their physical appearance is the icon identifying the tile type. This enables users who are not wearing an HMD to identify them correctly.

The interface model implemented in Tiles defines a systematic and generic set of operations that are the same across all objects, which is similar to a desktop GUI where a basic set of interactions is common for all GUI elements. *Data tiles* are generic data containers (Figure 12.12): the user can add and remove virtual objects to/from data tiles, and if a data tile is empty, nothing is rendered on it. *Operator tiles* are used to perform basic operations on data tiles, including *deleting* a virtual object from a data tile, *copying* a virtual object from a data tile to the clipboard or from

Figure 12.11 *Using the generic Tiles interface. (Photograph courtesy of Ivan Poupyrev)*

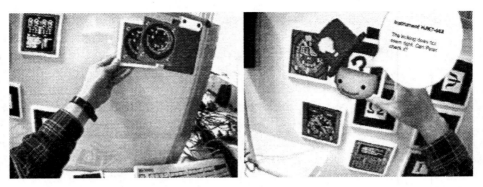

Figure 12.12   *Operations in the Tiles system: (a) copying data from the clipboard tile to an empty data tile; (b) obtaining help using the help widget. (Photographs courtesy of Ivan Poupyrev)*

the clipboard to a data tile, and requesting *help* and displaying annotations associated with a virtual object on the data tile. The operator tiles are identified by virtual 3D widgets attached to them. *Menu tiles* make up a book of tiles attached to each page (see Figure 12.11). This book works like a catalogue or a restaurant menu. As users flip through the pages, they can see the virtual objects attached to each page, choose the desired object, and then copy it from the book to any empty data tile.

Operations *between tiles* (Figure 12.13) are invoked simply by putting two tiles next to each other. For example, to copy information onto a data tile, users first find an object in the menu book and then place an empty data tile next to the object. After a one-second delay to prevent accidental copying, a copy of the object smoothly slides from the menu page to the tile and is ready to be arranged on the whiteboard. Similarly, if users want to remove data from the tile, they put the trashcan tile close to the data tile, thereby removing the data from it.

12.5.2. Time-Multiplexed Interaction in Tangible AR

The Tiles system was based on the principle of *space-multiplexed* interaction: each tile can operate with any other tile, and there is no single general-purpose input device like a mouse. The VOMAR system (Kato et al. 2000) explored how a *time-multiplexed* tangible AR interface could be designed, where the user is provided with a single universal tool that, like a mouse, acts on all objects.

Although the same interface could be applied to many domains, the system was evaluated for a virtual furniture layout task (Figure 12.14).

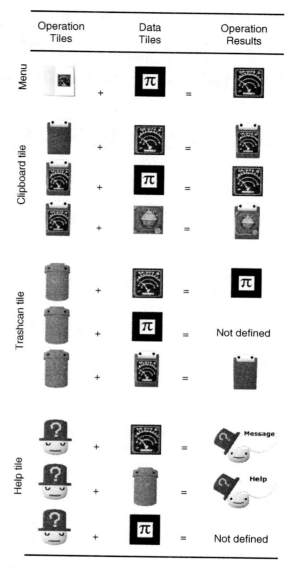

Figure 12.13 *Tiles operations semantics. (Image courtesy of Ivan Poupyrev)*

The user is provided with a paddle—a single input device that allows users to perform different tasks in a virtual-scene assembly application. The paddle is a paper object with an attached tracking symbol. It can be used by either hand and enables users to employ static and dynamic gestures to interact with the virtual objects. For example, to copy an object

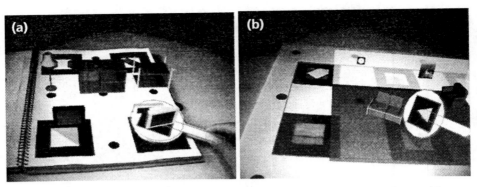

Figure 12.14   *Time-multiplexed tangible AR interface: (a) picking an object with a paddle; (b) nudging an object with a paddle. (Kato et al. 2000, © 2000 IEEE)*

from the book onto the paddle, users simply place the paddle beside the desired object. The close proximity is then detected, and the object is copied onto the paddle (Figure 12.14a). To place an object on the paddle at a desired location in the environment, the user simply shakes the paddle, which transfers the object from the paddle to the virtual scene. The user can adjust the position of the virtual objects by pushing them gently with the paddle (Figure 12.14b).

12.5.3. Advantages and Disadvantages of Tangible AR

There are several advantages of tangible AR interfaces. First, they are transparent interfaces that provide seamless, two-handed 3D interaction with both virtual and physical objects. They do not require participants to use or wear any special-purpose input devices to interact with virtual objects, such as magnetic 3D trackers. Instead, users can manipulate virtual objects using the same input devices they use in the physical world—their own hands—which leads to seamless interaction between the digital and physical worlds. This also allows the user to easily use both digital and conventional tools in the same workspace, for example by adding physical annotations, such as Post-it notes, to the virtual objects.

Tangible AR also allows seamless spatial interaction with virtual objects anywhere in their physical workspace. The user is not confined to a certain workspace, as in the case of augmented surfaces, but can pick up and manipulate virtual data anywhere and arrange it on any working surface, such as a table or a whiteboard. The digital and physical workspaces are therefore continuous, naturally blending together.

Figure 12.15 *AR Groove system. (Photograph courtesy of Ivan Poupyrev)*

The major disadvantage of tangible AR interfaces is that they require the user to wear an HMD, which might be a significant limitation for some applications. This problem can, however, be partially overcome by projecting the information on a screen in front of the user rather than using HMDs. For example, the AR Groove application (Poupyrev, Berry et al. 2000) is a simple music controller that uses tangible AR interaction without HMDs. In AR Groove, a camera was installed above a table. The user controlled the music by manipulating marked vinyl LP records, and the user's spatial gestures, expressed through object manipulations, were mapped into musical modifications. Three simple gestures were used to control performance: vertical translation, tilt, and rotation. At the same time, the performer was presented with a simple visual display on the state of the controller, which provided immediate feedback on the process of performance (Figure 12.15). No HMDs, wires, or special-purpose input devices were needed to play the music.

12.6. Agents in AR

Interaction and spatial seams are one of the main challenges in designing effective AR interfaces. Indeed, although the vision of AR is to make virtual objects a first-class part of the physical environment, indistinguishable from physical objects, it is challenging to develop interfaces that allow interaction with virtual objects as naturally as with their real-world counterparts.

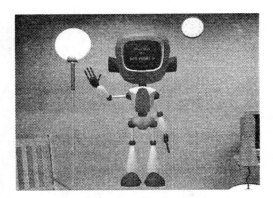

Figure 12.16   *Welbo: an AR agent. (Anabuki et al. 2000; reprinted by permission of the authors)*

One proposed approach for designing AR interfaces is to use agents, an approach that has been investigated in systems such as ALIVE (Maes 1997) and Welbo (Anabuki et al. 2000). The AR agent interface allows users to use gesture and speech commands (see Chapter 8) instead of direct manipulation techniques to control the system. The user asks virtual agents to perform simple tasks such as moving virtual furniture or bringing objects closer to the user for inspection (Figure 12.16).

Using AR agents can help to overcome some of the problems discussed above because the user does not have to manipulate virtual objects directly. However, the seam between the virtual and real still remains, because AR agents cannot act on physical objects. Another difficulty in agent interfaces is caused by the current limitations of gesture- and speech-recognition technology. Many tasks cannot be carried out effectively by using only verbal or gestural commands.

12.7. Transitional AR-VR Interfaces

Transitional AR interfaces attempt to cover a broad range of the MR continuum within one interactive system. The Magic Book project (Billinghurst et al. 2001) explored how a UI can smoothly transport users between reality and virtuality (Figure 12.17). The project used a physical book as the tangible AR interface object. The user could turn the pages of the book, look at the pictures, and read the text printed on them without using any additional technology. However, when they looked at the pages through an AR display, they saw 3D virtual models appearing out of the pages.

Figure 12.17 *Magic Book is a transitional interface between AR and VR. (Included by permission of HIT Lab, University of Washington)*

The AR view was therefore an enhanced version of a 3D "pop-up" book. Users could change the virtual models simply by turning the pages, and when they saw a scene they wanted to explore, they could fly into the page and experience the story in an immersive VE. While immersed in the VE, they were free to move about the scene at will and used traditional 3D interaction techniques to interact with the VE. Users could return to the real world by issuing an appropriate command.

The Magic Book interface therefore provided a technique for the seamless blending of VR experiences with everyday user activities. Transitional interfaces are important and are an interesting future research direction because they span the continuum between VR and AR interfaces.

12.8. Conclusion

Designing and evaluating 3D interfaces for physical environments augmented with virtual information is a new frontier in 3D UIs. As basic AR technology improves, it opens possibilities for many new and exciting developments.

There are many areas remaining to explore in AR UIs. Certainly, developing new input and output devices, tracking technologies, and registration techniques are vital for the future development and deployment of AR in practical applications. Designing new interaction techniques allowing users to interact seamlessly with both physical and virtual objects is one interesting direction for future research. The application and adaptation of existing 3D interaction techniques and interface design principles to AR interfaces is another fruitful area of future work. Finally, more work is needed on the human factors of AR interaction and the usability evaluation of AR interfaces.

Recommended Reading

An excellent starting point for AR interaction is a survey written by Azuma:

Azuma, R. (1997). A Survey of Augmented Reality. *Presence: Teleoperators and Virtual Environments* 6(4): 355–385.

The following are two classic papers that initially proposed the handheld AR interaction style and are still very relevant in AR interaction:

Fitzmaurice, G. (1993). Situated Information Spaces and Spatially Aware Palmtop Computers. *Communications of the ACM* 36(7): 38–49.

Rekimoto, J., and K. Nagao (1995). The World through the Computer: Computer-Augmented Interaction with Real World Environments. *Proceedings of the 1995 ACM Symposium on User Interface Software and Technology (UIST '95)*, ACM Press, 29–36.

The basic principles of tangible interfaces were proposed in the following two papers:

Ishii, H., and B. Ullmer (1997). Tangible Bits: Towards Seamless Interfaces between People, Bits, and Atoms. *Proceedings of the 1997 ACM Conference on Human Factors in Computing Systems (CHI '97)*, ACM Press, 234–241.

Fitzmaurice, G., H. Ishii, and W. Buxton (1995). Bricks: Laying the Foundations for Graspable User Interfaces. *Proceedings of the 1995 ACM Conference on Human Factors in Computing Systems (CHI '95)*, ACM Press, 442–449.

A discussion of tangible AR and the importance of considering seams in AR interaction can be found in the following paper:

Poupyrev, I., D. Tan, M. Billinghurst, H. Kato, H. Regenbrecht, and N. Tetsutani (2002). Developing a Generic Augmented-Reality Interface. *IEEE Computer* 35(3): 44–49.

There are a few readily available tools that can be used to develop AR interfaces. One of the most popular is the AR Toolkit, and its basic principles can be found in the following paper. The toolkit can be downloaded from the University of Washington's HIT Lab Web site (http://www.hitl.washington.edu):

Kato, H. and M. Billinghurst (1999). Marker Tracking and HMD Calibration for a Video-based Augmented Reality Conferencing System. *Proceedings of the 2nd International Workshop on Augmented Reality*, 85–94.

CHAPTER 13
The Future of 3D User Interfaces

Three-dimensional UI design is not yet a fully mature field. There are many questions still unanswered, many topics still relatively unexplored. In this final chapter, we present a list of 20 important questions that need to be addressed by researchers, students, or developers. Although we could have listed many more important questions, we've limited this list to "grand challenge" questions for 3D UI design. That means that finding the answers to these questions will not be an easy task and that the answers will change the landscape of the field dramatically. Of course, any such list will be subjective, speculative, and biased by the authors' presuppositions (not surprisingly, we are already working on projects related to many of the questions in the list!). Despite these flaws, however, we hope that this list will help you think about the next steps for 3D UIs and inspire you to tackle some of these important issues yourself.

13.1. Questions about 3D UI Technology

In Chapters 3 and 4, we looked at current hardware technology used in 3D interfaces. There are lots of people working on technological problems, and there are plenty of problems remaining. Although better technology alone won't ensure usable 3D UIs, this work is still necessary. Here are four problems we feel are very important.

Can we build systems that immerse all of the user's senses?

Most immersive technologies have been designed to provide a virtual stimulus to a single sensory modality (visual). We have surround-screen displays that flood the user's visual sense with realistic 3D stereo graphics, spatial audio systems that produce believable sounds from any 3D location, and haptic devices that display surfaces or textures with passable realism. Less work has been done on smell, taste, or vestibular displays, although some rough prototypes have been developed. The real challenge, however, is to integrate all of these single-sense display types into a seamless system. Similar to the Holodeck on *Star Trek*, in such a system, objects and environments would look, sound, feel, smell, and taste completely realistic. Before we achieve the Holodeck, however, there are many intermediate steps. One is to develop a haptic system that integrates all the different elements of haptic sensation: resistance, elasticity, texture, and temperature, at any number of points on the user's hand and body. A second step is to integrate haptics and immersive visuals. Current haptics devices are typically unusable in immersive displays, because they must sit on a desk or because they require so many wires, mechanical arms, and other hardware that they are too complex to integrate with a CAVE or HMD. A third challenge is to solve the "visual interference" problem. If we completely surround the user with virtual visuals, where do we put the tracking devices, haptic devices, speakers, and other components so that they do not interfere with viewing the virtual world? Retinal displays that draw graphics directly on the entire surface of the user's retinae could provide a solution here.

Can we completely remove the tethers and encumbrances in 3D interfaces?

Current immersive VE and AR systems either require tethers (wires between the user and the electronics) or are too cumbersome to be practical. Although the wires or heavy equipment are not typically considered part of the "interface design," they have a huge impact on the usability of the systems. Wireless tracking systems are now becoming more common; this makes it possible to have a completely untethered surround-screen display, for example. Wireless HMDs are not currently available, but there is no technical reason why such displays cannot be developed. Unencumbered mobile AR is a more difficult challenge because the user must wear the entire system (e.g., HMD, computer, inertial orientation tracker, GPS receiver, input devices).

Will "true 3D" displays ever become practical?

Today's 3D displays have a number of visual artifacts making them less then realistic. One is the so-called "accommodation–convergence mismatch" (see Chapter 3, section 3.2.2 and Figure 3.7). Because graphics are displayed on a fixed screen, the user must focus at the depth of that screen to see the graphics sharply. But when stereo graphics are used, the left and right eye images are drawn so that the user's eyes will rotate to see the object at its virtual depth. When the virtual object depth and the screen depth are different, the user's eyes send conflicting signals to the brain about the distance to the object. Another issue with projected displays (not HMDs) is the occlusion problem. This occurs when a physical object (like the user's hand) passes behind a virtual object. Because the virtual object is actually being displayed on a screen *behind* the physical object, the virtual object is occluded, even though according to the "real" positions of the objects, the physical object should be occluded. Both of these problems could be solved by "true 3D" displays—devices that display the graphics for a virtual object at the *actual depth* of that object. Small examples of such displays (volumetric or holographic displays) have been developed (see Chapter 3, section 3.2.3), but the challenge is to develop such displays that can work in large-scale immersive environments or in mixed reality contexts.

What are the best mappings between devices, tasks, interaction techniques, and applications?

The point of developing better 3D technology is to enable better 3D applications, but currently we know very little about the usefulness of specific technologies for specific applications. Ideally, we would like to have a set of guidelines (or even an automated process) that, given a description of an application (domain, tasks, users, requirements, constraints), would suggest an appropriate set of devices (input and output) and interaction techniques. In order for this to become a reality, a huge amount of empirical research needs to be performed. We need to compare the usability of various 3D display devices and input devices for particular tasks and domains; we need to evaluate the compatibility of input devices and interaction techniques; and we need to understand the ways in which input and display devices affect each other.

13.2. Questions about 3D Interaction Techniques

As we saw in Chapters 5 through 9, there has already been a large amount of research on 3D interaction techniques for universal tasks. This topic is still ripe for more research, however. We came up with six crucial questions about interaction techniques.

What travel techniques will allow users to navigate effectively through multiple scales?

One of the great advantages of virtual worlds is their flexibility—in a VE, whether on the desktop or using a fully immersive display, we can represent any type of real or fantasy world, and users can experience environments that are impossible or impractical to see in real life. Many such experiences, however, involve a huge range of physical scale. Consider the human body. We have the whole-body scale (meters), the organ scale (centimeters), the blood vessel scale (millimeters), the cellular scale (micrometers), and the atomic scale (nanometers), and users of a VE for anatomy education will need to visit them all. Larger scales will also be important—think of a VE allowing exploration of the galaxy. Such VEs must manage users' navigation such that they can achieve their goals without explicitly setting a scale factor or velocity. How will the system recognize the user's intent? How can we keep users from becoming disoriented during multiscale navigation?

Can we build usable hands-free 3D interfaces?

People are used to working with their hands, and as we saw in Chapter 5, there is a long history of research on manual interaction with both real and virtual objects. In some situations, however, a hands-free interface is called for. For instance, how will disabled persons without the use of arms or hands use an interactive VE? How will a driver interact with an AR system that displays travel information overlaid on the real world? We need to consider novel ways to make use of speech, head or eye movements, or even facial expression as input modalities for 3D interfaces.

How can users enter, edit, and mark up symbols efficiently in 3D UIs?

In Chapter 9 we looked at symbolic input techniques for 3D UIs, but the chapter was largely speculative—very little work has been done in this area. As 3D UIs become more prevalent and complex, the need for efficient, low-error, comfortable symbolic input will increase dramatically.

The most usable and effective techniques may come from outside of the 3D UI area, as we suggested in Chapter 9 by looking at techniques from the mobile and wearable computing world, but there may also be novel techniques designed specifically for symbolic input in 3D UIs. This topic is wide open.

How can MR interaction techniques allow seamless interaction in both the real and virtual worlds?

In completely virtual worlds, UI designers can opt for fully natural techniques or magic techniques, or something in between. In mixed reality, however, UI designers don't have as much freedom, because users will be interacting with real objects as well as virtual ones. In some cases, it may be appropriate and effective to use different methods of interaction in the real and virtual parts of the application, but it is likely that a seamless interface for both parts will be the best choice in most applications. The challenge, then, is to use the same interaction techniques to interact with both physical and virtual objects. The current trend in MR is to use a *tangible interface,* where virtual objects have an associated physical object. To manipulate the virtual object, therefore, the user simply picks up the associated real object. As we've seen, however, magic interaction techniques can be very powerful, so MR researchers should also consider whether it is possible to interact with real objects using magic interaction techniques. As a simple example, note that it certainly makes sense to select both virtual and real objects using a magic technique like ray-casting.

Can we provide integrated interaction techniques for multiple tasks?

In complex 3D UIs that involve many different tasks (travel, selection, manipulation, system control, and so on), the user is often forced to learn a different interaction technique for each task. An application may use gaze-directed steering, Go-Go selection and manipulation, and a pen-and-tablet–based menu, for example. From HCI, however, we know that interfaces that use a consistent metaphor are easier to learn and help prevent errors. Therefore, if we can provide multiple interaction techniques that use the same root concept, we can create more usable 3D UIs. One candidate metaphor is the aforementioned pen and tablet. Consider a tablet that displays a map of the virtual world, with icons representing the user and objects on the map. Dragging the user icon moves the viewpoint (travel), and the map provides spatial knowledge of the environment (wayfinding). Dragging the object icons causes the 3D objects to move (selection and manipulation). A menu (system control) and a virtual keyboard (symbolic input) can also be displayed on the tablet. By understanding one simple idea, the user can perform all the universal tasks. Another idea comes from noticing that at a very basic level, travel, selection, and manipulation are all about specifying a 3D position and orientation. This implies that the same interaction technique might work for all three tasks—such a technique is called a *cross-task* technique. For example, many manipulation techniques, such as Go-Go, can also be used for travel (grab an object or the "air" with your virtual hand, and pull yourself toward it). More research is needed to explore this idea fully.

How should interaction techniques be optimized for specific domains? Almost all of the existing research on 3D interaction techniques has focused on generic techniques for one of the universal tasks. This generality is an advantage, because the techniques that have been designed will work in any context. It is also a disadvantage, however, because there are no generic applications! A real-world application domain has specific properties, constraints, and requirements that should be taken into account when designing interaction techniques for that domain. To take a simple example, consider the domain of interior design. A travel technique for an interior design application will not require long-distance movements, should keep the viewpoint at "eye-level" above the floor, and should allow precise positioning of the viewpoint so that the designer can evaluate the design. Manipulation techniques in this domain should take into account the type of object being manipulated—furniture should remain on the floor and rotate only about its vertical axis, pictures should remain upright and on a wall. The design of domain-specific interaction techniques should be one of the next major research topics in 3D UIs. Two important subquestions: first, should we refine existing techniques or design completely new ones; and second, when is the benefit of a domain-specific interaction technique worth the cost of its development?

13.3. Questions about 3D UI Design and Development

Chapter 10 of this book focused on design and development strategies, and principles for 3D UIs. There is still a lot to learn in this area. Five of our "grand challenge" questions fit in this category.

How do we create a seamless 3D UI from a given set of 3D interaction techniques?

Part III of this book presented a large number of individual interaction techniques for the universal 3D interaction tasks and guidelines to help developers choose interaction techniques for their applications. But choosing usable interaction techniques for an application is only half the battle. *Integrating* the diverse techniques into a single, seamless 3D UI is another challenge that needs to be addressed. Take a simple example: suppose you choose the pointing technique for navigation and the HOMER technique for selection and manipulation, and that you are using an input device with only a single button. When the user points in a particular direction and presses the button, what does she mean? She could intend to travel in that direction, or she could intend to select an object in that direction. The integrated 3D UI must disambiguate this action in some way. For example, if the user clicks the button quickly, treat it as a selection action, but if the user holds the button down, treat it as a travel action. One solution to this integration problem is to use integrated or cross-task techniques, as discussed above, but more work is needed to determine the best ways to integrate techniques in general.

What does an effective 3D UI development environment look like?

Developing a 3D UI today requires the use of many tools (3D modelers, programming environments, libraries, and toolkits), none of which are specifically focused on the requirements of 3D UIs. If 3D UIs become more prevalent, however, we will need dedicated tools to design, implement, document, and maintain them, just as we have today for 2D UIs. There are many potential directions here. We might need a platform-independent description language that allows developers to specify 3D UIs without specifying the details of their implementation. Not only would this be a useful abstraction, it would also provide a way for researchers to share the details of their UI designs even though they are using different platforms or libraries. It would also be useful to have a plug-and-play 3D UI toolkit that has generic implementations of many common interaction techniques and allows developers to simply choose techniques (and devices) "a la carte," resulting in a complete working 3D UI.

Can we build software systems that allow 3D UIs to migrate intelligently between platforms?

A recent trend in 3D graphics and VE APIs is *device independence*: the idea that the application code does not know or care about the display or input devices being used, and that the same code can run equally well on a laptop, in a CAVE, or anywhere in between. User interaction is handled outside the application code, and the proper interfaces, interaction techniques, and so on are loaded at runtime when the devices are known. This scheme is extremely useful for developers who care primarily about the graphics and content of their environments and who will use only the basic interaction techniques provided by the API. For 3D UI developers who have complex interfaces and techniques, however, this type of device independence is not as helpful. They still have to write interface code for each combination of input and output devices, and their applications will not necessarily be usable on other platforms. The challenge, then, is to allow 3D UIs to *migrate* between platforms without requiring developers to implement special interfaces for each. The ultimate goal might be an intelligent system that took a single interface—one designed for an HMD and stylus, for example—and modified it appropriately for use on a workbench, on a desktop computer, or on a handheld. To accomplish this, we would need a way to specify abstractly the types of tasks the interface must be able to perform and a method of mapping those requirements onto interaction techniques that worked well with the available devices. The system would also need to understand usability guidelines. Just because a technique will work with a specific platform does not mean that it will be usable on that platform.

How should abstract information be managed in 3D UIs?

Most existing VE applications focus on the user's experience; therefore, they contain *perceptual* information—geometric objects, colors, textures, lighting effects, sounds, and so on. For many real-world tasks, however, we need both perceptual and *abstract* information (descriptions, classifications, statistics, numeric values, etc.). When a perceptual VE is enhanced with related abstract information, we call it an *information-rich virtual environment* (IRVE). IRVEs in many ways are similar to AR, which combines perceptual information (real) with abstract information (virtual). For both IRVEs and AR, there are a number of challenges related to the abstract information. How should it be stored and organized? How and where should it be displayed in the 3D environment? How should users access hidden information? How do we avoid information "clutter" in these environments?

How can multiple users collaborate effectively in a 3D UI?

We have focused almost exclusively on single-user interaction with 3D UIs in this book. But for many 3D UI application areas, collaborative, multiuser work is the norm. Consider automobile manufacturers: when a new car model is being designed, the work is not all done by a single person. A large team of specialists must work together over a long period of time to create the final design. But a collaborative 3D UI for such a team is not trivial—it's not simply the sum of several single-user UIs. Collaboration brings with it a multitude of interface challenges, such as awareness (Who is here? Where are they? What are they doing?), communication (speech, pointing, facial expressions), and "floor control" (Who is working on that object? How do I get the object?). There is existing work on interaction in collaborative VEs and MR, but there is still much to be done. One first step would be to perform a design case study: take an existing single-user application with a complex 3D UI and create a collaborative 3D UI with the same functionality.

13.4. Questions about 3D UI Evaluation

Although some work has been done to address the unique issues involved in evaluating 3D UIs (Chapter 11), there are still some important questions to answer. Here are two of them.

What specific heuristics or guidelines should we use to evaluate 3D UIs? Usability inspection methods, such as heuristic or guideline-based evaluation, are very popular for the evaluation of traditional UIs because of their low cost and complexity. In heuristic evaluation, a UI expert uses a small set of general principles to assess the usability of a system. Some existing sets of heuristics are generic enough that they can be applied to 3D UIs, but we also know from other domains that more specific heuristics can produce better, more consistent results. A simple, focused, validated set of heuristics for 3D UIs would make quality evaluations easier to perform.

How can we effectively evaluate MR applications? Evaluation of VEs can be difficult, as we saw in Chapter 11. But in some ways, the evaluation of MR applications is even more problematic. A typical MR setup might use an optical see-through HMD, so that the user sees the real world directly and graphics overlaid on the real world. In this configuration, there is no way for the evaluator to see exactly what the user is seeing! A video see-through HMD might be used, but the quality of the real-world visuals would be greatly reduced. A camera could be mounted on the optical see-through HMD and its image combined with the augmenting graphics, but it would be very difficult to calibrate the camera so that it captured exactly what the user could see through the HMD. This limitation makes it extremely difficult to understand what the user is doing, what problems she is having, or what she is pointing at or talking about. A solution to this problem would greatly enhance the ability of MR researchers to perform quality evaluations. One idea would be to let the evaluator wear an HMD as well, and stand behind or near the user. The system could even project a rectangle into the world to show the evaluator exactly what the user was looking at. But this solution might also cause the evaluator to get in the user's way, and might prevent the evaluator from taking notes or timing tasks.

13.5. Million-Dollar Questions

The 17 questions we've looked at so far are all extremely important and difficult to answer. However, if the use of 3D UIs is limited to a small set of people working in a very small set of domains, the answers to these questions will not have a very significant *impact*. Thus, in this final category, we take a look at three questions that could very well determine the future of 3D UI design as a field. If researchers and developers can provide positive and definite answers to these three questions, then suddenly all the information in this book will become much more important to many more people.

Can we quantify the real benefits of 3D UIs?

One of the major reasons that VEs, AR, and other 3D UI technologies are used in few industrial settings is that industries perceive these technologies to have a very high cost relative to their benefit. Most companies have little or no budget for research and no tolerance for large expenditures that will not improve the bottom line. Therefore, the challenge for the 3D UI community is to quantify the benefits of these technologies—demonstrate concrete results that will translate into dollars and cents. For different domains, these benefits might take on different forms. For manufacturers, the benefit might be increased productivity of the workers; for educators, the benefit might be increased student understanding; for scientists, the benefit might be greater insight into a dataset. These benefits are very difficult to prove, but even worse, it is difficult to even design a valid experiment to attempt to measure them. Suppose you run an experiment comparing task completion time on a typical HMD-based VE system and a typical desktop computer system, and that you find significantly faster times with the HMD. What would your conclusion be? What caused the difference? Was it physical immersion, head tracking, presence, the use of a 3D input device, the use of a 3D interaction technique, or some combination of these things? A first step toward quantifying the benefits of 3D UI technologies, then, is to develop a methodology that separates all these variables so that we know from where the benefit comes. In the example above, if the 3D input device was actually the crucial difference, perhaps we could achieve the same benefit by using the 3D input device with a standard desktop display monitor and avoid the high cost of the HMD and head tracker.

Will there ever be a standard 3D UI?

Computers would be unusable by the general population if the UI were not standardized to some degree. Because all PCs today use the WIMP (Windows, Icons, Menus, and Pointers) interaction style and the desktop metaphor, and because all applications make use of these same standard interface elements, users can start using applications right away, without lengthy training or even reading a manual. Currently, there is nothing even close to a standard for 3D UIs. The interface is designed and implemented separately for each new application. Some techniques and metaphors have become fairly common, but even when the same technique is used in two different applications, the implementation may be entirely different. In order to define a standard, we would need much more empirical evidence on the usability of various techniques and metaphors, and on the combination of these techniques and metaphors with various devices. In order for a standard to be practical, we would need a set of standard, generic implementations that could be reused in any application. But perhaps the bigger issue is whether we *want* a standard. One might argue that 3D UIs are much more complex than 2D UIs, that the input and output devices for 3D UIs are too diverse to match up to a single standard, and that 3D UI applications need specialized, domain-specific interface designs for optimum usability. Perhaps the answer to this question depends on the answer to the final question. . . .

What is the killer app for 3D UIs?

Almost all widely successful technologies became successful because of some application of that technology that made everyone feel that they couldn't do without it. For personal computers, the original "killer app" was the spreadsheet (pioneered in the VisiCalc project), which made complex and tedious business and accounting tasks simple, automatic, and visual (no programming required!). The Internet existed for many years before most people were aware of it, but then the World Wide Web and the Web browser gave everyone access to massive amounts of information, making the Internet a daily part of life around the world. So, what about 3D UIs? Will we someday find an immersive VE in every home? Will all business professionals need a mobile AR system to keep up? Or will 3D UIs remain restricted to specialized tasks in a few domains? Of course, this latter outcome would not mean that 3D UIs were a failure—there are many technologies that are used only in specialized contexts (consider submarines, night-vision goggles, and MRI machines) that are considered successful. But whether or not 3D UIs are widely adopted may determine whether or not there is ever a standard 3D interface.

APPENDIX A

Quick Reference Guide to 3D User Interface Mathematics

In this appendix, we provide a quick reference guide to working with scalars, vectors, points, matrices, and quaternions, which are important mathematical tools used in 3D UIs and 3D interaction techniques. It is not our intention to provide mathematical rigor in discussing these concepts but merely to provide practical descriptions and a common notation style to be used throughout the book. See the recommended reading list at the end of this appendix for more information.

We use the following notational conventions:

- Non-boldface letters (except for p and q) and lowercase Greek letters refer to scalars
  - Example: the scalar λ, the distance D
- Lowercase boldface type refers to vectors and points
  - Example: the vector $\vec{\mathbf{v}}$, the point $\mathbf{p}$
- Lowercase subscripted letters refer to vector and point components
  - Example: the x component of vector $\vec{\mathbf{v}}$ is v_x
- Uppercase boldface type refers to matrices
  - Example: the matrix $\mathbf{M}$
- Lowercase p, q, q_1, q', etc. refer to quaternions
  - Example: the quaternion $q + p$

A.1. Scalars

A scalar is a single number—that is, a quantity that has a magnitude but not a direction—and is thus different from a vector.

A.2. Vectors

A vector is a quantity that has both magnitude and direction. In our case, a vector in 3D space is expressed as the column vector

$$\vec{\mathbf{v}} = \left[v_x, v_y, v_z \right]^T,$$

and we refer to a 3D vector simply as a vector throughout this appendix. A vector multiplied by a scalar λ is

$$\vec{\mathbf{v}}' = \lambda\vec{\mathbf{v}} = \left[\lambda v_x, \lambda v_y, \lambda v_z \right]^T,$$

and is also equivalent to a uniform scaling of the vector about the origin. Vectors can be added and subtracted together as follows:

$$\vec{\mathbf{u}} + \vec{\mathbf{v}} = \left[(u_x + v_x), (u_y + v_y), (u_z + v_z) \right]^T,$$

$$\vec{\mathbf{u}} - \vec{\mathbf{v}} = \vec{\mathbf{u}} + (-1)\vec{\mathbf{v}} = \left[(u_x - v_x), (u_y - v_y), (u_z - v_z) \right]^T$$

Very often, we need to use a vector's direction or magnitude individually. A vector's magnitude (i.e., length) is calculated as

$$\|\vec{\mathbf{v}}\| = \sqrt{v_x^2 + v_y^2 + v_z^2}$$

and is a scalar quantity.

When we are interested in a vector's direction independent of its magnitude, a normalized vector is often used; that is $\|\vec{\mathbf{v}}\| = 1$. A normalized vector is calculated as

$$\vec{\mathbf{u}} = \frac{\vec{\mathbf{v}}}{\|\vec{\mathbf{v}}\|} = \left[\frac{v_x}{\|\vec{\mathbf{v}}\|}, \frac{v_y}{\|\vec{\mathbf{v}}\|}, \frac{v_z}{\|\vec{\mathbf{v}}\|} \right]^T.$$

There are two multiplication operations defined for vectors. The dot product is defined as

$$\lambda = \vec{\mathbf{u}} \cdot \vec{\mathbf{v}} = \left(u_x \cdot v_x \right) + \left(u_y \cdot v_y \right) + \left(u_z \cdot v_z \right).$$

The dot product represents the projection of vector $\vec{\mathbf{u}}$ onto the vector $\vec{\mathbf{v}}$, and the result of this operation is a scalar. Another way to write it is

$$\lambda = \vec{\mathbf{u}} \cdot \vec{\mathbf{v}} = \|\vec{\mathbf{u}}\| \, \|\vec{\mathbf{v}}\| \cos(\theta).$$

Therefore, the dot product is also calculated from the magnitudes of the two vectors and the angle between them, and is useful when we want to know the angle between two vectors. Assuming these vectors are normalized, we can find the angle between them using

$$\theta = \arccos(\vec{\mathbf{u}} \cdot \vec{\mathbf{v}}).$$

Note that because *arccos* takes values from –1 to 1, the range of possible values for θ is from 0 to 180°.

The second multiplication operation is the cross product, defined as

$$\vec{\mathbf{u}} \times \vec{\mathbf{v}} = \left[\left(u_y \cdot v_z - u_z \cdot v_y \right), \left(u_z \cdot v_x - u_x \cdot v_z \right), \left(u_x \cdot v_y - u_y \cdot v_x \right) \right]^T.$$

The result of the cross product is a vector perpendicular to the plane that contains $\vec{\mathbf{u}}$ and $\vec{\mathbf{v}}$. The direction this vector is pointing can be determined by the right hand rule, which states that if the two vectors are placed tail to tail and a person curls his fingers (using his right hand) in the direction from $\vec{\mathbf{u}}$ to $\vec{\mathbf{v}}$, then his thumb will be pointing in the direction of the resulting vector.

A.3. Points

A 3D point is a quantity that is used to specify a spatial position in three dimensions. Points are different from vectors because they do not specify a direction. However, they can be written as vectors relative to the origin. We can express a 3D point as a column vector

$$\mathbf{p} = \left[p_x, p_y, p_z \right]^T,$$

and, as with vectors, we refer to 3D points simply as points throughout this appendix.

We can find the distance between two points **p** and **r** using

$$\delta = dist(\mathbf{p},\mathbf{r}) = \sqrt{\left(p_x - r_x\right)^2 + \left(p_y - r_y\right)^2 + \left(p_z - r_z\right)^2}.$$

Two points can also be used to define a vector by subtracting point **r** from point **p**, as shown

$$\vec{v} = \mathbf{p} - \mathbf{r} = \left[\left(p_x - r_x\right),\left(p_y - r_y\right),\left(p_z - r_z\right)\right]^T.$$

A frequent occurrence in 3D interaction techniques is to translate points in 3D space. This operation is easily accomplished by translating a point using a vector, and is expressed in either of two ways:

$$\mathbf{p}' = \mathbf{p} + \vec{v} = \left[\left(p_x + v_x\right),\left(p_y + v_y\right),\left(p_z + v_z\right)\right]^T$$

$$\mathbf{p}' = \mathbf{p} + (-\vec{v}) = \mathbf{p} - \vec{v} = \left[\left(p_x - v_x\right),\left(p_y - v_y\right),\left(p_z - v_z\right)\right]^T.$$

Note that because points are just quantities that specify location in spatial dimensions, there is no *point + point* operator.

A.4. Matrices

A matrix is simply a rectangular array of elements. Matrices are used in many different applications, and in the domain of 3D user interfaces, they can be used to perform affine transformations on points and vectors such as rotation, scaling, translation, and shearing. For our purposes, we restrict the definition of matrices to square 3×3 matrices of real numbers that are used to rotate or scale points and vectors in 3D space. We express a 3×3 matrix as

$$\mathbf{M} = \begin{bmatrix} a_{00} & a_{01} & a_{02} \\ a_{10} & a_{11} & a_{12} \\ a_{20} & a_{21} & a_{22} \end{bmatrix}.$$

We can define rotation matrices that rotate points and vectors around the three principal axes, x, y, and z. For rotating a point or vector about the x-axis by an angle θ, we use

$$\mathbf{R}_x(\theta) = \begin{bmatrix} 1 & 0 & 0 \\ 0 & \cos(\theta) & -\sin(\theta) \\ 0 & \sin(\theta) & \cos(\theta) \end{bmatrix}.$$

For rotation about the y-axis, we use

$$\mathbf{R}_y(\theta) = \begin{bmatrix} \cos(\theta) & 0 & \sin(\theta) \\ 0 & 1 & 0 \\ -\sin(\theta) & 0 & \cos(\theta) \end{bmatrix}.$$

For rotation about the z-axis, we use,

$$\mathbf{R}_z(\theta) = \begin{bmatrix} \cos(\theta) & -\sin(\theta) & 0 \\ \sin(\theta) & \cos(\theta) & 0 \\ 0 & 0 & 1 \end{bmatrix}.$$

As an example, we can rotate the vector $\vec{v}$ about the y-axis by a given angle θ as

$$\begin{bmatrix} v_x\cos(\theta) + v_z\sin(\theta) \\ v_y \\ -v_x\sin(\theta) + v_z\cos(\theta) \end{bmatrix} = \begin{bmatrix} \cos(\theta) & 0 & \sin(\theta) \\ 0 & 1 & 0 \\ -\sin(\theta) & 0 & \cos(\theta) \end{bmatrix} \cdot \begin{bmatrix} v_x \\ v_y \\ v_z \end{bmatrix},$$

which can be written as

$$\vec{v}' = \mathbf{R}_y(\theta)\vec{v}.$$

Note that these rotation matrices can be composed by simply premultiplying the matrices together and then applying the result to the point or vector. As an example, if we want to rotate a point about the x-axis by an angle θ and then about the y-axis by an angle ϕ, we can express this as

$$\mathbf{p}' = \big(\mathbf{R}_y(\phi)\mathbf{R}_x(\theta)\big)\mathbf{p}.$$

Finally, we showed in section A.2 that multiplying a vector by a scalar is really scaling that vector uniformly about the origin. We can use a scale matrix to scale a vector with different scaling factors about the origin for each axis using the following:

$$\mathbf{S}(s_x,s_y,s_z) = \begin{bmatrix} s_x & 0 & 0 \\ 0 & s_y & 0 \\ 0 & 0 & s_z \end{bmatrix}.$$

A.5. Quaternions

Quaternions are another tool used to rotate points and vectors in 3D space. Two centuries ago, Leonhard Euler proved that the combination of any number of rotations of a rigid body is equivalent to a single rotation from a reference orientation. This single rotation can be conveniently represented using quaternions (Hamilton 1853).

A quaternion q is a 4D vector, defined as follows:

$$q = [\vec{\mathbf{v}}, \omega] = \left[\left(q_x, q_y, q_z \right), q_w \right],$$

where ω is a real number (a scalar) and $\vec{\mathbf{v}}$ is a 3D vector. Consequently, any real number s can be represented in quaternion form as $(\vec{\mathbf{0}}, s)$, and any vector $\vec{\mathbf{v}}$ as quaternion $(\vec{\mathbf{v}}, 0)$, which is referred to as a pure vector quaternion.

The magnitude of a quaternion q is

$$\| q \| = \sqrt{q_x^2 + q_y^2 + q_z^2 + q_w^2} \,,$$

and its *conjugate* is defined as $q^* = (-\vec{\mathbf{v}}, \omega)$. The inverse of a quaternion q is then

$$q^{-1} = \frac{q^*}{\| q \|}.$$

Given another quaternion q', we can define quaternion addition as

$$q'' = q + q' = \left[(\vec{\mathbf{v}} + \vec{\mathbf{v}}'), \omega + \omega' \right],$$

quaternion subtraction as

$$q'' = q - q' = q + (-q') = \left[(\vec{\mathbf{v}} - \vec{\mathbf{v}}'), \omega - \omega' \right],$$

quaternion multiplication as

$$q'' = qq' = \left[(\vec{\mathbf{v}} \times \vec{\mathbf{v}}' + w\vec{\mathbf{v}}' + w'\vec{\mathbf{v}}), ww' - \vec{\mathbf{v}} \cdot \vec{\mathbf{v}}' \right],$$

and the quaternion dot product as

$$\lambda = q \cdot q' = \vec{v} \cdot \vec{v}' + \omega \cdot \omega'.$$

Note that quaternion multiplication is associative ($q_1(q_2 q_3) = (q_1 q_2)q_3$) but does not commute ($qq' \neq q'q$) and has an identity element $1 = (\vec{0}, 1)$, so that $1q = q1 = q$ for any q.

There is a natural correspondence between unit length quaternions (i.e., $\|q\| = 1$) and 3D rotations: the rotation about unit axis $\vec{v}$ by angle θ can be represented as the following unit quaternion:

Eq. A.1
$$q = (\sin\frac{\theta}{2}\vec{v}, \cos\frac{\theta}{2})$$

Then, a rotation of a vector $\vec{u}$ about axis $\vec{v}$ by angle θ can be computed as a quaternion multiplication:

$$\vec{u}' = q\vec{u}q^{-1},$$

where the vector $\vec{u}$ is represented as a pure vector quaternion. Also note that rotations can be easily combined: rotation q_1 followed by q_2 can be computed as their multiplication $q_2 q_1$.

There are two useful ways to think about quaternions. One way is to consider quaternions as a numerical quantity that encodes a vector and a twist around this vector, or, in other words, encodes axis and angle of rotation.

Another way to think about quaternions is from a geometric point of view. Indeed, the set of all unit quaternions (i.e., $\|q\| = 1$) forms a unit three-sphere in four dimensions. If we consider the rotation of a rigid body, then each point on this sphere corresponds to a single orientation of the body. A single 3D rotation would "draw" an arc on the sphere, and the length of this arc is half of the rotation angle. By choosing quaternions with the scalar part set to zero, we can visualize rotation as a path on the quaternion sphere in three dimensions.

Constructing quaternions is easy if you can obtain an axis of rotation and angle: in this case, the values are simply plugged into Equation

A.1. Many 3D computer graphics APIs provide basic functions that allow you to convert matrices to the axis and angle of rotation. See Pique (1995) for information on how you can obtain rotation axis and angle of rotation from a rotation matrix.

Quaternions can be constructed from Euler angles as well. Although there are 12 possible axis conventions for Euler angles (Shoemake 1985), we use a convention commonly used in computer graphics; roll, pitch, and yaw corresponding to rotations about the x-, y-, and z-axes respectively. Therefore, a general rotation is constructed by rotating about the z-axis with an angle of ϕ, rotating about the y-axis with an angle of θ, and rotating about the x-axis with an angle of θ (note all angles are in radians). The quaternions that represent these rotations are

$$q_{roll} = \left[\left(\sin\left(\frac{\psi}{2}\right), 0, 0\right), \cos\left(\frac{\psi}{2}\right) \right],$$

$$q_{pitch} = \left[\left(0, \sin\left(\frac{\theta}{2}\right), 0\right), \cos\left(\frac{\theta}{2}\right) \right],$$

$$q_{yaw} = \left[\left(0, 0, \sin\left(\frac{\phi}{2}\right)\right), \cos\left(\frac{\phi}{2}\right) \right].$$

Multiplying these quaternions appropriately gives us

$$q = q_{yaw} q_{pitch} q_{roll},$$

which is the desired result.

Recommended Reading

For a detailed discussion of vectors, we recommend

Colley, S. (2001). *Vector Calculus*, 2nd ed., Prentice Hall.

Jones, H. (2001). *Computer Graphics through Key Mathematics*, Springer-Verlag.

General information on matrices can be found in these books:

Golub, G., and C. Van Loan (1996). *Matrix Computations*, Johns Hopkins University Press.

Pique, M. (1995). Rotation Tools. *Graphics Gems 1*, A. Glassner (Ed.), Morgan Kaufman Publishers, 465–469.

Note that in our discussion of matrices, we presented only rotation and scaling matrices. However, we said in the introduction to section A.4 that matrices can be used to apply other types of transformations such as translation and shearing. All of these transformations can be applied in the same way (i.e., composition of translation, rotation, scaling, and shearing into one transformation matrix) using homogeneous coordinates.

Homogeneous coordinates are a frequently used tool in computer graphics, and a nice discussion on them and their use can be found in the following:

Foley, J., A. van Dam, S. Feiner, and J. Hughes (1996). *Computer Graphics: Principles and Practice*, Addison-Wesley.

For more detail on quaternions, we recommend the following:

Kuipers, J. (2002). *Quaternions and Rotation Sequences: A Primer with Applications to Orbits, Aerospace and Virtual Reality*, Princeton University Press.

Grassia, F. S. (1998). Practical Parameterization of Rotations Using the Exponential Map. *Journal of Graphics Tools* 3(3): 29–48.

Bibliography

Accot, J., and S. Zhai (1997). Beyond Fitts' Law: Models for Trajectory-Based HCI Tasks. *Proceedings of the 1997 ACM Conference on Human Factors in Computing Systems (CHI '97)*, ACM Press, 295–302.

Agrawala, M., A. C. Beers, I. McDowell, B. Fröhlich, M. Bolas, and P. Hanrahan (1997). The Two-User Responsive Workbench: Support for Collaboration through Individual Views of a Shared Space. *Proceedings of SIGGRAPH '97*, ACM Press, 327–332.

Airey, J., J. Rohlf, and F. Brooks (1990). Toward Image Realism with Interactive Update Rates in Complex Virtual Building Environments. University of North Carolina at Chapel Hill, TR90–001.

Akenine-Möller, T., and E. Haines (2002). *Real-Time Rendering*, 2nd ed., AK Peters.

Alexander, C., S. Ishikawa, and M. Silverstein (1977). *A Pattern Language: Towns, Buildings, Construction*, Oxford University Press.

Allen, B. D., G. Bishop, and G. Welch (2001). Tracking: Beyond 15 Minutes of Thought. *SIGGRAPH Course #11*.

Allison, R., L. Harris, M. Jenkin, U. Jasiobedzka, and J. Zacher (2001). Tolerance of Temporal Delay in Virtual Environments. *Proceedings of IEEE Virtual Reality 2001*, IEEE Press, 247–256.

Anabuki, M., H. Kakuta, H. Yamamoto, and H. Tamura (2000). Welbo: An Embodied Conversational Agent Living in Mixed Reality Spaces. *Proceedings of the 2000 ACM Conference on Human Factors in Computing Systems (CHI 2000), Extended Abstracts*, ACM Press, 10–11.

Anderson, J. (1983). *The Architecture of Cognition*, Harvard University Press.

Angus, I., and H. Sowizral (1996). VRMosaic: Web Access from Within a Virtual Environment. *IEEE Computer Graphics & Applications* 16(3): 6–10.

429

Ayers, M., and R. Zeleznik (1996). The Lego Interface Toolkit. *Proceedings of the 1996 ACM Symposium on User Interface Software and Technology (UIST '96)*, ACM Press, 97–98.

Azuma, R. (1997). A Survey of Augmented Reality. *Presence: Teleoperators and Virtual Environments* 6(4): 355–385.

Azuma, R., and G. Bishop (1994). Improving Static and Dynamic Registration in an Optical See-Through HMD. *Proceedings of SIGGRAPH '94*, ACM Press, 197–204.

Bajura, M., H. Fuchs, and R. Ohbuchi (1992). Merging Virtual Objects with the Real World: Seeing Ultrasound Imagery within the Patient. *Proceedings of SIGGRAPH '92*, ACM Press, 203–210.

Bakker, N., P. Werkhoven, and P. Passenier (1998). Aiding Orientation Performance in Virtual Environments with Proprioceptive Feedback. *Proceedings of the 1998 IEEE Virtual Reality Annual International Symposium (VRAIS '98)*, IEEE Press, 28–35.

Balakrishnan, R., G. Fitzmaurice, and G. Kurtenbach (2001). User Interfaces for Volumetric Displays. *IEEE Computer* 34(3): 37–45.

Balakrishnan, R., G. Fitzmaurice, G. Kurtenbach, and K. Singh (1999). Exploring Interactive Curve and Surface Manipulation Using a Bend and Twist Sensitive Input Strip. *Proceedings of the 1999 ACM Symposium on Interactive 3D Graphics (I3D '99)*, ACM Press, 111–118.

Balakrishnan, R., and G. Kurtenbach (1999). Exploring Bimanual Camera Control and Object Manipulation in 3D Graphics Interfaces. *Proceedings of the 1999 ACM Conference on Human Factors in Computing Systems (CHI '99)*, ACM Press, 56–63.

Balakrishnan, R., T. Baudel, G. Fitzmaurice, and G. Kurtenbach (1997). The Rockin' Mouse: Integral 3D Manipulation on a Plane. *Proceedings of the 1997 ACM Conference on Human Factors in Computing Systems (CHI '97)*, ACM Press, 311–318.

Barrilleaux, J. (2000). *3D User Interfaces with Java 3D*, Manning Publications.

Basdogan, C., and M. A. Srinivasan (2002). Haptic Rendering in Virtual Environments. *Handbook of Virtual Environments: Design, Implementation, and Applications*. K. Stanney (Ed.), Lawrence Erlbaum Associates, 117–134.

Begault, D. R. (1994). *3D Sound For Virtual Reality and Multimedia*, Academic Press.

Begault, D. R. (1992). Perceptual Effects of Synthetic Reverberation on Three-Dimensional Audio Systems. *Journal of the Audio Engineering Society* 40(11): 895–904.

Bell, B., T. Höllerer, and S. Feiner (2002). An Annotated Situation-Awareness Aid for Augmented Reality. *Proceedings of the 2002 ACM Symposium on User Interface Software and Technology (UIST '02)*, ACM Press, 213–216.

Bier, E., M. Stone, K. Pier, B. Buxton, and T. DeRose (1993). Toolglass and Magic Lenses: The See-Through Interface. *Proceedings of SIGGRAPH '93*, ACM Press, 73–80.

Bier, E. (1990). Snap-Dragging in Three Dimensions. *Proceedings of the 1990 ACM Symposium on Interactive 3D Graphics (I3D '90)*, ACM Press, 193–204.

Bier, E. (1986). Skitters and Jacks: Interactive 3D Positioning Tools. *Proceedings of the 1986 Workshop on Interactive 3D Graphics*, ACM Press, 183–196.

Biggs, S. J., and M. A. Srinivasan (2002). Haptic Interfaces. *Handbook of Virtual Environments: Design, Implementation, and Applications*. K. Stanney (Ed.), Lawrence Erlbaum Associates, 93–115.

Billinghurst, M., H. Kato, and I. Poupyrev (2001). The MagicBook—Moving Seamlessly between Reality and Virtuality. *IEEE Computer Graphics & Applications* 21(3): 6–8.

Billinghurst, M., I. Poupyrev, H. Kato, and R. May (2000). Mixing Realities in Shared Space: An Augmented Reality Interface for Collaborative Computing. *Proceedings of IEEE International Conference on Multimedia and Expo (ICME 2000)*, IEEE Press, 1641–1644.

Billinghurst, M. (1998). Put That Where? Voice and Gesture at the Graphic Interface. *Computer Graphics* 32(4): 60–63.

Bimber, O., B. Fröhlich, D. Schmalstieg, and L. Encarnação (2001). The Virtual Showcase. *IEEE Computer Graphics & Applications* 21(6): 48–55.

Bishop, G., and D. Weimer (1986). Fast Phong Shading. *Proceedings of SIGGRAPH '86*, ACM Press, 103–105.

Blauert, J. (1997). *Spatial Hearing: The Psychoacoustics of Human Sound Localization*, MIT Press.

Bliss, J., P. Tidwell, and M. Guest (1997). The Effectiveness of Virtual Reality for Administering Spatial Navigation Training to Firefighters. *Presence: Teleoperators and Virtual Environments* 6(1): 73–86.

Blom, K., G. Lindhal, and C. Cruz-Neira (2002). Multiple Active Viewers in Projection-Based Immersive Environments. *Proceedings of the Seventh Annual Immersive Projection Technology Workshop*, Orlando, Florida.

Blundell, B. G., and A. J. Schwarz (2000). *Volumetric Three-Dimensional Display Systems*. John Wiley & Sons.

Bødker, S. (1991). *Through the Interface: A Human Activity Approach to User Interface Design*. Lawrence Erlbaum Associates.

Bolas, M. T. (1994). Human Factors in the Design of an Immersive Display. *IEEE Computer Graphics & Applications* 14(1): 55–59.

Bolt, R. (1980). "Put-That-There": Voice and Gesture at the Graphics Interface. *Proceedings of SIGGRAPH '80*, ACM Press, 262–270.

Bolter, J., L. Hodges, T. Meyer, and A. Nichols (1995). Integrating Perceptual and Symbolic Information in VR. *IEEE Computer Graphics & Applications* 15(4): 8–11.

Bordegoni, M., and M. Hemmje (1993). A Dynamic Gesture Language and Graphical Feedback for Interaction in a 3D User Interface. *Computer Graphics Forum* 12(3): 1–11.

Bowman, D. (2002). Principles for the Design of Performance-Oriented Interaction Techniques. *Handbook of Virtual Environments: Design, Implementation, and Applications*. K. Stanney (Ed.), Lawrence Erlbaum Associates, 277–300.

Bowman, D., A. Datey, Y. S. Ryu, U. Farooq, and O. Vasnaik (2002). Empirical Comparison of Human Behavior and Performance with Different Display Devices for Virtual Environments. *Proceedings of the Human Factors and Ergonomics Society Annual Meeting 2002*, 2134–2138.

Bowman, D., C. Rhoton, and M. Pinho (2002). Text Input Techniques for Immersive Virtual Environments: An Empirical Comparison. *Proceedings of the Human Factors and Ergonomics Society Annual Meeting 2002*, 2154–2158.

Bowman, D., C. Wingrave, J. Campbell, V. Ly, and C. Rhoton (2002). Novel Uses of Pinch™ Gloves for Virtual Environment Interaction Techniques. *Virtual Reality* 6(3): 122–129.

Bowman, D., D. Johnson, and L. Hodges (2001). Testbed Evaluation of VE Interaction Techniques. *Presence: Teleoperators and Virtual Environments* 10(1): 75–95.

Bowman, D., and C. Wingrave (2001). Design and Evaluation of Menu Systems for Immersive Virtual Environments. *Proceedings of IEEE Virtual Reality 2001*, IEEE Press, 149–156.

Bowman, D., C. Wingrave, J. Campbell, and V. Ly (2001). Using Pinch™ Gloves for Both Natural and Abstract Interaction Techniques in Virtual Environments. *HCI International*, New Orleans, Louisiana.

Bowman, D., E. Davis, A. Badre, and L. Hodges (1999). Maintaining Spatial Orientation during Travel in an Immersive Virtual Environment. *Presence: Teleoperators and Virtual Environments* 8(6): 618–631.

Bowman, D., and L. Hodges (1999). Formalizing the Design, Evaluation, and Application of Interaction Techniques for Immersive Virtual Environments. *The Journal of Visual Languages and Computing* 10(1): 37–53.

Bowman, D., D. Johnson, and L. Hodges (1999). Testbed Evaluation of VE Interaction Techniques. *Proceedings of the 1999 ACM Symposium on Virtual Reality Software and Technology (VRST '99)*, ACM Press, 26–33.

Bowman, D., D. Koller, and L. Hodges (1998). A Methodology for the Evaluation of Travel Techniques for Immersive Virtual Environments. *Virtual Reality: Research, Development, and Applications* 3: 120–131.

Bowman, D., J. Wineman, L. Hodges, and D. Allison (1998). Designing Animal Habitats within an Immersive VE. *IEEE Computer Graphics & Applications* 18(5): 9–13.

Bowman, D., and L. Hodges (1997). An Evaluation of Techniques for Grabbing and Manipulating Remote Objects in Immersive Virtual Environments. *Proceedings of the 1997 ACM Symposium on Interactive 3D Graphics (I3D '97)*, ACM Press, 35–38.

Bowman, D., D. Koller, and L. Hodges (1997). Travel in Immersive Virtual Environments: An Evaluation of Viewpoint Motion Control Techniques. *Proceedings of the 1997 IEEE Virtual Reality Annual International Symposium (VRAIS '97)*, IEEE Press, 45–52.

Bresenham, J. (1965). Algorithm for Computer Control of a Digital Plotter. *IBM Systems Journal* 4(1): 25–30.

Brewster, S. (1998). Using Nonspeech Sounds to Provide Navigation Cues. *ACM Transactions on Computer-Human Interaction* 5(3): 224–259.

Brogan, D., R. Metoyer, and J. Hodgins (1998). Dynamically Simulated Characters in Virtual Environments. *IEEE Computer Graphics & Applications* 15(5): 58–69.

Brooks, F. (1999). What's Real about Virtual Reality? *IEEE Computer Graphics & Applications* 19(6): 16–27.

Brooks, F., M. Ouh-Young, J. Batter, and P. Kilpatrick (1990). Project GROPE: Haptic Displays for Scientific Visualization. *Proceedings of SIGGRAPH '90*, ACM Press, 177–185.

Brooks, F. (1986). A Dynamic Graphics System for Simulating Virtual Buildings. *Proceedings of the 1986 Workshop on Interactive 3D Graphics*, ACM Press, 9–21.

Bruce, V., and P. Green (1990). *Visual Perception: Physiology, Psychology, and Ecology,* Lawrence Erlbaum Associates.

Bryson, S. (1996). Virtual Reality in Scientific Visualization. *Communications of the ACM* 39(5): 62–71.

Bukowski, R., and C. Séquin (1995). Object Associations: A Simple and Practical Approach to Virtual 3D Manipulation. *Proceedings of the 1995 Symposium on Interactive 3D Graphics (I3D '95),* ACM Press, 102–109.

Bullinger, H., P. Kern, and M. Braun (1997). Controls. *Handbook of Human Factors and Ergonomics.* G. Salvendy (Ed.), John Wiley & Sons, 697–728.

Burdea, G., and P. Coiffet (2003). *Virtual Reality Technology,* 2nd ed., John Wiley & Sons.

Burdea, G., G. Patounakis, and V. Popescu (1998). Virtual Reality Training for the Diagnosis of Prostate Cancer. *Proceedings of the 1998 IEEE Virtual Reality Annual International Symposium (VRAIS '98),* IEEE Press, 190–197.

Burdea, G. (1996). *Force and Touch Feedback for Virtual Reality,* Wiley Interscience.

Burdea, G., J. Zhufang, E. Roskos, D. Silver, and N. Langrana (1992). A Portable Dextrous Master with Force Feedback. *Presence: Teleoperators and Virtual Environments* 1(1): 18–27.

Butterworth, J., A. Davidson, S. Hench, and M. Olano (1992). 3DM: A Three-Dimensional Modeler Using a Head-Mounted Display. *Proceedings of the 1992 ACM Symposium on Interactive 3D Graphics (I3D '92),* ACM Press, 135–138.

Buxton, W. (1986). There's More to Interaction Than Meets the Eye: Some Issues in Manual Input. *User Centered System Design: New Perspectives on Human-Computer Interaction.* D. Norman and S. Draper (Eds.), Lawrence Erlbaum Associates, 319–337.

Buxton, W., and B. Myers (1986). A Study in Two-Handed Input. *Proceedings of the 1986 ACM Conference on Human Factors in Computing Systems (CHI '86),* ACM Press, 321–326.

Buxton, W. (1983). Lexical and Pragmatic Considerations of Input Structures. *Computer Graphics* 17(1): 31–37.

Campbell, D. (1996). *Design in Virtual Environments Using Architectural Metaphor: A HIT Lab Gallery,* Master's Thesis, HIT Lab, University of Washington.

Card, S., J. Mackinlay, and G. Robertson (1990). The Design Space of Input Devices. *Proceedings of the 1990 ACM Conference on Human Factors in Computing Systems (CHI '90),* ACM Press, 117–124.

Card, S., T. Moran, and A. Newell (1986). The Model Human Processor. *Handbook of Perception and Human Performance.* K. Boff, L. Kaufman, and J. Thomas (Eds.), John Wiley & Sons, Volume 1, 45-1–45-35.

Card, S., T. Moran, and A. Newell (1983). *The Psychology of Human-Computer Interaction,* Lawrence Erlbaum Associates.

Card, S., T. Moran, and A. Newell (1980). The Keystroke-Level Model for User Performance Time with Interactive Systems. *Communications of the ACM* 23(7): 398–410.

Carlile, S. (1996). *Virtual Auditory Space: Generation and Application,* R. G. Landes Company.

Carlin, A., H. Hoffman, and S. Weghorst (1997). Virtual Reality and Tactile Augmentation in the Treatment of Spider Phobia: A Case Report. *Behavior Research and Therapy* 35(2): 153–159.

Chance, S., F. Gaunet, A. Beall, and J. Loomis (1998). Locomotion Mode Affects the Updating of Objects Encountered during Travel: The Contribution of Vestibular and Proprioceptive Inputs to Path Integration. *Presence: Teleoperators and Virtual Environments* 7(2): 168–178.

Chen, M., S. Mountford, and A. Sellen (1988). A Study in Interactive 3-D Rotation Using 2-D Control Devices. *Computer Graphics* 22(4): 121–129.

Chinthammit, W., E. Seibel, and T. A. Furness (2002). Unique Shared-Aperture Display with Head or Target Tracking. *Proceedings of IEEE Virtual Reality 2002*, IEEE Press, 235–242.

Clark, F. J., and K. W. Horch (1986). Kinesthesia. *Handbook of Perception and Human Performance*. K. Boff, L. Kaufman, and J. Thomas (Eds.), John Wiley & Sons, Volume 1, 13-1–13-62.

Cohen, M., and E. Wenzel (1995). The Design of Multidimensional Sound Interfaces. *Virtual Environments and Advanced Interface Design*. W. Barfield and T. Furness (Eds.), Oxford University Press, 291–346.

Colley, S. (2001). *Vector Calculus*, 2nd ed., Prentice Hall.

Conkar, T., J. Noyes, and C. Kimble (1999). CLIMATE: A Framework for Developing Holistic Requirements Analysis in Virtual Environments. *Interacting with Computers* 11(4): 387–403.

Conner, B., S. Snibbe, K. Herndon, D. Robbins, R. Zeleznik, and A. van Dam (1992). Three-Dimensional Widgets. *Proceedings of the 1992 ACM Symposium on Interactive 3D Graphics (I3D '92)*, ACM Press, 183–188.

Cooper, W. (Ed.) (1983). *Cognitive Aspects of Skilled Typewriting*. Springer Verlag.

Coquillart, S., and G. Wesche (1999). The Virtual Palette and the Virtual Remote Control Panel: A Device and Interaction Paradigm for the Responsive Workbench. *Proceedings of IEEE Virtual Reality '99*, IEEE Press, 213–217.

Crichton, M. (1994). *Disclosure*, Knopf.

Crowford, B. (1964). Joystick vs. Multiple Levers for Remote Manipulator Control. *Human Factors* 6(1): 39–48.

Cruz-Neira, C., and R. Lutz (1999). Using Immersive Virtual Environments for Certification. *IEEE Software* 16(4): 26–30.

Cruz-Neira, C., D. Sandin, and T. Defanti (1993). Surround Screen Projection-Based Virtual Reality. *Proceedings of SIGGRAPH '93*, ACM Press, 135–142.

Cutler, L., B. Fröhlich, and P. Hanrahan (1997). Two-Handed Direct Manipulation on the Responsive Workbench. *Proceedings of the 1997 ACM Symposium on Interactive 3D Graphics (I3D '97)*, ACM Press, 107–114.

Darken, R., and B. Peterson (2002). Spatial Orientation, Wayfinding, and Representation. *Handbook of Virtual Environments: Design, Implementation, and Applications*, K. Stanney (Ed.), Lawrence Erlbaum Associates, 493–518.

Darken, R., and H. Cevik (1999). Map Usage in Virtual Environments: Orientation Issues. *Proceedings of IEEE Virtual Reality '99*, IEEE Press, 133–140.

Darken, R., and S. Goerger (1999). The Transfer of Strategies from Virtual to Real Environments: An Explanation for Performance Differences. *Proceedings of Virtual Worlds and Simulation '99*, 159–164.

Darken, R., and W. Banker (1998). Navigating in Natural Environments: A Virtual Environment Training Transfer Study. *Proceedings of the 1998 IEEE Virtual Reality Annual International Symposium (VRAIS '98)*, IEEE Press, 12–19.

Darken, R., W. Cockayne, and D. Carmein (1997). The Omni-Directional Treadmill: A Locomotion Device for Virtual Worlds. *Proceedings of the 1997 ACM Symposium on User Interface Software and Technology (UIST '97)*, ACM Press, 213–221.

Darken, R., and J. Sibert (1996). Wayfinding Strategies and Behaviors in Large Virtual Worlds. *Proceedings of the 1996 ACM Conference on Human Factors in Computing Systems (CHI'96)*, ACM Press, 142–149.

Davide, F., M. Holmberg, and I. Lundström (2001). Virtual Olfactory Interfaces: Electronic Noses and Olfactory Displays. *Communications through Virtual Technologies: Identity, Community and Technology in the Communication Age*. G. Riva and F. Davide (Eds.), IOS Press, Volume 1, 193–220.

Davies, C., and J. Harrison (1996). Osmose: Towards Broadening the Aesthetics of Virtual Reality. *Computer Graphics* 30(4): 25–28.

Davis, E., K. Scott, J. Pair, L. Hodges, and J. Oliviero (1999). Can Audio Enhance Visual Perception and Performance in a Virtual Environment? *Proceedings of the Human Factors and Ergonomics 43rd Annual Meeting*, 1197–1201.

Davis, E. (1996). Visual Requirements in HMDs: What Can We See and What Do We Need to See? *Head-Mounted Displays: Designing for the User*. J. Melzer and K. Moffitt (Eds.), McGraw-Hill, 207–249.

Davis, E., and L. Hodges (1995). Human Stereopsis, Fusion, and Virtual Environments. *Virtual Environments and Advanced Interface Design*. W. Barfield and T. Furness (Eds.), Oxford University Press, 145–174.

Defanti, T., and D. Sandin (1977). Final Report to the National Endowment of the Arts, University of Illinois at Chicago.

Deisinger, J., R. Breining, A. Robler, D. Ruckert, and J. Hofle (2000). Immersive Ergonomic Analyses of Console Elements in a Tractor Cabin. *Proceedings of the Immersive Projection Technology Workshop*, Ames, Iowa.

Demiralp, Ç., D. Laidlaw, C. Jackson, D. Keefe, and S. Zhang (2003). Subjective Usefulness of CAVE and Fish Tank VR Display Systems for a Scientific Visualization Application. *IEEE Visualization 2003—Poster Abstracts*, IEEE Press.

Dobashi, Y., T. Yamamoto, and T. Nishita (2003). Real-Time Rendering of Aerodynamic Sound Using Sound Textures Based on Computational Fluid Dynamics. *ACM Transactions on Graphics* 23(3): 732–740.

Downs, R., and D. Stea (1977). *Maps in Minds, Reflections on Cognitive Mapping*, Harper and Row.

Draper, M. (1995). *Exploring the Influence of a Virtual Body on Spatial Awareness*, Master of Science in Engineering, Dept. of Engineering, University of Washington.

Duchowski, A. T. (2003). *Eye Tracking Methodology: Theory and Practice*. Springer-Verlag.

Duchowski, A. T., E. Medlin, A. Gramopadhye, B. Melloy, and S. Nair (2001). Binocular Eye Tracking in VR for Visual Inspection Training. *Proceedings of the 2001 ACM Symposium on Virtual Reality Software and Technology (VRST 2001)*, ACM Press, 1–9.

Durlach, N., and A. Mavor (1995). *Virtual Reality: Scientific and Technical Challenges*, National Academy Press.

Durlach, N. (1991). Auditory Localization in Teleoperator and Virtual Environment Systems: Ideas, Issues, and Problems. *Perception* 20: 543–554.

Dvorak, A., N. Merrick, W. Dealey, and G. Ford (1936). *Typewriting Behavior*, American Book Company.

Ebert, D., E. Bedwell, S. Maher, L. Smoliar, and E. Downing (1999). Realizing 3D Visualizations Using Crossed-Beam Volumetric Displays. *Communications of the ACM* 42(8): 101–107.

Ellis, S., B. Adelstein, S. Baumeler, G. Jense, and R. Jacoby (1999). Sensor Spatial Distortion, Visual Latency, and Update Rate Effects on 3D Tracking in Virtual Environments. *Proceedings of IEEE Virtual Reality '99*, IEEE Press, 218–221.

Ellson, D. (1947). The Independence of Tracking in Two or Three Dimensions with B-29 Pedestal Sight, Aero Medical Laboratory, Wright Air Development Center, TSEAA-694-2G.

Elvins, T., D. Nadeau, and D. Kirsh (1997). Worldlets: 3D Thumbnails for Wayfinding in Virtual Environments. *Proceedings of the 1997 ACM Symposium on User Interface Software and Technology (UIST '97)*, ACM Press, 21–30.

Enderle, G., K. Kanasay, and G. Pfaff (1984). *GKS: The Graphics Standard, Computer Graphics Programming*. Springer-Verlag.

Englebart, D. C., and W. K. English (1968). A Research Center for Augmenting Human Intellect. *Proceedings of the 1968 Fall Joint Computer Conference*, 395–410.

Fairchild, K., L. Hai, J. Loo, N. Hern, and L. Serra (1993). The Heaven and Earth Virtual Reality: Designing Applications for Novice Users. Proceedings of the *IEEE Symposium on Research Frontiers in Virtual Reality*, IEEE Press, 47–53.

Feiner, S., B. MacIntyre, and D. Seligmann (1993). Knowledge-Based Augmented Reality. *Communications of the ACM* 36(7): 53–62.

Fels, S., and G. Hinton (1998). Glove-Talk II: A Neural Network Interface Which Maps Gestures to Parallel Formant Speech Synthesizer Controls. *IEEE Transactions on Neural Networks* 9(1): 205–212.

Fels, S. (1994). *Glove-Talk II: Mapping Hand Gestures to Speech Using Neural Networks: An Approach to Building Adaptive Interfaces*, PhD Dissertation, University of Toronto.

Figueroa, P., M. Green, and H. Hoover (2001). 3DML: A Language for 3D Interaction Techniques Specification. *Eurographics*, Manchester, UK.

Fitts, P. (1954). The Information Capacity of the Human Motor System in Controlling the Amplitude of Movement. *Journal of Experimental Psychology* 47: 381–391.

Fitts, P., and M. Jones (1953). Compatibility: Spatial characteristics of stimulus and response codes. *Journal of Experimental Psychology* 46: 199–210.

Fitzmaurice, G., H. Ishii, and W. Buxton (1995). Bricks: Laying the Foundations for Graspable User Interfaces. *Proceedings of the 1995 ACM Conference on Human Factors in Computing Systems (CHI '95)*, ACM Press, 442–449.

Fitzmaurice, G. (1993). Situated Information Spaces and Spatially Aware Palmtop Computers. *Communications of the ACM* 36(7): 38–49.

Foley, J., A. van Dam, S. Feiner, and J. Hughes (1996). *Computer Graphics: Principles and Practice*, Addison Wesley.

Foley, J. (1987). Interfaces for Advanced Computing. *Scientific American* 257(4): 126–135.

Foley, J., V. Wallace, and P. Chan (1984). The Human Factors of Computer Graphics Interaction Techniques. *IEEE Computer Graphics & Applications* 4(11): 13–48.

Foley, J., and V. Wallace (1974). The Art of Natural Graphics Man-Machine Conversation. *Proceedings of the IEEE* 62(4): 462–471.

Forman, E., and C. Lawson (2003). Building Physical Interfaces: Making Computer Graphics Interactive. *SIGGRAPH Course #30*.

Forsberg, A., M. Kirby, D. Laidlaw, G. Karniadakis, A. van Dam, and J. Elion (2000). Immersive Virtual Reality for Visualizing Flow through an Artery. *Proceedings of IEEE Visualization 2000*, IEEE Press, 457–460.

Forsberg, A., J. LaViola, and R. Zeleznik (1998). ErgoDesk: A Framework for Two and Three Dimensional Interaction at the ActiveDesk. *Proceedings of the Second International Immersive Projection Technology Workshop*, Ames, Iowa.

Forsberg, A., J. LaViola, L. Markosian, and R. Zeleznik (1997). Seamless Interaction in Virtual Reality. *IEEE Computer Graphics & Applications* 17(6): 6–9.

Forsberg, A., K. Herndon, and R. Zeleznik (1996). Aperture Based Selection for Immersive Virtual Environments. *Proceedings of the 1996 ACM Symposium on User Interface Software and Technology (UIST '96)*, ACM Press, 95–96.

Forsyth, D., and J. Ponce (2002). *Computer Vision: A Modern Approach*, Prentice Hall.

Foskey, M., M. Otaduy, and M. Lin (2002). ArtNova: Touch-Enabled 3D Model Design. *Proceedings of IEEE Virtual Reality 2002*, IEEE Press, 119–126.

Foxlin, E., and L. Naimark (2003). VIS-Tracker: A Wearable Vision-Inertial Self Tracker. *Proceedings of IEEE Virtual Reality 2003*, IEEE Press, 199–206.

Foxlin, E. (2002). Motion Tracking Requirements and Technologies. *Handbook of Virtual Environments: Design, Implementation, and Applications*. K. Stanney (Ed.), Lawrence Erlbaum Associates, 163–210.

Fröhlich, B., and J. Plate (2000). The Cubic Mouse: A New Device for Three-Dimensional Input. *Proceedings of the 2000 ACM Conference on Human Factors in Computing Systems (CHI 2000)*, ACM Press, 526–531.

Funkhouser, T., P. Min, and I. Carlbom (1999). Real Time Acoustic Modeling for Distributed Virtual Environments. *Proceedings of SIGGRAPH '99*, ACM Press, 365–374.

Gabbard, J., D. Hix, and J. Swan (1999). User-Centered Design and Evaluation of Virtual Environments. *IEEE Computer Graphics & Applications* 19(6): 51–59.

Gabbard, J. (1997). *Taxonomy of Usability Characteristics in Virtual Environments*, Master's Thesis, Dept. of Computer Science, Virginia Polytechnic Institute and State University.

Gale, N., R. Golledge, J. Pellegrino, and S. Doherty (1990). The Acquisition and Integration of Route Knowledge in an Unfamiliar Neighbourhood. *Journal of Environmental Psychology* 10: 3–25.

Galyean, T. (1995). Guided Navigation of Virtual Environments. *Proceedings of the 1995 ACM Symposium on Interactive 3D Graphics (I3D '95)*, ACM Press, 103–104.

Garas, J. (2000). *Adaptive 3D Sound Systems*, Kluwer Academic Publishers.

Gardner, W. (1998). *3D Audio Using Loudspeakers*, Kluwer Academic Publishers.

Garner, W. (1974). *The Processing of Information and Structure*, Lawrence Erlbaum Associates.

Gelfand, S. (1998). *Hearing: An Introduction to Psychological and Psychophysical Acoustics*, Marcel Dekker.

Gibson, W. (1984). *Neuromancer*, Ace Books.

Gleue, T., and P. Dahne (2001). Design and Implementation of a Mobile Device for Outdoor Augmented Reality in the Archeoguide Project. *Conference on Virtual Reality, Archeology, and Cultural Heritage*, ACM Press, 161–168.

Golledge, R. (1999). *Wayfinding Behavior: Cognitive Mapping and Other Spatial Processes*, John Hopkins University Press.

Golub, G., and C. Van Loan (1996). *Matrix Computations*, Johns Hopkins University Press.

Grammenos, G., M. Filou, P. Papadakos, and C. Stephanidis (2002). Virtual Prints: Leaving Trails in Virtual Environments. *Proceedings of the Eighth Eurographics Workshop on Virtual Environments (VE 2002)*, 131–138.

Grassia, F. S. (1998). Practical Parameterization of Rotations Using the Exponential Map. *Journal of Graphics Tools* 3(3): 29–48.

Grasso, M., D. Ebert, and T. Finin (1998). The Integrality of Speech in Multimodal Interfaces. *ACM Transactions on Computer-Human Interaction* 5(4): 303–325.

Greenburg, S., and M. Boyle (2002). Customizable Physical Interfaces for Interacting with Conventional Applications. *Proceedings of the 2002 ACM Symposium on User Interface Software and Technology (UIST 2002)*, ACM Press, 31–40.

Greenburg, S., and C. Fitchett (2001). Phidgets: Easy Development of Physical Interfaces through Physical Widgets. *Proceedings of the 2001 ACM Symposium on User Interface Software and Technology (UIST 2001)*, ACM Press, 209–218.

Grosjean, J., J-M. Burkhardt, S. Coquillart, and P. Richard (2002). Evaluation of the Command and Control Cube. *Proceedings of the Fourth International Conference on Multimodal Interfaces (ICMI 2002)*, IEEE Press, 14–16.

Grossman, T., R. Balakrishnan, and K. Singh (2003). An Interface for Creating and Manipulating Curves Using a High Degree-of-Freedom Curve Input Device. *Proceedings of 2003 ACM Conference on Human Factors in Computing Systems (CHI 2003)*, ACM Press, 185–192.

Guiard, Y. (1987). Symmetric Division of Labor in Human Skilled Bimanual Action: The Kinematic Chain as a Model. *The Journal of Motor Behaviour* 19(4): 486–517.

Hachet, M., P. Guitton, and P. Reuter (2003). The CAT for Efficient 2D and 3D Interaction as an Alternative to Mouse Adaptations. *Proceedings of the 2003 ACM Symposium on Virtual Reality Software and Technology (VRST 2003)*, ACM Press, 205–212.

Hackos, J., and J. Redish (1998). *User and Task Analysis for Interface Design*, John Wiley & Sons.

Hamilton, Sir W. (1853). *Lectures on Quaternions*, Hodges and Smith.

Hanson, A. (1992). The Rolling Ball. *Graphics Gem III*. D. Kirk (Ed.), Academic Press, 51–60.

Harmon, R., W. Patterson, W. Ribarsky, and J. Bolter (1996). The Virtual Annotation System. *Proceedings of the 1996 IEEE Virtual Reality Annual International Symposium (VRAIS '96)*, IEEE Press, 239–245.

Harris, L., M. Jenkin, and D. Zikovitz (1999). Vestibular Cues and Virtual Environments: Choosing the Magnitude of the Vestibular Cue. *Proceedings of IEEE Virtual Reality '99*, IEEE Press, 229–236.

Hartson, H., and P. Gray (1992). Temporal Aspect of Tasks in the User Action Notation. *Human Computer Interaction* 7(1): 1–45.

Henry, D., and T. Furness (1993). Spatial Perception in Virtual Environments: Evaluating an Architectural Application. *Proceedings of the 1993 IEEE Virtual Reality Annual International Symposium (VRAIS '93)*, IEEE Press, 33–40.

Herndon, K., A. van Dam, and M. Gleicher (1994). The Challenges of 3D Interaction. *SIGCHI Bulletin* 26(4): 36–43.

Herndon, K., R. Zeleznik, D. Robbins, D. Conner, S. Snibbe, and A. van Dam (1992). Interactive Shadows. *Proceedings of the 1992 ACM Symposium on User Interface Software and Technology (UIST '92)*, ACM Press, 1–6.

Hinckley, K., R. Pausch, D. Proffitt, J. Patten, and N. Kassell (1997). Cooperative Bimanual Action. *Proceedings of the 1997 ACM Conference on Human Factors in Computing Systems (CHI '97)*, ACM Press, 27–34.

Hinckley, K., J. Tullio, R. Pausch, D. Proffitt, and N. Kassell (1997). Usability Analysis of 3D Rotation Techniques. *Proceedings of the 1997 ACM Symposium on User Interface Software and Technology (UIST '97)*, ACM Press, 1–10.

Hinckley, K., R. Pausch, J. Goble, and N. Kassell (1994). Passive Real-World Interfaces Props for Neurosurgical Visualization. *Proceedings of the 1994 ACM Conference on Human Factors in Computing Systems (CHI '94)*, ACM Press, 452–458.

Hix, D., and J. Gabbard (2002). Usability Engineering of Virtual Environments. *Handbook of Virtual Environments: Design, Implementation, and Applications*. K. Stanney (Ed.), Lawrence Erlbaum Associates, 681–699.

Hix, D., J. Swan, J. Gabbard, M. McGee, J. Durbin, and T. King (1999). User-Centered Design and Evaluation of a Real-Time Battlefield Visualization Virtual Environment. *Proceedings of IEEE Virtual Reality '99*, IEEE Press, 96–103.

Hix, D., and H. Hartson (1993). *Developing User Interfaces: Ensuring Usability through Product & Process*, John Wiley and Sons.

Hodges, L., B. Rothbaum, R. Alarcon, D. Ready, F. Shahar, K. Graap, J. Pair, P. Herbert, B. Wills, and D. Baltzell (1999). Virtual Vietnam: A Virtual Environment for the Treatment of Chronic Post-traumatic Stress Disorder. *CyberPsychology and Behavior* 2(1): 7–14.

Hodges, L., B. Rothbaum, R. Kooper, D. Opdyke, T. Meyer, M. North, J. de Graff, and J. Williford (1995). Virtual Environments for Treating the Fear of Heights. *IEEE Computer* 28(7): 27–34.

Hoffman, H., A. Hollander, K. Schroder, S. Rousseau, and T. Furness (1998). Physically Touching and Tasting Virtual Objects Enhances the Realism of Virtual Experiences. *Virtual Reality: Research, Development and Application*, 3: 226–234.

Hogue, A., M. Robinson, M. R. Jenkin, and R. S. Allison (2003). A Vision-Based Head Tracking System for Fully Immersive Displays. *Proceedings of Immersive Projection Technology and Virtual Environments 2003,* ACM Press, 179–188.

Hollerbach, J. (2002). Locomotion Interfaces. *Handbook of Virtual Environments: Design, Implementation, and Applications.* K. Stanney (Ed.), Lawrence Erlbaum Associates, 239–254.

Höllerer, T., S. Feiner, T. Terauchi, G. Rashid, and D. Hallaway (1999). Exploring MARS: Developing Indoor and Outdoor User Interfaces to a Mobile Augmented Reality System. *Computers and Graphics* 23(6): 779–785.

Houde, S. (1992). Iterative Design of an Interface for Easy 3-D Direct Manipulation. *Proceedings of the 1992 ACM Conference on Human Factors in Computing Systems (CHI '92),* ACM Press, 135–142.

Howard, I. (1991). Spatial Vision within Egocentric and Exocentric Frames of Reference. *Pictorial Communication in Virtual and Real Environments.* A. Grunwald (Ed.), Taylor and Francis Ltd., 338–357.

Hua, H., C. Gao, L. Brown, D. Ahuja, and J. Rolland (2002). A Testbed for Precise Registration, Natural Occlusion, and Interaction in an Augmented Environment Using a Head-Mounted Projective Display. *Proceedings of IEEE Virtual Reality 2002,* IEEE Press, 81–89.

Hua, H., C. Gao, F. Biocca, and J. Rolland (2001). An Ultra-Light and Compact Design and Implementation of Head-Mounted Projective Displays. *Proceedings of IEEE Virtual Reality 2001,* IEEE Press, 175–182.

Hultquits, J. (1990). A Virtual Trackball. *Graphics Gems I,* Academic Press, 462–463.

Huopaniemi, J. (1999). *Virtual Acoustics and 3D Sound in Multimedia Signal Processing,* PhD Dissertation, Dept. of Electrical and Communications Engineering, Helsinki University of Technology.

Igarashi, T., S. Matsuoka, and H. Tanaka (1999). Teddy: A Sketching Interface for 3D Freeform Design. *Proceedings of SIGGRAPH '99,* ACM Press, 409–416.

Igarashi, T., R. Kadobayahi, K. Mase, and H. Tanaka (1998). Path Drawing for 3D Walkthrough. *Proceedings of the 1998 ACM Symposium on User Interface Software and Technology (UIST '98),* ACM Press, 173–174.

Ingram, R., J. Bowers, and S. Benford (1996). Building Virtual Cities: Applying Urban Planning Principles to the Design of Virtual Environments. *Proceedings of the 1996 ACM Symposium on Virtual Reality Software and Technology (VRST '96),* ACM Press, 83–92.

Insko, B. E. (2001). *Passive Haptics Significantly Enhances Virtual Environments,* PhD Dissertation, Dept. of Computer Science, University of North Carolina at Chapel Hill.

Ishii, H., and B. Ullmer (1997). Tangible Bits: Towards Seamless Interfaces between People, Bits, and Atoms. *Proceedings of the 1997 ACM Conference on Human Factors in Computing Systems (CHI '97),* ACM Press, 234–241.

Ishii, M., and M. Sato (1994). A 3D Spatial Interface Device Using Tensed Strings. *Presence: Teleoperators and Virtual Environments* 3(1): 81–86.

Iwata, H. (2001). GaitMaster: A Versatile Locomotion Interface for Uneven Virtual Terrain. *Proceedings of IEEE Virtual Reality 2001,* IEEE Press, 131–137.

Iwata, H. (1999). Walking about Virtual Environments on an Infinite Floor. *Proceedings of IEEE Virtual Reality '99*, IEEE Press, 286–293.

Iwata, H., and T. Fujii (1996). Virtual Perambulator: A Novel Interface Device for Locomotion in Virtual Environment. *Proceedings of the 1996 IEEE Virtual Reality Annual International Symposium (VRAIS '96)*, IEEE Press, 60–65.

Jacob, R. (1996). Input Devices and Techniques. *The Computer Science and Engineering Handbook*. A. B. Tucker (Ed.), CRC Press, 1494–1511.

Jacob, R. (1995). Eye Tracking in Advanced Interface Design. *Virtual Environments and Advanced Interface Design*. W. Barfield and T. Furness (Eds.), Oxford University Press, 258–288.

Jacob, R., and L. Sibert (1992). The Perceptual Structure of Multidimensional Input Devices. *Proceedings of the 1992 ACM Conference on Human Factors and Computing Systems (CHI '92)*, ACM Press, 211–218.

Jacobson, D. (1996). Talking Tactile Maps and Environmental Audio Beacons: An Orientation and Mobility Development Tool for Visually Impaired People. *ICA Commission on Maps and Graphics for Blind and Visually Impaired People.*

Jacoby, R., M. Ferneau, and J. Humphries (1994). Gestural Interaction in a Virtual Environment. *Stereoscopic Display and Virtual Reality Systems: The Engineering Reality of Virtual Reality*, SPIE, 355–364.

Johnson, A., M. Roussos, J. Leigh, C. Vasilakis, C. Barnes, and T. Moher (1998). The NICE Project: Learning Together in a Virtual World. *Proceedings of the 1998 IEEE Virtual Reality Annual International Symposium (VRAIS '98)*, IEEE Press, 176–183.

Johnson-Laird, P. (1993). *The Computer and the Mind: An Introduction to Cognitive Science.* Fontana Press.

Jones, H. (2001). *Computer Graphics through Key Mathematics,* Springer-Verlag.

Jorgensen, C., K. Wheeler, and S. Stepniewski (2000). Bioelectric Control of a 757 Class High Fidelity Aircraft Simulation. *Proceedings of the World Automation Conference.*

Kapralos B., M. Jenkin, and E. Milios (2003). Auditory Perception and Virtual Environments, Dept. of Computer Science, York University, CS-2003-07.

Kasik, D., J. Troy, S. Amorosi, M. Murray, and S. Swamy (2002). Evaluating Graphics Displays for Complex 3D Models. *IEEE Computer Graphics & Applications* 22(3): 56–64.

Kato, H., M. Billinghurst, I. Poupyrev, K. Imamoto, and K. Tachibana (2000). Virtual Object Manipulation on a Table-Top AR Environment. *Proceedings of the IEEE and ACM International Symposium on Augmented Reality.*

Kato, H., and M. Billinghurst (1999). Marker Tracking and HMD Calibration for a Video-Based Augmented Reality Conferencing System. *Proceedings of the 2nd International Workshop on Augmented Reality*, 85–94.

Kaufman, N., I. Poupyrev, E. Miller, M. Billinghurst, P. Oppenheimer, and S. Weghorst (1997). New Interface Metaphors for Complex Information Space Visualization: An ECG Monitor Object Prototype. *Medicine Meets Virtual Reality 5,* IOS Press, 131–140.

Kaur, K. (1999). *Designing Virtual Environments for Usability,* PhD Dissertation, Dept. of Computer Science, University College.

Kaur, K., N. Maiden, and A. Sutcliffe (1999). Interacting with Virtual Environments: An Evaluation of a Model of Interaction. *Interacting with Computers* 11(4): 403–426.

Keefe, D., D. Acevedo, T. Moscovich, D. Laidlaw, and J. LaViola (2001). CavePainting: A Fully Immersive 3D Artistic Medium and Interactive Experience. *Proceedings of the 2001 Symposium on Interactive 3D Graphics (I3D 2001),* ACM Press, 85–93.

Kendall, G. (1995). A 3D Sound Primer: Directional Hearing and Stereo Reproduction. *Computer Music Journal* 19(4): 23–46.

Kendon, A. (1988). How Gestures Can Become Like Words. *Crosscultural Perspectives in Nonverbal Communication.* F. Potyatos (Ed.), Hogrefe, 131–141.

Kennedy, R., K. Stanney, and W. Dunlap (2000). Duration and Exposure to Virtual Environments: Sickness Curves during and across Sessions. *Presence: Teleoperators and Virtual Environments* 9(5): 463–472.

Kennedy, R., N. Lane, K. Berbaum, and M. Lilienthal (1993). A Simulator Sickness Questionnaire (SSQ): A New Method for Quantifying Simulator Sickness. *International Journal of Aviation Psychology* 3(3): 203–220.

Kessler, G., D. Bowman, and L. Hodges (2000). The Simple Virtual Environment Library: An Extensible Framework for Building VE Applications. *Presence: Teleoperators and Virtual Environments* 9(2): 187–208.

Kessler, G., L. Hodges, and N. Walker (1995). Evaluation of the CyberGlove as a Whole-Hand Input Device. *ACM Transactions on Computer-Human Interaction* 2(4): 263–283.

Khotake, N., J. Rekimoto, and Y. Anzai (1999). InfoStick: An Interaction Device for Inter-appliance Computing. *Proceedings of Handheld and Ubiquitous Computing: First International Symposium,* Springer-Verlag, 246–258.

Kieseyer, U. (2001). *Georges Seurat: 1859–1891: The Master of Pointillism,* TASCHEN America LLC.

Kindratenko, V. (2000). A Survey of Electromagnetic Position Tracker Calibration. *Virtual Reality: Research, Development, and Applications* 5(3): 169–182.

Kiyokawa, K., H. Takemura, and N. Yokoya (2000). Seamless Design for 3D Object Creation. *IEEE MultiMedia* 7(1): 22–33.

Klatzky, R., J. Loomis, A. Beall, S. Chance, and R. Golledge (1998). Spatial Updating of Self-position and Orientation during Real, Imagined and Virtual Locomotion. *Psychological Science* 9: 29–298.

Klein, A., W. Li, M. Kazhdan, W. Correa, A. Finkelstein, and T. Funkhouser (2000). Non-photorealistic Virtual Environments. *Proceedings of SIGGRAPH 2000,* ACM Press, 527–534.

Kleiner, M., D. I. Dalenback, and P. Svensson (1993). Auralization: An Overview. *Journal of the Audio Engineering Society* 41(11): 861–875.

Knight, J. (1987). Manual Control and Tracking. *Handbook of Human Factors.* G. Salvendy (Ed.), John Wiley and Sons, 182–218.

Koller, D., M. Mine, and S. Hudson (1996). Head-Tracked Orbital Viewing: An Interaction Technique for Immersive Virtual Environments. *Proceedings of the 1996 ACM Symposium on User Interface Software and Technology (UIST '96),* ACM Press, 81–82.

Körner, O., and R. Männer (2003). Implementation of a Haptic Interface for a Virtual Reality Simulator for Flexible Endoscopy. *11th International Symposium on Haptic Interfaces for Virtual Environments and Teleoperator Systems,* IEEE Press, 278–284.

Kosslyn, S. (1993). *Image and Brain,* MIT Press.

Kramer, J. (1993). Force Feedback and Texture Simulating Interface Device, Patent No. 5,047,952.

Kramer, J. (1991). Communication System for Deaf, Deaf-Blind and Non-vocal Individuals Using Instrumented Gloves, Patent No. 5,047,952.

Krueger, M., T. Gionfriddo, and K. Hinrichsen (1985). VIDEOPLACE: An Artificial Reality. *Proceedings of the 1985 ACM Conference on Human Factors in Computing Systems (CHI '85)*, ACM Press, 35–40.

Krüger, W., C. Bohn, B. Fröhlich, H. Schuth, W. Strauss, and G. Wesche (1995). The Responsive Workbench: A Virtual Work Environment. *IEEE Computer* 28(7): 42–48.

Krüger, W., and B. Fröhlich (1994). The Responsive Workbench. *IEEE Computer Graphics & Applications* 14(3): 12–15.

Kruijff, E., S. Conrad, and A. Mueller (2003). Flow of Action in Mixed Interaction Modalities, *Proceedings of HCI International 2003*.

Kuipers, J. (2002). *Quaternions and Rotation Sequences: A Primer with Applications to Orbits, Aerospace and Virtual Reality*, Princeton University Press.

Kulkanri, A., and H. Colburn (1993). Evaluation of a Linear Interpolation Scheme for Approximating HRTFs. *Journal of the Acoustical Society of America* 93(4): 2350.

Kurtenbach, G., and W. Buxton (1991). Issues in Combining Marking and Direct Manipulation Techniques. *Proceedings of the 1991 ACM Symposium on User Interface Software and Technology (UIST '91)*, ACM Press, 137–144.

Lampton, D., B. Knerr, S. Goldberg, J. Bliss, M. Moshell, and B. Blau (1994). The Virtual Environment Performance Assessment Battery (VEPAB): Development and Evaluation. *Presence: Teleoperators and Virtual Environments* 3(2): 145–157.

Latoschik, M. (2001). A Gesture Processing Framework for Multimodal Interaction in Virtual Reality. *Proceedings of the 1st International Conference on Computer Graphics, Virtual Reality and Visualization in Africa*, ACM Press, 95–100.

LaViola, J., D. Keefe, D. Acevedo, and R. Zeleznik (2004). Case Studies in Building Custom Input Devices for Virtual Environment Interfaces. *Proceedings of the VR 2004 Workshop on Beyond Wand and Glove Interaction*, 67–71.

LaViola, J., D. Acevedo, D. Keefe, and R. Zeleznik (2001). Hands-Free Multi-scale Navigation in Virtual Environments. *Proceedings of the 2001 Symposium on Interactive 3D Graphics (I3D 2001)*, ACM Press, 9–15.

LaViola, J. (2000a). A Discussion of Cybersickness in Virtual Environments. *SIGCHI Bulletin* 32(1): 47–56.

LaViola, J. (2000b). MSVT: A Virtual Reality-Based Multimodal Scientific Visualization Tool. *Proceedings of the Third IASTED International Conference on Computer Graphics and Imaging*, 1–7.

LaViola, J. (1999a). *Whole-Hand and Speech Input in Virtual Environments*, Master's Thesis, Dept. of Computer Science, Brown University.

LaViola, J. (1999b). Flex and Pinch: A Case Study of Whole-Hand Input Design for Virtual Environment Interaction. *Proceedings of the IASTED International Conference on Computer Graphics and Imaging '99*, 221–225.

Liang, J., and M. Green (1994). JDCAD: A Highly Interactive 3D Modeling System. *Computers and Graphics* 18(4): 499–506.

Liang, J., C. Shaw, and M. Green (1991). On Temporal-Spatial Realism in the Virtual Reality Environment. *Proceedings of the 1991 ACM Symposium on User Interface Software and Technology (UIST '91)*, ACM Press, 19–25.

Liebe, B., T. Starner, W. Ribarsky, Z. Wartell, D. Krum, B. Singletary, and L. Hodges (2000). The Perceptive Workbench: Toward Spontaneous and Natural Interaction in Semi-immersive Environments. *Proceedings of IEEE Virtual Reality 2000*, IEEE Press, 13–20.

Lindeman, R., J. Sibert, and J. Hahn (1999). Hand-Held Windows: Towards Effective 2D Interaction in Immersive Virtual Environments. *Proceedings of IEEE Virtual Reality '99*, IEEE Press, 205–212.

Loftin, R. B., and P. Kenney (1995). Training the Hubble Space Telescope Flight Team. *IEEE Computer Graphics & Applications* 15(5): 31–37.

Loomis, J., and S. Lederman (1986). Tactual Perception. *Handbook of Perception and Human Performance*. K. Boff, L. Kaufman, and J. Thomas (Eds.), John Wiley & Sons, Volume 1, 12-1–12-57.

Lucente, M., G. Zwart, and A. George (1998). Visualization Space: A Testbed for Deviceless Multimodal User Interface. *Proceedings of Intelligent Environments '98, The AAAI Spring Symposium Series*, 87–92.

Lucente, M. (1997). Interactive Three-Dimensional Holographic Displays: Seeing the Future in Depth. *Computer Graphics* 31(2): 63–67.

Luebke, D., M. Reddy, J. Cohen, A. Varshney, B. Watson, and R. Huebner (2002). *Level of Detail for 3D Graphics*, Morgan Kaufmann.

Lynch, K. (1960). *The Image of the City*, MIT Press.

MacKenzie, C., and T. Iberall (1994). *The Grasping Hand*, North-Holland.

MacKenzie, I. S., and R. Soukoreff (2002). Text Entry for Mobile Computing: Models and Methods, Theory and Practice. *Human Computer Interaction* 17: 147–198.

MacKenzie, I. S. (1995). Input Devices and Interaction Techniques for Advanced Computing. *Virtual Environments and Advanced Interface Design*. W. Barfield and T. Furness (Eds.), Oxford University Press, 437–472.

MacKenzie, I. S. (1992). Fitts' Law as a Research and Design Tool in Human Computer Interaction. *Human Computer Interaction* 7: 91–139.

Mackinlay, J., S. Card, and G. Robertson (1990b). A Semantic Analysis of the Design Space of Input Devices. *Human Computer Interaction* 5, 145–190.

Mackinlay, J., S. Card, and G. Robertson (1990a). Rapid Controlled Movement through a Virtual 3D Workspace. *Proceedings of SIGGRAPH '90*, ACM Press, 171–176.

Maes, P. (1997). The ALIVE System: Wireless, Full-Body Interaction with Autonomous Agents. *ACM Multimedia Systems* 5(2): 105–112.

Mankoff, J., and G. Abowd (1998). Cirrin: A Word-Level Unistroke Keyboard for Pen Input. *Proceedings of the 1998 ACM Symposium on User Interface Software and Technology (UIST '98)*, ACM Press, 213–214.

Mapes, D., and J. Moshell (1995). A Two-Handed Interface for Object Manipulation in Virtual Environments. *Presence: Teleoperators and Virtual Environments* 4(4): 403–416.

Marr, D. (1982). *Vision*, W. H. Freeman.

Marras, W. (1997). Biomechanics of the Human Body. *Handbook of Human Factors and Ergonomics.* G. Salvendy (Ed.), John Wiley & Sons, 233–267.

Marriott, K., and P. Stuckey (1998). *Programming with Constraints: An Introduction,* MIT Press.

Massie, T. H. (1993). *Design of a Three Degree of Freedom Force Reflecting Haptic Interface,* MIT Press.

May, J., and D. Badcock (2002). Vision and Virtual Environments. *Handbook of Virtual Environments: Design, Implementation, and Applications.* K. Stanney (Ed.), Lawrence Erlbaum Associates, 29–64.

McCormick, B., T. DeFanti, and M. Brown (1987). Visualization in Scientific Computing. *Computer Graphics* 21(6).

McCormick, E. (1970). *Human Factors Engineering,* McGraw-Hill.

McMillan, G., R. Eggelston, and T. Anderson (1997). Nonconventional Controls. *Handbook of Human Factors and Ergonomics.* G. Salvendy (Ed.), John Wiley & Sons, 729–771.

McQuaide, S., E. Seibel, R. Burstein, and T. Furness (2002). Three-Dimensional Virtual Retinal Display System Using Deformable Membrane Mirror. *Society for Information Display (SID '02),* Boston, MA.

McTear, M. (2002). Spoken Dialogue Technology: Enabling the Conversational User Interface. *ACM Computing Surveys* 34(1): 90–169.

Melzer, J., and K. Moffitt (1996). *Head-Mounted Displays: Designing for the User,* McGraw-Hill.

Meyer, K., and H. Applewhite (1992). A Survey of Position Trackers. *Presence: Teleoperators and Virtual Environments* 1(2): 173–200.

Milgram, P., and F. Kishino (1994). A Taxonomy of Mixed Reality Visual Displays. *IECE Transactions on Information and Systems* E77-D(12): 1321–1329.

Milgram, P., H. Takemura, A. Utsumi, and F. Kishino (1994). Augmented Reality: A Class of Displays on the Reality-Virtuality Continuum. *Telemanipulator and Telepresence Technologies,* SPIE, 282–292.

Millán, J. (2003). Adaptive Brain Interfaces. *Communications of the ACM* 46(3): 74–80.

Mills, S., and J. Noyes (1999). Virtual Reality: An Overview of User-Related Design Issues. *Interacting with Computers* 11(4): 375–386.

Mine, M. (1997). ISAAC: A Meta-CAD System for Virtual Environments. *Computer-Aided Design* 29(8): 547–553.

Mine, M., F. Brooks, and C. Séquin (1997). Moving Objects in Space: Exploiting Proprioception in Virtual Environment Interaction. *Proceedings of SIGGRAPH '97,* ACM Press, 19–26.

Mine, M. (1995a). Virtual Environment Interaction Techniques, Dept. of Computer Science, University of North Carolina at Chapel Hill, TR95-018.

Mine, M. (1995b). ISAAC: A Virtual Environment Tool for the Interactive Construction of Virtual Worlds, Dept. of Computer Science, University of North Carolina at Chapel Hill, TR-95-020.

Moeser, S. (1988). Cognitive Mapping in a Complex Building. *Environment and Behavior* 20(1): 21–49.

Mouchtaris, A., P. Reveliotis, and C. Kyrakakis (2000). Inverse Filter Design for Immersive Audio Rendering over Loudspeakers. *IEEE Transactions on Multimedia* 2(2): 77–87.

Mulder, A. (1996). Hand Gestures for HCI, School of Kinesiology, Simon Fraser University, Technical Report 96-1.

Mundel, M. (1978). *Motion and Time Study*, Prentice-Hall.

Naer, M., O. Staadt, and M. Gross (2002). Spatialized Audio Rendering for Immersive Virtual Environments. *Proceedings of the 2002 ACM Symposium on Virtual Reality Software and Technology (VRST 2002)*, ACM Press, 65–72.

Neale, D. (1998). Head Mounted Displays: Product Reviews and Related Design Considerations. Blacksburg, Dept. of Industrial Systems and Engineering, Virginia Tech, HCIL-98-02.

Newell, A., P. Rosenbloom, and J. Laird (1989). Symbolic Architectures for Cognition. *Foundations in Cognitive Science*. M. Posner (Ed.), MIT Press, 93–131.

Nielsen, J., and R. Molich (1992). Heuristic Evaluation of User Interfaces. *Proceedings of the 1992 ACM Conference on Human Factors in Computing Systems (CHI '92)*, ACM Press, 249–256.

Noma, H., and T. Miyasato (1998). Design for Locomotion Interface in a Large Scale Virtual Environment—ATLAS: ATR Locomotion Interface for Active Self Motion. *ASME-DSC* 64: 111–118.

Norman, D. (1990). *The Design of Everyday Things*, Doubleday.

Normand, V., C. Babski, S. Benford, A. Bullock, S. Carion, Y. Chrysanthou, N. Farcet, J. Harvey, N. Kuijpers, N. Magnenat-Thalmann, S. Raupp-Musse, T. Rodden, M. Slater, and G. Smith (1999). The Coven Project: Exploring Applicative, Technical and Usage Dimensions of Collaborative Virtual Environments. *Presence: Teleoperators and Virtual Environments* 8(2): 218–236.

Noyes, J. (1983). Chord Keyboards. *Applied Ergonomics* 14: 55–59.

Ohshima, T., K. Sato, H. Yamamoto, and H. Tamura (1998). AR2Hockey: A Case Study of Collaborative Augmented Reality. *Proceedings of the 1998 IEEE Virtual Reality Annual International Symposium (VRAIS '98)*, IEEE Press, 268–275.

Olano, M., and A. Lastra (1998). A Shading Language on Graphics Hardware: The Pixel-Flow Rendering System. *Proceedings of SIGGRAPH '98*, ACM Press, 159–168.

Olwal, A., and S. Feiner (2003). The Flexible Pointer: An Interaction Technique for Augmented and Virtual Reality. *User Interface Software and Technology (UIST) 2003 Conference Supplement*, ACM Press, 81–82.

Omura, K., S. Shiwa, and F. Kishino (1996). 3D Display with Accommodative Compensation (3DDAC) Employing Real-Time Gaze Detection. *Society for Information Display Digest*, 889–892.

Osawa, N., X. Ren, and M. Suzuki. (2003). Investigating Text Entry Strategies for an Immersive Virtual Environment. *Information* 6(5): 577–582.

Oviatt, S., and P. Cohen (2000). Multimodal Interfaces That Process What Comes Naturally. *Communications of the ACM* 43(3): 45–51.

Oviatt, S. (1999). Mutual Disambiguation of Recognition Errors in a Multimodal Architecture. *Proceedings of the 1999 ACM Conference on Human Factors in Computing Systems (CHI '99)*, ACM Press, 576–583.

Pastoor, S., and M. Wopking (1997). 3-D Displays: A Review of Current Technologies. *Displays* 17: 100–110.

Pausch, R., D. Proffitt, and G. Williams (1997). Quantifying Immersion in Virtual Reality. *Proceedings of SIGGRAPH '97*, ACM Press, 13–18.

Pausch, R., J. Snoddy, R. Taylor, S. Watson, and E. Haseltine (1996). Disney's Aladdin: First Steps toward Storytelling in Virtual Reality. *Proceedings of SIGGRAPH '96*, ACM Press, 193–203.

Pausch, R., T. Burnette, D. Brockway, and M. Weiblen (1995). Navigation and Locomotion in Virtual Worlds via Flight into Hand-Held Miniatures. *Proceedings of SIGGRAPH '95*, ACM Press, 399–400.

Pausch, R., T. Crea, and M. Conway (1993). A Literature Survey for Virtual Environments: Military Flight Simulator Visual Systems and Simulator Sickness. *Presence: Teleoperators and Virtual Environments* 1(3): 344–363.

Perlin, K., S. Paxia, and J. Kollin (2000). An Autostereoscopic Display. *Proceedings of SIGGRAPH 2000*, ACM Press, 319–326.

Perlin, K. (1998). Quikwriting: Continuous Stylus-Based Text Entry. *Proceedings of the 1998 ACM Symposium on User Interface Software and Technology (UIST '98)*, ACM Press, 215–216.

Péruch, P., M. May, and F. Wartenburg (1997). Homing in Virtual Environments: Effects of Field of View and Path Layout. *Perception* 26: 301–312.

Pierce, J., B. Stearns, and R. Pausch (1999). Voodoo Dolls: Seamless Interaction at the Multiple Scales in Virtual Environments. *Proceedings of the 1999 ACM Symposium on Interactive 3D Graphics (I3D '99)*, ACM Press, 141–145.

Pierce, J., A. Forsberg, M. Conway, S. Hong, R. Zeleznik, and M. Mine (1997). Image Plane Interaction Techniques in 3D Immersive Environments. *Proceedings of the 1997 ACM Symposium on Interactive 3D Graphics (I3D '97)*, ACM Press, 39–44.

Pique, M. (1995). Rotation Tools. *Graphics Gem 1.* A. Glassner (Ed.), Morgan Kaufman Publishers, 465–469.

Polson, P., C. Lewis, J. Rieman, and C. Wharton (1992). Cognitive Walkthroughs: A Method for Theory-Based Evaluation of User Interfaces. *International Journal of Man-Machine Studies* 36: 741–773.

Poupyrev, I., D. Tan, M. Billinghurst, H. Kato, H. Regenbrecht, and N. Tetsutani (2002). Developing a Generic Augmented-Reality Interface. *IEEE Computer* 35(3): 44–49.

Poupyrev, I., D. Tan, M. Billinghurst, H. Kato, H. Regenbrecht, and N. Tetsutani (2001). Tiles: A Mixed Reality Authoring Interface. *Proceedings of INTERACT 2001*, 334–341.

Poupyrev, I., R. Berry, J. Kurumisawa, K. Nakao, M. Billinghurst, C. Airola, H. Kato, T. Yonezawa, and L. Baldwin (2000). Augmented Groove: Collaborative Jamming in Augmented Reality. *SIGGRAPH 2000 Conference Abstracts and Applications*, ACM Press, 77.

Poupyrev, I., S. Weghorst, and S. Fels (2000). Non-isomorphic 3D Rotational Interaction Techniques. *Proceedings of the 2000 ACM Conference on Human Factors in Computing Systems (CHI 2000)*, ACM Press, 540–547.

Poupyrev, I., and T. Ichikawa (1999). Manipulating Objects in Virtual Worlds: Categorization and Empirical Evaluation of Interaction Techniques. *Journal of Visual Languages and Computing* 10(1): 19–35.

Poupyrev, I., S. Weghorst, T. Otsuka, and T. Ichikawa (1999). Amplifying Rotations in 3D Interfaces. *Proceedings of the 1999 ACM Conference on Human Factors in Computing Systems (CHI '99)*, ACM Press, 256–257.

Poupyrev, I., N. Tomokazu, and S. Weghorst (1998). Virtual Notepad: Handwriting in Immersive VR. *Proceedings of the 1998 IEEE Virtual Reality Annual International Symposium (VRAIS '98)*, IEEE Press, 126–132.

Poupyrev, I., S. Weghorst, M. Billinghurst, and T. Ichikawa (1998). Egocentric Object Manipulation in Virtual Environments: Empirical Evaluation of Interaction Techniques. *Computer Graphics Forum, EUROGRAPHICS '98 Issue* 17(3): 41–52.

Poupyrev, I., S. Weghorst, M. Billinghurst, and T. Ichikawa (1997). A Framework and Testbed for Studying Manipulation Techniques for Immersive VR. *Proceedings of the 1997 ACM Symposium on Virtual Reality Software and Technology (VRST '97)*, ACM Press, 21–28.

Poupyrev, I., M. Billinghurst, S. Weghorst, and T. Ichikawa (1996). The Go-Go Interaction Technique: Non-linear Mapping for Direct Manipulation in VR. *Proceedings of the 1996 ACM Symposium on User Interface Software and Technology (UIST '96)*, ACM Press, 79–80.

Preece, J., Y. Rogers, and H. Sharp (2002). *Interaction Design: Beyond Human-Computer Interaction*, John Wiley and Sons.

Prince, S., A. Cheok, F. Farbiz, T. Williamson, N. Johnson, M. Billinghurst, and H. Kato (2002). 3-D Live: Real Time Interaction for Mixed Reality. *Proceedings of the ACM Conference on Computer Supported Cooperative Work,* ACM Press, 364–371.

Pulkki, V. (2001). *Spatial Sound Generation and Perception by Amplitude Panning Techniques,* PhD Dissertation, Dept. of Electrical Engineering and Communications Engineering, Helsink University of Technology.

Raskar, R., G. Welch, M. Cutts, A. Lake, L. Stesin, and H. Fuchs (1998). The Office of the Future: A Unified Approach to Image-Based Modeling and Spatially Immersive Displays. *Proceedings of SIGGRAPH '98*, ACM Press, 179–188.

Razzaque, S., D. Swapp, M. Slater, M. Whitton, and A. Steed (2002). Redirected Walking in Place. *Proceedings of the 2002 Eurographics Workshop on Virtual Environments,* Eurographics Association, 123–130.

Regenbrecht, H., T. Schubert, and F. Friedman (1998). Measuring the Sense of Presence and Its Relations to Fear of Heights in Virtual Environments. *International Journal of Human-Computer Interaction,* 10(3): 233–250.

Rekimoto, J. (2002). SmartSkin: An Infrastructure for Freehand Manipulation on Interactive Surfaces. *Proceedings of the 2002 ACM Conference on Human Factors in Computing Systems (CHI 2002),* ACM Press, 113–120.

Rekimoto, J., and M. Saitoh (1999). Augmented Surfaces: A Spatially Continuous Work Space for Hybrid Computing Environments. *Proceedings of the 1999 ACM Conference on Human Factors in Computing Systems (CHI '99),* ACM Press, 378–385.

Rekimoto, J. (1998). Matrix: A Realtime Object Identification and Registration Method for Augmented Reality. *Proceedings of Asia Pacific Computer Human Interaction (APCHI '98).*

Rekimoto, J., and K. Nagao (1995). The World through the Computer: Computer Augmented Interaction with Real World Environments. *Proceedings of the 1995 ACM Symposium on User Interface Software and Technology (UIST '95),* ACM Press, 29–36.

Robertson, G., M. Czerwinski, and M. van Dantzich (1997). Immersion in Desktop Virtual Reality. *Proceedings of the 1997 ACM Symposium on User Interface Software and Technology (UIST '97),* ACM Press, 11–19.

Rosenfeld, R., D. Olsen, and A. Rudnicky (2001). Universal Speech Interfaces. *Interactions* 8(6): 33–44.

Rosson, M., and J. Carroll (2001). *Usability Engineering: Scenario-Based Development of Human Computer Interaction,* Morgan Kaufmann Publishers.

Ruddle, R., S. Payne, and D. Jones (1999). The Effects of Maps on Navigation and Search Strategies in Very-Large-Scale Virtual Environments. *Journal of Experimental Psychology* 5(1): 54–75.

Ruddle, R., S. Payne, and D. Jones (1998). Navigating Large-Scale "Desktop" Virtual Buildings: Effects of Orientation Aids and Familiarity. *Presence: Teleoperators and Virtual Environments* 7(2): 179–192.

Rumsey, F. (1994). *MIDI Systems and Control,* Focal Press.

Sachs, E., A. Roberts, and D. Stoops (1991). 3-Draw: A Tool for Designing 3D Shapes. *IEEE Computer Graphics & Applications* 11(6): 18–26.

Salvendy, G. (1997). *The Handbook of Human Factors and Ergonomics,* John Wiley and Sons.

Schell, J., and J. Shochet (2001). Designing Interactive Theme Park Rides. *IEEE Computer Graphics & Applications* 21(4): 11–13.

Schkolne, S., M. Pruett, and P. Schröder (2001). Surface Drawing: Creating Organic 3D Shapes with the Hand and Tangible Tools. *Proceedings of the 2001 ACM Conference on Human Factors in Computing Systems (CHI 2001),* ACM Press, 261–268.

Schmalstieg, D., M. Encarnação, and Z. Szalavári (1999). Using Transparent Props for Interaction with the Virtual Table. *Proceedings of the 1999 ACM Symposium on Interactive 3D Graphics (I3D '99),* ACM Press, 147–154.

Schmalstieg, D., A. Fuhrmann, Z. Szalavári, and M. Gervautz (1996). Studierstube: An Environment for Collaboration in Augmented Reality. *Proceedings of the Collaborative Virtual Environment '96 Workshop.*

Schmandt, C. (1983). Spatial Input/Display Correspondence in a Stereoscopic Computer Graphic Work Station. *Proceedings of SIGGRAPH '83,* ACM Press, 253–262.

Schwerdtner, A., and H. Heidrich (1998). Dresden 3D Display (D4D). *Stereoscopic Display and Virtual Reality Systems V,* 3295: 203–210.

Scriven, M. (1967). The Methodology of Evaluation. *Perspectives of Curriculum Evaluation.* R. Stake (Ed.), American Educational Research Association, 39–83.

Sedwick, H. (1988). Space Perception. *Handbook of Perception and Human Performance.* K. Boff, L. Kaufman, and J. Thomas (Eds.), John Wiley & Sons, Volume 1, 1–21.

Sekuler, R., and R. Blake (1994). *Perception,* McGraw Hill.

Senders, J., J. Christensen, and R. Sabeh (1955). Comparison of Single Operator Performance with Team Performance in a Tracking Task, Aero Medical Laboratory, Wright Air Development Center.

Serruya, M., N. Hatsopoulos, L. Paninski, M. Fellows, and J. Donoghue (2002). Instant Neural Control of a Movement Signal. *Nature* 416: 141–142.

Shaw, C., and M. Green (1994). Two-Handed Polygonal Surface Design. *Proceedings of the 1994 ACM Symposium on User Interface Software and Technology (UIST '94)*, ACM Press, 205–212.

Shepard, R., and J. Metzler (1971). Mental Rotation of Three-Dimensional Objects. *Science* 171: 701–703.

Sherman, B., and A. Craig (2003). *Understanding Virtual Reality*, Morgan Kauffman Publishers.

Shilling, R., and B. Shinn-Cunningham (2002). Virtual Auditory Displays. *Handbook of Virtual Environments: Design, Implementation, and Applications.* K. Stanney (Ed.), Lawrence Erlbaum Associates, 65–92.

Shneiderman, B. (2003). Why Not Make Interfaces Better than 3D Reality? *IEEE Computer Graphics & Applications* 23(6): 12–15.

Shneiderman, B. (2000). The Limits of Speech Recognition. *Communications of the ACM* 43(9): 63–65.

Shneiderman, B. (1998). *Designing the User Interface: Strategies for Effective Human-Computer Interaction,* 3rd ed., Addison Wesley.

Shoemake, K. (1992). ARCBALL: A User Interface for Specifying Three-Dimensional Orientation Using a Mouse. *Proceedings of Graphics Interface (GI '92)*, 151–156.

Shoemake, K. (1985). Animating Rotations with Quaternion Curves. *Proceedings of SIGGRAPH '85*, ACM Press, 245–254.

Simon, A., and B. Fröhlich (2003). The YoYo: A Handheld Device Combining Elastic and Isotonic Input. *Proceedings of INTERACT 2003*, IOS Press, 303–310.

Siochi, A., and D. Hix (1991). A Study of Computer-Supported User Interface Evaluation Using Maximal Repeating Pattern Analysis. *Proceedings of the 1991 ACM Conference on Human Factors in Computing Systems (CHI '91)*, ACM Press, 301–305.

Slater, M., A. Steed, and Y. Chrysanthou (2002). *Computer Graphics and Virtual Environments: From Realism to Real-Time,* Addison Wesley.

Slater, M., M. Usoh, and A. Steed (1995). Taking Steps: The Influence of a Walking Technique on Presence in Virtual Reality. *ACM Transactions on Computer-Human Interaction* 2(3): 201–219.

Slater, M., M. Usoh, and A. Steed (1994). Depth of Presence in Virtual Environments. *Presence: Teleoperators and Virtual Environments* 3(2): 130–144.

Smith, R. (1987). Experiences with Alternative Reality Kit: An Example of Tension between Literalism and Magic. *IEEE Computer Graphics & Applications* 7(8): 42–50.

Smith, T., and K. Smith (1987). Feedback-Control Mechanisms of Human Behavior. *Handbook of Human Factors.* G. Salvendy (Ed.), John Wiley & Sons, 251–293.

Snow, M., and R. Williges (1998). Empirical Models Based on Free-Modulus Magnitude Estimation of Perceived Presence in Virtual Environments. *Human Factors* 40(3): 386–402.

Song, D., and M. Norman (1993). Nonlinear Interactive Motion Control Techniques for Virtual Space Navigation. *Proceedings of the 1993 IEEE Virtual Reality Annual International Symposium (VRAIS '93),* IEEE Press, 111–117.

Srinivasan, M., and J. Chen (1993). Human Performance in Controlling Normal Forces of Contact with Rigid Objects. *Advances in Robotics, Mechatronics, and Haptic Interfaces,* ASME, 119–125.

Stanney, K. (Ed.) (2002). *Handbook of Virtual Environments: Design, Implementation, and Applications,* Lawrence Erlbaum Associates.

Stanney, K., M. Mollaghasemi, and L. Reeves (2000). Development of MAUVE, The Multi-Criteria Assessment of Usability for Virtual Environments System. Orlando, Florida, Naval Air Warfare Center, Training Systems Division.

Stanney, K., and L. Reeves (2000). COVE Evaluation Report. Orlando, Florida, Naval Air Warfare Center, Training Systems Division.

Stanney, K., R. Mourant, and R. Kennedy (1998). Human Factors Issues in Virtual Environments: A Review of the Literature. *Presence: Teleoperators and Virtual Environments* 7(4): 327–351.

Starner, T., J. Weaver, and A. Pentland (1998). Real-Time American Sign Language Recognition Using Desk and Wearable Computer-Based Video. *IEEE Transactions on Pattern Analysis and Machine Intelligence* 20(12): 1371–1375.

Stassen, H., and G. Smets (1995). Telemanipulation and Telepresence. *Proceedings of the 6th IFAC/IFIP/IFORS/IEA Symposium on Analysis, Design, and Evaluation of Man-Machine Systems,* 13–23.

State, A., M. Livingston, G. Hirota, W. Garrett, M. Whitton, H. Fuchs, and E. Pisano (1996). Technologies for Augmented Reality Systems: Realizing Ultrasound-Guided Needle Biopsies. *Proceedings of SIGGRAPH '96,* ACM Press, 439–446.

Steck, S., and H. Mallot (2000). The Role of Global and Local Landmarks in Virtual Environment Navigation. *Presence: Teleoperators and Virtual Environments* 9(1): 69–83.

Steed, A., and J. Tromp (1998). Experiences with the Evaluation of CVE Applications. *Proceedings of Collaborative Virtual Environments 1998,* Manchester, UK.

Stefani, O., and J. Rauschenbach (2003). 3D Input Devices and Interaction Concepts for Optical Tracking in Immersive Environments. *Proceedings of Immersive Projection Technology and Virtual Environments 2003,* ACM Press, 317–318.

Stephenson, N. (1992). *Snow Crash,* Bantam Books.

Stevens, A., and P. Coupe (1978). Distortions in Judged Spatial Relations. *Cognitive Psychology* 10: 422–437.

Stiles, R., L. McCarthy, A. Munro, Q. Pizzini, L. Johnson, and J. Rickel (1996). Virtual Environments for Shipboard Training. *Intelligent Ships Symposium.*

Stoakley, R., M. Conway, and R. Pausch (1995). Virtual Reality on a WIM: Interactive Worlds in Miniature. *Proceedings of the 1995 ACM Conference on Human Factors in Computing Systems (CHI '95),* ACM Press, 265–272.

Stuart, R. (1996). *The Design of Virtual Environments,* McGraw Hill.

Sturman, D., D. Zeltzer, and S. Pieper (1989). Hands-On Interaction with Virtual Environments. *Proceedings of the 1989 ACM Symposium on User Interface Software and Technology (UIST '89)*, ACM Press, 19–24.

Sullivan, A. (2003). A Solid-State Multi-planar Volumetric Display. *Society for Information Display Digest*, 354–356.

Sutherland, I (1968). A Head-Mounted Three Dimensional Display. *Proceedings of the Fall Joint Computer Conference*, 757–764.

Sutherland, I. (1965). The Ultimate Display. *Proceedings of the IFIP Congress*, 505–508.

Swan, J., J. Gabbard, D. Hix, R. Schulman, and K. Kim (2003). A Comparative Study of User Performance in a Map-Based Virtual Environment. *Proceedings of IEEE Virtual Reality 2003*, IEEE Press, 259–266.

Szalavári, Z., D. Schmalstieg, A. Fuhrmann, and M. Gervautz (1997). Studierstube: An Environment for Collaboration in Augmented Reality. *Virtual Reality: Systems, Development and Applications* 3(1): 37–49.

Tan, D., K. Stefanucci, D. Proffitt, and R. Pausch (2002). Kinesthetic Cues Aid Spatial Memory. *Proceedings of the 2002 ACM Conference on Human Factors in Computing Systems, Extended Abstracts (CHI 2002)*, ACM Press, 806–807.

Templeman, J., P. Denbrook, and L. Sibert (1999). Virtual Locomotion: Walking in Place through Virtual Environments. *Presence: Teleoperators and Virtual Environments* 8(6): 598–617.

Thomas, B., S. Tyerman, and K. Grimmer (1998). Evaluation of Text Input Mechanisms for Wearable Computers. *Virtual Reality: Research, Development, and Applications* 3: 187–199.

Thorndyke, P., and B. Hayes-Roth (1982). Differences in Spatial Knowledge Obtained from Maps and Navigation. *Cognitive Psychology* 14: 560–589.

Tidwell, M., R. Johnston, D. Melville, and T. Furness (1995). The Virtual Retinal Display: A Retinal Scanning Imaging System. *Proceedings of Virtual Reality World '95*, 325–333.

Tlauka, M., and P. Wilson (1996). Orientation Free Representations of Navigation through a Computer-Simulated Environment. *Journal of Environmental Psychology* 28(5): 305–313.

Tsang, M., G. Fitzmaurice, G. Kurtenbach, A. Khan, and B. Buxton (2002). BOOM Chameleon: Simultaneous Capture of 3D Viewpoint, Voice, and Gesture Annotations on a Spatially Aware Display. *Proceedings of the 2002 ACM Symposium on User Interface Software and Technology (UIST 2002)*, ACM Press, 111–120.

Tsingos, N., T. Funkhouser, A. Hgan, and I. Carlbom (2001). Modeling Acoustics in a Virtual Environment Using the Uniform Theory of Diffraction. *Proceedings of SIGGRAPH 2001*, ACM Press, 545–552.

Tufte, E. (1990). *Envisioning Information*, Graphics Press.

Ullmer, B., and H. Ishii (2001). Emerging Frameworks for Tangible User Interfaces. *Human-Computer Interaction in the New Millennium*. J. Carroll (Ed.), Addison-Wesley, 579–601.

Ullmer, B., and H. Ishii (1997). The metaDesk: Models and Prototypes for Tangible User Interfaces. *Proceedings of the 1997 ACM Symposium on User Interface Software and Technology (UIST '97)*, ACM Press, 223–232.

Underkoffler, J., and H. Ishii (1998). Illuminating Light: An Optical Design Tool with a Luminous-Tangible Interface. *Proceedings of the 1998 ACM Conference on Human Factors in Computing Systems (CHI '98)*, ACM Press, 542–549.

Usoh, M., E. Catena, S. Arman, and M. Slater (2000). Using Presence Questionnaires in Reality. *Presence: Teleoperators and Virtual Environments* 9(5): 497–503.

Usoh, M., K. Arthur, M. Whitton, R. Bastos, A. Steed, M. Slater, and F. Brooks Jr. (1999). Walking > Walking-in-Place > Flying in Virtual Environments. *Proceedings of SIGGRAPH '99*, ACM Press, 359–364.

van Dam, A., A. Forsberg, D. Laidlaw, J. LaViola, and R. Simpson (2000). Immersive VR for Scientific Visualization: A Progress Report. *IEEE Computer Graphics & Applications* 20(6): 26–52.

van Dam, A. (1997). Post-WIMP User Interfaces: The Human Connection. *Communication of the ACM* 40(2): 63–67.

Viirre, E. (1994). A Survey of Medical Issues and Virtual Reality Technology. *Virtual Reality World*, 16–20.

Vinson, N. (1999). Design Guidelines for Landmarks to Support Navigation in Virtual Environments. *Proceedings of the 1999 ACM Conference on Human Factors in Computing Systems (CHI '99)*, ACM Press, 278–285.

Waller, D., E. Hunt, and D. Knapp (1998). The Transfer of Spatial Knowledge in Virtual Environment Training. *Presence: Teleoperators and Virtual Environments* 7(2): 129–143.

Wann, J., and M. Mon-Williams (2002). Measurement of Visual Aftereffects Following Virtual Environment Exposure. *Handbook of Virtual Environments: Design, Implementation, and Applications*. K. Stanney (Ed.), Lawrence Erlbaum Associates, 731–750.

Ward, D., A. Blackwell, and D. MacKay (2002). Dasher: A Gesture-Driven Data Entry Interface for Mobile Computing. *Human Computer Interaction* 17(2/3): 199–228.

Ware, C. (2000). *Information Visualization: Perception for Design*, Morgan Kaufman.

Ware, C., and J. Rose (1999). Rotating Virtual Objects with Real Handles. *ACM Transactions on Computer-Human Interaction* 6(2): 162–180.

Ware, C., K. Arthur, and K. Booth (1993). Fishtank Virtual Reality. *Proceedings of INTERCHI '93*, 37–42.

Ware, C., and S. Osborne (1990). Exploration and Virtual Camera Control in Virtual Three Dimensional Environments. *Proceedings of the 1990 ACM Symposium on Interactive 3D Graphics (I3D '90)*, ACM Press, 175–183.

Ware, C., and D. Jessome (1988). Using the Bat: A Six-Dimensional Mouse for Object Placement. *Proceedings of Graphics Interface '88*, 119–124.

Watsen, K., R. Darken, and M. Capps (1999). A Handheld Computer as an Interaction Device to a Virtual Environment. *Proceedings of the Third Immersive Projection Technology Workshop*, Stuttgart, Germany.

Watson, B., V. Spaulding, N. Walker, and W. Ribarsky (1997). Evaluation of the Effects of Frame Time Variation on VR Task Performance. *Proceedings of 1997 IEEE Virtual Reality Annual International Symposium (VRAIS '97)*, IEEE Press, 38–44.

Watt, A., and M. Watt (1992). *Advanced Animation and Rendering Techniques: Theory and Practice*. ACM Press.

Weiser, M. (1991). The Computer for the 21st Century. *Scientific American* 265(3): 66–75.

Welch, G. (2004). Tracking Bibliography, http://www.cs.unc.edu/~tracker/ref/biblio/index.html.

Welch, G., and E. Foxlin (2002). Motion Tracking: No Silver Bullet, but a Respectable Arsenal. *IEEE Computer Graphics & Applications, special issue on "Tracking"* 22(6): 24–38.

Welch, G., L. Vicci, S. Brumback, K. Keller, and D. Colucci (2001). High-Performance Wide-Area Optical Tracking: The HiBall Tracking System. *Presence: Teleoperators and Virtual Environments* 10(1): 1–21.

Welch, G., G. Bishop, L. Vicci, S. Brumback, K. Keller, and D. Colucci (1999). The HiBall Tracker: High-Performance Wide-Area Tracking for Virtual and Augmented Environments. *Proceedings of the 1999 ACM Symposium on Virtual Reality Software and Technology (VRST '99)*, ACM Press, 1–10.

Welch, R., and D. Warren (1986). Intersensory Interactions. *Handbook of Perception and Human Performance*. K. Boff, L. Kaufman, and J. Thomas (Eds.), John Wiley & Sons, Volume 2, 25-1–25-36.

Wellner, P. (1993). Interaction with Paper on the Digital Desk. *Communications of the ACM* 36(7): 87–96.

Wellner, P., W. Mackay, and R. Gold (1993). Back to the Real World. *Communications of the ACM* 36(7): 24–27.

Wells, M., B. Peterson, and J. Aten (1996). The Virtual Motion Controller: A Sufficient-Motion Walking Simulator. *Proceedings of the 1996 IEEE Virtual Reality Annual International Symposium (VRAIS '96)*, IEEE Press, 1–8.

Wickens, C., and C. Carswell (1997). Information Processing. *Handbook of Human Factors and Ergonomics*. G. Salvendy (Ed.), John Wiley & Sons, 130–149.

Wickens, C., S. Todd, and K. Seidler (1989). Three-Dimensional Displays: Perception, Implementation, Applications. Ohio, CSERIAC SOAR-89-01 Wright Patterson AFB.

Wickens, C. (1986). The Effects of Control Dynamics on Performance. *Handbook of Perception and Human Performance*. K. Boff, L. Kaufman, and J. Thomas (Eds.), John Wiley & Sons, Volume 2, 39–60.

Wiener, N. (1948). *Cybernetics, or Control and Communication in the Animal and the Machine*, John Wiley & Sons.

Wilder, J., G. Hung, M. Tremaine, and M. Kaur (2002). Eye Tracking in Virtual Environments. *Handbook of Virtual Environments: Design, Implementation, and Applications*. K. Stanney (Ed.), Lawrence Erlbaum Associates, 211–222.

Williams, G., H. Faste, I. McDowall, and M. Bolas (1999). Physical Presence in Virtual Spaces. *Proceedings of SPIE, Stereoscopic Displays and Virtual Reality Systems VI* 3639: 374–384.

Winston, P. (1993). *Artificial Intelligence*, 3rd ed., Addison-Wesley.

Wiseman, J. (1995). *The SAS Survival Handbook*, Collins Publications.

Witmer, B., and M. Singer (1998). Measuring Presence in Virtual Environments: A Presence Questionnaire. *Presence: Teleoperators and Virtual Environments* 7(3): 225–240.

Wloka, M., and E. Greenfield (1995). The Virtual Tricorder: A Uniform Interface for Virtual Reality. *Proceedings of the 1995 ACM Symposium on User Interface Software and Technology (UIST '95)*, ACM Press, 39–40.

Wormell, D., and E. Foxlin (2003). Advancements in 3D Interactive Devices for Virtual Environments. *Proceedings of Immersive Projection Technology and Virtual Environments 2003*, ACM Press, 47–56.

Yamada, H. (1980). A Historical Study of Typewriters and Typing Methods: From the Position of Planning Japanese Parallels. *Journal of Information Processing* 2(4): 175–202.

Yost, W. A. (1994). *Fundamentals of Hearing: An Introduction*, 3rd ed., Academic Press.

Zeleznik, R., J. LaViola, D. Acevedo, and D. Keefe (2002). Pop-Through Buttons for Virtual Environment Navigation and Interaction. *Proceedings of IEEE Virtual Reality 2002*, IEEE Press, 127–134.

Zeleznik, R., and A. Forsberg (1999). UniCam: 2D Gestural Camera Controls for 3D Environments. *Proceedings of the 1999 ACM Symposium on Interactive 3D Graphics (I3D '99)*, ACM Press, 169–173.

Zeleznik, R., A. Forsberg, and P. Strauss (1997). Two Pointer Input for 3D Interaction. *Proceedings of the 1997 ACM Symposium in Interactive 3D Graphics (I3D '97)*, ACM Press, 115–120.

Zeleznik, R., K. Herndon, and J. Hughes (1996). SKETCH: An Interface for Sketching 3D Scenes. *Proceedings of SIGGRAPH '96*, ACM Press, 163–170.

Zhai, S., and R. Woltjer (2003). Human Movement Performance in Relation to Path Constraint The Law of Steering in Locomotion. *Proceedings of IEEE Virtual Reality 2003*, IEEE Press, 149–158.

Zhai, S., M. Hunter, and B. Smith (2000). The Metropolis Keyboard: An Exploration of Quantitative Techniques for Virtual Keyboard Design. *Proceedings of the 2000 ACM Symposium on User Interface Software and Technology (UIST 2000)*, ACM Press, 119–128.

Zhai, S., E. Kandogan, B. Smith, and T. Selker (1999). In Search of the "Magic Carpet": Design and Experimentation of a Bimanual 3D Navigation Interface. *Journal of Visual Languages and Computing* 10: 3–17.

Zhai, S. (1998). User Performance in Relation to 3D Input Device Design. *Computer Graphics* 32(4): 50–54.

Zhai, S., and P. Milgram (1998). Quantifying Coordination in Multiple DOF Movement and Its Application to Evaluating 6 DOF Input Devices. *Proceedings of the 1998 ACM Conference on Human Factors in Computing Systems (CHI '98)*, ACM Press, 320–327.

Zhai, S., P. Milgram, and A. Rastogi (1997). Anisotropic Human Performance in Six Degree-of-Freedom Tracking: An Evaluation of Three-Dimensional Display and Control Interfaces. *IEEE Transactions on Systems, Man and Cybernetics* 27(4): 518–528.

Zhai, S., and J. Senders (1997a). Investigating Coordination in Multidegree of Freedom Control I: Time-on-Target Analysis of 6 DOF Tracking. *Human Factors and Ergonomics Society 41st Annual Meeting*, 1249–1253.

Zhai, S., and J. Senders (1997b). Investigating Coordination in Multidegree of Freedom Control II: Correlation Analysis in 6 DOF Tracking. *Human Factors and Ergonomics Society 41st Annual Meeting*, 1254–1258.

Zhai, S., P. Milgram, and W. Buxton (1996). The Influence of Muscle Groups on Performance of Multiple Degree-of-Freedom Input. *Proceedings of the 1996 ACM Conference on Human Factors in Computing Systems (CHI '96)*, ACM Press, 308–315.

Zhai, S. (1995). *Human Performance in Six Degree of Freedom Input Control*, PhD Dissertation, Dept. of Computer Science, University of Toronto.

Zhai, S., W. Buxton, and P. Milgram (1994). The "Silk Cursor": Investigating Transparency for 3D Target Acquisition. *Proceedings of the 1994 ACM Conference on Human Factors in Computing Systems (CHI '94)*, ACM Press, 459–464.

Zhai, S., and P. Milgram (1993). Human Performance Evaluation of Manipulation Schemes in Virtual Environments. *Proceedings of the 1993 IEEE Virtual Reality Annual International Symposium (VRAIS '93)*, IEEE Press, 155–161.

Zimmerman, T., J. Lanier, C. Blanchard, S. Bryson, and Y. Harvill (1987). A Hand Gesture Interface Device. *Proceedings of CHI+GI '87, Human Factors in Computing Systems and Graphics Interface*, ACM Press, 189–192.

Zwaga, H., T. Boersema, and H. Hoonhout (1999). *Visual Information for Everyday Use: Design and Research Perspectives*, Taylor & Francis.

Index

Numbers